TRUE GHOST STORIES

FROM AROUND

THE WORLD

D0262663

TRUE GHOST STORIES

FROM AROUND

THE WORLD

Bounty
Books

First published in 2005 by Bounty Books,
a division of Octopus Publishing Group Ltd
2–4 Heron Quays, London E14 4JP

ISBN 0 7537 1118 4
ISBN13 9780753711187

A CIP catalogue record for this book is available from
the British Library

Printed and bound in Great Britain

CONTENTS

THE FIRST GHOST IN AMERICA
by Karen Froehlich

On August 9, 1799, Abner Blaisdel first heard the knocking noises in his house in Machiasport, Maine. Then on January 2, 1800, Abner and his daughter heard a woman's voice coming from the cellar. The voice said she was the dead wife of Captain George Butler and that her maiden name had been Nelly Hooper. Accounts of Nelly Butler made her what many believe is America's first documented ghost.

After hearing Nelly's message, Abner sent for David Hooper, Nelly's father, who happened to live only five miles away. Once again, Nelly spoke and Hooper became a believer. "She gave such clear and irresistible tokens of her being the spirit of my own daughter as gave me no less satisfaction than admiration and delight," he later wrote.

Shortly after her father's return home. Nelly first appeared to Abner's son Paul as he was walking through nearby fields. Terrified, he ran home and reported that an apparition had floated behind him and had chased him. That night Nelly spoke to the Blaisdel family, and she scolded Paul for not talking to her when he saw her.

By February 1800, Nelly was becoming famous in Machiasport and the surrounding towns. People crowded into the Blaisdel house to see and hear her. She was described by a female witness as at first being a mere mass of light, then growing into a human form about the size of the woman describing her. The glow from the ghost had a constant, tremulous motion. Then it became shapeless, expanding in every direction. Finally, it simply vanished.

Before the end of the year more than 100 people had seen or heard Nelly Butler's ghost, and most had given sworn testimony to the local pastor, Reverend Cummings. He didn't believe in ghosts and didn't think his flock should either.

Angrily, Cummings decided to see for himself. As he strode through the fields to the Blaisdel home, a woman suddenly appeared before him. "Surrounded by bright light, at first her form was no bigger than that of a toad," he wrote. As he watched, Nelly Butler grew to normal height before his eyes. Seeing that convinced him.

Maybe Nelly had made her point, or maybe she just got tired, but after her encounter with Reverend Cummings she was only seen one more time. Captain George Butler, Nelly's husband, reported that she appeared to him one night in his bedroom. She gave him a tongue-lashing for remarrying after promising her on her deathbed that he would never marry again.

SPECTACLE ON 37TH STREET
by Mary R. Woods

An intense haunting at a Vancouver, Washington, home becomes a media sensation.

In December 1994, my family moved into a quiet neighbourhood in the Orchards area of Vancouver, Washington. Like many homes built in the early 1970s, ours is a plain, four-bedroom, ranch-style home in the centre of a cul de sac. The last thing we expected to find was the remnants of previous occupants.

I've come to realize that the activity in the house began not long after we moved in, with little incidents that at first I chalked up to either imagination or the natural sounds of an older home. I was up late one night and heard the front door open and the doorknob rattle. It woke my husband, who grabbed a torch and shotgun and went to investigate. I called the police and reported an attempted break-in. Yet when we investigated, we found no marks on the door and no footprints in the wet mud by the door. The police found no evidence of intruders in the neighbourhood.

Not long afterwards, I began hearing footsteps late at night in the hall. I suspected that it was my older daughter Heather, who had a history of sleepwalking. Yet when I went to check on her, she would be in bed, sound asleep.

I started to notice that the pictures in the hall would be rearranged, and occasionally I would find one or two on the floor. I would also catch sudden movements out of the corner of my eye, as if I were in a crowded room and someone had just walked in. I would turn to look, but nothing would be there.

I tried to find as many rational explanations as I could. To no avail, I even called the U.S. Geological Survey to find out if we were above a fault line or underground aquifer that could cause vibration or shifting of the house. But in early 1996, an occurrence in my bedroom made me finally realize that there was someone or something else with us. I was in the small bathroom off the bedroom, getting ready for bed. I heard the water in our king-size waterbed move, and I looked out to see which of our daughters had come in and sat down. I saw an impression form on the end of the bed, as if someone were sitting on

11

the end of it, yet there was no physical being there. A few seconds passed before the mattress wobbled again and the impression was gone.

I went to check on the girls. Angel was asleep in her room and Heather was in the living room watching TV. My husband was in the computer room. I went to him and told him that I thought I was losing it. It was then that he confessed his own unusual experiences – hearing footsteps in the hall, seeing shadows out of the corner of his eye and noticing items being moved around.

He also told me of an uneasy feeling he had, centred in the small bathroom off the master bedroom. He always had a thing about keeping its door shut when he went to bed. Once when he had left the door open, he was awakened in the middle of the night. He felt as if something was sitting on his chest, smothering him. It scared him, and he managed to get out of bed and shut the door. Once the door was closed, the feeling left.

This little room has always been strange. It is always cold, even on the hottest day of summer. Our first thought was that the vent in there was stuck open and we were getting a draft from outside, but that did not explain the icy coldness in the middle of the summer. In the spring of 1996, the roof was replaced and new fans and vents were installed. But the coldness persists.

The activity began to happen more frequently. It could be called poltergeist activity, but personally, I think it was more of an attempt by some entities to get our attention. For three months, we couldn't keep anything on the shelf or in the medicine cabinet in the little bathroom. When leaving the bedroom, we would always make sure that everything in the bathroom was put away, the medicine cabinet was closed and the light was turned off. Shortly afterward we would hear a loud crash and find the bathroom door open, the light on, and everything scattered on the shelf and floor – yet none of the glass or porcelain items would be broken. Once we acknowledged the entity's presence, it would stop.

Even today, I may go in there and find something on the floor. I simply pick it up and tell the entity to cut it out, almost as if it's a game.

Kathy, Duane and the Letter K
Not long after the bathroom incidents began, I first saw the figure of a

woman in a long nightdress near the end of the hall. I was startled by it, but not frightened. She appeared to be looking for someone or something. She was also seen and felt by my daughter Heather. We nicknamed her "the lady in white", after one of our favourite films.

I learned that a woman named Kathy had died in the house in the spring of 1994, after a prolonged fight against cancer. The odd part was the tie she had with Heather. Kathy had left behind a teenage daughter who had been Heather's friend since primary school. Kathy had known Heather quite well, although they had drifted apart when Kathy's family moved to the Orchards neighbourhood. Her family moved out a few months after she died, and the house was empty until we moved in. I soon grew used to Kathy's presence and came to realize that she was here watching over both of our daughters.

I also believe that her presence in this dimension has caused an opening between this plane of existence and the spirit plane. Following her appearance, other entities began to appear, including two men, a female in the front bathroom and a young girl in the hall. To go into all of the strange happenings and people involved would take a book. But being naturally curious, I began to dig into the history of the area and the house itself.

The property had been part of a large farm owned by a Wagner family, which was very prominent in the area around the turn of the century. Some scandal that involved the Wagners had been hushed up, and I haven't been able to find out more about it. In August 1996, due to my digging, our local newspaper *The Columbian* published an article on the haunting. KING-TV in Seattle then contacted me. They did a piece on the haunting for their show *Evening Magazine*.

I was introduced to Shirlee Teabo, a local psychic investigator. I had been sceptical about psychics, but considering all that had been going on, I decided to see what would happen. Although she was told nothing about the house and the activity here, I was quite surprised at her abilities, especially when she began to tell me things that even I didn't know about.

One bizarre incident occurred when Shirlee, a cameraman, reporter Jon Stoffled and I were in the back garden. I started to tell her about the uneasy feeling my husband and I had had in this area, when I began to sense a cold chill down my back. I felt surrounded by a grey fog and I had a feeling of being suffocated. I remember backing up and saying that I had to get away. I couldn't see the reporter or cameraman even though they were right in front of me. Shirlee put her hand on my shoulder, and the touch broke whatever had hold of me. Since then, I have not returned to that area of the garden. Even now, when I look out of the kitchen window, I glimpse a greyish fog rising from the ground. I now know what horror writers are referring to when they use the phrase *abject terror*.

Shirlee was adamant about the importance of two details she sensed: the name "Duane", and the letter "K". She felt the name Duane very strongly at the end of the hallway where I and several others had seen the figure of a man. I did some more digging and found out about a double murder that took place on January 1, 1974, a couple of streets away. Shirlee knew details of the murder that weren't in the paper, and I was able to verify them through one of the victim's families. That victim's name was Charles Duane Gibson. He never used the name Charles; he was known as Duane. Also, the description of the figure that I had seen matched that of Gibson, according to the family member I spoke to.

It would be nearly six months after Shirlee's visit before I discovered a possible connection to the letter K. My husband and Heather were cleaning up the side patio of the house after a storm. My daughter came in and said they had found the "K" Shirlee had been talking about. Written in the patio concrete was the name Kimball, as well as the names Sally, Terry or Jerry and Paul, and the date 1971, which was the year the house was built. Coincidence? Maybe, maybe not. For now I prefer to keep an open mind.

Eventful Investigation

A week after Shirlee's visit, I was watching a locally produced TV programme known as *Town Hall*. One of the guests was paranormal investigator (and FATE columnist) Loyd Auerbach. Auerbach requested that anyone who believed they had had a paranormal experience get in touch with the show, and he would be glad to hear about it. The producer put me in touch with Auerbach, and through him, I was contacted by *Unsolved Mysteries* and was asked if they could do a segment for a special to air in early 1998. I agreed, and for two weekends in November, my house became a set.

Even that didn't seem to affect the ghosts, who made their presence known. While setting up, the sound engineer noticed something odd on one of his meters. The remote mike I was wearing and the boom mike he carried were off, yet his meters spiked when he was halfway down the hall. He also said he felt like a cold breeze was blowing through him. Later, Auerbach would find this spot to be a source of electromagnetic activity.

Prior to the arrival of the crew and producers, I met with director Bob Wise at my home. It was an informal meeting involving myself and two women whose family owned property nearby and were familiar with local history. During the meeting, one of the women remarked about a sudden draft in the dining room, which we all felt, and the sensation of small hands touching her through the back of her chair. At first I thought it might have been five-year-old Angel, but she was in the computer room with her dad, playing games.

When this happened, I had been telling Wise about Pinky, the little girl we often see crossing the end of the hall. She does the same thing every time we see her. We call her Pinky because of the long pink dress she wears. Our guest may have encountered Pinky's way of letting us know she was aware of us talking about her.

The filming was far from uneventful. As part of it, the producers asked Shirlee Teabo to return to the house. Shirlee was accompanied by her daughter Xanthea, a psychic in her own right. Whether or not it was related to the presence of two psychics, the house had a very strong effect on Shirlee. Standing in the middle of the hall, she was suddenly no longer herself. An entity had taken her over and was trying to speak through her. Her entire demeanour changed instantly and she became angry and spiteful. She hunched over with her hand on her lower back, and complained of back pain, saying, "The bitch double-crossed me. I wouldn't be here if it wasn't because of that bitch. It was her fault." She also kept referring to "Naomi".

When Wise tried to ask her what she was saying, she either couldn't hear him or wasn't able to answer. The experience upset her so much that the crew had to finish their interview with her outside. It had a rather upsetting effect on me, too. I had been standing behind her. As her transformation took place, I swear that the entire hall dropped in temperature. I felt like I had stepped back in time and was witnessing an actual event that may have taken place in the house. I saw the shadow of a man behind her, similar to the figure I'd seen many times in the hall. The whole thing lasted for five or ten minutes, but it seemed longer.

Two weeks later, the film crew returned with Auerbach to film reenactments for the show. Auerbach's only equipment was two EM meters and a Polaroid camera. After making observations, he agreed that something was definitely going on, and whatever it was, it was cyclical. Every seven to ten minutes, the needles on his meters would surge deep into the red, staying there for two to two and a half minutes.

To rule out the possibility of appliances or other electronics causing it, we shut down everything. It continued to happen. Finally, my husband went to the garage and turned all the power off. The spikes on the meter continued in the same cycle, and by this time, Auerbach was suffering from a serious sinus headache – his reaction to paranormal activity. I began to think the hair on the back of my neck was going to stay permanently on end and I was going to end up with permanent goose pimples.

I can't begin to explain what is going on in this house. We've had just about every type of paranormal manifestation happen in the last three years. None of it, though, has been harmful or directed at anyone in the family. Auerbach believes that at least two of the entities we've seen are not actually ghosts but "psychic recordings" or "residual hauntings". I'm inclined to agree, because they are like seeing a photograph or a quick glimpse of something out of the past, like Pinky running across the hall.

Kathy, on the other hand, is an actual apparition or ghost. She's here, I believe, because of unfinished business from her life, and because she is a protective spirit. At times I have felt comforted by her presence. As for the other two entities – the young lady in the bathroom and the angry man in the hall – I'm at a loss to explain them. All that I know is that what I have written here has truly happened, and it continues to happen.

Mary R. Woods *is a housewife, needlework designer, and mother of three. She is working toward a university degree in maths and civil engineering.*

Spectacle on 37th Street: An Investigator's Comments
by Loyd Auerbach

The episode of *Unsolved Mysteries* featuring the Vancouver case aired on April 17, 1998. As is typical with TV, it's nearly impossible to cover all the intricacies of a haunting/apparition case in the eight to ten minutes allotted. The show left out most of my assessment, preferring to leave the case "unsolved" – not that it's actually solved in any real way.

The case is quite interesting because of the variety of figures seen by Mary and Ed Woods and others, and because of the combination of subjective experience (that which is seen, heard and felt) with objective phenomena (the physical disruption of items in the bathroom, for example).

When I first walked around the house, my Tri-Field meter did in fact read higher than the standard "background" level in spots where Mary and Ed reported phenomena, although generally not significantly higher. The background reading was between 0 and 0.6 milligauss, normal for most homes, but the "spots" read anywhere from 2 to 4 milligauss. There was no technology in those locations to account for the change.

As time went on, two things started changing. First, I began getting sinus pressure in the front of my head. While I do suffer from minor allergies, I have learned over the years to associate that feeling with "something" happening (especially when I've already taken allergy tablets). That "something" is often in spots where these higher magnetic readings are taken. So I switched on the Tri-Field and got a reading that ran from 50 to ostensibly more than 100 milligauss – the top of the meter's scale. Then, a few minutes later, the reading skyrocketed again...and again...and again. There appeared to be a pattern of about 7.5 minutes of normal levels, followed by two to three minutes of very high levels. When I asked Ed to turn off the power in the house, the high reading still came every couple of minutes, but with no regularity. Was this an indication of ghosts?

At issue is whether the phenomena should be classified as apparitions or as a haunting. Mary senses that most of the figures are "aware" of the family and interact with them, which would indicate apparitions. Other reported phenomena, including a "gambler" and a female "groper" in the shower, seem to recur in a pattern, indicating a haunting (also called "residual memory" or "energy imprint"). Consistent with a haunting, an imprint is left on the environment by people and events in the past that the Woods family perceives.

The magnetic fields that I measured also seem to correlate more closely with hauntings than apparitions, because high readings in hauntings tend to be stationary. With apparitions, there are usually moving energy fields. However, the pulsating field I mentioned could be related to either category. This is the first time I've come across such a pattern.

So is it an apparition moving items around? Or could Mary or Ed be subconsciously using psychokinesis to interact with a haunting?

This case really *is* unsolved, as we still don't have all the specific phenomena diagnosed. What is solved, in my mind, is that there is psychic phenomena in that house, be it apparitional or a haunting...or both.

THE CASTLE AT 658 WAYNE STREET
by Maggie L. Cooper

Built in around 1875, this Victorian house was the epitome of regal gentility for the small town of Defiance in northwestern Ohio. The builder had spared no expense, using the finest materials – teak mosaics for the dining room floor, stained glass windows, oak sliding doors and a hand-carved banister from Europe for the front stairs. A long verandah hugged the back and one side of the house. Eight concrete steps led to a smaller verandah at the front door. The front wall of the house was a semicircle with bay windows, crowned with a half-circle roof. This appearance prompted many neighbourhood children to refer to the house as a castle, especially as years went by and Victorian-style homes became a rarity.

As with all castles, this one had its own ghosts. By 1948, when my father bought the house, there seemed to be an ominous reflection of ghostly inhospitality within its walls. The four large bedrooms and bathroom upstairs opened to a gloomy landing. While three of the bedrooms were sunny, with large windows, the back bedroom was dismal, with two small gabled windows and a door leading to a storage room that had one small, square window on the outside wall.

To the left of the storage-room door, a walled-in back staircase curved sharply at the top – which presented a danger to any unwary person, who could easily enter the storeroom, take one step to the left, and tumble down a flight of about 20 steps to another sharp curve that opened to the kitchen.

The ground floor was typically Victorian with a closed-off room for company only, family living room, dining room and a large kitchen and pantry. Closed-in stairs led from the kitchen to a basement laundry room complete with a pantry and a stove for making preserves and making soap. The next room was the furnace room with a long red stain running across the floor from the oversized furnace to a drainpipe. The front basement room was used to hang the washing on rainy Mondays.

John and Ester
Several stories existed about the ghosts, whom I called "John" and "Ester". The blandest one was that John, the original owner, was given

to fits of depression. After one such serious fit, he committed suicide. I preferred the following more complicated and colourful story.

Agreeing that John was the original owner, the tellers of this story said that John had murdered his wife Ester during an argument in one of the upstairs bedrooms. Since John was a respected businessman, he had no desire to confess to this murder and decided to secretly dispose of Ester's body. For reasons unknown (or perhaps to make the plot more exciting), the storytellers said that John cut off Ester's head and shoved it all the way to the back of a deep alcove above a closet in the bedroom where they'd argued. After doing this, John dragged Ester's headless body through the dark upstairs hall to the back bedroom and stuffed the gory corpse into the dark recesses of a cupboard that had a storage area to the left of the hanging clothes.

When the cook and maid left for their homes that night, John dragged Ester's body out of the cupboard, down the back stairs, through the kitchen, down the basement steps, through the laundry room and into the furnace room, where he burned it in the furnace. The long stain on the floor, they explained, was Ester's blood. Critics of this story said that the furnace was not installed until the 1920s and the stain was nothing but rust. They insisted that John had cut Ester's body into pieces and burned various parts in each of the fireplaces situated in almost every room of the house. A third version was that John had buried Ester's body under the furnace-room floor, but few people accepted this since there was no evidence of the cement floor having been disturbed.

Although they disagreed on how John had disposed of Ester's body, all agreed that John explained Ester's sudden absence by saying she'd gone on an emergency trip to visit her father in California. Because John was highly respected in the community, no one doubted his words.

Unfortunately for John, Ester was one of those people able to carry a grudge beyond the grave. A few days after her murder, a guest chose to sleep in the room with Ester's head in the cupboard alcove. The story didn't explain why he never noticed the smell of Ester's head decomposing but told how he ran out, screaming that he had seen Ester's head floating around the room. Martha, one of Ester's friends, smelled a rat and sent a letter to Ester's father. After learning that Ester had never come to visit, Martha hired a detective to investigate.

John had covered his tracks quite well, and the detective

found no evidence of murder. When it seemed as if John was going to get away with the crime, Ester apparently decided to make him admit his guilt. The maid and cook gossiped about John walking daily for hours along the upstairs landing, babbling that Ester's head was floating after him as she cried to him from the back bedroom cupboard. He refused to go to the basement any more, insisting that he could see Ester's headless body wandering around the furnace room.

One morning when the maid and cook entered the kitchen to start their day, they heard a strange sound coming from the stairs to the storeroom. They opened the door, peered up the flight of steps, and saw John's body swinging from a rope above the curve in the stairs. Some people said that John had killed himself out of grief for his missing wife. Others said that Ester had executed him for his crime.

For many years afterwards, more than a few people reported seeing strange lights in the house when the occupants were gone, or hearing terrified screams from the upstairs. Most people who moved into this majestic building never stayed long and refused to discuss their reasons for moving.

Dad had pooh-poohed any notion about ghosts or flying heads while we lived there. Although I was only eight when we moved in, I – like Mum – enjoyed the idea of living in a real haunted house.

"Look Here, Mr Ghost"

Nothing happened for the first few months until Mum and I were changing the beds. Clean sheets and blankets, stacked on a chair, suddenly began flying around the room.

Seeing me cry at the possible reality of a ghost, Mum stared with maternal sternness in the direction where the bedding had been.

"Now look here, Mr Ghost," Mum said, shaking a scolding finger at the air, "you can stay here if you want, but if I ever see you bothering anyone, I will call for an exorcist."

Perhaps Mr. Ghost, as we named him, had been a lawyer in his lifetime, because he found a loophole in Mum's warning. He waited until she was not looking before he bothered anyone for the next seven years that we lived there.

In order to help pay the hefty mortgage of $9,500, Mum rented out the upstairs bedrooms to the college football team. They were a handful for Mum, who was hard pressed to keep them on the straight and narrow. There was the day when one of them sneaked a couple of female students into his room. Hearing the rumpus, Mum charged upstairs and dragged the two girls down while shouting stern warnings at the football player.

None of us knew what happened to the football player that night, and I slept through the incident, but this is the story Mum told me the next day. It seems that the football player had awakened suddenly from a sound sleep and ran (according to Mum) hell-bent-for-breakfast down the hallway while screaming at something behind him. Not watching where he was going, he fell over the banister at the top of the stairs and toppled down to land on a bench in the foyer. He hit the bench with such force that it broke in six pieces. Mum and Dad tried to check him for injuries, but he pushed them away and ran outside, screaming as he disappeared into the darkness. He never returned to our house, not even to get his possessions.

Mum and I insisted Mr Ghost had intervened with his own justice on that football player.

Dad replied, "Stuff and nonsense. The idiot was just drunk."

Angel's Nightmare

Dad had a way of spoiling a perfectly good ghost story for Mum and I, but there were moments which even he could not explain away. The most remarkable instance was what I call "Angel's nightmare".

I had a pet cat named Angel who, Mum shut in the basement at night or whenever we were away from the home. Dad insisted a cat should never be confined. He always left one of our coal chute doors open to allow Angel a means of escape. Mum complained that tramps could easily sneak into the basement to sleep or steal anything. Dad grumped that even tramps needed food and shelter. The door remained open.

One morning when we were leaving for a day trip to the Toledo Zoo, Mum sent Angel to the basement and locked the door between the kitchen and basement. As we drove home that night, I began to worry about Angel. For some inexplicable reason, I believed something bad had happened to him. I could almost hear him crying for me. In spite of my parents reminding me about Angel's easy access outside in case of danger, my bad feelings did not go away.

The moment Dad stopped the car by our garage, I jumped out and ran into our kitchen. I yanked open the basement door. Too afraid to go down there, I called for my pet. A faint, terrified meowing responded. Panicky, I called harder.

Mum listened and said the sounds were coming from the downstairs. We located the cries coming from the locked front parlour. Mum unlocked the door, and I found Angel crouched under a desk in the far corner of the room. He was trembling, and his eyes were open wide in fear. When Angel recognized us, he bolted past us and ran out of the house. Neither Mum nor Dad could explain how Angel could have entered the downstairs on his own, let alone get into the parlour. Angel did not return for over a week. Dad explained his absence by saying that Angel was a tom cat and toms always prowled for days on end. Mum, in her usual way to remove my fears, turned the incident into a joke about "Mr Ghost".

After four years, the football players moved out, allowing us to occupy the upstairs bedrooms. Mum and Dad remained downstairs and continued using the study for their bedroom.

Finding a Bedroom
I moved into the front bedroom. Nothing bothered me until I entered my teens and became more receptive to the strangeness of our house. Hearing gentle tapping on my door every night, I decided to move to the room across the hall from the "head room". This room was even more frightening, as I kept seeing a vague form sitting in the rocking chair at the foot of my bed every night. I often woke up to the sounds of male footsteps walking down the hall dragging something along the floor. I moved to the head room and lasted there for two sleepless nights while I visualized a woman's head staring at me from the alcove.

The only room left to me was the back bedroom. I constantly heard someone walking up the back stairs and felt a frightening presence near the cupboard. Whenever I went down the back stairs, I always felt someone touching me at the top curve of steps. Ironically, the only pleasant place upstairs for me was the store room at the top of the back stairs. This pleasantness was not strong enough to take away my fear, and I finally returned downstairs to sleep in the front room.

I began to question some of Dad's explanations about the unexplicable; for example, the stain on our basement floor. If it was rust from hard water like Dad said, why was it the only rust stain in the home and why did it run only from the furnace to the drain instead of appearing in other places? Why couldn't Mum, who was an immaculate housekeeper, remove the stain? Dad never answered my questions. He just grumped at my notion about the stain being blood instead of rust.

When I was 15, Dad sold the house because it was too expensive to maintain. We moved to a ranch-style home next to a cemetery, of all places. The people who bought our castle home lived there for just a short time and sold it for almost nothing.

Nightmares

I left Defiance when I turned 18 and forgot about my haunted house. Seven or eight years later, I began to have nightmares about the house. The dreams were always the same: My husband Bob and I and our five children moved back into the haunted castle house. I knew we should not go upstairs, but Bob insisted we go up and sleep in the back bedroom. Refusing to enter that room, I remained on the landing while Bob and our children slept there. Within a short time, a man began screaming in horrible shrieks of agony, sending Bob racing with our children out of the room towards me. I hesitated only long enough to see what could have been a handsome man if his face were not so distorted in pain. He lumbered from the store room into the back bedroom and then down the landing towards me. He wore rotted clothing and kept his arms stretched out with his hands trying to grab me. We always escaped the house in my dreams. The house crashed to the ground, swallowing the phantom with it. I woke up screaming.

These nightmares happened every month for several years, then stopped as mysteriously as they had begun. Later I learned the final chapter in the history of our house. The last people to live there, a man and his wife whom I shall call Frank and Edna, had moved into our home around the same time my nightmares had begun. Feeling uncomfortable about sleeping upstairs, Frank and Edna also used the downstairs study for a bedroom.

Screams From the Storage Room

On the first night of the next month, husband and wife were awakened by the tortured screams of a man in the store room. They guessed the man was a tramp who had come into the basement from the cold and somehow wandered upstairs.

Frank ran to the kitchen and pulled open the door leading to the back stairs. Warning Edna to stay in the kitchen in case of trouble,

Frank dashed up the steps toward the voice, now shrieking and laughing like a madman. Edna waited. Then came silence. After no more than a few seconds, she heard Frank scream, "God, oh God! No! No!" Frank ran back downstairs (some people said his hair had turned white) and told Edna to help him barricade the door. When Edna asked him what he'd seen, Frank only said, "Don't ask me. Don't ever ask me."

The next day Frank sealed off the back bedroom and walled up the kitchen door leading to the back stairs. For the rest of the time that they lived there, this unwelcome intruder cried his hellish wails on the first of every month, the same night I had my recurrent nightmare.

Finally, Frank sold the property to a nearby church. The house was torn down, the basement filled in, and the ground paved over for a parking lot. Rumours circulated about workmen having found a skull above the "head room" cupboard. I don't know if that happened, but I do know my nightmares ended then, even though I would not know about the fate of our house for another two years.

I can't explain the circumstances concerning this house that we children called a castle. I won't even try. But I like to think that somehow the destruction of this castle house at last brought peace to John and Ester.

A ROMANIAN TEMPLE BUILT WITH THE AID OF A SPIRIT

by Boczor Iosif

Bogdan-Petriceicu Hasdeu (1838–1907) was a famous Romanian writer, linguist, and Spiritualist. He was a member of the Romanian Spiritualist Society and the Romanian Academy of Science. In 1888 his only daughter, Iulia, went to live and study in Paris. This very gifted young girl could read and write at the age of three, and at the age of five wrote short plays.

One night in February 1889, Hasdeu was working in his sitting room when he received the following telepathic message from his daughter: "Daddy, I'm very happy. I believe we'll meet in the other world."

The next day he received a telegram informing him that his daughter had passed away after his reception of her message.

In the last two decades of his life, Bogdan-Petriceicu Hasdeu took part in many séances and wrote a book about Spiritualism. In a séance he attended, a medium named Sperantia received a message by automatic writing from the other world. Hasdeu attributed this message to his daughter's spirit. The message contained a detailed plan of a temple.

"You must build this temple at Campina, at the foot of the Carpathians," it stated.

Hasdeu fulfilled the wish of his daughter's spirit in 1896. The mystical number three, denoting spiritual harmony, can be found in many elements of the building. There are three rows of halls, three floors, an isosceles triangle on the front, three steps leading to a statue of Christ, and candlesticks with three arms. Hasdeu had a small observatory on the third floor. Near the statue of Christ was a picture of Iulia covered with a white veil.

The atheist Communist regime closed the Spiritualist temple in 1948, but its archive was saved. After the collapse of the dictatorship in December 1989, this sacred building was reopened as a museum.

THE GHOST OF THE ALAMO
by Nick Howes

On March 6, 1836, a massed ground attack by Mexican regulars breached the walls of an old Franciscan mission that was being used as a fortress. The mission was known as the Alamo. Within minutes, the soldiers of General Antonio Lopez de Santa Anna swept through the Alamo, killing every armed defender in a bitter combat. Thus ended 13 days of siege.

Among the dead were Lt Col William Barret Travis, a 26 year-old quick-tempered lawyer and the author of impassioned appeals to the outside world; Jim Bowie, 40, commander of the volunteers, a slave trader, entrepreneur, land speculator, and wielder of the deadly Bowie knife; and Davy Crockett, 50, world-famous frontiersman, former congressman and lively symbol of rough-and-ready America. Santa Anna ordered the 184 dead Texans should be buried in a mass grave.

In the meantime, he prepared to strike out for the north in search of Gen. Sam Houston. Houston was raising an army, using the time the Alamo's defenders had bought.

The Alamo stood silent, secure in enemy hands. But tradition says that the defenders continued their resistance, even from beyond the grave.

It is one of the least-known stories connected with the Alamo, and an authentic ghost story.

The legend is recounted in a 1917 book by Adina de Zavala entitled *History and Legends of the Alamo and Other Missions In and Around San Antonio*. De Zavala notes that the story is taken from a folk tale, which claims the incident occurred after Santa Anna's capture at the battle of San Jacinto, shortly after the fall of the Alamo. Mexican General Andrade ordered the mission to be razed. Only rubble should remain where the Texans had defied Santa Anna's army.

Ghostly hands protruded
Demolition began without incident. But when attention was turned to the walls themselves, ghostly hands protruded from them, brandishing flaming torches that sent the Mexican engineers running in terror.

Accompanying the flaming torches was a spectral verbal

27

warning: "Depart! Touch not these walls. He who desecrates these walls shall meet a horrible fate. Multiple afflictions shall seize upon him and a horrible and agonizing and avenging torture shall be his death."

The tale claims that several relays of engineers sent to demolish the mission were frightened off by the apparitions. Whatever the truth of the story, the Alamo was not demolished.

De Zavala wrote "The Alamo was dismantled of its works, guns, etc. the fosse filled up and the pickets torn up and burned, but only the single outer walls of the mission-square were injured."

The man most directly responsible for the destruction of the Alamo's second story, De Zavala noted, was subsequently killed, "entombed alive and consumed by flames." Or at least, that was the common claim of those telling the tale.

THE GHOSTS OF ASCENSION ISLAND
by *Preston Dennett*

If you don't find Ascension
Your wife will get a pension
– USAF airmen's song

One of the strangest and most isolated places on Earth is a little island called Ascension. Located in the middle of the South Atlantic Ocean, this tiny, unassuming speck of land has a long, remarkable history filled with bizarre and paranormal events. Despite its isolated location (or rather because of it), the island ended up playing a vital role in many major world events.

Ascension Island's fascinating story begins with its discovery on Ascension Day in 1501 by Portuguese mariner Juan de Nova Costella.

Hell on Earth

Immediately, the island earned a reputation as a hellish place. It covers approximately 35 square miles and contains no fresh water and virtually no life. In 1600, explorer John Davis wrote, "This Isle has neither wood, water nor greene thing upon it, but is a fruitlesse greene Rocke of five leagues broad."

The infamous pirate, explorer, and writer William Dampier was shipwrecked on the island in 1701. He called it, "a blot on the fair surface of the earth, an awful wilderness, in the solitude of the ocean."

For centuries, the island was considered a useless, godforsaken place, and was avoided by all seafarers. Even the names of its geological features – Devil's Cauldron, Dark Slope, Devil's Ashpit – reveal what a dismal place it is. Ironically, however, this little island out in the middle of nowhere turned out to be vitally important to a large number of people and nations across the world.

The strategic location of the island was first put to use in 1815 by the English, who garrisoned it with marines to guard Napoleon after he had been exiled to the island of St Helena, 800 miles to the south.

Following the death of Napoleon in 1821, the island assumed another world-changing role: it became the base for ships engaged in the suppression of the West African slave trade. Freed slaves were taken to Ascension Island where they were rehabilitated and liberated.

In 1836 Charles Darwin, then a 27-year-old unknown naturalist, heard about the island and its unusual wildlife. He landed on Ascension and by observing the varieties of the rat population, verified his theory of evolution through natural selection.

In 1899, the first transatlantic submarine cable was installed at Ascension, making it the crossroads of international communication.

By now, it was clear that Ascension was a very important place, and other nations clamoured to use it. During World War II, the United States government built a landing strip on the island. Three hundred enlisted men and a squadron of planes were stationed there, and so Ascension again played a crucial role in world events.

In 1960, NASA established a satellite tracking station at 1,750 feet above sea-level, the highest point on Ascension, firmly establishing the tiny island as one of the most important places on earth.

The Abandoned Sailor
While Ascension's role in world events is undeniable, the saddest and strangest story of the island is that of Jan Svilt, aged 39, a bookkeeper turned sailor, with a wife and two children, who was forcibly marooned on the island on May 5, 1725, after being accused of homosexual acts while at sea.

Svilt's incredible story would have remained unknown if not for a gruesome discovery. In 1747, Captain Mawson of the ship *Compton* was forced to land on Ascension Island for repairs. While there, his crew found the skeleton of Jan Svilt in a small cave. Lying next to Svilt's body was his diary, which told the sad story of his doomed struggle for survival on the dry, deserted island.

What makes Svilt's story so riveting, however, is the amazing series of supernatural events that he experienced prior to his death.

In 1725, life at sea was harsh. Before Svilt was marooned, more than 20 sailors on his ship had been killed through accident and disease, and more than half were ill. Punishment for any infraction was swift and merciless. Svilt was actually going to be thrown overboard before the decision was made to maroon him on Ascension.

So began Ian Svilt's ordeal. He was abandoned on the island with only a small amount of food, supplies and water. He built a camp near the shore and began to explore the island. After a few weeks of exploration, he found the island to be completely desolate, with almost no life except for hordes of rats.

In a matter of weeks, his food ran out and he began to suffer badly from starvation and exposure. Svilt was a religious man, and he turned to prayer and reading his Bible to help him through his ordeal.

Things soon went from bad to worse. Svilt was forced into a constant search for food and water. He managed to catch just enough food to keep himself alive. When his shoes and clothes disintegrated, he moved his campsite into a more sheltered cave farther inland. On June 16, shortly after he moved into his cave, and a month and a half into his ordeal, Svilt had his first supernatural encounter. It was to be the first of a series of encounters that would plague him until his death.

A Plague of Demons

Although he was the only living human being on the island, Svilt was to discover that he wasn't alone. As he wrote in the diary that he kept the entire time he was on the island, "I took my walk on the beach as usual and with as little success as ever, then returned to my tent to repose myself, where in the solemn gloom and dead of night I was surprised by uncommon noises surrounding my tent. Bitter cursing and swearing mixed with the most blasphemous and libidinous expressions that I ever heard. My hair stood on end with horror and cold sweat trickled down my cheeks. Trembling I lay, fearful to speak, least some vile fiend more wicked than the rest should make prey of me. I fear that the Devil has forsook his dark abode and come attended by infernal spirits to keep his hell on Ascension, for I was certain there was not a human creature on the island except myself, never having observed the footsteps of a man since my being there.

"Their discourse and their actions was such that nothing but devils could be guilty of; one more busy than the rest kept such a continual whisking of his tail about my face that I expected nothing than to be torn to pieces by them. Among the rest I imagined to have heard the voice of a friend of mine, with him in this lifetime I was very conversant."

Svilt knelt in prayer for forgiveness and deliverance. But the devils continued their onslaught until three o'clock in the morning, at which point he finally fell asleep. He awoke early the next morning to hear a disembodied voice again screaming vile curses at him. Svilt wrote grimly, "I cannot afford paper enough to set down every particular of this unhappy day." From this point on, Svilt was tormented by the ghosts of Ascension Island. Perhaps he was mad with thirst and starvation. However, Svilt made it very clear in his diary that he believed the ghosts were real and not hallucinations.

A Friendly Spirit

The next day, June 17, Svilt had another dramatic encounter. This one, however, involved the benevolent spirit of his friend and shipmate, Piek Houtman, who had actually died early on the ill-fated voyage. Never again would Svilt laugh at people who talked of ghosts. As he wrote, "Before I came to this miserable island I was a true Calvinist and used to laugh at the Romans when they talked to me of apparitions; but to my great sorrow now find smarting reasons to the contrary and shall henceforth embrace their opinions. This day, as I stood under the bright sun near the peak of a volcano, an apparition in the likeness of Piek Houtman appeared on a black plateau near me. He conversed with me. I did not know whether to run or to cower, but remained rooted to the spot as he talked to me of the sins of my past life, of which I have a sincere and heartfelt repentance. Houtman's nearness shocked me so that I became unsure whether I was already dead, or whether the vision was sent me to prepare me for death. Perhaps the sun has befuddled my brain. I dropped to my knees and prayed to the Father, the Son and the Holy Ghost."

After a few moments, the apparition disappeared and Svilt returned to his cave. The very next day, however, after Svilt dragged a log up to his cave, he had another encounter. "Whilst I was resting my wearied limbs and seriously reflecting with myself the apparition again appeared to me, which gave me horror inexpressible. His name I am unwilling to again mention, not knowing what the consequence may be. He haunted me so long that he began to be familiar with me."

On the next night, the evil spirits returned, and this time they physically attacked Svilt, proving once and for all that they were no hallucination. Instead, it seemed that the evil spirits and the spirit of Svilt's friend, Piek, were in a battle to save Svilt's soul.

"When night came on, to my great surprise the restless apparitions grew more enraged and doubled their fury, tumbling me up and down so in my tent that in the morning my flesh appeared like an Egyptian mummy. Piek Houtman spoke several times to me, nor I could think he meant me any harm, for when he was living we were as friendly as brothers. The saucepan was thrown down, the light put out and all my things left in a strange disorder."

Svilt prayed to God to end his suffering. "My death begins to draw near, my strength decays and life is become a great burden to me."

Nevertheless, Svilt continued his struggle to survive. It was nearly two months into his ordeal and Svilt had still seen no ships. He was utterly alone on the island.

Then, on June 29, Svilt made a horrible discovery. He was exploring the island when he came across the old gravesite of another castaway. This threw him into a great depression, and he hiked forlornly back to his cave. It was then that he experienced his next supernatural encounter.

Writes Svilt in his diary, "I was no sooner come to my cavern but I heard a dreadful noise, resembling many coppersmiths at work. The din stopped as suddenly as it had begun."

Svilt shook his head and wondered if his long sufferings were causing him to lose his mind. He sat down and prayed. By this point, Svilt was so severely dehydrated, he was sure he would die from thirst. While Providence had so far managed to provide enough food and water to survive, he was growing steadily weaker.

The next night he woke up to a terrifying apparition. "I saw a skeleton appear next to my tent with his hand uplifted. Strange to relate, I was not afraid."

On July 9, Svilt had yet another supernatural encounter. "I was walking pensively on the sand, half-dead with thirst. I heard a dismal noise of cursing and swearing in my own language."

Svilt looked around, but there was no one; only a cloud of birds rose up, obscuring the sun for a moment. But he was becoming convinced that evil spirits were taunting him and trying to capture his soul.

Over the next few weeks, Svilt began to deteriorate further. He was reduced to drinking turtle blood and then his own urine. He spent every waking moment searching for food and water. He was weak and dizzy all the time, and was barely able to walk. He prayed constantly for death and to be forgiven for his sins.

The Beatific Vision

On September 6, starting his fifth month upon the island, Svilt lay in his cave, near death. He was no longer able to roam the shoreline for fish or turtles. He was too weak to even stand up. Instead, Svilt lay on his deathbed, consumed with guilt over his sins.

It was then that he had his final and most profound supernatural encounter. Although he refers to it as a dream, it contains all the features and the emotional impact of a typical near-death experience: "I lay down in despair and fell into a fitful sleep. After a while I dreamed that as I walked through the wilderness full of hardships I came upon a place where there was a cave, and I laid me down in that place to rest. I dreamed that I was sadder than at any time in all my life; all my sin and vileness appeared before me great and consuming. I saw that I was fit for nothing but hell and for the everlasting damnation of my soul – and I despaired. Then suddenly, before me the Lord Jesus who looked down from heaven and said to me in a gentle voice, 'Believe in the Lord Jesus Christ and thou shalt be saved.' But I could only whisper, 'I am a great and monstrous sinner.' He smiled and answered, 'My grave is sufficient for thee.' At this my heart was full of joy. He said to me, 'You will reach the Celestial City. Look it is over yonder,' and he pointed above. 'Follow me.' And I did, and as I entered the golden gates I was given a raiment of golden cloth, light as spiders' down. We were met by sweet angels with harps and flutes who sang the praises of God. The city spires shone like gold, the streets were paved with sunlight. In the radiant streets walked men and women wearing crowns on their heads and carrying palm fronds in their hands. All were singing hymns of praise....Then I awoke to find two rats nibbling at my hands."

This experience gave Svilt some renewed hope, and he continued his struggle to survive. He clung to life through the rest of September. He marked off the days in his diary, making only one written entry: "I am so decayed that I am a perfect skeleton and cannot write the particulars, my hand shakes so. I resign my soul wholly to Providence."

Svilt lived for another two weeks. His last entry was dated September 14. He had survived for more than four months, leaving only his diary and a few belongings. It would take more than 20 years for them to be discovered by a passing ship. Fifteen years later, in 1762, Jan Svilt's story was published as a book in Amsterdam, ensuring that his incredible ordeal would never be forgotten.

Preston Dennett is a MUFON field investigator, the author of four books, and a long-time FATE contributor.

ATTACKED BY A BODILESS HAND

By C. V. Jench

***The icy hand was joined to nothing more than a wrist –
but slowly it was strangling me.***

WHEN I ARRIVED at Goli, Matabeleland, Southern Rhodesia, Africa, on that July morning in 1950, it was for the purpose of collecting from the locals the annual hut tax of one pound. For this small amount the locals received full police protection and other aids. That was but one of my many duties as local Native Commissioner, appointed by the British Colonial Office, Department of Colonial Affairs, African Division.

My party consisted of six well-armed local policemen, 20 porters and camp helpers, my own personal servant, Yubi, and myself.

Notice an empty hut standing somewhat isolated from the others, I told Yubi to have it cleaned out and then put my personal belongings in it and set up my cot.

At that I noticed the locals who had gathered to welcome me stopped talking and smiling and fell to staring at me somewhat affrightedly. The head man, Sura, then begged me not to stay in that hut as it was haunted; he said that the white man who had built it had been killed inside it as he slept, by whom or what they did not know.

Thinking myself thoroughly conversant with native fears and superstitions, I merely shrugged and smiled. Had I known what I was going to experience that night I would have taken their advice and slept out-of-doors.

Runners having told them of my coming, locals had arrived and continued to arrive from far and wide to pay their taxes. Setting up a table and chair under a tree I commenced collecting. By evening I had taken in several hundred pounds. Locking the cash box I then took it into the hut and placed two policemen on guard.

I next had my evening meal and then joined the locals around the huge fire they had built. Presently, feeling sleepy, I retired to the hut. Yubi had made a good job of fixing it up and in the glow of the hurricane lamp my cot looked inviting.

Dismissing the local policemen, I placed the cash box under my bed, checked my revolver and placed it handy, undressed and got into bed.

It was pleasant restfully lying there listening to the drone of voices around the fire. Soon I dropped off to sleep.

The next thing I knew I was half awake, gasping agonizingly for breath. Something was pressing hard on my windpipe, shutting off air. A thief after the money, I thought, and instantly came wide awake. In the darkness I groped for my revolver but failed to find it.

Now the "something" at my throat tightened its grip. It was icy cold and clammy and did not feel like a human hand. A snake must have coiled itself around my neck, I decided. I grabbed at it, and seized not a snake but a wrist, cold as ice.

Clutching the wrist with my right hand, I wrenched it sideways, and once again breathed freely. With my left hand I reached for the spot where the attacker's body should be, at the same time sitting up on the cot.

But I could feel no body – only the cold wrist and hand.

Hanging on to it with all the strength in my right hand I felt along the wrist with my left, and found myself clutching only empty air. There was seemingly only a wrist and a hand, both as cold as death. It writhed and struggled furiously to reach my throat, and seemed slowly to be winning the struggle. At that stark fear engulfed me and, still clinging desperately to that struggling, bodiless hand, I began shouting wildly for help.

"Help! police, police! Leta Malampur! Pangisa!" (Bring lamps! Hurry!)

There were grunts, then shouts, as the startled policemen roused each other.

Meanwhile, I hung on to the ice-cold hand and wrist, although my teeth were chattering and my brain reeling. It seemed like hours but was actually only short minutes before the police, carrying lighted lanterns, came racing to my aid. And even as they burst into the hut I felt that chilly wrist slipping from my grasp. It didn't so much slip as it faded. It seemed to *dissolve* in my grasp.

I struggled to my feet, found my revolver and ordered the hut thoroughly searched.

We found nothing.

My personal servant, Yubi, had come running to my aid with the policemen, and I now asked him to look at my throat. Picking up a lantern he looked closely. His face went grey and he drew back shuddering. When I asked him why he reminded me that a thorough search had turned up no one, yet the distinct marks of human fingers were on my neck. They had not been made by any living man, he assured me, but by a dead hand – an *isituhwane* – the spirit of a man from another world.

The whole camp now was aroused and a huge fire lighted the scene. Sura, the head man, came hurrying up. After being told what had occurred he nodded sagely. He said he had warned the other white man, who had been choked to death in his sleep on the first night he slept there, not to build the hut over that spot. He had told him it was directly over the site of a *Makalanga* village whose inhabitants had been massacred one night by a Matabele *impi* many years before. Undoubtedly, the severed hand and wrist of one of the victims still sought revenge, he said.

I accepted Sura's explanation, for I could offer no other and cannot to this day.

Ordering my belongings and cash box taken to another hut, I then had the haunted one burned to the ground. I can only hope that the bodiless hand was destroyed with it.

I am now retired, living in modest comfort at Hampton-on-Thames in Middlesex. But even yet, on rare occasions, I start up from my sleep with a frightened cry, dreaming that a strangling, bodiless hand is at my throat.

BALTAZARINI'S GHOST

By Rev. Irene Farrier

The word of one of France's most estimable gentlemen
substantiates this apparition of Baltazarini, creator
of the opera.

King Henri III, the last of the Valois, was the favorite son of Catherine de Medici, and is best known for his one great crime, his assent to the St Bartholomew's Day Massacre.

Less well known is the part he played in one of the world's most famous ghost stories, his composition of a mournful song in memory of Marie de Cleves, his beloved, and his gift of a spinet piano to his favourite musician, Baltazarini, to whom the world owes the invention of the opera.

On May 4, 1865, Leon Bach, great-great-grandson of Johann Sebastian Bach, the famed composer, discovered an unusually preserved and remarkable beautiful spinet in a Paris shop, and bought it as a gift for his father N.G. Bach.

It was very old, of oak, ornamented with delicate carving in tasteful gilded Arabesques, encrusted with turquoise and intermingled with gilt fleur-de-lys. It was about five feet long by two wide; it had no legs; but it was packed away, like a violin, in a wooden case. When about to be used, it was set on a table or stand. As a musical instrument, it was little to be desired, having a bad tone.

Upon examination, however, the elder Bach made a discovery which atoned for all imperfections. On a narrow bar supporting the sounding-board was a written inscription which revealed that the spinet had been made in Rome in 1564 by Antonius Nobilis of Milan, and finished on April14 of that year.

This certification of the antiquity of the spinet greatly added to its value since even in those days value was placed on antiques.

Much pleased, Mr. Bach retired for the night – and dreamed of his son's gift. There appeared to him a handsome young stranger, with a carefully trimmed beard, and elegantly dressed in the ancient costume of the French court – rich doublet with ample lace collar and close-fitting sleeves that were slashed in the upper part; large slashed trunk-hose, long stockings and low shoes with rosettes. Doffing a high-pointed, broad-brimmed and white-plumed hat, this young man advanced, bowing and smiling, toward Mr Bach's bed.

"The spinet you have, belonged to me," said the ghostly visitor. "I often played on it to amuse my master, King Henri. In his youth he composed an air with words which he was fond of singing while I accompanied him. Both words and air were written in memory of a lady whom he greatly loved. He was separated from her, which caused him much grief. She died, and in his sad moments he used to hum this air."

The strange visitor added, "I will play it to you, and I shall take means to recall it to your recollection, for I know you have a poor memory."

Seating himself at the spinet he accompanied himself as he sang the words.

The old man awoke in tears, lighted a taper and discovered that it was two o'clock. He returned to his rest, much disturbed.

As he opened his eyes to broad daylight, he saw, to his amazement, a sheet of paper lying on his bed inscribed with score and words of a song and headed "Air and lyrics by King Henri III."

His astonishment increased when he examined the sheet more closely. It was a rare archaeological specimen: the notes were minute, the clefs those used in former times, the writing careful and old fashioned, with here and there the Gothic tails similar to those attached to certain letters in the manuscripts of the sixteenth and seventeenth centuries, with the orthography, too, that of two or three hundred years previous.

It was the song the ghost of the dream had sung to him!

He hastened to his piano and soon convinced himself beyond any possible doubt that it was indeed the same song.

The mysterious message was written on the back of a four-page sheet of music-paper, two pages of which contained a composition of his own which he had sketched the day before, leaving the sheet in his escritoire. Who had taken it and filled the two blank pages with this mysterious music from a bygone age? The ghost?

Or had it been himself, walking and writing in his sleep? He was mystified, the more so when he noticed the remarkable coincidence of names and dates. The name in the vision had spoken of "his master, King Henri," the song itself purported to have been written by Henri III; but the spinet was made in 1564 when Henry (then Duke d'Anjou) was fourteen years old.

The elder Bach spoke of his strange experience to his friends, and among them was one who suggested that he was a "writing medium" and that his hand might be guided while he slept.

Intrigued by this suggestion, one day three or four weeks after the dream, feeling a headache and nervous trembling of the arm, the idea struck him that the friend's explanation might be the correct one; so, seating himself with paper and pencil, he waited. Almost immediately he lost consciousness, and, while in that state, wrote – in French – "King Henri, my master, who gave me the spinet you now possess, had written a four-line stanza on a piece of parchment, which he caused to be nailed to the case (*etui*), when one morning, he sent me the instrument. Some years afterward, having to travel and take the spinet with me, fearing that the parchment might be torn off and lost, I took it off, and for safe-keeping put it in a small niche, on the left of the keyboard, where it still is."

This communication was signed Baldazzarini, and then followed the stanza alluded to, as follows:

"Le roy Henri donne cette grande espinette
A Baldazzarini, tres-bon musicien.
Si elle n'est bonne ou pas assez conquette,
Pour souvenir, do moins, qu'il la conserve bien."

The stanza, literally translated, reads:

"King Henri gives this large spinet
To Baldazzarini, an excellent musician.
If it is not good, or not stylish enough,
At least, for my sake, let him preserve it carefully."

Here, at last, was a chance to obtain tangible evidence in connection with these mysteries. Here was a test to determine whether this Baldazzarini was a myth or a real person, capable of disclosing unknown facts.

Father and son explored the old spinet in vain for several hours, then, having raised the keyboard and removed some hammers, they detected, underneath, on the left, a narrow slit in the wood containing what proved to be a bit of parchment eleven and a half inches long and two and three-quarter inches wide, on which was written, in a bold dashing hand, four lines, similar to those the elder Bach's hand had traced in his trance. And there was a signature – Henri's!

"Moy le Roy Henri trios octroys cette espinette
A Baltasarini mon gay musicien
Mais s'il did mal sone, ou bien (ma) moult simplette
Lors pour mon souvenir dans l'estuy garde bien.
HENRI."

The stanza, literally translated, reads as follows:

"I, King Henri III, present this spinet
To Baltasarini, my gay musician:
But if he finds it poor-toned, or else very simple,
Still for my sake, in its case let him preserve it."

Here was proof, substantial, but not literal. For instance, "King Henri" in the ghost message, "I, King Henri III" in the original: a variation in the spelling of the recipient's name, and "excellent" written "gay" in the original; also "not good" replaced by "poor-toned"; and "not stylish enough" by "very simple"; finally in the last line, the original refers to the case, while in the stanza written by Mr. Bach there is no such reference.

The interpolated *(ma)* in the discovered stanza, greatly puzzling at first, was explained by the elder Bach. "No one could imagine the meaning of the word *ma*, surrounded by lines. But one day my hand was again moved involuntarily and there was written, "Amico mio: the King joked about my Italian accent in the verse he sent with the spinet. I always said *ma* instead of *mais.*'"

The original parchment was taken to the *Biblioteque Imperiale*, France's great national library at that time, and compared with original manuscripts. In these Henri's hand was found to vary, as in that age handwritings often did; but with some of the acknowledged originals the writing on the parchment – verse as well as signature – was found to correspond. Various experienced antiquarians also pronounced the parchment to be a genuine autograph of Henri, no matter where obtained.

Minute holes visible along the upper edge of the parchment indicated that it had originally been attached to some wooden surface, sustaining the allegation that Henri had caused it "to be nailed to the case". On the lower edge it seems to have been cut off inside the nail-holes; but the marks of four larger holes, one at each corner of the parchment, are distinctly visible.

Is this the actual proof of a ghostly visitant, dead several hundred years? There seems to be no reason for the eminently respectable descendant of the celebrated Johann Sebastian Bach, himself an accomplished musician with unimpeachable social and professional standing, to perpetuate a fraud of such exact skill. All France believed the proof to be authentic.

The song (see cut B for first two lines) was published. As no treble accompaniment, but only the air with bass, was given in the original, the elder Bach had to supply the accompaniment for the right hand, which he did with taste and judgment.

The Athenaeum Library of Boston, in a *French Dictionary of Musicians* lists Baltasarini as follows, "An Italian musician, known in France under the name of Beaujoyeux, was the first violinist of his day. The Marechal de Brissac brought him from Piedmont, in 1577, to the court of Queen Catherine de Medici, who appointed him her Director of Music, the first *valet de chamber*. Henri III entrusted to him the management of the court fetes; and he long discharged the duties of that post with credit. It was he who first conceived the idea of a dramatic spectacle, combined with music and dancing." (Opera.)

Baltazarini was, then, at Henri's court, called "the handsome and the joyous," a final link in the chain of evidence of the reality of a ghost!

FOLLOW THE BEACON TO THE GHOST
by Nick Howes

Ghosts reportedly walk at the Ponce de Leon Lighthouse, a site just south of Daytona Beach, Florida, that is visited by hundreds of tourists daily. After climbing to the top of the tower, visitors exit onto the gallery deck to view the Ponce de Leon Inlet, once known as Mosquito Inlet, the Atlantic Ocean beyond and, on the inland side, the Halifax River.

Between 1884 and 1887, 1.25 million bricks were used to build the lighthouse. At 175 feet, the tower is Florida's tallest, second only in the U.S. to the Cape Hatteras, North Carolina, lighthouse.

After decades of service, the lighthouse was abandoned by the Coast Guard in 1970 and replaced with a beacon on the south side of the inlet. A preservation association restored the facility and opened it to the public as a museum. Today, tourists can explore the three keepers' homes, watch a film about the lighthouse, and examine artefacts and numerous displays.

The lighthouse returned to active duty in 1982 with the installation of a new beacon, which doesn't interfere with visitors who climb the tower for the view.

The Haunting

The chief haunting stems from a Sunday in October 1919, when assistant keeper Joseph Davis filled in for the principal keeper. Half an hour before sunset, Davis' initial evening task was to lug a heavy container of paraffin, then referred to as mineral oil, up the tower steps to refuel the beacon. Visible 20 miles out at sea, the light burned about five gallons a night. But on the seventh landing, Davis slumped to the floor, struck by his third heart attack, this time fatal. When the light failed to come on with the darkness, the second assistant keeper climbed the tower stairs and found Davis.

According to a current employee, maintenance men report smelling paraffin fumes on that landing, although the paraffin-fueled light gave way to a revolving electric beacon in 1933.

From the era of principal keeper Tom O'Hagen, during the first decade of the 20th century, comes another haunting. It is believed to be that of his son, who died of injuries after being kicked in the head by a horse. This presence manifests itself as eerie footsteps, closing doors and other activities that, as the employee I spoke to put it, suggest childish pranks.

During its maiden investigation of the site, the Daytona Beach Paranormal Research Group, Inc., arrived with an assortment of electronic equipment on the afternoon of April 4, 2002. Doris "Dusty" Smith, author of *Haunts of the World's Most Famous Beach*, said their early results indicated high orb activity near the oil house, where paraffin for the light was once kept. Orbs are small, round balls of light, often emitting light or, conversely, transparent, associated with haunted locations. The group took a break until after dark.

At 9.30 p.m. a preliminary examination was made. Smith and another member, monitoring the south gate with a videocamera, saw through the LED an orb exiting through the gate and turning east every 11 minutes, 11 seconds. "The anomaly was captured 13 times throughout the course of the night," said Smith, "and was found to be the same size, shape, and colour each time it was in the shot."

Resuming at 10:37 p.m. investigators detected substantial orb activity at the boatyard, keeper's house, and south gate. Video footage, 35mm photos, and digital photos showed the orb passing through the south gate as before, with corresponding EMF (electromagnetic field) fluctuations.

The site exhibited signs of paranormal activity and deserves to be researched at length, said Smith. The investigation into the haunting of the Ponce de Leon Lighthouse is ongoing.

Nick Howes *is news director at WNSVFM, Nashville, Illinois.*

A HOUSE ON BEECH STREET
by Ron Halbritter

Chula Vista, California. The city's name comes from the Spanish, *que chula vista* – what a beautiful view. And so it is, as we sit near San Diego Bay with San Diego to our north and Tiajuana, Mexico, to our south.

Chula Vista's streets are named in alphabetical order, north to south. There aren't enough streets to complete the alphabet, so we travel through Orange and Palomar, and end at Quintard. Not many exciting events occur on our neatly organized streets. The rock group Cream once was arrested in Chula Vista for being disorderly when they stopped at a service station to ask directions, and in November 1960, two backyard astronomers observed a UFO that later became one of the famous Project Blue Book unsolved cases.

But nothing had ever prepared me and two of my friends for the events that occurred in a house on Beech street.

Nearly every Friday, my co-worker Marie and I would stop by a well-known watering hole along "F" street. Sometimes Marie and I would share a drink or two with Marie's friend Olivia, affectionately called Ollie, and Ollie's husband, Steve. Together, we would enjoy a stunning view of Chula Vista and share notes about the week that had just passed.

One Friday evening, Steve and Ollie were thrilled to announce that they had just bought a house at the north end of town, on Beech Street. It was warm and cosy, just like most of the homes in Chula Vista. And like all new homeowners, Steve and Ollie spent hours decorating their house and making it a comfortable, inviting place for friends and family to visit.

Sadly, however, Ollie and Steve divorced within a year or two. Ollie kept the house. She and Marie had always been good friends, but now they became almost inseparable.

One night at our favourite "F" street hangout, Ollie and Marie took me into their confidence. Something strange had been occurring at Ollie's house on Beech Street. Ever since the divorce, the house had been inexplicably filled with cold drafts. Strange sounds emanated from nowhere and some items had been moved. Ollie thought she was living with a ghost. I asked her what her neighbours knew about the house, but Ollie explained that her neighbourhood was largely populated by Navy officers, who move often. None of Ollie's neighbours had lived there long.

Ollie and Marie were clearly shaken by the mysterious events on Beech Street.

"Maybe there's a logical explanation," I said. "Let me take a close look at the house."

I'm not a professional investigator, but I thought I knew where to start. I began with a thorough visual inspection. I sought small holes in the foundation and in the eaves. I had heard that many a potential ghost has been found to be mice, birds or even bees. When my visual inspection showed nothing unusual, I went to the city's building inspection department, where I found a microfilm of the house's original 1955 blueprints. Careful study showed no secret rooms or surprises; the blueprints matched my visual survey. I went to the county tax assessor's office and looked up past property owners. It was a short list. The original owners were husband and wife. But the next owner's information was curious; the house had been sold by "the executor of the estate". That seemed to indicate that the second owner had died there.

With the second owner's name and the date of the house sale, I next went to the library's genealogical society. I knew they have an index of all the obituaries in the local papers. I found an obituary that described the suicide of the homeowner, who had been in despair after his wife's death.

I reported my findings to Ollie and Marie. The two were now more convinced than ever that a supernatural presence was, in fact, haunting the house.

I wasn't prepared to deal with a real ghost – so I called one of the area's leading experts on the afterlife, Lady Sabrina of the Circle of Our Lady of Endora. Lady Sabrina listened carefully to our story and offered to come to the house on the following new moon. She explained that the full moon is appropriate for many activities but for beginnings, one should work from the new moon.

That evening, Lady Sabrina arrived at the house before sunset. She introduced herself, then quickly, confidently, prepared a broom from straw and swept the entire house, high and low. When she was finished sweeping, we sat around a Ouija board. Lady Sabrina prepared a circle, calling on the guardians of the four elements (Earth, Air, Fire and Water) to protect us. We put our hands onto the planchette.

Lady Sabrina asked, "Is anyone here? Is there anyone we can speak to?"

The planchette responded almost immediately: "Yes."

"What is your name?"

"E-r-i-c."

Shivers ran up and down my spine.

"Are you the person who has been disrupting this home?"

"N-o." The word was spelled out. "N-o … T-h-i-s … h-o-u-s-e … h-a-p-p-y … n-o-t … w-a-n-t … f-i-g-h-t."

"Eric, are you saying that the fighting and unhappiness in this house is what caused you to react?"

"Y-e-s … T-h-i-s … h-o-u-s-e … l-o-n-g … h-a-p-p-y … n-o … f-i-g-h-t."

"But Eric, Steve is gone. There hasn't been any fighting."

"A-n-g-e-r … s-t-i-l-l … h-e-r-e … w-a-n-t … p-e-a-c-e."

"Eric, do you want peace for Ollie, or for yourself?"

"B-o-t-h."

"Would it make you happy if we did a ritual of dismissal and allowed you to leave, to cross over and join your wife?"

"V-e-r-y … h-a-p-p-y."

Lady Sabrina asked that we not reveal the details of the dismissal ritual, but she has allowed me to report one significant sentence:

"May all beings and elementals attracted to this rite, depart, on their way harming none…"

After the dismissal ritual, the Lady opened the circle:

"The circle is open, but unbroken…"

We then proceeded with a cleansing ritual that included tying a thread to the front door. The four of us walked through every room in the house trailing the thread, then gathered the thread in a ball and burned it in the back yard.

Since then, the house hasn't had any recurrence of paranormal activity. Once again, it's just another comfortable home in Chula Vista.

Ron Halbritter *is a shipbuilder and ship repairman in Chula Vista. He owns every issue of FATE ever published.*

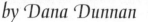

THE BELLMAN HELPS OUT
by Dana Dunnan

In 2001, on the weekend of a provincial holiday called Family Day, the Banff Springs Hotel was very noisy and active. After Family Day, the hotel fell dramatically quiet. The next day, I spent some time in the $12,000,000 Solace Spa. Soothing music played underwater as a computer controlled the mineral content.

A guest reported that James Coburn was holidaying with his wife at the hotel. A second person said he had heard Cuba Gooding, Jr., was at the hotel doing scenes for a Disney film about dog sledding in nearby Canmore. A third person disapprovingly said that he had seen a male guest heading through the lobby with two clearly underage women on his arm.

Given the new solitude of my wing, I went to sleep at 10 p.m. without using the earplugs on my nightstand.

Around midnight, there was a loud banging from the wall in back of the headboard. Such noises aren't unknown in hotels, although perhaps more often at the lower end of the economic spectrum. I put in the earplugs and went back to sleep.

Within ten minutes the banging woke me up again. My headboard seemed as solid as concrete, so enthusiastic neighbours seemed an unlikely explanation.

Even after I switched to a new pair of earplugs, the pounding continued – this time in the ceiling.

When I checked in, there had been confusion at the front desk. The hotel had just completed a new lobby as another step in the $75,000,000 renovation, restoring the craftsmanship from 1928. Perhaps construction was going on around the clock, to meet a deadline. But the noise was not like construction, and it was not the sounds of steam pipes in an old heating system.

Determined to sleep, I called the front desk. Like the car that works perfectly when you finally get it to a mechanic, the sound stopped as soon as the operator answered, and never returned. The operator said they would send security.

After hearing my story, Kyle, a security guard, asked, "Are you a spiritual person?"

I didn't want to hurt his feelings, so I offered a tentative "yes".

Meet Sam McCauley

So began my introduction to Sam McCauley.

Kyle explained to me that Sam had been a bellman who died some years ago, and he came when people needed help.

Kyle and I walked together on his rounds.

Back when Sam patrolled the corridors of his beloved hotel in the spring of 1969, there was hope that it might return to its glory days. It would be a welcome change, since recent talk had been of tearing it down. Decades earlier, he'd come to the Banff Springs Hotel as a bellman. He had worked in the mines each winter, so summer in the hotel was heaven.

Walking the worn carpeting of its hallways, he remembered when guests would come for the entire summer. The Canadian Pacific Railroad had built the hotel in 1888. The bellmen would bring the huge steamer trunks up to the rooms while the guests checked in, often setting up lines of credit for $50,000.

With the rich came the famous: Benny Goodman, Helen Keller, Jack Benny and Cole Porter all stayed in the great castle.

As he walked from turret to turret on the top floor, Sam remembered becoming head of the bellmen. The little Scotsman was proud when a summer staff-member had written that he was "a kind but firm and sometimes tyrannical individual" who was "the iron will behind these men who thought themselves the epitomes of staff-persons." His boys were the first representatives of the hotel to greet guests. They needed his discipline. He enjoyed a joke during the slow times that occurred, but guests must see them as professionals.

Signs of Decay

As he climbed the stair up into the turrets, it saddened him to see the cracked plaster. While the advent of jet travel had brought guests like the Kennedys and Queen Elizabeth, it had also brought bus tours to fill rooms and wander the corridors. What they saw was a crumbling reminder of its former glory.

Sam passed through the great halls, the furniture covered with sheets. As winter caretaker, he tried to get the more worn furniture out of sight. Some found the sheets ghostly; to him, it was just familiar.

Old steam pipes banged, attempting to heat the 845-room hotel. The stone castle that was finished in 1928, meant to replace the original wooden hotel, hadn't been engineered for year-round use.

Yet there was talk that a new general manager coming in might open the hotel year round to take advantage of the expanding skiing market. That revenue might bring renovation to what had been a grand hotel before the effects of the Depression wore it down and World War II closed it completely for a while.

Sam loved the top floor. There were many little hiding places where he could keep his tips. Although the sloping roof made the corridor narrower, the views out over the confluence of the Bow and Spray Rivers and up Sulphur Mountain reminded him why the hotel was situated here.

Sam had told the boys that he would come back and haunt the hotel after he died. He had been with the hotel in its best times and its worst. Maybe he would stay there forever.

In the security centre, Kyle introduced his colleague Kerri. Afterwards, fully awake, I wandered the hotel.

As dawn drew nearer, I saw Kerri again at the convenience store off the lobby. She said she hadn't seen Kyle in a couple of hours.

She called him on the radio. He responded, sounding extremely upset. Kerri asked what was wrong. He said he would come and tell her.

The Wandering Girl

Kyle had been outside the lobby smoking when he saw a young girl, poorly dressed and with the beginnings of hypothermia. She told him it was her intent, after a night of partying, to wander off into the woods to die.

It was a very cold night, in a town that was then home to about 20 wolves and seven cougars. While wolves aren't known to attack humans, a cougar had killed a woman cross-country skiing a month earlier.

The despondent girl resisted Kyle's attempts to detain her there. However, he kept her talking until the Mounties arrived and took her into custody.

She was very uncooperative with them also. She was unwilling to give her name or age, but eventually it was determined she had run away from Toronto, so she was put on a bus back home the next day.

Kyle had saved her life. And the pounding on the wall and ceiling had set in motion the sequence of events that put him in the right place to do so. Was Sam helping out again?

Before I checked out, I asked at the front desk about the occupancy of the rooms behind and above me.

They were both empty.

The Blazing Bride

At the bookshop the next day, I learned that Sam wasn't the only legend in the hotel. Edmonton native Barbara Smith has written several books of ghost tales in Canada and the Rockies, and the Banff Springs Hotel is included.

Supposedly the gown of a bride making her grand entrance had caught on fire from the candles illuminating a staircase. The bride was originally described as having tripped over her dress, fallen and broken her neck. Only in later articles was her dress reported to have been been ignited by candles, leaving it unclear as to whether she was merely clumsy or a fire hazard. In the one instance that a year is identified, the local paper has no reference to any such tragedy at the hotel, although it reports other explosions, fires, accidents and deaths associated with the Canadian Pacific Railroad and the hotel.

In later years, a spectral bride was seen dancing a waltz alone. Other ghosts in formal wear have been seen in the Rob Roy Room, but they appear only from the waist up. The new lounge has its floor some three feet above the old floor, but the dancers seem to prefer the old floor.

The Headless Bagpiper

The Banff Springs prides itself on taking good care of its guests. The same lounge frequented by the ghostly bride also featured a long-deceased bartender who would inform patrons when they had enough to drink. Since entertainment is crucial to high society a headless bagpiper was seen in the lounge. A male voice was once heard singing in the ladies' rest room at 3:00 a.m. and an entire men's chorus echoed in the men's room. In each case, the rooms proved to be empty.

An error made in construction of an added wing produced a room with no door or windows. The blueprints were altered to cover the error, and the room wasn't discovered until a fire in 1926. A spectral figure had been seen outside the room by security guards, but, after the fire, the figure never reappeared. Whether the spectre was a guilt-ridden architect or a spirit-world lawyer will remain a mystery.

The books contain all these stories, but with few names, quotes or dates.

Barbara Smith's books are also filled with stories about Sam, the only ghost with a name. Lights seen shining outside windows in rooms lacking any ledge to stand on are attributed to Sam.

Two years after Sam had died, two guests who had checked in late inquired about the elderly man who had helped with their bags. Told that there were no bellboys over 30, the couple insisted and proceeded to describe Sam.

Employees also shared stories with me. Sam particularly liked working with honeymooners, which would have placed him on my wing and the floor above.

Sam had been forced to retire. Insisting that he had to keep working, he was sent home and supposedly died without coming back for his last paycheque.

Stories From Employees

Some employees said they had been told the ghost stories in their orientation. Others said they had been told not to discuss them, that they were untrue and demeaning to a great hotel.

A friend of Sam's, Louis Trono, played trombone in the hotel orchestra for over six decades. Now 93, Trono described Sam as rather difficult in the last years of his life. When Sam's widow was asked if she minded all the ghost stories about her late husband, she replied, "Not as long as he stays up in that hotel."

The public relations director for the hotel is Holly Wood. Wood considers the topic of Sam and other ghosts "bullhooey". She maintains that the stories of Sam and the burning bride were fabrications of a public relations director 20 years ago. She has been there 12 years, and she says there are no ghosts.

However, when the hotel ran a Halloween package in 1994, Wood was sharing the legends of Sam and the bride with the *Calgary Herald*. Similarly, the Canadian Broadcasting Corporation ran a show on Sam and the bride in 1995.

A column called "The Psychic" from *The Edmonton Journal* in 1980 describes the general manager of Banff Springs speaking about "their ghost". Details on Sam's ghost were produced in a letter from the then-Banff Springs public relations director, Elise Williamson.

Robert Sandford is historian-in-residence for the Alberta region of the Fairmont hotel chain. He "gets calls all the time about these stories". Sandford sees the persistence of the stories as a result of "the nature, scale, and architecture of the building". Conditioned by Shakespeare and other writers, "people in an unfamiliar setting like this are hypersensitive to sounds and circumstances they haven't experienced before".

Many Legends Debunked

"In my investigations [of the bride]," Sandford said, "I could not find any record of said guest and said event. You would think it would be in the security records.

A public relations person took the various noises and rattles of an old hotel and built them into five different story lines that she shared with over a thousand different journalists.

It finally became so big she stopped doing it, because the stories were taking on lives of their own. They were backfilling with dates and details that she hadn't concocted. When I came in 1997, I wanted to know the historical basis for the legends. Gradually, it became apparent there was less and less substance to this. Still, I got a fair amount of resistance from people who insisted there were ghosts."

Elise Williamson had come to the Banff Springs Hotel soon after college. She said that on her first day on the job, the head of the bellboys told her about Sam's ghost.

"True or not, it's mythology; it's something people want to hear. I embraced the story, because I do believe in ghosts personally. I thought 'this hotel needs ghosts'". From then on, she talked to writers "as often as I could".

"I never fabricated things. I listened to what I heard. I listened to the guests, I listened to what other people told me and I embraced those stories. I probably enhanced them a little bit. I'm the one who got the stories going."

The legends seem to exist at the intersection of public relations and cultural anthropology. The demographics and culture of the skiing clientele in the 1970s made the ghost tales an acceptable way to get the hotel greater recognition. In 1976, Sam died. Two years later, the first stories began to arise.

A friend and fellow employee says of the hotel and Sam, "It's an old place, and old places always have something or other. It's what you believed in, I think, or what you wanted to believe."

I had heard nothing of the Banff Springs legends when I carried my bags into Room 667. The hotel didn't strike me as eerie, and I am hardly predisposed to look for the supernatural.

Experience Confirms Ghosts

But the pile of earplugs on the nightstand would serve as testimony to something that went bump in the night. The front desk confirmed that the rooms behind and above me were unoccupied. The RCMP did confirm that they had sent the underage runaway back to Toronto.

Perhaps Sam McAuley is still in the Banff Springs Hotel, helping those in need.

Dana Dunnan is a retired high school teacher who has a master's degree from Stanford. He lives in Greenland, New Hampshire.

LOVE FROM BEYOND THE GRAVE

An ethereal romance leads a young woman to her death

by Corrine De Winter

It was a story of love beyond the grave – two people from different times drawn to each other in a mysterious and ethereal union that ultimately led to death. In 1886 Mrs Julia Bowles Phillips recorded the strange story that began when her family moved into a beautiful colonial-style mansion, now known as the Alexander Phillips House, in Springfield, Massachusetts. Julia's son gave her account to the Society for the Preservation of New England Antiquities in 1949.

"When my father bought this place, I was very young, only seven years old, but my first recollection of the house is quite distinct. I was brought here one afternoon when he came to talk over some business arrangement with the former owner, an elderly southern lady who had used it as a summer residence, bringing with her a family of two sons and a beautiful daughter, a retinue of slaves, a fine yellow coach and thoroughbred horses.

Soon we were established, and I and my younger sister roamed at our own sweet will through the lofty rooms and the lovely gardens. The flower garden was the delight of us both. Our dining room was then in the eastern wing and the library in the western.

We were still quite young when we learned that the library and the little room that opened out from it had been inhabited for years by a young man, one of the sons of the southern lady, and that during the time he had lived there, no one looked upon his face. He was very handsome, they said, clever and fascinating in his manner, but, like many attractive men with plenty of money, and with the Southern abhorrence of work, he had become dissipated and led a very fast life. Then, satiated with what he supposed to be the only pleasures of this world, he decided to isolate himself from his fellows and spend his remaining years in study and self-communion.

My sister was a strange child, fanciful and dreamy. The house seemed to hold a special charm for her, and the young man's story in particular made a great impression on her.

One warm summer afternoon in early June, when Leila was 16, she stood in the garden facing the library and looked toward it, feeling drawn to do so by some strong impulse. There in the window sat a young man, beautiful as a god he seemed to her, and his large dark eyes rested on her with a gaze of burning intensity.

She walked through the garden and up the library verandah steps, but the chair was empty. She asked the family for the identity of the man who had been in the library. We laughed and replied that she must have been dreaming. She turned from us with a troubled look in her eyes.

"Several days later, Leila came to me and said, 'I have seen him again.' She told me that she had stepped out on the eastern verandah for a moment and was astonished to see, standing in the driveway, a spirited black horse saddled and bridled with rich silver-mounted trappings. She turned her head and encountered again the face of the man she had seen at the library window. Before she had time to speak or even think, he leaned toward her, eagerly grasped her hand on which he pressed a burning kiss, mounted the horse, and galloped away in the dusk. As Leila related this to me, she trembled with intense excitement. She begged for me to say nothing of the matter to our parents, and I consented, although I was greatly troubled.

The sultry days of August had come. It seemed to me that I had never known such oppressive heat. For weeks, we had no rain. At last, one evening we felt a slight breeze as we started for bed.

I must have slept heavily for several hours when I was awakened by a frightful flash of lightning followed by a deafening crash, and before I could gather my senses, down came the longed-for rain.

My first thought was of the open windows, and I flew from room to room closing them. On reaching Leila's room, a sudden flash illuminated the entire chamber and showed me that the bed was empty!

'Leila is out in the storm!' I cried out. We took a lantern and went into the garden. Halfway down the walk we found her – her sweet life shattered by a thunderbolt!

We bore her up to her bed. It was then we realized that she was dressed in Mother's bridal dress. She had arrayed herself in this quaint, old-fashioned gown and around her head had wrapped the bridal lace. The cruel lightning had failed to mar her exquisite beauty. It wasn't until we had laid her away in the grave that everything was explained.

A few days after the funeral I was in her room. When I opened a little escritoire, I found a folded letter addressed to me in Leila's handwriting.

The letter told me of the first time the handsome stranger in the garden spoke. 'Leila, the power of love has drawn me from a far-off country to your side. Without question or fear, will you put your trust in me?'

The letter ended, 'I am going to that far-off country from which he came to me, and it may be many years before I shall see you all again.'"

The amazing confession in Leila's letter was never known outside the family. As the years passed and the city grew, the house was moved to the side lawn where it now stands. In the process of moving it, the library wing had been removed and the workmen discovered the skeleton of a man in the cellar beneath the bedroom. Leila's father had the bones buried next to her grave. But were they the remains of the handsome lover from a "far-off country?"

The house still stands on State Street in Springfield, without tenants but well preserved as an important landmark in New England. Some people claim they have seen figures in the windows and mysteriously blinking "ghost lights". So far no phenomena have been captured on film. But if you stand in the now barren gardens on a sultry August night, will you also run the risk of being swept away by the desire and passion from another world?

Corrine De Winter *is the author of five books, including* Wishcraft *and* One Side of Heaven *(Black Arrow Press). Her work has appeared in the* Palo Alto Review, The New York Quarterly, Chrysalis, Space & Time, *and* Atom Mind. *She is currently working on a compilation of supernatural tales from New England.*

BILLY COMES BACK

A memorable phenomenon took place on Christmas Eve 1908 in the tiny farm village of Ethelbert, Manitoba, at least to the youngest members of my grandmother's family.

The area was settled by Ukrainians in the 1890s. Farms in all directions were owned by people who came primarily from Galicia, in what was then Austria-Hungary. They were hard-working people who barely scratched a living from the stony ground.

They told a wealth of legends and stories, and a strong belief in the supernatural was common. Belief in the beyond was as certain and inevitable as we believe that if today is Sunday tomorrow must be Monday. These beliefs had a steadying influence on people.

On Orthodox Christmas Eve, January 6, 1908, my grandmother, Pearl Zabinski, was busily setting the large homemade table in her family's chilly, seldom-used dining room in preparation for the next day's Christmas dinner, when neighbours would come by horse from miles around.

Some of the children were helping their mama (my grandmother) get the room ready. As is the Ukrainian tradition, there was hay on the floor and the best heads of wheat were lightly spread under the tablecloth on the table before it was set with 12 traditional meatless dishes. Each dish represented one of Christ's 12 apostles.

The table was set against the wall and an oil lamp glowed on the table, showing off the treasures of the new settlers, which were brought out and used only on these high holidays. The children's mother had just finished saying that she hoped everybody would come, when eight-year-old Ann yelled out, "Billy has come! Billy has come!" There, on the floor beneath the table, illuminated by the dull glow of the table lamp, stood a two-year-old figure dressed in white, as their brother Billy had been when he was buried in the village cemetery two years before. All the children were jumping about with delight. Billy had come home at last!

But his mother could see nothing. The smiling figure held his little hands clasped together, just as he had when he was buried. The vision lasted a considerable time before it gradually began to fade, leaving an aural light under the table. All the children thought it was the best Christmas ever, but it was some time before their mother regained her composure. This story was told at many Christmas Eves up to the present, celebrating an event that took place 87 years ago.

There is an unshakable belief in our extended family that death opens a door into an unknown world. Billy's visit had imparted a broader belief in a subject that only some people were previously aware of in our little farming town. Years later, mama, now a grandmother and very advanced in years, still expressed sorrow that she saw nothing, but the children of the house were treated by their brother Billy to a Christmas Eve visit from the vast beyond.

– *Walter Krivda, Manitoba, Canada*

BISBEE BED & BREAKFAST

A team of psychics and students spend the night in a historic haunted house.

By William G. Everist

Built in 1909 by Edith Ann Oliver, wife of mining tycoon Henry Oliver, the Oliver House in Bisbee, Arizona, has a violent history. This may explain the ghostly presences that today scare staff members and guests at the house, which now serves as a bed and breakfast.

The Oliver House was originally designed as a boarding house and planning centre for executive members of the Arizona and Calumet Mining Company. No identities for the non-living inhabitants of the house have been established, but it is believed that several killings took place during the hotel's early days.

One murder involved a mining company employee named Nat Anderson, who was shot at the top of the staircase to the first floor on February 22, 1920. According to the *Bisbee Daily Review*, Anderson was shot in the head and back during the early morning hours as he was entering Room 13. His assailant was never captured and the incident remains an unsolved mystery.

Another story – unconfirmed by public record – relates that in 1932, a man found his wife in bed with another man in what is now the Blue Room. Enraged, he shot them both and then killed himself.

Warnings

In 1986, Dennis Schranz began negotiating to buy the Oliver House. He thought he was buying the perfect old building for restoration as a bed and breakfast. Before he could complete the purchase, however, one of the owners suddenly announced that she couldn't go through with the deal in good conscience. "The place is haunted," she confessed. "There are five ghosts in the house, one of them violent."

Since Schranz didn't believe in ghosts at the time, he said that wouldn't worry him, and they concluded the sales transaction. Later, however, as he settled down to spend his first night alone in the house,

Schranz began to hear water running through pipes that no longer existed. This alone would have been a strange occurrence, since he was supposed to be the house's only occupant; then, when the water sound stopped, he heard footsteps approaching down the hall. As he listened to them, Schranz was glad he had locked the door. But to his surprise and dismay, the steps continued into his room and up to his bed.

This incident was only an initiation for Schranz, a taste of what he and others who have stayed in the house since have experienced.

Terri King, former manager of the Bisbee Bed and Breakfast, reported that she experienced a presence in both the Blue Room and in Room 13, as well as in several other locations throughout the house. One incident occurred when she went into the Captain's Room to change the sheets. Upon entering the room, she sensed a hostile presence and then heard a voice yell "Get out!" Since she was the only person in the room, she challenged the formless voice and replied in an equally authoritative voice, "What do you mean 'Get Out'? Who else is going to clean up this room? You get out!" Evidently it did. She never heard the voice again.

Another incident involved the Grandma Room. In this room, various guests have reported what appeared to be an older woman watching over them during the night. Although the sightings reportedly made guests nervous, it was thought to be a benevolent spirit offering its presence as a protection.

A Formal Investigation

In mid-October 1992, in response to numerous requests from graduates of my parapsychology and intuition classes at Pima Community College in Tucson, I organized a group of interested students to serve as sensitives for an investigation team in an attempt to establish the validity of these haunting claims. We planned on using the methodology of well-known parapsychologist Gertrude Schmeidler.

The investigation team consisted of 19 student sensitives, two local residents and two professional psychics. None of them was given information about the building's history.

Since the facility is a bed and breakfast, we had the advantage of being able to stay overnight in the house. Special accommodation included overnight lodging, three meals, and the possibility of a paranormal experience.

Following dinner on the eve of our investigation, I established two baseline levels of information. The first information source was provided by walking the two professional psychics through the house and recording their impressions as we travelled from room to room. At the same time, I had each student participant complete a variation of the "Auerbach Psychic Dreaming, Psychic Experiences, Psychic Beliefs Survey" in order to establish a measure of their individual experiences.

Once this information was independently established, the main walk-through began. Participants were given a floor plan of the house and asked to record the location of any ghosts they might experience. A list of adjectives was also provided to describe the nature of the ghost. Independent hall monitors assured that only one person occupied any room at one time as they progressed through the house.

Upon completion of the tour, personalized journals were distributed for the students to record overnight experiences and impressions. Evening room assignments were also announced and anyone who felt uncomfortable with their designated room was offered the opportunity to request another. Much to my surprise, no one felt room changes were necessary.

Guests Who Never Leave

The wife of the participant assigned to the Grandma Room, however, did feel a slight uneasiness. Describing the experience in her journal, she reported:

"It was an uncomfortable room at first. A heavy fragrance was in the room. I felt something in the left corner by the chair.

After being assigned the room – June, Shirley and Tina all visited the room. Each felt that there was a child there (unhappy, timid, and probably abused).

Shirley [one of the professional psychics] felt particularly uncomfortable, so she asked us to join hands and repeat after her – asking [the] spirit to seek the white light."

Tina's account reflected an original intuitive impression she received earlier that evening:

"When I first came across the bridge [leading to the house] I looked at the side of the house and the adjoining yard. I immediately sensed a little girl, five to seven years old. She liked to play in that area.

Later, discussing the little girl in the Grandma Room with the couple that would be staying there, the window to the right (the one I was drawn to look out of) brought to me the feeling again that this had been a sort of playroom and she would look out this window, onto her favorite play area. She was lonely."

After breakfast the next morning, we gathered to exchange experiences from the night before. Still unaware of the house's published history, various participants reported their experience. The man who had been assigned to the room at the top of the stairs on the first floor, near the alleged location of Nat Anderson's shooting, reported hearing metallic sounds in the night, like jewelry or coins rattling.

"At about 3:30 a.m.," he stated, "I awoke to hear a voice. It was my roommate having a dream. As I went back to sleep, I heard two female voices in the distance. A short while later, I heard another female voice whispering near me, but when I opened my eyes, no one else was in the room.

"Shortly thereafter, I had an unusual dream. I dreamt that someone from our group had laid down on the bed to my right. I told them that they did not belong there and I woke up to find no one there. I went back to sleep and began to dream again. This time I was walking the darkened halls of the Oliver House, first upstairs then downstairs. Then I sat with someone in the parlour where we had dinner earlier last night. After that I went back up to my room. As I went back to sleep in my dream, the same person again laid down on my right side. I told them they did not belong there and they left."

The man woke when he heard the metal rattling sound next to his right ear. It was about 5:30 a.m., and he noticed the sound at poker chips from the right corner of the room and the sound at coins being poured into a sack.

"I felt nervous about this," he said. "I felt the presence of a man about 45 to 50 years old. I also felt frustration from this person – possibly anger."

He described this man in his journal. "He has a craggy face, dark hair (some grey), and a beard. He's about six feet tall with a medium build.

I also have the impression of the woman who whispered in the night. She was about five feet eight inches tall, slender to medium build, in a red frilly dress with white lace trim, and long sandy brown hair." (No one in our group wore this style of clothing.)

Recalling the events again later, he said he was impressed with the realism of the experience. "It seemed as though the series of events were really happening," he said. "The sound of the coins and voices were very realistic and have made a lasting impression."

Two women who stayed next door in Room 13 had a similar experience.

"I was awakened in the middle of the night by a loud noise and then heard my roommate crying loudly in her sleep," one of the women wrote. "I called out to her to wake her up and told her she had been dreaming.

I then went back to sleep and dreamed I was staying at the Oliver House. I was walking through the house and then dreamt I was in my room."

Looking back on the experience, she said she felt as though there was a reason she had been awakened in time to be a support for her friend Molly. "Although we had both planned to bring a rosary and leave it by our beds, I was the only one who did."

Molly also dreamt she was in the room she slept in.

"I dreamt I woke up from the dream and saw the clothes rack on the other side of the room in front of me. To the left of the clothes rack, I felt a presence. The presence was just watching us sleep. I didn't know what to do, so I began crying. I was terrified, but this was in my dream and then Janice woke me up. But it felt real to me.

We went back to sleep, but I think we woke up again. I felt a presence right in front of me. All I said was 'go away from here' and then I went to sleep."

Another woman, who roomed with three others, reported a male presence in her room. She stated in her journal:

"I felt very uncomfortable upon retiring for the evening. I felt the presence of a male entity and I did not like the feeling I got from him. I felt that he had done something terrible to someone while he was alive and was somehow being punished. I refused to open my eyes, the presence was so strong. I later had a dream where I saw his face and then watched as he melted."

A man in the room at the far end of the upstairs hall reported the following in his journal:

"Before falling asleep, but with my eyes closed, I saw an image of a hand holding a tiny bouquet of flowers. The bouquet was large, but the flowers were small – like dried flowers or baby's breath.

Earlier, when I first walked into the room after I was assigned, I felt a tingling (as if touched) in my fingers of both hands. It was like a warm greeting. My first thought was that it was female.

As I lay in bed, before falling asleep, I felt a heavy sensation on my right arm, as if someone was resting their arm on it. I felt that it was a woman."

Later that evening, the man recorded this dream:

"I sat up in bed (in my dream) and looked in a mirror, which reflected the image of a young woman with light on her face, who was sitting to the left of the bed, watching. She had short brown hair.

When I turned to my left to look at her directly, I couldn't see her and it was dark there. I think this happened twice in succession, but the second time it was a different woman – about the same age, but with longer dark hair.

"I then heard a lot of talking or some sort of commotion out in the hall. I woke up immediately, but noticed the place was silent.

As I was going back to sleep after the previous dream, I felt the presence of a male, who wanted to be recognized. He had some connection with the military, as though he had to go to war, or had just returned. He had dark, somewhat curly hair and a medium build."

This participant later commented that the experience had definitely confirmed his beliefs in the paranormal. "I don't normally remember my dreams," he said, "but these dreams were different. I was much more aware. The vividness was outstanding."

The next morning, before our discussion and stories revealing the history of the Oliver House, the same man added this journal entry:

"Just after visiting the various rooms last night, as I was walking down the stairs from the first floor, I felt the back of my neck prickle. It kept that prickly feeling as I turned on the landing and began down the second flight to the ground floor. I felt the need to turn back, just to check and see if something was there. It seemed as though the presence was near the foot of the top flight of stairs."

This type of feeling was also experienced by several others, four of whom reported it on their walk-through experience. The same sensation was also noted by both professional psychics and confirmed by stories reported to the manager by various guests during the previous year.

Dream Hauntings Analysed

Although a formal statistical analysis of the walk-through data has yet to be performed, a review of the overnight dream journals has proven interesting.

One common experience reported by half of those who offered

journal episodes included the traditional out-of-body experience disguised as a dream of walking through the halls of the Oliver House. A correlating experience, which could also be considered an out-of-body episode was reported in five out of six accounts. This was the feeling of being awakened within their dream and, rather than travelling about, becoming aware of a presence in their room. Some of these individuals were able to physically describe the entity.

Could these episodes be the haunting visitations of former residents within a dream state? Those who reported being aware that they were dreaming of being in their own room (a reality simulation) yet experiencing someone not actually there (at least physically) may have been contacted by a ghost. Although actual communication was not reported in these episodes, the manner in which the individuals were aroused to awareness within their sleep seems like an effort to attract attention. Those who indicated they felt as though they had been awakened were aroused through extraneous voices or noises only to witness a paranormal event within the altered state of sleep – characteristic of a haunting incident.

One person who has looked into a variation of this phenomenon is Helen Solem. As reported in the March 1984 issue of FATE, she has studied numerous dream accounts reported by individuals who have received information in their dreams from sources who were known to be dead. Paranormal credibility was enhanced by the fact that many of the dreams contained information that was not available to the dreamer prior to the episode.

In reviewing the Bisbee dream haunting experiences, one might logically ask, "Could these experiences be nothing more than dream incubation?" That is, were the dreamers experiencing something similar to collective programming or self-fulfilling prophesy since each of them were at the Oliver House for the specific purpose of having some sort of paranormal experience?

Since the events reported were not a formal part of the intended investigation, but merely additional accounts of spontaneous experiences, I believe they should be considered merely as observations. We are planning future inquiries, structured to incorporate control factors, in hopes of better understanding the "dream haunting experience".

THE BLACK FOREST HAUNTING
by Dennis William Hauck

The Lee family spent nearly $70,000 trying to find the source of the paranormal activity that filled their house for years.

Steve and Beth Lee and their two sons dreamed of living in the beautiful Black Forest region of Colourado. For four years they rented homes in the densely forested area northeast of Colourado Springs before finding a spacious, two-storey log home off Swan Road in the thickest part of the woods. What they did not know was that the former tenant of the house was convinced the property was haunted, but had not mentioned anything for fear of being ridiculed. The unsuspecting Lees signed a lease in May 1991 and moved into the picturesque house. A year later they decided to purchase the five-acre plot.

Within weeks of buying their new home, the gates of hell opened up on them. "One day we came home," said Beth, "and it was like the Fourth of July in our living room and master bedroom. We had all kinds of lights flashing, and it sounded like people stomping across the roof. We would lie in bed at night and hear chains rattling. One night we woke up and heard orchestral music. Strange things started happening every day." Their sons complained of weird lights and shadows in their rooms. Lights and appliances started going on and off by themselves, and untraceable chemical odors burned family members' eyes and throats.

Steve Lee, a 34-year-old professional truck driver, believed that someone was trying to scare his family out of their new home. But the Louisiana-born man had "just enough redneck left" to fight back against the elusive presence, no matter what it took. He installed a state-of-the-art security system with video surveillance cameras and motion detectors, although the system often sounded alarms with no one around to trigger them. Over the next four years, they would have 62 inexplicable break-ins. The El Paso County Sheriff's Department opened an investigation in April 1993 and conducted 45 follow-ups, but could find no evidence of a crime. When the sheriff stopped responding, the Lees hired private investigators to solve the mystery.

Steve noticed that photographs and videotapes taken in certain locations on the property had strange light streaks running through them, and sometimes translucent faces appeared on the film. Three parts of the Lee house seemed especially prone to these unusual photographic effects: the outside wall next to their satellite dish, the living room and the master bedroom. Determined to document the activity, Steve borrowed or bought every type of camera he could think of to see if the bizarre images appeared. No matter what type of camera or film he used, he captured evidence of unexplainable light phenomena, including brilliant beams, floating balls of light, and glowing outlines of humans and animals. Sometimes the mysterious lights could be seen with the naked eye, although more often they lasted just a split second and showed up only on film. Steve and Beth finally agreed that something paranormal might be going on in their home, and in early 1995 they sent some of the pictures and videotape to the *Sightings* television show.

Sightings Investigates

Hollywood special-effects technician Edson Williams examined the Lee films and told the producers of the show that most of the light images would be extremely difficult to reproduce and some seemed to defy the laws of optics entirely. *Sightings* dispatched a film crew and Minneapolis ghostbuster Echo Bodine to the Black Forest to document some of the weird phenomena the Lees had witnessed.

When they got to the Lees' home, Bodine quickly identified a threatening male spirit in the living room. A sophisticated thermal imaging camera showed the presence of the ghost who, according to Bodine, was "responsible for things happening here and considers this to be his place". Bodine determined the presence of at least 20 more spirits and judged the level of otherworldly activity in the house as "monumental". She felt especially uncomfortable in the upstairs bedroom, which she said was "full of spirits – not a restful room".

During the filming of a discussion between Bodine and Beth Lee at the kitchen table, Beth suddenly felt like someone was holding her down. She asked to halt the interview and staggered from the table, obviously distraught. Then Sherry, a member of the backup film crew, felt "something go into her", as her chest, arms, and legs became numb. She fell into a chair and started crying uncontrollably in abject terror as some unseen force seemed to possess her. She had to be escorted off the set and did not recover fully until she was off the property. To this day, she is convinced that something in the Lee house tried to take over her body.

During both of these emotional outbursts, the *Sightings* equipment recorded unusual electromagnetic interference in the room. After the crew returned to Los Angeles, Steve Lee got a photo back from some film he shot during that period. It showed a white dagger of light pointed directly at his forehead.

Sightings returned six months later with renowned psychic investigator Peter James, who immediately sensed the pull of a powerful psychic energy vortex on the property. Then, while touring the house, James was overwhelmed by a burning, chemical odour and suddenly asked if the name "Howard" meant anything to the Lees. Steve and Beth were both startled by the unexpected mention of the name of a dear friend, whom Beth called their "adopted granddaddy for the last ten years". As the Lees revealed more about the old man, the connection with the chemical smell became obvious.

Apparently, Howard's son, Howard, Jr., died of a drug overdose in the 1960s. The youth's best friend was a pharmacist, and the two stole prescription drugs and got high together. Peter James felt that Howard, Jr., had entered a "rift in space-time" on the Lee property, because he wanted to make contact with his father to explain that he had not really died of a drug overdose – he had, in fact, been murdered. Steve was impressed with James's revelation and asked to stop filming so he could compose himself. "There's no way on God's earth he could have known about Howard," Steve said.

About a year after their first visit, *Sightings* returned a third time to the Lee house. This time Peter James concentrated his efforts on the most active spot in the house – the master bedroom on the second floor. Many anomalous events had been recorded near the entry to a small cupboard in the room as well as in a hundred-year-old mirror on the Lees' dresser. Several psychics had pinpointed the cupboard as the gateway to the Other Side, and the mirror was an endless source of photographs of apparitions and floating faces.

James believed the mirror reflected the faces of the spirits going in and out of the room's gateway in search of the lifeforce they had lost. Several photographs of the mirror were computer-enhanced to show scores of eerie faces peering back. In summarizing the Lee haunting for viewers, James said, "There is an energy here unlike any I've ever experienced in all the years I've investigated anomalous activity."

The Black Forest Vortex

A Hopi shaman consulted on the Black Forest hauntings said that the area is a "Rainbow Vortex", one of only a few psychic energy spots on the planet that connect our world with the next. Currently there are only two other locations where photographic phenomena similar to those from the Black Forest are being recorded. Both are private residences – one in Arizona and the other in London. Visits by psychics to each of these locations seem to cause the paranormal activity to increase in frequency and intensity, and today at the Lee house, doors open and close by themselves, appliances turn on and off, objects disappear or are hidden away, alarms go off for no reason, shadowy figures move silently through the house and disembodied voices can be heard.

Red, yellow and white lightforms are seen and recorded, as well as apparitions of an old lady, a little girl, a burly man dressed in 1800s clothing, and a "flying dog", not to mention the hundreds of forlorn faces seen floating in the Lees' bedroom mirror. When asked why they hadn't abandoned the abode, Beth Lee replied, "Because we want it solved and we want to keep our house. Until you walk in our shoes, you won't understand. Mainly, though, I just want a normal life again, so we can get on with our lives."

By the beginning of 1997, the Lees had spent nearly $70,000 trying to find the source of the paranormal energy. They had collected over 3,000 photos and 400 videotapes showing anomalous phenomena. Steve Lee continues to try to capture the activity on film, and last October he purchased expensive infra-red lenses with ultrasonic trip mechanisms to take automatic photographs of the ghostly intruders.

The Lees have also called in more than 30 different specialists, including some of the best paranormal researchers in the country, private investigators, members of the clergy, psychics and quantum physicists. Several scientists have stated that the lightforms recorded on film at the Lee house do not behave according to accepted laws of physics.

Bill Gibbens, an electromagnetics expert from Denver, who specializes in exposing fraudulent hauntings, was hired to sweep the house for electronic bugs, but he witnessed so many paranormal events that he has returned several times on his own to try to trace the source of the projected energy. Gibbens believes the energy is coming from a stationary source under the house. He plans to bring in ground sonar equipment and spectrum analysers to track it. "I saw spectacular light shows that could be seen with the naked eye," he admitted. "It's an extremely active site, and there's nothing that Steve or his wife are doing to cause this."

The Lees even persuaded a Colourado state senator to investigate their home. Charles Duke, a Republican senator from Monument, brought his own camera and film and was able to take several photographs that showed lights and apparitions. "There are things happening that defy explanation around his house," Duke told reporters, "but I must admit I went over there with a great deal of scepticism. It's really bizarre. I was shocked. I'm not a believer yet, but certainly there is something going on there. I don't believe in ghosts and neither does Mr Lee. He's just trying to get someone to listen." Senator Duke asked the FBI to investigate but they declined, saying they would visit the house only if there were evidence federal law had been violated.

In November 1996 I went to the Lee property to take infrared photographs. Three months earlier, Senator Duke had taken a picture of a cloudy image that he said was "clearly a dog" – an apparition that had been photographed repeatedly on the property and which Steve believes might be his own dog who died ten years ago. I was able to capture this "flying dog" on film, as well as the frightening face of another ghost, possibly the "old woman" or "burly man" described by witnesses. Like most researchers who visit the Lee property, I experienced the usual inexplicable equipment problems and odd physical sensations. While Steve was showing Bill Gibbens and me a corner of the cellar that had been "active" lately, we all felt an uneasy, heavy presence pulling at us.

Alchemy of the Paranormal

Although I try to document the physical parameters of the cases I investigate, the focus of my research is on the changes wrought by paranormal events on the people involved. I have identified a kind of paranormal alchemy that produces fundamental changes in the personalities of experiencers, whether the events centre around apparitions, UFOs, sacred energy vortices, mystical states or near-death visions. In genuine cases, the subject undergoes a threefold process of transformation that begins with the fiery destruction of personal ego and material concerns.

This conflagration of ego can be quenched only by surrendering to the dissolving waters of the sub-conscious mind and integrating the paranormal viewpoint through processes like visualizations and dreams. Finally, the essence of the personality surfaces and the belief system of the individual is overhauled to accept and live with the reality of another, unexpected side to our existence.

Paranormal events can even be prompted by this loss of ego, as in the blurring of personal identity that takes place in deep meditation or with mind-altering drugs, although it can be forced on people by circumstances such as illness, isolation or withdrawal. In many instances the breakthrough event is perceived negatively, because it blows away the values of everyday life and it challenges our most basic assumptions.

Depending on their belief systems, subjects want paranormal events to have a specific explanation, and they end up blaming aliens, devils, religious cults or secret government agencies.

In Steve Lee's case, it was the latter. "I truly think the U.S. government has a hand in this," he told a television reporter. "I don't think any one individual could get away with this for this period of time without getting caught. The government does testing out here that has military implications."

Steve was convinced that the government was using his family as human guinea pigs to test laser holograms and biological weapons for psychic warfare. He saw figures in military fatigues carrying assault rifles and he spent hours trying to photograph them. One of his neighbours obtained a restraining order to keep him from taking any more pictures across property lines.

Steve accused government agents of cutting off the electricity to his home whenever it was vacant, so they could enter it without being detected. He also accused them of spraying illness-causing chemicals in his van and truck. He believes the secret agents even followed him when he visited his mother-in-law's ranch in Gunnison, Colourado, and his father's home in Louisiana.

My limited investigation uncovered no direct evidence of government surveillance, although it certainly wouldn't surprise me if certain government agencies took a covert interest in this case. Actually, Steve's explanation seemed to fit the facts as well as any other theory. However, as the unexplainable events continued to evolve, Steve eventually incorporated their reality into his own world view and is learning to live with it.

What has changed most over the last five years is not the Black Forest's mysterious vortex of otherwordly energy, but the Lees' definition of what is "normal" for them. "It would scare other people," notes Steve, "but it doesn't scare us. It's kind of a normal way of life now."

Dennis William Hauck *is a paranormal investigator and an internationally recognized authority on the paranormal. He is the author of* Haunted Places: The National Directory *(Penguin, 1996).*

THE HAUNTED BLASKE BUILDING
By Mike Heil

For years, the haunted history of Alton, Illinois, has been attracting the attention of ghostbusters and psychics, adding mystique and intrigue to this small city nestled along the muddy Mississippi River.

Historic Alton is located about 15 miles east of St Louis, Missouri. It received national attention in 1837 when a pro-slavery mob killed abolitionist newspaper editor Elijah P Lovejoy. It was in the national spotlight again in 1858 when Abraham Lincoln and Stephen A Douglas held their seventh and final debate there. During the Civil War it was the main supply point for the Union armies and a key link to the underground railway. It's not surprising that Alton, with its rich and colourful past, has about 50 nineteenth- and early twentieth-century homes and buildings that are haunted.

Alton's Haunted Blaske Building
The two-storey Blaske Building was built in 1916 by the Sparks Milling Company as a company office. Since 1941 it has had several owners, who have rented it to other businesses in the area for storage or office use. It is owned today by ConAgra of Alton, which allows it to be used by a social services agency. Built of stucco and timber-framed, the exterior of the building has retained much of its early twentieth-century charm. Despite its pleasant appearance, unsettling paranormal activities have been reported inside by ConAgra employees and social workers whose offices are in the building.

Well-known psychic Shirley Blaine of Belleville, Illinois, has investigated 30 to 40 haunted houses during the last two years in the St Louis metropolitan area and neighbouring Illinois communities and has cleansed several of their lingering ghosts. Known as the Belleville ghostbuster, she recently became intrigued by paranormal activities inside the Blaske Building. With permission from ConAgra, on September 8, 1995, she spent part of the evening there with five members of a paranormal investigating team that included me.

A nocturnal quiet had fallen over Alton when we arrived at the building at about 8:30 p.m. with a social worker who was there to take care of the paperwork involved in our visit.

I had been there for about 15 minutes when Shirley arrived with James Woods and Jeff and Chou Campbell, all of whom were part of the team that assisted her with other paranormal investigations. The other team member, John Kropf, arrived at 10.30 p.m. to operate a video camera that picks up light-sensitive materials. He set up his equipment in two areas where Shirley and James could sense a presence.

An Angry Spirit Makes Its Presence Felt

Shortly after 9.00 p.m., we gathered around a small table near the front door to prepare our strategy. We decided to investigate the ground and first floors, then the basement. This was the first time I had participated in a paranormal investigation. My adrenaline was flowing and my heart was pumping. I was ready and so were the others. For almost 10 minutes we combed the ground floor like detectives searching for evidence to solve a murder mystery, but we came up empty-handed. Shirley searched every nook and cranny, but she didn't sense anything.

It was on the first floor in the large conference room that she felt what she called a "fierce man, very angry, very mean". James felt the presence, too, exclaiming, "Something poked me. I think I'm being stabbed." While it was in the room, I centreed my attention on James, who looked annoyed. He kept insisting that he was being poked and stabbed.

At 10.00 p.m., it was time to rid him of his discomfort and investigate the basement. We were at the steps within a minute, looking down into eerie darkness. As we hesitantly crept downward, my legs became wobbly. We tightened three light bulbs hanging from the cobweb ceiling. They emitted enough light to define the cellar. It was a spooky-looking place that had what looked like two vaulted rooms and one large room cut into three smaller sections. The walls were decrepit and crumbling. In one of the vaulted rooms Shirley felt an abhorrent presence. We stood near it for what seemed like an eternity. During that time James blurted out that he was being poked and stabbed again, while I felt as though I had just run a mile in 90-degree heat. The others also felt intense heat. I was incessantly wiping sweat from my forehead. Addled and fidgety, I wanted to leave. Finally, I did, with Chou, Jeff, James and Shirley right behind me.

We were upstairs, trying to discern what had occurred, when John arrived with his camera and video-recorder. He had his equipment set up on the first floor in the far corner of the conference room by eleven o'clock. Shirley and James sat next to each other at the large conference table at the other end of the room. I was behind Shirley, to her left, Chou was next to me and Jeff may have been in the hall. At midnight, several hair-raising events took place, beginning when John exclaimed, "Did you hear that loud click?" (Presumably it was the cellar door opening.) Shirley then stated that something had rushed by her.

James, looking distraught, shouted, "This thing doesn't like me, but I'm not afraid. It's poking and stabbing me." Meanwhile, John was clicking his camera rapidly while Chou remained still. Wide-eyed, I was trying furiously to write down what everybody was saying. During the crucial moment, when the presence charged into the room, John's video recorder mysteriously lost power and didn't recharge until whatever was there left 10 minutes later.

Eventually we went downstairs. It would be almost two hours before we regrouped and again turned our attention to the basement. Chou and Jeff had left, but the rest of us got ourselves in place for the coming events.

A little after 2.00 a.m., John had his equipment propped up near the vaulted room where we had felt intense heat. Shirley decided to put a chair in front of the entrance of the room. She and James exchanged seats at five-minute intervals, channelling energies. About 2.45 a.m. Shirley felt uneasiness, then a presence. "He's a big man, very, very angry. I feel he's a captain, a captain," she stated resolutely several times.

John said he saw behind her what looked like grey mist filling the entrance. Although I, too, saw a mist, I couldn't focus on it well. Grey mist or not, whatever it was James felt it, too. He kept repeating, "He doesn't like me. He wants me out of the basement. He wants me out of here." After being in the building for nearly five and a half hours, I was drained. We left the squalid cellar a little after 3.00 a.m. I arrived at my apartment in St Louis 25 minutes later, weary-eyed and dumfounded.

The Illinois Historical Site
I returned to the Blaske Building the next day with my girlfriend

Antonella. I wanted to take more pictures. I knew I had an incredible story. That afternoon when I pulled into the parking lot adjacent to it, I saw that the lot foundation was made of cut stones. We found a plaque that said the stones were part of the first Illinois prison.

Antonella said she felt raindrops near the historical site, and they intensified as we neared the Blaske Building. I kept shooting photos, though, turning a deaf ear to her complaints, which seemed baseless to me because the bright blue sky was filled with puffy, pillowy clouds. Antonella was adamant, however, reiterating, "I can feel raindrops on my legs and arms." I tried to reason with her, telling her that if she felt raindrops, we should be able to see small droplets on her body. She looked, but didn't see any. We walked around the building. Antonella stopped at times to look through the basement windows. When we reached the front steps, she looked at me and said, "I know what is happening. It's all right."

I then went across the street and shot the rest of my roll of film while trying to grasp what had happened. On the way back home, Antonella told me she was frightened, adding, "They weren't God's raindrops."

I agreed, shaking my head.

More Witnesses

On September 11, I went back to the Blaske Building to talk to the social worker whom I had met on September 8. I also chatted with another person who has been employed by the social service agency for a number of years. They asked that I keep them anonymous. During our conversation they told me several fascinating stories. For years, they said, social workers in the building have heard doors inexplicably open and close. In the evenings, at around 8.30 or 9.00 p.m., they felt compelled to gather their belonging and leave the building. In 1993 a social worker who no longer works there saw a lady donning a white and black dress materialize in front of her in the large conference room on the first floor.

BLUFF CITY TOURS

The "Haunted History" Tour by Bluff City Tours is turning sceptics into believers.
FATE contributor Mike Heil was there for the tour in October 1995. Here is his fascinating report.

by Mike Heil

For the past few years Bluff City Tours has explored people's fascination with Halloween by featuring special tours of haunted sites in Alton and nearby Godfrey, Illinois. In 1995, I joined the tour for FATE Magazine.

Most of the people on the tour I joined thought that ghosts and spirits were a figment of a crafty imagination to be read about in short stories or viewed on spooky, late-night TV shows. Many had a change of heart, however, when they toured Alton's haunted Durie Home, built in 1896 by a prominent jeweller.

Shirley Durie, present owner of the home with her husband Cameron, reported, "One woman came running down the steps and just about flew out the front door. She was breathing heavily and looked pale. She said she would never enter the house again because she felt a presence in the master bedroom that scared her to death."

Shirley is an Alton historian who in her hundreds of explorations of old buildings over the years has come in contact with several ghosts and spirits. Two of those spirits inhabit the home she and Cameron purchased in 1983. Shirley believes one is the spirit of her father, who died in the house in 1986; the other, she thinks, is that of Cameron's Aunt Elva. The spirits, whoever they are, gained quite a reputation as pranksters during the tours. One was standing by the family Bible when a tour guest entered the room.

Encounters with Apparitions

Many people felt the presence of the spirits on this ghostly tour. An elderly gentleman may have been accosted by one of the rambunctious phantoms when he was smacked in the buttocks by a door that mysteriously swung open. Countless people felt a spirit or two lurking in the bedrooms. Some were shaken by what happened. "If they didn't believe in spirits or ghosts before they came into the house," Shirley said, chuckling, "I would think they do now."

The 100-year-old Durie Home was one of seven haunted houses and several historical sites that were part of the tour. The infamous Blaske Building, also known as the Sparks Building, was another. For years paranormal activities have frightened employees there. I participated in a remarkable paranormal investigation in the building one evening in September 1995 with noted psychic Shirley Blaine of Belleville, Illinois, and others intrigued by the paranormal. My report in FATE, August 1996, described the paranormal activities that manifested that night.

I was a sceptic until that incredible evening, like the many people who were sceptical before they participated in the Bluff City Tour. More than a handful of previous sceptics told me after their tour that they now believe in the paranormal. Their experiences at the Durie Home and other sites on the tour convinced them, affording them a different outlook on life after death.

Many of the tour locations, including the Durie Home, are covered in Jim Longo's book *Ghosts Along the Mississippi: Haunted Odyssey II*. Longo considers Alton to be one of the most haunted towns in rural America. Those who experienced the paranormal for the first time at the Durie Home would probably agree with his assessment.

GHOSTS, GOBLINS, & APPARITIONS OF THE CALIFORNIA GOLD COUNTRY

By Richard Giannone

The California Gold Rush began in 1848. Small mining towns sprang up overnight all over the foothills of the sprawling Sierra Nevada mountains. Men and supplies flooded areas previously trod only by occasional Indians and the abundant game indigenous to the area. But then, almost as quickly as it started, the Gold Rush ended, leaving in its wake deserted towns, empty mines and cemeteries filled with unlucky prospectors unable to elaborate on their tales of woe. So say the historians...

Many believe that those deserted towns are not so empty, those mines are not so vacant and those long dead and buried prospectors are not so silent. In fact, the California Gold Country is abundant with stories of ghosts, strange happenings and tales of the unexplained.

Highway 49, named after the prospectors that flocked to the area in 1849, runs through the heart of the Gold Country and also through many of the towns that residents claim are filled with supernatural beings. One of those towns is Nevada City, California. Now a touristy recreation of its past splendour, Nevada City has a museum that contains more than just artefacts. According to locals, the Firehouse Number 1 Museum is a spookhouse. Located on Main Street, the converted firehouse has been the site of ghostly occurrences, most centred around the 1,000-year-old Taoist shrine located near the back of the museum. The golden shrine reaches to the ceiling of the museum and is truly a sight to behold. Large Chinese letters adorn the ornate posts that support the top of the structure.

But some things about the shrine are not so apparent to the naked eye. Museum visitors regularly report seeing full-sized, standing figures near the golden altar. As many as three of these ghostly figures have been seen at one time, and there have also been reports of ghostly tripping, shoving and pushing. During the Gold Rush era, the shrine was in a Chinese Joss House that stood in Grass Valley, a town just down the road from Nevada City. Are ghosts of the devout Chinese who worshiped at the altar angered by the procession of nonbelievers standing at their shrine? Or is this old firehouse just a fertile ground for the imagination? To the right of the shrine, stairs take visitors to the museum's first floor. At the top of the stairs, the curious are greeted by the strange portrait of a Mr Carrigan. The photo, taken in 1880, shows Carrigan, a former president of a local mine, seated next to the faded image of a young boy. When the photo was taken, however, no boy was sitting there!

At the time, Carrigan said that he recognized the image as that of himself as a youngster, and he recollected that at the time of the sitting, he had been thinking about his childhood. Whatever the case, the photo seems harmless. Or is it? According to former museum director Hjaimer Berg, a female visitor started up the stairs one day, saw the photo, and ran out of the museum screaming, "They're after me!"

The Tommyknockers
Not far from Nevada City is the Empire Mine. Located in Grass Valley, the Empire Mine was one of the largest gold mines in California. Founded in 1850, the Empire was just that: an underground empire. More than 367 miles of tunnel thrust deep into the ground in a complex maze that went to depths of almost a full mile below the surface.

This empire was populated by hard-rock miners, many of whom had recently emigrated from Cornwall. The Cornish miners were skilled workers who were part of a mining tradition dating back over 1,000 years. They brought many things to California from the old country – the latest mining technologies, English food such as pasties and saffron buns and, according to some, the Tommyknockers.

Something like a leprechaun, a Tommyknocker would warn miners of dangerous underground gases and impending tunnel cave-ins by knocking on the wall of the mine shaft. In return, the thankful miners would leave crusts of bread broken from their meat pasties for the Tommyknockers. Given to pranks, the magical little men would also on occasion lead the miners to a rich gold-bearing spot in the mine.

The *New Larousse Encyclopedia of Mythology* describes little men much like the Tommyknockers, "Dwarfs may be considered a subclass of Elves. They too were small of stature, lived in secret places, usually underground, and were endowed with supernatural intelligence and foresight....Miners, they said, frequently met Dwarfs in the galleries they dug in the flanks of mountains. It was said that these Dwarfs were themselves often dressed as miners and wore leather aprons and carried lanterns, picks and hammers. More ingenious and learned than men, they only frequented places where useful and precious metals abounded; hence, to come across them foreshadowed the discovery of rich booty."

This description seems to fit the Tommyknockers perfectly. If the stories of the little men are true, could they still be down in the dark, empty tunnels of the Empire Mine?

The original miners from Cornwall are now all gone, and most of the tunnels of the mine have been flooded by underground water sources. But noises are still heard from deep down in the main shaft. Are the noises simply those to be expected from damp creaking timbers? Or are they caused by the Tommyknockers, calling to long-dead miners, trying to point out yet another rich vein of gold ore?

Coloma – Ghost Central

Following Highway 49 south from Grass Valley, travellers will come to the spot that started it all – Coloma, California. This is where, in 1848, lumber mill foreman James Marshall discovered the small gold nuggets that would eventually transform the area into a hustling gold town, filled with all manner of men, good and bad. The town of Coloma is now a state park, and many of the original buildings from the 1800s remain standing. Old cemeteries hide in the rolling hills among 500-year-old oak trees that dot former Indian trails. Coloma is the kind of place that makes people feel as if they could step back through time and join the prospectors as they avidly hunt for gold.

Of course, this is also the kind of environment that breeds strange happenings, and, as one would expect, ghost stories abound.

One of the more famous stories revolves around the Vineyard House. Built in 1878, the Vineyard House is a rather large Victorian-style hotel that was built by Robert and Louise Chalmers. Popular with the miners, the Vineyard House enjoyed success until Robert Chalmers began to suffer from mental problems. Some claim he went quite insane. His fits of violence and strange paranoid behaviour culminated in residents finding Robert lying in an open grave to "see how it would fit". Eventually, according to local lore, he was locked in the cellar of the Vineyard House, where he starved himself to death because he thought that his wife was trying to poison him.

The Vineyard House is still open for business, and reports of ghosts are common. Most people think they are seeing Louise Chalmers roaming the halls of the inn, dressed as she was more than 100 years ago. Going about their unearthly business regardless of guests, the ghosts of the Vineyard House haven't hurt business, and despite the ghostly screams that have sometimes prompted guests to call the police, the hotel has become a well-known bed and breakfast spot for curious travellers.

Across the street from the Vineyard House sits the Pioneer Cemetery. The hills of the cemetery contain 400 to 500 graves. Most of these burial plots belong to miners, prospectors and merchants from the Gold Rush days. Murderers are also buried there, and the cemetery is the site of the famous double hanging of convicted murderers Jerry Crane and Mickey Free in 1855. Old-fashioned headstones mix with clinging vegetation to create a scene of horror. Fanciful ironwork surrounds some of the tombs, while the ground collapses and sags in the spots where bodies were laid to rest many years ago. Most of the very old markers are gone. Because they were made only of wood, the elements made short work of them long ago. As a result, a great number of the buried are unknown, their stories a mystery. Unfortunately, this makes it difficult to make sense out of persistent ghosts like the Lady in Burgundy.

The Lady in Burgundy has been seen many times around the old Pioneer Cemetery, trying to beckon onlookers to her side. Her long, flowing, burgundy skirt moving in the wind, she seems intent on showing the unwary visitor something urgent, but no one has yet been able to discover what her pressing problem is. When spotted, she is usually standing near the tombstone of Charles Schieffer and two of his children.

One clue to the Lady in Burgundy's identity might be a tombstone on the other side of the cemetery. Here, a small stone marks the grave of Catherine Schieffer. By the dates on the marker, it can be seen that Catherine was two years old when Charles died. Was she related? Is she requesting a burial place closer to her loved ones? Or does she have nothing to do with the Schieffers? Perhaps one of the unmarked graves belongs to her and she longs to have someone recognize the fact that at one time she did exist.

My Own Story

My own experience with Coloma started in 1991, when I was sent to write a story on the park by a magazine that specializes in factual accounts of the Old West. Ghosts were the farthest thing from my mind as my brother and I walked around the old buildings and made notes on when they were built and by whom.

Walking up a hill just west of the town, we came upon James Marshall's original cabin. Near his grave site and monument, the wooden cabin also sits next to an old cemetery. Because it was the middle of the week, the park was fairly deserted, and my brother and I found ourselves eerily isolated among the gravestones and the small rustic buildings. I snapped some photos of the cabin, graves and surrounding area, feeling uneasy because of the spooky surroundings. A few days later, after developing my film, I was looking at the photograph of Marshall's cabin when a cold chill ran up my spine. Two bearded men appeared to be looking back at me from inside one of the cabin windows. They looked remarkably like old miners from the 1800s. One seemed to be holding a hat, and as I examined the photo, I saw another face in a different window of the cabin. I was spooked.

Thinking that these just might be strange reflections in the old cabin glass, I drove back to Coloma with a few friends and walked to the cabin. The time of day was very close to the time that the original photo had been taken, but when we looked in the windows for reflections, nothing even remotely similar was visible. Only a distinctive oak tree was reflected in the window – nothing that could be confused with the images I had captured on film.

So, what could be in the windows of Marshall's cabin? Residents of the nearby cemetery? Or are these mysterious images those of old miners who feel comfortable in a cabin much like the ones they lived in so many years ago?

Recently, I went back into the darkroom and made photographic enlargements of the faces in the windows. To my surprise, they held up in an extreme blow-up. Detail can still be seen, and they look remarkably like people looking out the windows.

After I finished printing the Coloma photos in my darkroom, I placed them on my dresser next to my bed. Not needing any excuses for nightmares, I took the photos out of my room and placed them in the family room in a nice, neat stack. When I awoke the next morning, I was surprised to find the photo of Marshall's cabin sitting defiantly propped up on my dresser next to my bed! No one in the household admitted to touching the photos, so I grudgingly had to conclude that somehow this enigmatic photo travelled into my room overnight and set itself on the dresser from which I had so fervently removed it the night before.

So, now I become a reluctant proponent with those who would tell you of the very real existence of strange happenings in California Gold Country. Whether it's aggressive spirits in the Fire House Museum, Mrs Chalmers in the Vineyard House or nameless faces lurking in John Marshall's cabin, something is definitely going on in Gold Country. Maybe the powerful draw of gold that called out to early miners and prospectors is so strong that it holds them there still.

Richard Giannone *is a writer and photographer living in California.*

THE MOST HAUNTED CAPITOL IN AMERICA
Part I
by Patty A. Wilson

Early in 2003, the Rhine Research Centre of Durham, North Carolina, contacted me about my work. Some members of the Rhine staff were interested in learning about the role of field investigators in paranormal studies.

The late Dr J.B. Rhine became famous for debunking psychics and also for the controlled investigation of human anomalies such as ESP. Dr Rhine began his work under the auspices of Duke University but later conducted independent investigations through his institute. The subject of human life after death was his initial area of concentration. Over the years, the organization that Dr Rhine created came to focus only on the area of ESP and left field research on ghost phenomena untouched. Recently, however, some of the staff have worked to steer the research back to its original mission.

Scott Crownover and I run the Ghost Research Foundation. We were cautious but happy when asked to speak at the Rhine Research Centre. We were doubly cautious but happier yet when they asked us to conduct a teaching investigation. We were emailed a list of potential sites for investigation and asked to choose one. Scott and I were the first group honoured to both speak and teach. We reviewed the various sites, looking for a site that had a good mix of paranormal activity, from sightings to sounds, and an indoor location out of the elements. We knew that we'd only have one chance to show what we did and we didn't want rain stopping us. Only one site met all of our criteria – North Carolina's State Capitol.

The Haunted Capitol
The Capitol is now a State Historic Site but continues to house the offices of North Carolina's governor and his staff. The hauntings there were varied and had been witnessed over the years by a broad spectrum of the public – from past governors, site staff, and State Capitol police officers to property guards and custodians.

Maggie Blackman and Lynette Minnich, then of the Rhine

Research Centre, arranged for our visit. Their time and dedication locating sources and history was invaluable to us. They also made contacts with the staff at the site. Criminal profiler and psychic Anne Poole was also instrumental in assisting Maggie and Lynette.

However, none of our research would have been possible without the assistance of the Capitol's historian, Raymond Beck. Beck agreed to help us while we worked at the site, to share the building's history and hauntings and to otherwise aid us during our investigations. Scott and I had worked with professional historians before. They were typically stuffy gentlemen who scoffed at our studies of the paranormal. However, Beck was not only gracious, but he willingly shared both his interest in our proposed investigation and his personal encounters with the building's "other occupants". He was happy to assist us without bias in order to learn more about the Capitol's paranormal activities.

The night of our initial investigation arrived and we travelled from Durham to the State Capitol in Raleigh. From the Rhine Centre, we brought staff, family and friends of the staff and interested individuals who had been charged a small fee to learn how a haunting is documented.

The group was broken into three smaller parties, each assigned to one of the Capitol's three floors. They had been told nothing of the reported paranormal activities within the Capitol. Even Maggie and Lynette of the Rhine staff had only slight knowledge of the activity there, and they were asked to remain silent until the end of the evening.

Historic Background

I usually conduct interviews prior to arriving at a site, but due to the 420-mile distance from my home to Raleigh, I waited until the night of the investigation to interview Beck. Scott did much of the teaching and instruction that night, while Beck and I sat in the old House of Representatives chamber for my interview. Beck sat in a representative's chair and I set up my equipment nearby at the 1850s newspaper reporters' table at the front of the chamber. Beck provided much historical background about the Capitol, including the fact that it is the least altered 19th-century state capitol in America. Between 1990 and 2000 the North Carolina Capitol's interiors were restored to their early grandeur with their documented 1840 colours and varied decorative finishes.

Raleigh was established as the state's permanent capital in 1792 and was modelled after Philadelphia, Pennsylvania, the nation's capital at that time. A State House was constructed on Union Square near the centre of the city, where it stood until its accidental destruction by fire in 1831. The present State Capitol was constructed between 1833 and 1840 and stands on the site of the earlier building.

The Capitol was initially designed by William Nichols, Jr., who was soon replaced by the New York architectural partnership of Ithiel Town and Alexander Jackson Davis, advocates of the Greek Revival style in its purest form. In 1835, Town and Davis were replaced by David Paton of Edinburgh, Scotland, who served as both the sole architect and project superintendent until the Capitol's completion in 1840. As completed, the building is 160 feet in length by 140 feet in width and stands 97.5 feet in height to the top of the building's central dome. The Capitol was built entirely by hand without the use of any power-driven equipment. It was warmed by 32 fireplaces and was originally lit by candled chandeliers and whale-oil lamps.

North Carolina's Capitol housed all of the state's government until 1888. The executive branch was assigned to the ground floor, the legislature sat in the old House and Senate chambers on the first floor from 1840 to 1961, and the State Library occupied the second floor from 1840 until 1888, along with the state Supreme Court (1840–43) and later the state geologist (1852–63). The geologist's office was also used to store an overflow of library books and documents. Both rooms on the second floor have been recreated to their mid 1850s appearances.

At the outset of the Civil War, the House chamber (then called the House of Commons) was the site of the May 1861 Secession Convention, and the Ordinance of Secession was adopted and signed there. During the war, the Capitol stored war materials along with serving its governmental functions. One can only speculate on the building's uses during the war; however, we can reasonably assume that great passions were expended there throughout the four-year conflict.

In April 1865, the city of Raleigh was surrendered to Union general William T. Sherman. During the following three weeks, Union forces plundered the state geologist's "cabinet" or mineral display and recovered many captured Union banners. The extent of theft from the building has never been ascertained, although Raleigh was much luckier than many other Southern capital cities, and the State Capitol was not burned. We know of no deaths in the building during this period, but several Confederate officers killed in battle were allowed the honour of lying in state in the Capitol's rotunda. Following the war, during the Reconstruction era, one large committee room on the first floor was used as a bar by the notorious carpetbagger and former Union general Milton Littlefield. That room was known as the "Third House" of the legislature – both for its alcoholic "treats" and the influence peddling that took place there. In later years, it was the office of the Keeper of the Capitol and later both a post office and snack bar for legislators.

The building's full history is too extensive to document thoroughly here but, through my conversations with Beck, I was greatly awed by the building's well-preserved history, architecture and symbolism.

Amused Phantom

Approximately 40 minutes into my interview with Beck, I noticed a blur of motion off to my right, in the third row behind Beck at the far right side of that aisle. I was surprised to see a man sitting there watching us. He appeared to be in his thirties and was dressed in clothing from the mid-to-late 1800s. He was dressed as a gentleman, had clark hair brushed to one side and was quite pleasant looking. The thing that struck me most about his appearance was his smile. He was laughing at us as we talked about the ghosts of the building and seemed immensely amused.

I thought over what to do. Should I call Beck's attention to the gentleman? Chances were, by the time Beck turned to look, the fellow would have disappeared. Should I keep quiet and observe him for as long as possible? I followed the second option keeping him in view for several minutes while Beck and I chatted.

Beck recounted three legends connected with the Capitol. The first concerned the so-called "secret rooms" above the House chamber. The spaces above the House offices were not accessible from the second-floor public gallery. (The two rooms in the Senate chamber's gallery are.) In the mid1920s the spaces above the House offices were finally finished with floors and made accessible via cast-iron spiral staircases.

A second Capitol legend recalls a "secret tunnel" used as a means of escape by the governor during the Civil War. However, there was no such tunnel. There are low crawl spaces beneath the Capitol used for utility access, but the first tunnel was constructed for the addition of steam heat and electricity to the building in the 1880s.

The third legend states that the west staircase between the ground and first floors was damaged by "whiskey barrels" associated with General Littlefield's bar.

The gneiss (granite) steps are chipped, but the west stairs served as the service entry for the building and they were more likely damaged by wheelbarrows with iron-rimmed wheels hauling great quantities of wood to the more than 14 legislative and office fireplaces above.

Yet we were there for more than legends. We came to hunt for ghosts, and Beck was anxious to tell me all of the ghost stories he had collected through the years.

He gave me quite a tour of the hauntings. Beck had two experiences himself while he was recreating the library room's interior late at night when he had to stop working due to the chilling presences he encountered there.

When our group gathered in the House chamber later that evening to summarize our findings, we found much activity throughout the Capitol. An EMF meter spiked near the second-floor library stair, where at least two people have had paranormal encounters. Energy orbs were digitally photographed and moving orbs were videotaped with infrared equipment. Cold spots were found in locations where the Capitol staff had reported paranormal activities.

The Rhine staff members left that evening with a better understanding of what we do and why we do it. For example, we never allow an investigator to know a site's history in advance so that their imagination is not working against our investigative methods. We also do not allow anyone to speak of their experiences until the end of the evening. That validates personal experiences without the power of imagination and possible suggestion from another source.

The Rhine staff later prepared a paper recommending our methodologies of unbiased and uninformed individual study followed by a group discussion of the investigative evening's events as witnessed by each investigator.

Beck concluded the evening by inviting us to return with our regular staff for an in-depth ghost hunt and study.

THE MOST HAUNTED CAPITOL IN AMERICA
Part II
by *Patty A. Wilson*

He Suddenly Felt a Hand On His Shoulder...

My first contact was Mrs Jane Barbot, a member of the board of the nonprofit State Capitol Foundation who had volunteered to install Christmas decorations in the Capitol in the early 1980s. Her initial story involved her husband James and a friend, Ernie Fuller. The three of them were in the Capitol at 1.30 a.m. one night decorating each of the four first-floor rotunda niches that originally contained that area's lighting fixtures. Large urns were placed in each of the niches and a Christmas tree was placed in the urn occupying the northwestern niche. They completed that arrangement and were decorating another niche when they realized that the tree in the northwestern niche had nearly tipped and fallen over. It happened again several times throughout the night.

When the Barbots and Fuller left the Capitol the next morning all was well – until they received a phone call that the northwest arrangement had shifted yet again. The following night, Fuller returned to the Capitol with plywood to support and stabilize the tree. While he worked, he suddenly felt a hand on his shoulder, but no one was near him. He did not panic but calmly completed his work and left the building.

Mrs Barbot related that on another occasion while they were at work on the decorations, her husband was pushed, although no one was close to him at the time.

Former governor James B. Hunt, Jr., told Mrs Barbot that he often sensed unexplainable presences while he worked alone late into the night in his first-floor office. Mrs Barbot no longer doubted the Capitol was haunted, and she wondered who might be responsible. She found some answers in a most unlikely place.

The Barbots attend Christ Episcopal Church across from the Capitol. One Sunday she brought up the question of ghosts at the Capitol. One elderly member told her that the building had a long history of being haunted. He said that as a child, he and other children were warned by a night watchman that they had better stay away from the Capitol because it was haunted. At the time he thought this was just a story to scare children, but now he wondered if the night watchman was serious.

Another person told the Barbots that a former governor had lost his wife in an accident in the Capitol in the 1800s. The governor was supposedly furious with the workmen at the building. He blamed them for his wife's untimely death and returned after his own passing to haunt the building where his wife had died. (I could find no credible historical documentation for this tale.)

"I Don't Want To Be In No Lift With No Ghosts...."

I met with Owen Jackson at his home in a nearby community where he agreed to tell me of his many experiences and encounters in the historic Capitol. Jackson served for 12 years (1980–91) as a Capitol police property guard assigned to the Capitol and other state government buildings. He worked in the Capitol after it closed to the public each workday, from 4.30 p.m. until 12.30 a.m. He said that several members of the Capitol's staff liked to work late into the evening.

One night during his first week on the job, Jackson clearly heard a hymn being sung: "Nearer My God To Thee". He looked unsuccessfully for the music's source. The hymn was repeated for over a half an hour as he searched each floor for a radio, tape recorder or someone outside the building who might be playing it. At approximately 12.15 a.m., he reported to the State Capitol police headquarters on his two-way radio and told the dispatcher (who took notes) about the music. The dispatcher told him, "You won't catch me up there!" They just left the music playing.

Throughout his 12 years of working in the building, Jackson heard many unaccountable sounds that were more than the old structure "settling". He heard doors slamming late at night, though he knew he was alone. He heard keys jingling and a man's footsteps walking. He heard glass breaking but never found a broken window or any other damage. The most disturbing sound that Jackson ever heard was that of a woman giving out a single piercing scream – seemingly from the Capitol's second floor. One night he heard what sounded like an armload of books drop in the second-floor library. Prior to the 1980–81 re-creation of the library's interior there were no books in the room. Jackson searched the empty room, and no books were found anywhere within the space. (Mrs Barbot reported that former Governor Hunt confided to her of hearing books falling one night in the late 1970s. The sound seemed to come from the second floor, prior to the library's refurnishing.)

When I mentioned former governor Jim Hunt, Jackson remembered an incident that happened in the governor's office. A door of the suite made a particular sort of squeak – a different sound than any other in the governor's offices.

One night he heard that door squeaking as it did when being opened. He hurried to that area directly across from the office of the governor's security guard. He looked at the guard and asked, "Did you hear that door open?" The guard said he had. Both men stared at the door and realized that they could not have heard it open. A display case stood in the doorway so that no one could walk through. The governor's office doors were all locked and no one was inside his office. So who had done it? What had they heard?

Jackson told me that the Capitol's hauntings went far beyond sights and sounds. "One night I was fixing to get up and go somewhere. I don't remember where I was going. Somebody laid their hand upon my shoulder right there and I said that I wasn't going nowhere. And you'd be sitting there at night and you'd hear that lift come down and the door would never open up. I wouldn't ride it, if I were in there by myself. I would always use the stairs. I don't want to get trapped in no lift with no ghosts!" (The area of the present lift and men's room on the ground floor was originally the office of the House of Commons' doorkeeper.)

One evening, Jackson was sitting at the receptionist's desk in the east hall across from the lift when a lady came out of the men's room next door. The woman had on a blue choir robe with white trim. Jackson described her as a short, slightly-built white woman. She walked toward the double glass entry doors and went through them without opening them. As he watched in amazement, she simply faded away on the other side.

Jackson's most dramatic sighting was yet to come. "I was getting ready to leave one night and I was parked out in the north driveway out there. I had a car that if you didn't let it warm up in the wintertime it would stall out on you. I was looking up at the second floor, you know; the shades were pulled. And there was a fellow standing there and you could see from here to here [he indicated from neck to chest]. And he had on a Confederate soldier's uniform. You could see them brass buttons up and down that uniform. He was just standing there looking out that window.... It was about 12.15 am. I said, 'Well, he'll take care of it; I'm gone.'"

Jackson believes that at least one of the Capitol's ghosts is that of a crooked legislator who stole a couple of million dollars and hid it in the building. He speculated that the loot was probably Confederate money and is hidden behind one of the building's massive blocks of stone.

"You Could Always Hear Something All The Time"
John Johnson worked for approximately 18 years at the Capitol on the custodial staff of the North Carolina Department of Administration's Facilities Maintenance Division. He entered the Capitol each workday at 4.30 a.m. and was almost alone in the building until at least 7.00 a.m. During his first few years at the building, Johnson heard others' ghost stories but had no encounters himself. However, that would change.

Johnson's first experience was hearing a crying baby. In fact, he said that many on the custodial staff had heard the infant's wails. (Johnson later introduced me to Patricia, a woman on the current custodial staff, who has also heard an infant crying.) The sound came from somewhere on the second floor or perhaps in the attic area.

One of the most disturbing incidents in Johnson's career occurred one morning when he walked by the lift doors in the eastern area of the ground floor. The doors of the lift suddenly closed and the lift started to the first floor. He heard the doors open again on the first floor. He pressed the call button to bring the lift back down but it would not return, so he took the stairs. On the first floor he could find no one. He has always wondered who rode the lift up to the legislative floor that morning. After that experience, Johnson decided that the stairs were safer.

Johnson's daily activities became a routine. "I always closed the doors behind me, you know. I always worked with my doors locked behind me 'cause you could always hear something all the time. Doors closing, people walking.... I'll tell ya what I'd hear, somebody walking with spurs on – like you ride a horse. You could hear them – clink, clink, clink.... I guess they was going up to the second floor.... I could feel the presence of someone sometimes – especially when I came up here, you know [the first floor]. And frankly, I'd be afraid to look back. I'd just try to move as quickly as possible."

Johnson's most personal experience came many years into his service at the Capitol. He had worked with a man named Jesse for several years. Jesse was transferred to the custodial staff of the nearby old State Revenue Building where he died of a massive heart attack on the job one night. Several months later, Johnson entered the Capitol at 4:30 a.m. and turned on the office lights throughout the building. He entered the old House chamber to make sure its lights were on and turned to leave. On the balcony above him stood Jesse. For a split second, Johnson forgot that Jesse was dead. Jesse was leaning forward on the balcony rail and slightly lifted his hands and seemed to fade backward toward the balcony's rear wall. Once he was gone, Johnson never saw him again.

Johnson's words of advice regarding the Capitol's other occupants was simple: "You see what you have to do, if you got to work here, you got to put that stuff out of your mind. You don't stop and try to listen for something, 'cause you'll sure hear something!'"

The G Word...

Members of the maintenance and security staff are not the only people to notice the ghosts of the Capitol. Samuel P. Townsend, Sr., served as administrator of the State Capitol from 1975 until 1998. His opening statement to me set the tone for our interview. "I never use the G word. I have always looked for explanations for what has happened and I have found them. I will not use the G word." Townsend was very clear that he had found explanations for many of his experiences – even if he had to stretch to make his explanations seem logical.

In the summer of 1976, while the Capitol was undergoing an earlier restoration, Townsend was using the historic governor's office as his own. The governor's suite is located in the southwest corner on the building's ground floor.

It was late June. Townsend was still at his desk at 8.00 p.m.and because of daylight saving time it remained light outside. He heard the north door of the building opening, then footsteps, keys rattling in a lock and an inside door opening. Townsend knew that then-Secretary of State Thad Eure had been out for the day. He thought Eure might have returned to his office in the northeast suite of the ground floor. Townsend needed to speak to Eure, so he walked up the halls toward his office. The secretary's office was dark – no one was there. Puzzled, Townsend returned to his office, where he soon heard more footsteps and keys opening the Capitol's south door. Townsend stepped into the central rotunda and there realized that the Capitol's south entry door was bolted from the inside.

Townsend searched the entire ground floor and looked around the Capitol's exterior. Not a single person was nearby.

"All of this happened rather quickly," said Townsend. "I believe that there is the greatest chance that a policeman was checking the doors. However, I was not able to catch up with him."

Soon after this initial event, the governor returned to his office on the ground floor. Townsend moved to the northeast corner of the first-floor Senate chamber.

One night a few months later, Townsend was in his office at 8.30 p.m. when he heard what he took to be the footsteps of a colleague coming around the Senate chamber toward his office. His door was slightly ajar and he looked up to see who it might be…but no one appeared. He took a few steps outside his office. No one was there and the footsteps stopped. Townsend said, "I have to tell you that I was never afraid of this. I was mystified by it." The same experience recurred several times over the years. The footsteps always started from a small committee room at the rear of the Senate chamber and progressed toward Townsend's office. At one point, it was happening two to three times per week.

In true sceptical style, Townsend concluded that the Senate's floors were expanding and contracting because of the weather. As further proof of his theory, Townsend stated that after a large copy machine was placed in the Senate committee room he only heard the steps two to three times per year.

Townsend worked until 1.00 a.m. one morning. On the way to his car he realized that he had forgotten an item inside and re-entered the Capitol. As he stepped into the Senate chamber, he found himself moving quickly to one side as if to avoid someone. It startled him, for he knew the Capitol was empty. "I think that possibly the mantelpiece and iron sign stand that sat at the near edge of the fireplace appeared to take the shape of a human being, due to the glare from the outside lights on my steel-rimmed glasses. At the time, it was quite real." There was no room in Townsend's world for the possibility of a ghost that night.

The State Library room is on the second floor of the Capitol. After 1.00 a.m. one morning, Townsend found he needed to obtain the dimensions of a table in the library. Upon entering the library, he sensed that he was not alone. He feared that a tramp had surreptitiously entered the Capitol to sleep there. He looked toward the Senate chamber gallery but saw no one. He started toward the library doorway and was three feet from it when he felt a chill on his neck and the hair stood up on his arms. He entered the library and felt the same chill at its north window at the far end of the room. The same experience occurred again at the doorway.

Townsend told no one of these events until a few weeks later, when Capitol historian Raymond Beck recounted a similar experience. Townsend jotted a few notes, and when Beck finished his story, he showed them to Beck. They had shared a similar experience. However, Townsend again refrained from using the G word, even for this unusual coincidence.

The most intriguing and dramatic story of recent times was recounted by Arlene "Dutchic" Sexsmith, who works in a small Senate committee room. In August 2002, as she was completing necessary work prior to a holiday, she heard the sound of a small crowd on the ground floor. The voices and accompanying sounds of doors opening and closing were typical of a working day. Dutchie assumed the governor's staff members were at work and paid little attention. The noises continued until she completed her work at 7.00 p.m. As she descended to the first floor the noises ceased, and she realized that all of the office lights on the first floor were out and all of the offices had been locked. Where were all of the people she had heard so clearly?

"We're Around Here!"

Throughout the winter and spring of 2002 – 03, Beck and I stayed in contact. He sent information for our planned return to the North Carolina Capitol for a full investigation of the building. The first investigation was used as a teaching tool, and now we were offered an opportunity for the Ghost Research Foundation to have unrestricted access to the entire building. In June 2003, we travelled to North Carolina and set up our equipment. We would be observed by students from the Rhine Centre as well as a TV crew from the University of North Carolina's Centre for Public Television (PBS).

I was surprised by the cooperation we received from the

Capitol's staff and the courtesies extended to us by Governor Michael F. Easley's administration.

On the evening of June 28, 2003, we set up our equipment throughout the Capitol and divided our team among the three floors. Linda was assigned the second floor, where a woman had been heard either screaming or crying. Interestingly, two of the Rhine observers insisted they had heard a woman sobbing that evening. The television crew captured the sounds on their video equipment. Linda also captured those sounds on her audiotape.

At 10.30 p.m., Beck and television reporter Rebecca Lindstrom sat at the top of the east staircase from the ground floor discussing the investigation. When they got up to walk over to the second-floor staircase they heard the distinctive sounds of a person ascending the staircase behind them and breathing extremely hard, as if asthmatic. Lindstrom left the area, but Charlie H., one of the Ghost Research Foundation staff members, was nearby and snapped two quick digital photos. Two large orbs were captured on the staircase. The second image showed the orbs passing into the wall of the staircase.

We gathered in the House Chamber at 11.00 p.m. to perform an experiment. Linda placed a CD of Civil War music on her computer and began to play it. Within minutes, many orbs were photographed in the House Chamber. The argument that the phenomenon was caused by dust was negated by the fact that everyone in the room was stationary. Linda's husband, a confirmed sceptic, reported seeing dark circles that when photographed appeared as orbs of energy. Suddenly, when the computer began playing the tune "John Brown's Body" or "Battle Hymn of the Republic," the CD would stop suddenly in mid-tune and move to the next song.

We have found no logical explanation for the switching CD – the disc was not damaged, the computer was not faulty, and every time we played it later outside the Capitol, it played through.

All of our attempts to play the song failed while we were in the House chamber.

The highlight of our visit occurred the next day, after the events in the Capitol were concluded. We had dozens of audio and video tapes to review, but the next night Steve asked to be allowed to sit alone in the Senate chamber the previous night. Steve is from the South and felt an affinity for the Capitol that a "Yankee" could never understand. On his tape, you could hear him sitting down, sighing, and saying, "I know there's something up here. I sure hope it ain't no damn Yankee!"

Following that statement, Steve was quiet for several seconds. He later found that he had captured a gruff male voice that said, "We're around here…" in a thick Southern accent, different from our Pennsylvania voices. The voice print analysis determined that Steve spoke at a level of 4,000 hertz. The unknown male voice modulated at 22,000 hertz – well above the normal range of human speech! It was clear that the voice was neither Steve's nor that of anyone who participated in the evening's study. I can only recall Owen Jackson's story of sighting a Confederate officer in the Senate window over a decade earlier. Whoever the fellow is, he remains there and is willing to communicate.

The haunting of the North Carolina State Capitol is significant due to the sheer number of paranormal events that occur. This is a very active historic site. There are at least five known entities that haunt the building consistently, and many more shades of former occupants occasionally frequent its halls and offices. There are probably many unreported sightings.

The current levels of activity will likely continue for many years into the future – perhaps until their reasons for residing there are better understood. The State Capitol was the focus of North Carolina's government from 1840 to 1888 (when the State Library and Supreme Court departed) and until 1961 for the Legislature. Perhaps the spirits who dwell there are being held by the power and passions bottled up within its walls – especially those of the 1861–65 era. It is well worth seeing for its beauty and grandeur, and for its more recent acclaim as the most haunted capitol in America.

Patty A. Wilson lives in central Pennsylvania, where she has chronicled the paranormal for several years. She is the author of six books and writes for various area newspapers. She also runs the Ghost Research Foundation and can be reached at ghostsrus.com.

SUMMONING THE CHEVALIER

It is commonly supposed that the modern era of mediumship began in 1848, when the Fox sisters of Hydesville, New York, conversed (they claimed) with the ghost of a murdered peddler.

The entire Spiritualist movement dates from that time, and the Fox sisters are often considered the first physical mediums – those mediums who produce physical phenomena, noises, apports, etc. In the following century, many famous physical mediums appeared in America and Europe. Names like D.D. Home, Eusapia Palladino and the Davenport brothers fill the annals of Spiritualism, but their kind can scarcely be found today. Fraud and fakery were always rife in the ranks of physical mediumship.

It was a hard life. Alcoholism plagued many, including Kate Fox. Many mediums lived short lives of furious fame, before exposure or emotional collapse claimed them.

It is therefore surprising to find a man whose career as an occultist and medium predates the Fox sisters by 70 years. His name was Johann Georg Schropfer, and in his day, his name was known across Europe as the most accomplished occultist alive. His reputation was fearsome, and outshone such contemporaries as Cagliostro and the Comte de St Germain.

Born in 1730, Schropfer came to Leipzig in 1768 and opened a coffee house. In those days, Leipzig was one of the most cultured cities on the Continent. It was considered much more refined than austere centres of power, such as Berlin or Moscow.

Leipzig was the co-capital of the small but wealthy kingdom of Saxony. Situated between two great powers – Prussia and Austria – Saxony was constantly threatened by war and invasion. During the Seven Years War (1756–1763) Saxony was ravaged by the armies of Frederick the Great. Leipzig, and the other great city of the kingdom, Dresden, underwent a great social and cultural revival. Johann Schropfer fitted nto that lively scene quite well.

Schropfer soon made it known that he had a strong interest in the occult sciences. Despite the fact that this was the peak of the sceptical Age of Enlightenment, occultism was all the rage.

Soon the habitués of the Schropfer cafe took on a more

esoteric cast. Rumours spread that an occult lodge, formed by Schropfer, met in the coffee shop. Whispers linked it to the Freemasons.

Masonry was not the respectable fraternity that it is today. Masonic ideals of equality and brotherhood were regarded as subversive by many royal governments. Schropfer's brand of Masonry seems to have been tinged with Rosicrucianism – making them a lodge interested in the pursuits of alchemy and ritual magic.

A highly successful magician

Schropfer soon emerged from among his fellow occultists as a highly successful magician. He particularly excelled in summoning spirits to physical form, considered one of the most difficult feats of magic.

As his reputation spread, so did rumours of fraud. This anticipated exactly the pattern of events experienced by mediums in the 19th century.

No exact account of Schropfer's methods has survived, but it appears from eyewitness accounts that he followed the precepts of classical high magic, as described in works like *The Key of Solomon* and the grimoires attributed to Henry Cornelius Agrippa and Dr Johannes Faust.

Schropfer followed a rigorous discipline of ritual cleanliness, prayers, and fasting before his magical operations. He maintained a special room draped in black, with an altar, candles and skulls.

His usual procedure was to invoke good spirits first, as protection for himself and his guests, and then summon evil spirits to do his will. Witnesses recalled that Schropfer's workings were noisy – indeed, he claimed to recognize spirits by the sounds they made. At times these spirits were quite violent, shaking his whole house as they roared and pounded on the walls.

Schropfer carefully kept visitors to his black room inside a magic circle. He burned incense to propitiate the spirits. His detractors claimed that the special spirit room was a theatre of fakery, and that Schropfer's effects were performed by hidden confederates. Whether or not that was true, Schropfer's reputation grew mightily. Soon he was attracting the attention of the highest in the land.

Prince Karl of Saxony, uncle of the reigning elector, was related to half the royalty of Europe. A cultured man, he was described by the English diplomat N. William Wraxall as being "not only elegant in his person and manners, but highly amiable and accomplished". Karl was intrigued by the miracle man in Leipzig, and sent a proposal to Schropfer that he perform a rite of necromancy for the prince. Schropfer declined rather acidly, saying that the summoning of the dead was too hazardous to undertake to gratify the whim of a bored aristocrat.

It may be that Schropfer's Masonic ideals had got the better of his good sense, for in the 18th century, a commoner did not speak so rudely to a prince. Infuriated, Prince Karl sent an officer of his household guard to chastise the insolent cafe owner.

The soldier burst into Schropfer's house and attacked him. After a short struggle, Schropfer broke free and ran to one corner of the room. He knelt down and began to invoke the spirits he had called so often to help him. The soldier, no doubt aware of the tales of Schropfer's powers, grew terrified and fled without finishing the thrashing.

Alarmed by the attack, Schropfer ran away to Dresden, assuming a clumsy false identity when he arrived. (He claimed to be a colonel in the French Army – the French consul promptly exposed him as an impostor.)

While in Dresden, Schropfer resumed his magical operations, to the wonder of the entire town. Word of this got back to Prince Karl, who decided he would get farther with the magician by acting humbly than by being imperious. He then astonished all of Saxony by going to Dresden and presenting himself at Schropfer's residence, the Hotel de Pologne, and asking the sorcerer's forgiveness.

Whatever else he may have been, Schropfer wasn't a fool. He saw the benefit of having a princely patron instead of a royal enemy, and made peace with Prince Karl. To satisfy the prince's desire for wonders, he performed some minor magic for Karl. This only whetted the prince's appetite for more. Would Schropfer undertake to summon the dead?

The magician dissembled. Summoning the dead was most arduous, and dangerous for the necromancer. It amounted to blasphemy in the eyes of the Church. Moreover, the appearance of the dead would cause untold horror to the living. Was Prince Karl prepared for such an ordeal?

He was, and insisted upon the rite without delay. Schropfer agreed.

The next question to consider was, who to summon? Unlike the blackest type of necromancer, Schropfer did not literally raise up a corpse to answer questions, so no grave robbery was necessary. Still, the spirit called had to be someone well known to the prince, someone not too long dead and someone with strong ties to the living. (Schropfer obviously did not want to be put in the position of summoning Julius Caesar or Cleopatra for the prince.) After some thought, Karl decided the perfect ghost to summon was that of his late uncle, the Chevalier de Saxe.

De Saxe was the illegitimate son of King Augustus II of Poland and Princess Lubomirska. His half-brother was the famous soldier, Maurice, Marshal de Saxe. The Chevalier had lived for many years in Dresden, and died there only a few years before Schropfer arrived. De Saxe was very rich as a result of inheriting his mother's estates in Poland, so he built a fine palace in Dresden. He died in the palace and, having no children of his own, willed his estate to Prince Karl.

When a reckoning of the Chevalier's wealth was made, the amount was believed to be too low. Rumour had it that a large amount of hard cash had been hidden in his Dresden palace. Prince Karl found this an excellent collusion of interests. Not only would he witness a demonstration of Schropfer's powers, he would be able to ask his uncle's ghost just where he'd hidden his cash.

The rendezvous was set. Besides Karl and Schropfer, 19 other men, "persons of consideration, character, and respectability," were let in on the secret as witnesses. Secrecy was essential, for the Elector of Saxony frowned on illicit magic.

The men assembled on a dark night in the grand gallery of the de Saxe palace. The first order of business was to secure the gallery's doors and windows, to prevent intrusion or deception. With bolts thrown, nothing human could get in, they thought.

Then Schropfer explained the ritual to them. Courage was required, he said, as terrifying things might occur. Schropfer offered everyone an alcoholic punch he'd prepared, to steady their nerves.

This aroused some suspicion. Two men refused the drink, preferring to keep their wits intact. All of the others, including Prince Karl, partook of the punch. (The principle account we have of this affair comes from one of the teetotallers, who related it to N. William Wraxall.)

One of the sober sceptics took a position by the gallery's main door, to make certain no confederates were admitted during the ritual.

Schropfer retired to a corner, alone. He knelt and commenced what were discreetly called "mysterious ceremonies" From the *Grand Grimoire* we find this conjuration, which may resemble Schropfer's:

"By the virtue of the Holy Resurrection, and the torments of the damned, I conjure and exorcise thee, Spirit of N... deceased, to answer my liege demands, being obedient unto these sacred ceremonies, on pain of everlasting torment and distress... Berald, Beroald, Balbin, Gab, Gabor, Agaba. Arise, arise, I charge and command thee...".

Schropfer repeated his invocation again and again. A long time passed without any outward sign that anything was responding to his commands. More punch was drunk. The witnesses were impressed by the magician's great effort; he soaked himself with sweat and shook hard, almost in convulsions.

After a long interval, a loud rattle sounded on the window panes. Then high, bell-like tones filled the gallery. Wraxall's sober witness described the latter noise as resembling "the effect produced by a number of wet fingers drawn over the edges of glasses".

A howling in the gallery

Schropfer declared that these strange sounds heralded the arrival of his good guardian spirits. He redoubled his efforts, and there followed a frightful howling in the gallery. Those, Schropfer told the assembly, were evil spirits. (It is worth noting that one species of black magic has been known as *Goetia*, which means "The Howling".)

The men were petrified by these manifestations. Neither the magician's warning nor the hearty punch had really prepared them. Worse was to follow.

Schropfer's invocation reached a crescendo, and suddenly the gallery door flew open. In through the door rolled a large, black globe emitting a thick vapour.

In the cloud above the globe appeared a disembodied human face, strongly resembling the Chevalier de Saxe. The men stared in amazement. A great voice boomed out angrily, "*Karl, was wolte du mit mich?*" ("Karl, what wouldst thou with me?")

The answer to the spirit's query was total panic. No-one dared leave the magic circle and approach the phantom, much less speak to it. Prince Karl was so terrified he fell to his knees and prayed aloud to God for mercy and protection from the enraged, disturbed ghost.

Others begged Schropfer to send the spirit away. He tried. Schropfer used every command he knew to force the phantom out, but the booming Chevalier remained for almost an hour while the witnesses cringed and prayed.

When the apparition finally withdrew, some order was regained. The shaken men tried to fathom what had happened. Others simply wanted to get out of the palace as soon as possible.

At that moment, the door banged open again, and there was the smoking black globe and floating face of the Chevalier! Pandemonium struck, as it now became every man for himself. Schropfer confronted the phantom and, by forceful recitation, exorcised the ghost. That done, the terrorized men fled the palace, lest the Chevalier de Saxe return again.

The affair at the de Saxe palace was too bizarre to keep secret long. The Elector caught wind of it, and issued an injunction against any more necromantic experiments in his domain.

Schropfer went back to Leipzig. His fame was at its highest, and he gathered to him a crowd of students eager to learn his mysteries. It is reported that he performed many magical feats for them, though none matched the Gothic heights of his encounter with the Chevalier de Saxe.

The summoning of the Chevalier took place in 1773. By the next year, Johann Georg Schropfer was dead under peculiar circumstances.

It happened in the summer of 1774. He asked three of his most promising students to meet him in the park of Rosendaal, just outside Leipzig, between three and four a.m. They met as arranged in a grove of trees. Schropfer asked them to stay where they were while he went off a short distance to begin his invocation. He promised his students "an exhibition more wonderful than any at which they had yet assisted."

The trio waited patiently, but presently they heard a pistol shot. Running toward the source of the sound, they found Schropfer on the ground, a pistol by his side. He never regained consciousness, and died. The verdict was suicide.

Stories started at once about the cause of Schropfer's death.

His partisans claimed that frequent close contact with spirits had resulted in his being obsessed by them and, despairing of ever getting rid of them, he killed himself.

Detractors believed that all his achievements had been faked, and that he shot himself to escape exposure as a fraud. He could live with anything, it was said, but the collapse of his reputation.

Schropfer clearly belongs to the older tradition of wonder-workers who travelled about Europe in the period from 1450 to 1789 – men like Paracelsus, Cagliostro, St Germain, and Anton Mesmer, who all flourished briefly and died in obscurity. But his career also mirrors quite well those of the Spiritualist mediums who were to follow, even to his strange and lonely end.

Created phenomena?
The phenomena described during the de Saxe affair could have been created artificially – knocks, bells, and yells could easily have been done by confederates outside the gallery. The black globe spewing smoke might have been a pyrotechnic device – the head of the Chevalier a projected image from a magic lantern. All this is possible, amplified by the strong drink and heady incense Schropfer always used.

Only the staging of the apparition seems genuine – why else would Schropfer have risked exposure by producing the phantom twice in one evening? If anyone had stepped forward and laid hands on the spectre, the game might have been up.

But no one dared, and we shall never know if the Chevalier de Saxe returned that night, or if the coffee house owner from Leipzig played the greatest joke in history on a temperamental prince and 19 sceptical witnesses.

A GHOST WITH A BAD CONSCIENCE
by *Boczor Iosif*

One of the most well-documented ghost apparitions in central Europe happened in the 17th century in what is today Bratislava, the capital of Slovakia. Founded by the Romans, Bratislava was the seat of the Hungarian government from 1526 until 1844.

Clemens Janos, a respectable citizen of Bratislava, died in 1640. After a year, Fischer Regina, a modest, intelligent 20-year-old Austrian girl came from Hallstat to Bratislava. Clemens' ghost first appeared before her in Hallstatt as an old man in a white robe. He stood silently near her bed for a few minutes. In Bratislava the phantom visited her late at night twice a week. The appalled girl prayed and fasted in vain. After the spirit visitor tried to touch her in front of a cellar door, Regina was ill for three weeks. Once she tried to get rid of him by reciting the following words, "Every good soul praises the Lord."

"Me too," answered the ghost.

After that night the spirit often spoke. Once he confessed to Regina that he felt remorse because he possessed money stained with blood.

"Visit my mother, ask her for 200 forint and give it to the people in need. My widow must commission a statue of St Mary with the Infant for the cathedral of Bratislava because I want to escape from hell," explained the phantom to the girl.

After the widow failed to fulfill this request, the ghost plagued Regina again. Once the desperate girl told the ghost, "Scram, old rascal!" The next day an invisible hand slapped her. Three reliable witnesses saw the traces of five fingers on her face.

"You must visit my widow again," the phantom ordered her.

"I'll go there only if you can prove to me with three proofs that you really are a ghost," Regina answered him.

Very soon, she got the three proofs. There was a wooden box covered with cloth in Regina's flat. The spirit put his hand on this box and cloth. His fingerprint remained on the box. Clemens' acquaintances confirmed that this was the print of his fingers because a knuckle was missing from the forefinger. A surgeon had amputated this knuckle when Clemens had an infection.

A cross appeared on the box, too. It seemed that it was burned with a hot iron.

Regina saw another example of proof the next week. Kopcsanyi Mihaly, a bishop, asked the girl to give a sealed letter to the ghost. Traces of burning appeared on the letter when the unseen hand of the spirit took it away. The phantom answered the bishop's questions precisely. He explained where the money stained with blood was hidden. Later, the money was found in that place.

That same week, flames shot up from a piece of wood when the unseen hand of the phantom touched it.

The proofs given by the spirit aroused the interest of many clergymen of high rank in the Roman Catholic church. Every night, 18 to 20 of them stood before the door of Regina's room waiting for the appearance of the mysterious phenomenon. On one occasion the phantom splashed water on them. On another night, the ghost answered the clergymen's questions for 30 minutes.

Soon St Mary's statue was finished and consecrated in the cathedral of Bratislava, and Clemens' money was distributed to poor people. Later, the phantom vanished forever.

In 1643, in Bratislava, Kopcsanyi Mihaly published a book about this apparition. It contains the declarations of 32 witnesses. Later this book was translated into German and Dutch. With a decree of November 11, 1646, Ferdinand III, Holy Roman Emperor and King of Hungary, gave a pension to Regina Fischer.

Boczor Iosif *is a retired teacher in Transylvania. He is a regular contributor to several Hungarian paranormal magazines and a correspondent for the* Fortean Times.

GHOST OF THE CRYSTAL ROSE INN
by M. Maureen McNulty

A ghost child shares her story.

I have never actually seen a ghost, but on Monday, September 23, 1996, I may have had the privilege of seeing through the eyes of one.

When my sister Donna, my friend Sue and I arrived in Arroyo Grande, California, we had no trouble locating the Crystal Rose Inn. It stood out against the surrounding fields with its bright pink coat of paint, grand spiral points, elaborate white woodwork, and lush, multicoloured gardens. It was a haven of majesty and beauty against the commonness of its surroundings.

The sun burned hot and the air was still, holding the spicy fragrance of hundreds of roses and flowers. As Donna, Sue and I stepped inside it was as though we had entered a long-forgotten era of exquisite taste, manners and gentility. All our senses were embraced; scented candles glowed from every corner, and the smells of tea, sweet cakes, and fresh roses drifted past our noses. Light music and the tinkling of teaspoons against fine china filled our ears. The reception rooms were aglow with polished antique furniture, original art and even a three-dimensional puzzle of a similar Victorian house laid out on a desk for guests to work on at their leisure.

I immediately sensed peace as well as playfulness in this house. We were shown to a huge, crisply white bedroom which the proprietor said was used as a honeymoon suite. Everything was meticulously clean. There was even a golden ribbon tied across the tiolet seat – and a new white gardenia floating inside. Every conceivable comfort was anticipated. We were giddy.

There was another large room across the hall, and although simpler, it was just as lovely. Donna and Sue decided they would take the white room together so they could catch up . I dropped my bags in the second room. The energy in the house felt loving and cheerful.

As we stood in the white room, gazing at the bridal dolls and baskets of amenities, a cold chill suddenly enveloped me. My skin became covered in goosepimples and my hair stood on end. It was so shocking, inside this sun-warmed room, that an expression must have crossed my face which alarmed Sue and Donna. As they came to my side, the chill subsided, yet it took several moments to feel warm again. The other women had not felt anything, and the lace curtains against the open windows had not moved. I dismissed the incident, and we unpacked and changed for the High English Tea being presented in the garden. As I moved between the rooms, the cold surrounded me several more times. It was heavy, but not malevolent, and I was sure it was meant simply to capture my attention. Donna and Sue continued to insist they felt no draft.

A Haunting Revealed

Following the scrumptious tea service, I cornered a secretary who worked at the inn. I whispered to her of my experience and told her that I was a sensitive. I asked her if the house was haunted. She instantly pulled away, covering her mouth.

Finally, after much coaxing and a promise on my part not to say anything to the other guests, she spoke softly, constantly turning to check that no-one else was listening.

She knew of a writer and his wife who had come from England to stay in the Queen Elizabeth room, which was at the end of our landing. He had heard rumours of a ghost and wanted to find out for himself. As it turned out, he slept peacefully all night. His wife, a sceptic, had been frightened by what she perceived as a child crawling into bed next to her. The woman witnessed the tiny form under the blanket and heard a little girl's voice calling for her mother. By the time the guest recognized that she was not dreaming, the form had disappeared. The woman woke her husband, who was quite perturbed over missing the experience.

The secretary followed that with other tales, leading me through the house to where the inn stored the diaries kept in every room. In a tiny office adjoining the kitchen she rustled through a mound of small books. Suddenly she stood and said as if in disbelief that the diary from the English couple was missing.

I asked her if there was any possibility that I could take a peek at the room. She said she would mention it to the guest currently inhabiting it, but I was only to say that I wanted to view it for the purpose of a future booking. She grew noticeably nervous, but guided me toward the sitting room where the other guests were talking and enjoying a glass of wine.

She bent and whispered to a handsome, older woman, who

handed her a key. I nodded when the guest glanced in my direction. The secretary and I left for the room.

She unlocked the door to the Queen Elizabeth Room. It was a bit smaller than ours, but just as richly appointed, gay and beautiful. I noticed a darkened, narrow staircase beyond the bath and inquired where it led.

It had been the turret room, she explained, but it was being used as a sitting room. I tiptoed alone up the narrow, painted staircase. The room contained a couple of overstuffed chairs and a coffee table, and it was as spotless and comfortable as the rest of the inn. I walked over to one of the room's many windows and peeked out over the front door. I saw the fields we had passed on our arrival. Then, quite unaccountably, I pictured everything outside in black and white, and I was filled with overwhelming joy.

I kept my eyes on the country road until I saw a massive old-fashioned car drive slowly by. I touched my cheek to see if I was there, because I somehow felt distanced from my body. With a jerk I spun around to see inside the room again. Here also I saw only in black and white, and the room appeared fuzzy and somehow different. I thought I saw toys and a cat! I could not recall now how the room had looked only a moment ago.

I suddenly realized that I was seeing what a young girl had seen here years before. I was seeing through *her* eyes, though I didn't understand why she would have seen things without colour.

It hardly mattered. I spoke out loud as my mind telepathically communicated with this child's, who I felt was crowded inside my body. She was extremely happy that I could see what she saw. I could sense that she was content there, and this is what she wanted me to know. She wanted everyone to know. She had many pleasant memories of playing in this room and watching out the window for her father returning from work. She did not feel trapped or displaced here, but secure.

She had long before determined that she was usually invisible to the people who came and went in the house. She had also learned how to enjoy their company and how to play silly tricks on them to get their attention when she desired it. She was having such fun! Hers were all the wonderful emotions I had felt upon first entering this unique bed-and-breakfast.

I caught a glimpse of the secretary peeking into the turret

room. Regardless, I found that I could not stop saying aloud, "I understand, and I see what you see."

The child seemed to need reassurance that people knew of her existence in this house.

I realized that talking as I was might be an odd spectacle to someone watching, so I finally forced myself away from the window and went toward the door. Instantly I felt released by the entity. I was weak and trembling but able to see normally as I made my way down the stairs. It had been only minutes, but the secretary was gone. I quickly left the room, locking the door behind me.

I rushed to our rooms and found Sue and Donna sprawled across the bed reading magazines. I could hardly catch my breath. I began to hyperventilate and wave my hands toward the hall. At the same time tears broke out all over my face. Sue and Donna came over to me and directed me to an easy chair. Eventually they got the story from me.

Afterward we all laid on the bed, exhausted and astonished. I could not say enough times that the spirit I had encountered was benevolent, joyous and innocent. I was compelled to relay its message.

A Night's Unrest

That night I slipped into the bed in the spare room and, remembering the story of the writer's wife, pulled down the comforter on the other side to welcome the ghost. Sue and Donna collapsed in their own bedroom.

At midnight, Sue woke abruptly and noticed the figure in the open doorway. A girl approximately nine years old stood in the frame. She had shoulder-length, blonde, corkscrew curls tied back with a wide ribbon. Her white dress reached to her ankles, under which a hint of lace and ribbon could be seen. She was solid and perfect in every detail. Sue said later that she was not frightened, but rather curious as to how the child had opened the locked door, and why she would be about at such a late hour.

The girl pointed to the bed and giggled. Sue gazed down at the fluffy quilt that covered her. Donna snored peacefully beside her. Instantly, Sue saw a deep, circular depression near her feet, and then several more all over the bed. She recognized that there were cats running from the direction of the open door and leaping up on the bed.

Sue jumped out of bed. She is not particularly fond of cats.

She called out to Donna, who immediately woke and asked about the commotion. Donna saw the cats dashing about the bed, then noticed the girl at the door.

Just then, a piercing car horn cut through the darkness. The child and cats vanished, and the door was once again shut. Sue and Donna ran to the door, unlocked it, and crossed the hall to a massage room. They peered out the windows and saw our car, the only one in the car park. Sue recognized the sound of the car alarm. Street lights clearly bathed the car and it was obvious there was no intruder near it. The horn bleated six times and stopped. Sue was terrified at this point. She informed Donna that the alarm was programmed to sound as many as 20 times if she did not turn it off with the key.

The two women ran into my room and tried to wake me. I only remember them screaming and flitting about the bed. They yelled about the car alarm, the cats, and the little girl, and they wanted me to go with them down to the car park. I was as if in a coma, too exhausted to respond. They gave up and returned to their room.

The next morning Donna had a plane to catch, so we had to leave long before breakfast. I was concerned about Sue and Donna, as they were dishevelled and bleary eyed. As we quietly left the house, I asked them why they were so tired? That is when I heard their part of the story, and I knew that the long-dead child wanted me to tell her story.

M. Maureen McNulty *is a recognized "sensitive" who has known a lifetime of accurate predictions. She is studying parapsychology at Indiana University.*

GUERNAVACA'S HOUSE OF TERROR
By Emil Zubryn

This apartment building in a crowded Mexican city is modern and attractive – yet nobody dares to live in it.

THERE is a modern, five-storey building in the centre of Cuernavaca, resort town 48 miles from Mexico City, which has been tenantless since shortly after it was built 10 years ago.

The edifice is said to be the favoured meeting place of ghostly apparitions. The building is known to Cuernavacans as *La Casa de Los Espantos* (The House Of Terror). This, despite the fact that it stands near Cuernavaca's City Hall, the Cathedral of Cuernavaca, the Borda Gardens, the Civil Hospital, the Red Cross Hospital and two funeral directors.

Just why the spectres have chosen this particular house for their meetings is a mystery. But the fact remains that Mrs Elisa Rodriguez, who owns the building, is making no profits on her investment. Apartments remain vacant; even the commercial quarters below, suitable for a store, find no tenant.

Mrs Guadalupe Villegas de Nunez, who lives on Zapata Avenue in the immediate neighbourhood of the house, says that on one occasion when she happened to pass the "haunted house" at midnight, she was greatly surprised to see a priest leave the uninhabited structure. He crossed the street and entered the cathedral by a gate that was chained and bolted. Mrs De Nunez swears that what she saw was a visitation from the other world. She takes special pains not to pass the House of Terror at night now.

Some tenants, in the beginning, did occupy the premises, but they stayed for short periods only. For some one night was enough; others stayed a week. All said they were "molested" by the "apparitions" and reported hearing various sinister sounds during the nights.

Jesus de Eguiluz, of Spanish descent and a long-time resident of Cuernavaca, still speaks of what happened to him there some years ago. One midnight he was driving home in a pick-up when suddenly the car stopped as though held by an invisible force. The vehicle halted precisely in front of the empty house, and he says he saw "mysterious shadows" leave the building. Then his car once again became mobile and, frightened out of his wits, he went straight to the nearest police station.

Policemen Eucario Arce and Baltasar Diaz, as well as the superintendant, scoffing, accompanied him back to the house. But once there they also saw "peculiar shadows". However, as minions of the law, they would not say they were ghosts.

Only one man ever lived on the site for any length of time, although not in the present structure. One Jesus Pintos lived in an old adobe structure which stood there before the present building was erected. Nothing bothered him there, although other tenants even of the old structure would leave suddenly, without explanation. Some of them hastily departed to sleep in the nearby Borda Gardens for the balance of the night, returning by daylight only to pick up their belongings and move to a less disturbing spot.

The citizens of Cuernavaca foster this story of their city's House of Terror. They even embellish it for the ears of foreign tourists. Nevertheless, and tall tales notwithstanding, the plain fact is that a modern, attractive building, with graceful iron balconies and large airy windows, remains empty in the crowded city of Cuernavaca. No one dares to live in it!

THE HAUNTING OF CURRY HILL

by *Kim Linn Lohret*

Tucked in the rolling foothills of the Catskills, about 30 miles from Albany, New York, there's a winding dirt road known as Curry Hill. Unless a local resident pointed it out, you probably wouldn't notice the tall, spindly tree that marks the location of a small, untended graveyard. The side of the road slopes up there, and clinging to the exposed roots of old trees is the only way to reach the plateau where the graveyard rests.

Although untended, the ivy-covered ground stays neat. Wild rose bushes provide fresh pink flowers for the nearly forgotten graves. Driving by the quiet country houses that lie on either side of the graveyard, you probably wouldn't believe the strange occurrences that have taken place there.

Kate Smith lives in a small, grey house about 200 feet from the graveyard. She vividly remembers an incident that involved her adopted son, Dave.

"One night, we were all asleep and he came running into my room," Kate recalls. "'There's something in my room,' he said. He was very frightened. It was obvious in his voice." Frightened herself, Kate asked Dave what he meant. "He said he saw someone. That there was somebody in his room. My first reaction was that he was dreaming. But he said, 'No, there's something in my room. I saw it.'"

Unnerved, Kate rose from her bed and walked with Dave back to his room, assuring him that there was nothing to fear. Kate sat with him as he explained what he had seen. "There's a little area against one wall near his door where if someone was leaning flat against it, you wouldn't see them from where he was lying," Kate says. Dave explained that he had been awakened by the sound of a girl crying. When he looked toward the doorway, he saw a young girl rocking, moving in and out of his view.

"At that point, I got a little scared," Kate admits. "I was thinking that he could've been dreaming, but it was so vivid in his mind, and he was so frightened. It wasn't like when you wake up from a scary dream and you're scared but you realize it was a dream." As Kate and Dave talked, Dave recalled a younger sister from whom he'd been separated in Korea. "I think in his mind, he was wondering if it was her. Maybe she had passed over and was somehow trying to connect with him."

Dave didn't want to sleep in his room, so Kate told him to sleep on the couch and they closed his bedroom door. As Kate walked down the hall to the bathroom, she heard Dave's voice again. "'What's the matter?' I asked, running back to him. He said 'My doorknob is turning!' So, I went over to the door and I pushed it open. There was a mist in the room – this white thing just hanging there. It didn't have a defined shape, but you could sense that something was there."

Mustering her courage, Kate commanded the phantom to leave. "You're not welcome in this house!" she cried out. "Get out! Leave this house!"

"I don't know where I got the courage to do that," she recalled. "I threw the light switch on at that point, and it was gone. It just disappeared."

Kate moved Dave into her room for the rest of the night. "By that point, I was pretty scared myself. I'm lying there trying to fall back asleep when Dave started again. 'Do you hear that?' he asked. I told him I didn't hear anything. 'You don't hear that? It's coming. It's coming down the hall. You don't hear that?'" Kate grabbed Dave and pulled him up into her bed, assuring him that everything would be fine.

"Finally, we fell asleep," she said. "The next day we woke up and everyone went off to school. I couldn't stand to be alone in the house. I've never gotten ready for work so quick."

Knowing that Dave would be alone after school, Kate made arrangements with her husband in the weeks that followed so that one of them would be there when Dave came home. "Nothing happened in his room after that, but he used to tell me that when he was alone in the house and it was getting dark outside, he felt like someone was watching him."

The ghost never appeared again, and neither Kate nor Dave ever discovered who she was. A careful examination of one of the tombstones in the nearby graveyard reveals the names of two young girls – Mary Kelly who died in 1852 aged 15, and her sister, Irene, who died in 1853 aged 14. Although Kate still wishes she could have found out more about the ghost and what she wanted, it appears that her identity will forever remain secret. She's chosen to remain silent, just like the cold stones in the hushed, country graveyard.

DAIRY FARM POLTERGEIST
By John P. Bessor

The milking machine disintegrated before their eyes and went
flying through the air at fantastic speed.

Early in 1949 strange things happened on the lonely dairy farm of
Lawrence A. Wilkinson, in the fertile Tarcutta Valley of New South
Wales, Australia.

His milking machine and the dairy shed which housed it
became the focal point of mysterious phenomena. The machine's brass
pulsator plates, three inches long and weighing 13 ounces, flew over
the adjoining field for 200 yards and more. Public works officials, dairy
inspectors and scientists of the Commonwealth Scientific and
Industrial Organization, were called in to observe the manifestation
and to help, if they could, bring order out of chaos.

Before their startled eyes hundreds of metal parts, weighing
from two ounces to two pounds, were thrown great distances by an
invisible force. The brass pulsator plates flew, without the slightest
noise and invariably in a northerly direction, so rapidly that their actual
flight could not be followed by the naked eye.

Alexander Porter, a local garage proprietor and acquaintance
of Wilkinson's, found one of the discs buried in mud. Oddly, a queer
haze hung over the place of fall for which he could not account.

Wilkinson's 15-year-old son, Robin, tried to dislodge one of
the plates with the aid of an iron bar but the bar was wrenched forcibly
from his hands by some unseen force which then hurled the point of
the bar deep into the concrete floor. The plate he had sought to move
rose into the air and landed 200 yards away.

At first the plates were hurled shorter distances.
Experimenting, Wilkinson removed the fibre facing and substituted
leather whereupon the plates were thrown farther.

A reporter for the Australian paper, the *Sunday Herald*, wrote
that at least 15 eyewitnesses had, at different times, observed the
phenomenon. Alexander Porter told the reporter:

"I was standing in the creamery with some friends. Mr
Wilkinson had just left the engine-room when an empty one-pound
grease tin, which had been standing on top of the vacuum pump,

began to rise in the air. We saw it spinning as it rose. It cleared a six foot wooden partition with 18 inches to spare, then turned and fell with terrific force to the ground about two feet from where I stood."

Amazed, they had decided to place an empty cigarette tin on the pump where the grease can had formerly rested. After several minutes they saw it, too, rise into the air.

A radio and electrical engineer who, with Mr Porter, had observed the levitation of the can and cigarette tin, stated that he once kept a four-hour watch on the master pulsator block in the creamery. Suddenly he became aware that it was gone although he had not seen it move. Later it was found in the paddock, 50 yards away. At another time he peered through the engine-room door to see the lid of a milk can rise off the creamery shelf, soar through the air and bang against the opposite wall. "It's impossible to explain these things by any known law," he told the reporter. "I've thought of magnetic deflection and electrical interference and I made a lot of electro-physical tests with instruments I brought to the farm. But my tests proved nothing. It's the biggest mystery I've ever experienced."

On one accasion Wilkinson securely fastened all the movable objects in the creamery to the rafters and walls. This had no effect. Parts of the milking machine continued to fly about. Heavy iron dog chains were twisted as though made of soft, copper wire. Not a single part of the machine escaped the strange force. Twelve of the moving parts were completely lost.

Agents for the milking machine, departmental experts and several other neighbourhood farmers who used the same make of milking machine could offer no mechanical explanation for its singular antics. They pointed out, however, that the majority of the machine parts were of non-magnetic brass and several tests made for ground magnetism proved negative.

Robin Wilkinson, the adolescent son, was present during some of the manifestations, but was miles away when others took place in the creamery. However he told the *Sunday Herald* reporter, "Not much happens when I'm away."

Perhaps it is significant that the machine began its strange antics when the power was switched off and it had to be worked by hand. The phenomena lasted for eight consecutive days, stopped for an interval of several days, then resumed.

Psychical researchers believe that certain people, particularly adolescent boys and girls, either possess strange supernormal potentialities in themselves or are acted upon by disembodied entities who use their psychic energy or nerve force as a means to perform physical phenomena. Did Robin Wilkinson so wish to be relieved of the drudgery of farm chores, especially the milking, that he subconsciously caused the milking machine to "fly apart and never be found"?

THE DEATH OF A POPE
by Maggie L. Cooper

On the sixth of August, 1978, Pope Paul VI's secretary went to the papal bedroom and spoke to the Bishop of Rome lying in his bed with his eyes closed: "Are you dead?"

The Pope made no reply.

The Pope's secretary picked up a silver hammer and tapped the Pope on his head, then repeated his question. "Are you dead?"

The Pope made no reply.

The Pope's secretary declared the Pope to be dead.

This is the way the Church has determined papal deaths for centuries. The Church changes slowly, except for the changes it made after the Vatican II Council from 1962 to 1965. Catholics back then felt that the Church was changing too soon and too fast. A deep split that still hasn't healed tore among hierarchy and laity, causing the Church to lose (according to some counts) almost half of her members. Some complained that the Church was still too conservative. Most complained that the Church had become far too liberal.

Italy Mourns

In all this chaos, two things did not change. The first was the silver hammer declaration of papal death. The second was the traditional mourning of Italy over a Pope's passing. I don't mean just the mourning of good Catholics, or all Catholics, or even all the people in Italy. I mean all of Italy – people, trees, rocks, mountains, water, wind, everything. There is no way I can testify about Italy's periods of mourning when the previous 261 Popes met their demise, but I can tell you with accuracy how Italy mourned when Popes Paul VI and John Paul I died, since I was living in Italy at the time.

Although Pope Paul VI was not the one who began the Second Vatican Council, he was the one who received the brunt of fury and condemnation from most Catholics. In the States, my friends had told me that he was everything from an anti-Catholic Mason to the Antichrist. I didn't feel any personal revulsion or anger towards him. To me, he was just a man. But, in the name of friendship, I offered no argument in his defence and remained neutral in my opinion of him.

That was one reason why I turned down my husband Bob's offer to take me to Rome for the funeral.

My second reason was that we had recently moved with our children – 15-year-old Diana, 12-year-old Patrick, and 10-year-old Teresa – into a first-floor apartment in the village of Gianola and still had much unpacking to do. The scenery surrounding what would be our home for the next two years was impressive. When we stood on our front balcony, we could see Via Appia, the famous road travelled by everyone from ancient Romans to modern-day tourists. Beyond Via Appia was a brutal-looking mountain range.

Exit From Purgatory
Our Italian neighbours told us legends (which they swore were true) that when the wind howled, souls in purgatory entered the world from those mountains and wandered the land to beg the living for prayers. They warned us to be careful when opening our doors or windows on windy days, since there was no telling who or what night be on the other side.

After we finished supper that fateful day, we spent some time unpacking, then went to bed at ten o'clock. The weather was still warm and breezy. We left all our windows and balcony doors open.

A little after midnight, I awoke to eerie wailing sounds slithering down from the mountain range and toward our apartment building. These cries were mingled with a howling wind that forced rain through the open doors and windows. I shook Bob to wake him up so he could help me close everything. Bob rolled over, never pausing between snores.

Muttering unkind words about sleeping husbands and Italian weather, I crawled out of bed, pushed our balcony door shut, then closed the windows and doors in Teresa and Patrick's rooms. Son and daughter slept undisturbed as I tripped over clothes, books and boxes. I stepped into the hall and struggled to see through its pitch blackness before going to Diana's bedroom by the front door.

The strange wailing sounds mixed with the wind and entered the building to spiral up the stairwell. It sounded as if hundreds of people in agony were out there. I told myself I was hearing only the wind. But no wind had ever sounded like this – not even the winds of the three hurricanes we had gone through one year in Key West, Florida.

Thinking there had been an accident and some of the victims were coming to us for help, I hurried blindly down the hall. The sounds changed from many low cries to one deep, cackling laugh. I stopped, my heart racing in fear, as I believed someone was in Diana's bedroom.

Panic forced me to run until I crashed into a stack of packing boxes. Screaming and cursing, I pushed the boxes aside and stood up. By then, the wailing had returned and was outside the front door. I raced to open the door, but my hand froze above the knob as I remembered our neighbours' advice. The cries drifted down the stairwell and then seemed to be outside Diana's window.

I ran into Diana's room and peered out her window. Looking down at Via Appia, I was certain I saw lines of vague forms walking past our building. Not ready to admit I was seeing ghosts, I closed my eyes and opened them again. The barely visible forms were still there, still walking in a misty procession. I closed the window and pulled down the *persioni*, a metal protective window covering, then returned to the hall.

Standing there, I heard the cries coming this time from the living-room balcony. I remained in the hall and stared through the living room to the window across from me. Drenched curtains blew inward like arms stretching toward me. The moanings became louder, more persistent. I could see what seemed to be outlines of human forms on the balcony, stretching their arms through the window.

"Stop it!" I screamed and ran back to bed. Bob was still snoring. Our children were still peacefully asleep.

Prayers for the Pope
The purgatorial storm that continued howling the next day covered almost all of Italy. I decided to go to my favorite church and pray for the Pope. On the ten-mile ride to church, the bus bounced like a fragile toy over the streets. Large tree branches tumbled to the ground. Debris swirled in little whirwinds. Sharp pellets of rain pounded me and the hundreds of Italians around me as we walked up the pathway of a small mountain to the church.

The Italians entered the church sanctuary. I went to a small chapel built in the side of the mountain over the beach area. There I knelt on cold rocks and prayed. Wind and rain sliced through openings in the granite walls of the chapel, hitting me with freezing bites. Waves a hundred feet below the chapel cried in woeful sounds as they crashed against the mountain's rocky sides. Even the image of Jesus on a large crucifix in the chapel seemed to be weeping.

Unable to spend more than a few minutes there, I struggled up wet stone steps and hurried past the church. The wind pelted me with needle-like raindrops. My hair was drenched. The thin coat I wore over my cotton dress did little to keep me dry. I hurried to a bus stop. By the time I returned to our apartment, I was exhausted. The storm and those agonizing ghostly cries continued in full fury until the day of the papal funeral.

After it was over and had become a memory, I decided it had all been coincidence. The storm just happened to arrive after the Pope had died and just happened to end on the day of his funeral. My imagination had turned the howling wind into moaning ghosts only I could see and hear.

Death of John Paul I

I was satisfied with this conclusion until September 28 of that year, when Pope John Paul I suddenly died in his sleep. It took only minutes for people to begin shouting that this Pope had been murdered. While the reasons for his alleged assassination were many, all the evidence pointed back to a statement he was supposed to have told the cardinals when they'd elected him: "May God forgive you for what you have done to me."

One of our Catholic saints (St Malachy 1095–1148) predicted who each Pope would be until the end of the world. His prediction for Paul VI was "Flower of flowers", which matched the three flowers on Paul's coat of arms. Since Malachy gave us only four more popes after Paul VI, many Catholics were startled at John Paul I's sudden death.

Confusion reigned supreme at his death. Before one ghost moaned or one breeze blew or one raindrop fell, whispers of holy intrigue and rumours of subversives planning to attack the Vatican raged across the country. The news media gave many conflicting accounts about John Paul I's death. The day of the funeral remained unannounced until the last moment. The hour of the funeral was never told. So many rumours abounded that the Italian military police were put on alert.

If all this wasn't bad enough, reports of flying saucer sightings came in from Sicily, Tuscany and Sardinia. When two employees of Alitalia Air Lines were credited as reliable eyewitnesses to some of these sightings, devout souls listened in terror for the sound of Armageddon's battle cry.

Italy was struck with another storm similar to the one when Paul VI had died but not quite so intense or over such a wide area. It did, however, flood Rome and cause massive traffic jams that stranded motorists.

Trip to the Funeral

I was determined to go to the funeral. Since Bob was away at the time, Patrick insisted on going along to protect me in case anything strange happened. The night before the day of the funeral, the storm pounded with full fury against our apartment. I sat up most of the night, wondering if the weather was too dangerous for Patrick and me to make the train trip to Rome. As dawn arrived, the storm let up somewhat. Patrick and I agreed to at least try to make the trip.

Dark storm clouds hung over St Peter's Square when we arrived. We could sense the feeling of dread and suspicion as we waited in line to view the papal body. Back outside, we were approached by various people shoving pamphlets and brochures into our hands about horrible times ahead. Four thousand armed policemen and military guards patrolled the Vatican grounds.

Rain came and went as Patrick and I tried to find out when the funeral would begin. Most often, our question was answered with, "I was hoping you knew."

In spite of the rain that came and went, we decided to wait it out. We looked at the three clocks on the front of the basilica. One said two o'clock, another said 3:30, the third said 4:15. That seemed to sum up the entire circumstances there.

The rain was still falling five hours later when the Pope's body was carried out to the basilica steps. Beside his wooden coffin was a candle and a Bible open to the Book of John. In spite of the wind and rain, the candle flame never went out, and the pages of the Bible never moved.

Not until the funeral ended did the storm stop.

LEGEND OF THE DEVIL MONKS
by *Andy Ellis*

Most legends have a basis in fact, although it is often impossible to find corroborative evidence. Every so often, however, things happen that confirm our worst fears. Such is the case of the Devil Monks.

A group of monks came to England from Europe in Saxon times and asked the local lord, the Earl of Leeds, if they could build a monastery on some nearby common land. The earl, assuming they belonged to a religious order, agreed.

Ten years later, the abbey was complete and the monks went about their business, keeping themselves to themselves. When young women started to disappear from the surrounding villages of Harthill and Todwick, however, people began asking questions.

After the fifth disappearance, the villagers decided to confront the monks and marched *en masse* to the abbey. There the abbot was able to quiet the crowd and convince the villagers that the monks did not interfere in village life and really had no idea where the girls were.

The father of one of the missing girls, Tom Moody, was not content with the abbot's response. He decided to take a look inside the abbey, which no one beside the monks had seen. According to legend, Moody saw the monks acting out a black mass and sacrificing a young woman he didn't recognize on the Devil's sign, the pentagram.

Terrified, he ran back to the village and reported what he had seen to the earl. The earl decided to wait until morning, despite the fact that the new sacrifice would by then be dead. He rounded up as many villagers as dared to come with him and rode to the abbey. There he confronted the abbot with Moody's evidence and smashed down the door. After searching, he found all the paraphernalia connected with devil worship. The monks were thrown into the local jail to await sentence.

The earl was also the magistrate, and it was left to him to deal with crimes that took place within the boundaries of his estate. The monks were convicted and burned. As they slowly died, they cursed the earl and his line for all time. Oddly enough, they also cursed the ground, saying it would never be happily inhabited.

One coincidence does not make the curse or the legend real, but the earl's family did die in the great plague. The monks' land remained barren for 700 years, until it was sold to a property developer. He sold it to the Rank Organization, which built a cinema on it, the Regal.

All was quiet for six months. Then the activity began: knocks, bangs, lights going out and equipment failure. Several employees said that they felt sudden temperature drops and they felt as if they were being watched all the time. Eventually, no one would work at the theatre and the place closed.

The developer sold the place to a local businessman in 1938. The man brought his family in to operate the machinery and do everything necessary to make the new company flourish. In October of that year, a fire burned the building to the ground, killing 25 people. They were all young, unmarried women.

Almost 40 years passed. The land was sold once again, this time to a brewery. Forewarned about the area's evil past, the owners had the land exorcised before building the Saxon pub. The Saxon is still intact. It has had five landlords, however, and each has confirmed strange happenings, usually in the cellar and usually at night.

The first landlord, Dick Strange, refused to ever again go into the cellar after one incident. He said, "I was down there changing a barrel over, when I suddenly felt very cold. I was aware that someone was watching me, and I thought perhaps that one of the bar staff had followed me down, leaving the door open. I turned around just in time to see a black, hooded figure walk through the far wall. I swear to God he walked straight through it. It made my hair stand on end, and I got out of there as fast as I could."

Three months later, Dick and his wife died in a mysterious car accident. The car just burst into flames. Dick's 24-year-old unmarried daughter also died later, in a hospital.

The next two landlords were single, unmarried men. Their tenure at the bar was uneventful.

The fourth landlord, however, was a different story: Maurice Smith had been happily married for over 20 years and had twin 19-year-old daughters. Several of the pub's regulars told him about the legend and what had happened to Dick Strange, but Smith just laughed it off as superstition.

For three months, nothing happened. Then, on November 5, 1989, three regulars were patiently waiting for the pub to open. Opening time came and went. They decided, after shouting and trying several windows, to call the police.

The police broke in and searched. The last room they came to was the cellar, and what they found was horrifying.

Maurice was hanging by his belt. In one corner, his wife and two daughters had been tied up, and each had stab wounds to the heart. A police pathologist later said that it looked like an attempt had been made to remove their hearts. A roughly drawn pentagram had been chalked onto the floor, and the couples' bedroom had been ransacked. Instead of the bed and the usual furnishings, there was a pile of wood in the centre of the room – a bonfire – soaked in petrol and ready to go.

Was Maurice taken over by the spirit of a devil-worshipping monk, or was he compelled to carry out their diabolical trade by some unseen force? We will never know.

Whether the pub owners believe in the legend or not, they have at least shown common sense. From that day on, the pub has only been managed by single men or childless couples.

The phantom, the cold spots and the feeling of being watched are still reported by regulars and staff at *The Saxon*. The legend lives on.

THE PRICE OF DISOBEDIENCE

My father had an old car, and it was common among his grown-up children to drive it through the streets of Benin City, Nigeria, in search of any passenger who might not be able to afford the normal taxi fare.

A local slang we adopted for this practice is *Kabubu*. Like all youngsters, we indulged in *Kabubu* when we were out of cash. Our father, a strict disciplinarian who knew of our escapades, usually administered his horse-whip or *bulala* on our bare buttocks when he caught us in the act. He warned us to refrain from it and would even give us chores to prevent us. But these and other measures were like water off a duck's back.

One weekend in June 1990, on holiday from our university, I headed for what I knew would be another boring three weeks at home. It also happened to be my father's seventy-fifth birthday. Knowing he was in a good mood that day, I asked to borrow the car from him. Contrary to my expectations, the old man agreed to my wish, instructing me to return by dusk.

I visited the amusement park and the zoo. As dusk neared, I decided to head straight home. Not far away, voices and drums rent the air and I could tell a party was going on. *This might be a real cool spot to find one or two passengers, I thought.*

The party was over, but people were gathered outside engaged in discussion. From the crowd emerged a pretty lady with a proposition: "Young man, would you drop me at my doorstep for 400 naira?"

Hardly had she said her last word than I agreed to the bargain. I couldn't believe my ears. Me, a mere undergraduate, to receive such an enormous sum in a single swoop? Unbelievable!

She got into the car and introduced herself as Stella. I saw nothing strange in my passenger, except that she would ask me to stop at intervals while she waved at imaginary objects. Initially, this queer behaviour surprised me and I wanted to ask her about it. But on second thoughts, I concluded her actions must have been caused by the booze she'd had at the party.

A glance at my wrist-watch revealed that we had been travelling for 90 minutes. When I asked Stella where to stop, she pointed to a sharp bend at the next junction.

She got out of the car hurriedly and asked me to hang around while she fetched the fare. There were no houses in sight. It was quiet and very dark. I got out my torch, and found a sign that read, "Area Cemetery. Do not trespass."

A chill ran over me. In my community there are myths surrounding sacred places and the dead. Lost in deep thought over this, I heard a loud guttural laugh from behind me; I turned sharply, and there was Stella sitting on a tomb, encircled by an indescribably bright light. As I rubbed my eyes to ensure it was not a nightmare, my passenger roared once again and beckoned to me with an outstretched arm, which seemed to wither!

I realized that I had encountered a ghost. My head became heavy and my limbs weakened. I wanted to drive off immediately, but my strength failed me, and I fell down, unconscious.

The next day, I awoke in a hospital. I had been brought there by a Good Samaritan who had found me lifeless under the hot afternoon sun, with a paltry sum of 10 naira placed carefully on my forehead. I was at a complete loss, unable to recollect what had occurred.

My father consulted a local herbalist, who ordered that I be brought to him immediately. Upon my arrival, the herbalist brought out two cowrie shells, chanted an incantation and rubbed me all over with a hot concoction. The more the potion penetrated my skin, the more the man confronted me: "What really happened to you, my son?" he demanded. He sipped a little of the concoction and offered the rest to appease Stella's lurking spirit.

After 75 minutes of excruciating pain, I could recall vividly everything that had transpired. I still do not know how I got the courage to recount the story. But nobody can refuse to dance to the tunes of this powerful herbalist who doubles as a witch hunter.

The herbalist and my father made for the cemetery, where they performed some rituals. On the same tomb my passenger had been sitting on, they found an epitaph which read, "In loving memory of Miss Stella Karowa (1949–1988) R.I.P." This was no surprise to me, after what I had witnessed the night before. The two men drove home in my father's car, which they found not far from the scene.

The next day, I left to stay with my Aunt about 1,200 miles away. I feared that Stella would somehow learn where I lived and would haunt me. My father tried to calm my mind, but who on Earth could explain how a lady who died and was buried years ago would still be hanging around, seeking people to torment? What if I had been mutilated or torn asunder by Stella? Thank goodness I am alive today to recount my ordeal and show that ghosts do exist. Anytime I reminisce about that fateful Saturday, I develop goosepimples, not to mention whenever I meet anyone who goes by that name

– *Martins Agbonlahor, Turin, Italy*

IN THE DOGHOUSE
by John J. Lamb

**A sceptic touring the haunted Whaley House changes his views
after seeing a spectral terrier.**

"The only reason I'm taking this tour is because my girlfriend is
interested in this kind of crap," announced the young man in a sardonic
voice. "But I think this stuff is laughable. There is no such thing as
ghosts, and anyone who believes in them needs his head examined."

It isn't often a ghost researcher can luxuriate in the sublime
pleasure of watching a doubting Thomas eat a large plate of humble
pie. But on this evening I was privileged to behold just such an
unpleasant meal.

The date was November 2, 1997 – a Sunday evening – and the
sceptic and his date had just purchased tickets for the ghost tour I lead
along the streets of San Diego, California. Since July 1997, I've taken
people on walking journeys through the Old Town district, acquainting
them with the spectres. The business allows me to pursue my two
greatest passions – ghosts and history.

The stories I share are neither folklore nor fiction. They've
been collected from credible witnesses who have seen ghosts in the old
buildings. As a ghost researcher I've taken special pains to separate the
genuine spectral encounters from legend. On a few occasions we've
been fortunate to witness spectral phenomena, but this happens very
infrequently.

The young man and his female companion were students at a
local university. By chance, they had discovered my tour while
exploring Old Town, and the young woman eventually cajoled her
unwilling date into buying tickets. She possessed a general interest in
paranormal matters, while he was a bellicose disbeliever.

Throughout the first half of the journey the arrogant critic
maintained a barrage of rhetorical questions and thinly veiled insults
regarding the sanity of the folks who had seen ghosts. His ill-tempered
comments were so disruptive I was tempted to refund their money and
give the tour up as a bad effort. But I persisted, little suspecting that,
before the evening was concluded, a ghost would come to my rescue.

Around 8.00 p.m. we arrived in the grounds of the infamous

haunted Whaley House. Over the years, a small army of ghost researchers, including Hans Holzer, Arthur Myers and Antoinette May, have examined the site. Stories of the spectres who inhabit the Victorian-era home have appeared in many books and are a staple feature in television programs on the paranormal. Among the more famous resident phantoms are Thomas and Anna Whaley, the noisy Yankee Jim Robinson and a young girl who met her death in the grounds. But it was one of the most obscure ghosts who provided that evening's entertainment.

As my guests sat on the low brick wall outside the home, I began recounting the long history of ghostly phenomena on the site. Soon, however, my attention was drawn to the increasingly curious behaviour of the insolent sceptic. He had removed his glasses and was peering intently toward a spot near the southeast corner of the house. He vigorously rubbed his eyes and cocked his head to look at the spot with his peripheral vision. It was clear he was observing something, but when I looked at the spot I saw nothing out of the ordinary. Finally, I asked the man what he had seen.

"Nothing," the disbeliever declared in an uncertain voice. "Nothing at all. I'm just getting a headache."

The explanation was feeble and unconvincing, but I let it go, happy that the cynic was, for the moment, quiet.

Near the end of my talk, I began to tell of the numerous sightings of a spectral dog in the Whaley House and its grounds. Her name is Dolly and she is often seen by Whaley House employees and visitors. In fact, there is far more evidence of Dolly's existence than that of the notorious Yankee Jim Robinson.

Upon hearing this story the sceptic raised his hand and asked, "So, what breed of dog was she?" Suddenly suspecting the young man had seen Dolly, I posed him a question in return, "What kind of dog did you see?"

"I'm not saying for a fact I saw a dog," the doubting Thomas unhappily replied. "Maybe it was just my imagination. For argument's sake, let's just say I thought I saw something that looked like a Scottish Terrier near those bushes."

Trying to conceal the triumph in my voice, I said, "That was Dolly. People have been seeing her for at least the last three decades."

"You're making that up," protested the young man.

"I'm not," I replied. "You can look up the information in any number of books on the Whaley House. I'll give you a list of the titles so you can look it up for yourself."

The disbeliever looked at the other customers and asked, "Did anyone else see it?" No one else had. I suppressed a grin as the young man's date began to giggle.

"Maybe it was a real dog," he said hopefully.

I encouraged him to examine the bushes to confirm that I hadn't concealed a genuine terrier there. Together we poked through the foliage but saw nothing. When he returned to his seat, the sceptic was plainly disturbed. In a small voice he described the sighting.

While listening to my commentary on the Whaley House ghosts, he'd observed the diffuse image of a Scottish Terrier amble from the house toward the clump of bushes. He was perplexed that he could not focus his direct gaze on the dog, but could clearly see the animal in his peripheral vision. Then, without warning, the dog vanished.

The distressed witness concluded his account with a weak objection. "But there's no such thing as ghosts," he said.

"Well, tonight is as good a night as any to start believing in them," I countered. "Face the facts. Either you saw a ghost or you've begun to hallucinate. Would you rather admit to being mentally ill or concede you might have been wrong about ghosts? Besides, how could you have known what Dolly looked like before I described her?"

For the remainder of the tour, the sceptic was silent, seemingly lost in contemplation. Meanwhile, his date wore a smug grin and she would periodically nudge the young man in the ribs and murmur, "Woof, woof."

After the tour, I paused for a moment at the Whaley House. The garden was dark and the bushes were motionless. I squinted into the foliage, hoping to catch a glimpse of the spectral terrier. Suddenly, I envied the doubting Thomas, for despite my belief in ghosts, I'd never been fortunate enough to see Dolly. It was, I reflected, quite unfair.

In the end, I whispered, "Good dog," and resumed my journey homeward.

John J. Lamb *is a retired police sergeant who lives in Oceanside, California. He is the Southern California regional coordinator for the Ghost Research Society.*

❦ THE STRANGE CASE OF ELEONORE ZUGUN ❧
By Harry Price

Were poltergeists mysteriously able to obtain energy for their mischief from this young girl?

AFTER a lifetime spent in the investigation of four-dimensional mysteries, I have formed the opinion that poltergeists are invisible, intangible and malicious noisy entities. They are able, by laws as yet unknown to our physicists, to extract energy from living persons, often from the young, and usually from girl adolescents. By using these young people as a fulcrum, lever or support, they are able to increase and nourish this energy, and to direct intelligently this stolen power and use it telekinetically for the violent propulsion or displacement of objects, for purposes of destruction and especially for the production of every variety of noise – from the "swish" of a silk skirt to an "explosion" that makes windows rattle. And they can do many other strange things, as the reader will discover.

It is a maxim that in poltergeist cases the investigator practically never witnesses the displaced objects in flight or the beginning of telekinetic movements. A classic example to the above rule was Eleonore Zugun, a little Romanian girl whose psychic life-story is known almost from her cradle to the present day. She was born at Talpa, Romania, on May 24, 1913 and lived with her parents until she was 12 years old, at which time she went to live with her grandparents.

A few days after Eleonore's arrival at her new home, a shower of stones entered their cottage, smashing several windows. Then in full sunlight a big stone, a piece of porcelain and half a brick also entered the house, breaking more windows. No one was seen to throw the missiles which invariably fell at the child's feet. The simple peasants thought that the girl was possessed by the Devil and sent her back home.

Home once more, Eleonore and the Zugun family were having a meal in the kitchen when a stone from outside came crashing through the window pane. The stone was wet and round, similar to those found in the river Seret, a few yards from their cottage. A priest was called. He marked the stone with a cross, threw it back into the river, and then returned to the house. A little later the same stone, recognizable from by the priest's mark, was flung into the house again.

The villagers were more and more convinced that *Dracu*, the Devil, was the cause of all the trouble, especially as the manifestations followed the girl from place to place. They threatened to put her in an asylum. Her father then resolved to take the child to a priest, and next morning he, together with 14 other peasants, conducted Eleonore to the old Greek Orthodox priest of Zamostea, named Macarescu, a bedridden old man of about 80.

Soon after Eleonore entered his room an iron vessel suddenly burst into many pieces. Immediately afterwards an earthenware jar which had been on the hearth also burst and the pieces were thrown into the court. Scarcely had the witnesses recovered from this shock than both inner windows broke and one of the splinters fell into the room. The outside windows remained intact.

During these events the old priest, his son and a school teacher, Teolorescu, were all present. Startled, they ran out of the room. The teacher looking through the window saw a chest, which normally stood against the wall, move backward and forward and from side to side of its own volition. Only one young man, John Ostafe, had remained in the room. When he saw the chest moving about he stopped it, saying, "Wait, devil, I see you cannot do it alone; I will help you." At that instant a plank, hidden in a corner, sprang upon the young man and injured him.

Then all again entered the room and one of them proposed going on a pilgrimage to St Johannes at the Convent of Suczava. The name of the saint being pronounced, a stone was thrown against a picture of him which hung on the wall. Now only the teacher was sufficiently courageous to remain in the room. He sat opposite a bench on which was a can of water. Suddenly the can was levitated 18 inches, described a half circle, and came down on the other end of the bench without spilling a single drop. The peasants begged the priest to hold a mass in order to cast out the "devil" that possessed Eleonore.

The mass was not successful, and the girl was sent to the Convent of Gorgvei, near Talpa. The priests said masses for her, she was exorcised; and examined by psychiatrists, but the phenomena still continued. At this juncture the Countess Wassilko-Serecki, a Romanian living in Vienna, received permission to take the little girl into her home.

Eleonore arrived in Vienna in September, 1925, to puzzle the Austrian scientists, especially the physicists. Her phenomena grew stronger and more spectacular. My friend Prof. Hans Thirring, the distinguished physicist of Vienna University, was especially interested and wrote to me about the girl and invited me to investigate her phenomena.

I arrived in Vienna on April 30, 1926, and began my observational periods next day. I found Eleonore living in the Countess' charming flat, and I at once set about arranging a test. I decided to use the bedroom-study for my experiments. This room was divided by a matchboard partition about six feet high, with an opening at one end for communication between the two divisions. A pair of French windows leading to a balcony overlooking a quiet wooded garden provided ample illumination for both study and bedroom.

I examined the study and bedroom minutely after carefully fastening both doors and windows. A bed, table and chairs comprised the bedroom furniture; and a bookcase, filled with books, a couch, a writing table and chairs were placed in conventional positions in the study portion of the room.

Having completed my examination of the room, I turned my attention to Eleonore and the Countess who, with amusement, were watching my precautionary measures.

Eleonore was an intelligent, well-developed girl with a sunny disposition. She was then nearly 13 years old and physically strong and healthy. The Countess and I seated ourselves on the couch and watched her play with a toy gun that projected a celluloid ping-pong ball which was caught in a sort of conical wire basket. As we watched the ball came to pieces, its component halves falling at our feet. The girl ran to the Countess and asked her to mend it. As I watched our hostess examining the join, a steel stiletto used for opening letters shot across the room from behind me and fell against the closed door. I instantly turned around but a minute investigation revealed nothing.

Let me say that no one in that room, and certainly not Eleonore, could have thrown the paperknife. We were at least 10 feet from the table and I had both Eleonore and the Countess in full view. Eleonore had one half of the ball in her right hand and the toy gun in her left; the Countess had the other half of the ball in her hand. It was a brilliant introductory phenomenon.

I witnessed many other manifestations during the days I spent in Vienna, including the precipitation of a small mirror over the partition from the bedroom side while we three were in the study portion. Then a metal cap followed the mirror. A large black cloth dog shot from the study side of the room, over the partition, and fell onto the coal shuttle near the bed. No one was nearer to the dog (which was lying on a chair near the French windows) than 10 feet, and Eleonore at the moment of the flight was pushing a table against a wall, using both her hands. Then I saw a cushion on one of the chairs begin to move. As I watched it slid slowly off the seat and fell to the floor. No one was near it. After each of these phenomena I examined the room, the furniture, and the accessories, but everything was normal. I was so impressed with what I had seen that I extended an invitation to Eleonore and her benefactress to pay a visit to my London laboratory in order to witness again the wonders I had seen in Vienna.

The afternoon of October 5 I made my way to the laboratory suite and found that my secretary had not returned from lunch and Eleonora had not yet arrived. I unlocked the various rooms of the suite, opened the doors, and sat down to do some writing. At 2:15 Eleonore appeared and I rose to greet her. She took off her coat and hat and went into the passage to play with her toys. I unlocked the séance room in order to prepare it for the afternoon's observation period.

I had thirteen Danish and French coins and decided to mark and place them about the room. Four of the coins I placed on an ultraviolet ray cabinet spaced evenly, five inches apart. The one on the extreme right was a Danish copper. On the lintel of the door leading to the cloakroom I placed four more coins, about six inches apart. The third coin from the left was a brass 1 franc piece. I placed other coins in various positions and then returned to my writing. During this checking of the coins Eleonore was playing in the passage, the whole length of which I could see through the open office door. At exactly 2:30 I heard a coin drop in the séance room. I looked at Eleonore who also looked up at the same time. She said *"Dracu!"* I immediately entered the séance room followed by Eleonore.

I examined the coins which I had so recently arranged, and found that the Danish copper from the right of the row on the ultraviolet cabinet was missing. The others on the lintel of the door had not been touched. After about two minutes Eleonore found the coin in the far corner of the room. As a matter of fact, we saw the coin simultaneously.

While she was stooping to pick up the Danish copper, the French franc – which two minutes previously I had seen firmly in position on the wide lintel of the door – fell from its place. No other person was on the laboratory floor. No one was nearer than the ground floor, four storeys below.

The fall of the franc was a true poltergeist phenomenon. It would have remained on that lintel (six feet, ten and three quarters inches from the floor) for a thousand years without falling. Nothing but an earthquake would have shifted it unless it was removed paranormally. The diameter of the coin was 23 mm, the depth of lintel was 24 mm, and all coins were purposely placed hard against the wall so that if they did fall there would be no ambiguity about the matter. I am as convinced of the reality of this particular phenomenon as I am of the fact that I am breathing. At one moment the coin was securely resting on the lintel and two minutes later it was flicked a distance of five feet nine inches with no one nearer to it than 13 feet. Here we have a characteristic example of a so-called poltergeist displacement witnessed under ideal conditions.

I could fill many pages with accounts of the phenomena we witnessed, under scientific conditions, during Eleonore's stay in London. Her visit caused the greatest interest among scientists and others who attended many of the observational periods, and those whom I invited included Dr R.J. Tillyard, F.R.S., Prof. William McDougall, F.R.S., the Hon. Everard Fielding and Dr Theodore B. Hyslop.

As remarkable as this case is, it does not compare with that of a little Indian boy named Damodar Ketkar, whom I investigated, vicariously, in 1929. Here are a few of the strange things that happened: Food and drink disappeared and sometimes returned, dropping "from nowhere"; household goods were flung all over the place, more violently when the boy was asleep; furniture wandered from room to room; small coins, of unknown origin, were seen to materialize in the air and then fall to the floor; loud explosions were heard; a waste-paper basket "walked" across the room; food and toys were repeatedly snatched from the boy's hands; objects suddenly "appeared" in the boy's hands – "from nowhere"; fruit left in a room overnight was eaten and the skins flung back, with teethmarks clearly visible on them.

Damodar was not only levitated, but was "transported" on more than one occasion; articles missed would return, weeks later, "from nowhere"; eggs were seen by two witnesses to vanish, one by one, from the dish on which they had been placed; two pound packets of butter on a shelf were seen by two witnesses to change places twice in five minutes; mosquito curtains around the boy's bed had to be dispensed with as stones and toys would appear inside the net and jump about while he was sleeping.

Some people are lucky! What wouldn't I give to have a boy like Damodar in my house for a few months – or even days. I attempted to get the boy over from India but the difficulty of finding someone to accompany him was an insuperable one. The subsequent case history of this boy is the same as Eleonore Zugun's; the phenomena ceased when they reached maturity.

ENCOUNTER IN THE DESERT
by Margaret Rau

Actor Anthony Quinn recalls a powerful spiritual experience during the filming of Lawrence of Arabia

"I will tell you about some strange experiences that I've had all through life," said actor Anthony Quinn. "When I was a child about five years old, for some unknown reason, I suddenly became a very religious boy."

Quinn was born in 1915 of Irish-Mexican heritage in the town of Chihuahua, Mexico. As he grew, Quinn said, he searched for reality and truth. To that end he began to investigate many avenues.

"I studied theosophy. I studied Judaism. I studied Brahmanism. I studied Buddhism. I studied Yogi. I studied so many religions, until I realized that the summation of it all is that I have faith in all faiths."

His search for truth continued after he became a film actor in the mid-1930s. Influenced by Aldous Huxley, he tried LSD once under the supervision of a doctor. He said the experiment revealed much about himself.

"I found out that we are the prisoners of our own cultural background and our own prejudices," he said. "LSD showed me I still had some [prejudices] left. The problem with LSD, as with hard drugs, is that under its influence you begin questioning all the morality and the institutions set up to enforce it. That's a rather dangerous moment because unless you have tremendous moral strength, you could become an anarchist wanting to destroy all institutions, all morality."

Quinn said the dangers of LSD caused him to drop his brief experimentation with it. But his search for truth continued. He explained that much of this search was in the interests of his acting – to make it as true as possible.

"One of the great problems of the artist," he pointed out, "whether he or she is an actor, a painter or a writer, is that the byways and the strange routes one has to travel in the quest for truth can be very dangerous."

Quinn described how one strange byway led him to an overpowering mystical experience. It happened during the filming of the 1962 film *Lawrence of Arabia*, in which Quinn had one of the leading roles. Director David Lean shot much of the film in the Sinai Desert, through which Moses had led the children of Israel long ago.

The shooting location was about five miles from the road where the company's cars were parked. After each day's shooting, crew and actors would travel by horse, camel or Jeep to the cars that were waiting to take them back to their headquarters in town.

One day Quinn finished shooting early. He loved to hike and he loved the desert so he decided to walk alone back to the road and the cars.

He had covered two or three miles when suddenly he stopped and looked around in shock. For the first time in his life he felt a terror of open spaces. There he stood, in the midst of miles of empty sand and sky. In that moment he experienced time – not time as measured by clocks or the Earth's revolutions, but time as time itself.

"I had never been so aware of time in all my life as then," Quinn said. "I felt not just the present, but all of time. I was back two thousand years. I was also in the year AD 5000. I was beyond infinity, because all of time had become one for me – past, present, future – indivisible."

Quinn stood motionless. He felt the desert come alive with prophets, those ancient men who had once travelled through the desert, where Christ himself had walked.

"I couldn't see them but I felt them all around me," Quinn explained. "And I was overcome with one of the most fantastic fears of my life. I suddenly felt that I was going to hear a Voice."

Quinn trembled with terror at the feeling that at any minute the silence of the desert could be broken by an awful Voice. He fell to his knees, shut his eyes and put his hands over his ears, covering his head.

"I said, 'No! Please! Don't talk to me! Don't talk to me!'" He cried aloud. "I couldn't bear it."

Still the prophets clustered around him. He knew they had prophecies to tell, secrets to divulge. They were almost insistent that he listen. But he felt he could not bear the weight of the wisdom they wanted to impart. For ten minutes he stayed on his knees with his ears covered and eyes closed, pleading, "No, please don't talk. Please, please don't."

Suddenly it was as though the prophets had given up. There

was a strange sound of exploding air, a *whoosh* that shook the day.

"In that moment I felt the congregation of prophets pass over me. It was only after they were gone that I realized I had been travelling through a deep tunnel and had just now come out safe at the far end. I stood up and there was nothing but the familiar stretches of sand below, sky above. Still, I felt that I really had experienced Space, Time, God – whatever you want to call it. And it left me with such fear.

I don't think it was the fear of God, because I truly believe our hope and mankind's hope is the verification that this great deity does exist and that we will truly come face to face with it. And I believe that the truest emotion God arouses is the emotion of love. Outside all this talk about visions that some people set so much store by, the one truth underlying everything else is that feeling of universal love enfolding us."

Then how to explain the fear that invaded Quinn as he knelt alone in the desert? "I think what I was truly afraid of was coming face to face with my deep inner self," Quinn said thoughtfully. He went on to explain that there are truths buried deep inside all of us that we're too terrified to explore. Those truths concern the brutal animal drives of our primordial heritage, drives that it takes a great deal of courage to admit and explore in order to know the whole truth about ourselves.

"Fear is the signal that we are approaching the truths we are seeking," Quinn explained. "That's why I have always found fear to be a very dear friend.

If we treat fear like an enemy, we shy away from the signals it sends us. These signals tell us we're on the path to some new truth. If only we can outride our initial storm of fear, we'll come into possession of it and be enriched."

Margaret Rau *is a writer who lives in California. She has published many books for juvenile audiences, and collaborated with her late husband, Neil Rau, on three adult books. She has lectured at schools in China, Australia and the United States.*

Some people don't believe in ghosts. I have never seen one myself. But I know they exist, because my grandmother's spirit has appeared to different family members over the years.

The first time my grandmother appeared was at her funeral in April 1969. My mother was sitting in one of the front pews in the deserted church after the funeral. As she sat, she remembers feeling something brush up against her. She believes it was her mother comforting her. My grandmother was only 45, my mother just 23. My mother took on more responsibility in caring for my grandfather and paying household expenses.

The second time was in late autumn of 1975. We were in Norwich at the time. I was three years old, and my mother had not yet discovered she was pregnant with my sister.

It was in the dead of night. Mum doesn't remember if there was a clock in the room or not. She sat bolt upright in bed straight out of a deep sleep, terrified, knowing something wasn't right. There was a factory across the street from our house. The lights were glaring through my parents' bedroom window, painting the closet door a solid white. She heard workers talking as they left the night shift, getting into their cars and driving off.

The room was ice cold. Mum was rigid with fear. She looked instinctively toward the closet door. There was a dark outline in the light shining on it. From the style of her hair, Mum knew it was my grandmother. Looking back on it, my mother feels it was Grandma reassuring her that everything would be all right.

One of my cousins related the following story to my mother. Years ago, my cousin and her brother spent the night at our house, in my parents' bed. My parents slept downstairs. She woke up in the middle of the night to find my grandmother sitting on the bed. She was looking straight at her, smiling.

I believe I know why my grandmother keeps coming back. She died extremely young, never getting to know her future grandchildren. She has appeared to my mother in trying times to reassure and comfort her. Grandma obviously feels she didn't accomplish enough while alive. She continues to protect and guide her family.

– *Kristen Voegeli, Georgetown, Ont.*

The Haunted House

Nestled in the wooded hills just south of Mishawaka, Indiana, stands a beautiful two-storey home. It was once owned by the parents of my best friend, Pam Krizman. Pam had one of the two bedrooms upstairs and her cousin Robbie (Roberta Banach) had the other.

One night while Pam was sleeping she thought she heard a rustling sound coming from her closet. Moonlight was shining through the window so she was able to see fairly well in the dark. She looked over to where she heard the noise and as her eyes adjusted to the light she saw what looked like a tall, dark shadow moving across her room. It made a rasping sound as if it were someone having trouble breathing. As she watched it floated through her closed door. She was terrified and like most kids who get scared she pulled the covers up over her head. After a while she fell asleep.

The next morning when she awoke she decided not to say anything to the rest of the family because she thought no one would believe her. She went downstairs to breakfast. A few minutes later, Robbie came and sat at the table. Pam could hardly believe it when Robbie started talking about seeing a black figure floating through her room, making a sound like someone having trouble breathing. When Pam told her the same thing had happened in her room, they knew they had both seen the same ghost.

Pam's mum told her the previous owner of the house was an elderly woman who had passed away in the bedroom that was now Pam's. The woman had severe asthma and had a hard time breathing. So now they knew who their ghostly visitor was.

This was not the only time the ghost made its presence known. One night, Pam's brother Art and some of his football friends came to the house after a game. The rest of the family was out for the evening, so the house was empty. As Art walked upstairs and into the hall, there was a mist-like fog in the middle of the hall right next to Pam's bedroom door. When Art and his friends saw it, they ran down the stairs and left a note for his mum and dad that said, "I'm staying over at my friend's for the night – the house is acting up again!"

This all happened back in the 1960s. Many times I have driven past the house and wondered if the new owners ever had any ghostly happenings. I've been tempted to knock on their door and tell them they live in a haunted house. But, then again, maybe it's just as well I don't. Some things are best left alone.

– *Mishawaka, Ind.*

Since 1989, FATE magazine has been published in St Paul, Minnesota, from a converted Coca-Cola bottling plant on the banks of the Mississippi. At FATE's headquarters, editors and writers have a panoramic view of the downtown city skyline, as well as the grain-laden barges and tourist paddleboats that ply the river. A sense of history is almost palpable in St Paul – and, in fact, many of those who made their homes here in life seem to linger long after their deaths.

Family Ties

Peter says his sister Pamela has a special sense for the spiritual realm and Pamela says the same about Peter. Maybe it runs in the family, but these siblings weren't the only people who experienced old-man Mausburger's presence in their old house on Congress Street in Saint Paul. Peter enthusiastically recalls his experiences:

"We had all kinds of weird stuff take place when we lived there – like the cherry pipe tobacco smoke hanging in the air in the attic. And, as it turns out, we weren't the only ones who attracted ghostly friends.

"When my sister Pamela first toured the house with the estate agent, she saw a distinguished-looking old man dressed in a tuxedo standing at the end of the first floor landing. Just as plain as day. No see-through stuff. Pamela didn't mention it to the agent at the time, but it turned out the agent also had seen the man!"

When the former owners of the house dropped off the keys, they asked if Peter had met the "old man" in the attic who paced back and forth at night. They told Peter their toddler daughter kept pointing to the attic door saying, "Grandpa! There grandpa!"

During their stay in the house on Saint Paul's West Side, Peter says they experienced a lot of peculiar things – like objects being rearranged in the house. Yule logs were apparently disturbing to Mr Mausburger, the turn-of-the-century socialite who built the house.

"Once, the (the ghost) removed all the logs and placed them neatly on the floor about four feet away from the hearth," says Peter. Another time a log rose up in mid-air and hit Pamela on the back of the head – sort of whacked her with a fair amount of force – and then dropped to the floor."

Peter moved out when his sister got married, and according to

Pamela there hasn't been much ghostly activity since.
    – *Susan Omoto*

A Real Hamm

Karin and Rich DuPaul have had a 20-year love affair with their historic house, a mansion built in 1892 on North Greenbrier Street by William Hamm of Hamm Brewery fame. They are convinced that their home, the very bricks and mortar, is possessed with a spirit of its own. The way they explain it, there are no ghosts *per se*. Instead, they feel the structure somehow influences what happens.

"Even before we moved into the house we were called to it. We were sitting around in our former home and felt this incredible urge to go see the house. We both got the urge at the same time. After we arrived we found that the water pipes had burst and water was dripping all over. Our arrival helped avert a very expensive disaster."

Still, Karin didn't fall in love with the house at first sight. "When I first saw the house I thought, 'You've got to be kidding:'" Karin recalls. The old mansion was a wreck.

"It was a monumental home that would require a monumental effort to restore. I said 'no' at first, but pretty soon it was like the house wouldn't let me go. Even after we bought it I wouldn't stay overnight in the house for a long time," Karin said.

"Funny things happen here. Like when our furnace broke down and we had to use the fireplace. For some strange reason Rich got up suddenly and said he felt he had to go down to the basement It was like something was pulling him down there. Sure enough, when he got down there several boxes that were stacked next to the chimney were smouldering."

Like many other haunted house stories, most of the activity at the house has tapered off over time. It could be a case of the ghosts and the people getting comfortable with each other and learning to co-exist. As Karin says, "After a while, you just get used to each other."
    – *Susan Omoto*

The Haunted Halls of Justice

The Ramsey County Courthouse, which sits almost directly across the Mississippi River from FATE's St Paul office, has been a centre of community activity for 65 years. For many of those years it has also been the centre of poltergeist activity.

Late-night cleaners and security guards alike report frequent encounters with spirits: They see and hear laughing, playful ghosts who cavort throughout the building in suits from the '30s and '40s. A phantom shoe repairman reportedly still works in the courthouse lobby. Doors open and close when no-one is around. The quiet tapping of women's high-heeled shoes echoes through empty hallways. And metal coat hangers jingle in the still night air.

Psychic Samantha Hernandez conducted a late-night séance at the courthouse in 1995. "There's a lot of history there," she said of the 18-story Art Deco building. "There have been a lot of famous and wonderful people going through there. When I was there, I felt like I was going to a spirit party. They [the spirits] love coming to visit there. We should be grateful there aren't demonic spirits in the courthouse. And there aren't."

The only frightening sight she noted was that of a hanged man swinging from a noose – apparently one of the convicts who was executed at the site.

"I definitely know the courthouse is haunted," Tim Mahanna told the St. Paul *Pioneer Press*. He was one of the workers who helped renovate the building five years ago. Tools and panelling moved, pipes sat disconnected and dry for weeks – and then water poured from them. "Strange things happened there that never happened at another job site," he said. "I think there are people there who died and never left."

– *Corrine Kenner*

Behind the Scenes
In the theatre world, drama is supposed to occur on stage. However, the antics of a ghost named Ben have brought spooky drama behind the scenes at the Fitzgerald Theatre in downtown St. Paul.

The history of this spectre is relatively unknown. The Fitzgerald underwent renovations in 1985, and the removal of a false ceiling revealed an additional balcony and an old note to a stagehand named Ben.

Around this time, unusual and inexplicable things began to happen to people working in the theatre. Members of staff began to experience cool drafts and often witnessed a dark, shadowy figure. Puzzled crew members discovered their tools had moved or disappeared. And bottles of muscatel, always empty, appeared mysteriously.

Apparently, the construction within the building aroused the dormant spirit of the old stagehand.

While Ben is not considered malicious or harmful, there was one experience that made two people rather leery of his presence. A collaborator on one of the theater's productions and his friend were walking backstage, guided by torchlight. Suddenly, a large chunk of ceiling plaster came crashing down between them. They quickly directed their beams above and viewed a hazy figure moving around, nearly 60 feet off the ground. What makes this experience all the more bizarre is that there is no plaster on the ceiling.

Theatre workers say that Ben occupies most of his time with his treasured muscatel and another ghost, his girlfriend, Veronica, an over-the-hill actress doomed to bit parts. While she has not been spotted, she has made her presence known through her singing, which can drown out a playing radio.

Recently, Ben and Veronica seem to be keeping quiet. Almost everyone at the Fitzgerald hopes they won't be attempting to make a comeback any time soon.

– *Lauren Skubick*

Shadow Boxer

In April, 1983, a young man named Clyde Mudgett decided to burgle a two-story meat plant on the East Side of St Paul. The 30-year-old had just served 18 months in the Indiana State Reformatory on a burglary conviction, which apparently had given him time to come up with a foolproof plan. On a quiet Sunday, he tied a rope to the chimney and climbed in, planning to scale his way down the stack and climb out through a waste door inside the building.

Unfortunately, the short-sighted Mudgett used a 40-foot rope – in a chimney that was 60 feet long. Because the stack was attached to the building's furnace and water heater, Mudgett was quickly asphyxiated. His body dangled for three days before an anonymous caller advised the building's owner to look in his chimney. By the time firefighters recovered the young man's body, Mudgett was already partially smoked.

The meat plant was converted into a boxing gym in 1991 – setting the stage for Mudgett's comeback. For in addition to his short-lived career as a burglar, Mudgett had been a two-time Indiana Golden

Gloves champion in the mid-1970s. After he turned pro in Texas, he boasted a 30–22 record, and he once even fought a televised match in Madison Square Garden.

Soon after he opened the gym, owner Jim Glancey began hearing noises late at night – the quick-hitting, hard-pounding jabs of an experienced boxer working the punching bags on the first floor. He would investigate, only to find the gym dark and empty.

When journalist Bill Alkofer decided to investigate last year, he, too, noticed the punching bags moving on their own. He helped write a tongue-in-cheek newspaper account of his night in the haunted gym. "It was really spooky," he said. "The bag was just swinging on its own. We looked for drafts, or vibrations, or anything that could explain it, but there was nothing."

Months later, he went back for an unrelated story, about father-and-son boxing referees. And then, he said, Mudgett got his revenge.

"I wanted to take a picture of them in the ring," he said, "but I needed to get up high for the shot. So I stood on a solid-looking little table. I took a few photos, but then suddenly, three of the legs just collapsed, and I went head over heels. I got a huge gash in my shin, which left a scar … and when we looked at the table, we noticed that all three screws had been completely removed. They were just nowhere to be found. There's no way that table should even have stood on its own.

"Its my feeling that Mudgett decided to get back at me for making fun of him. He just knocked me down a peg."
– *Corrine Kenner*

Phantom of the Fairgrounds
Chris Tahti isn't the kind of man you'd expect to discuss seeing ghosts. The easy-going entertainment superviser at the Minnesota State Fairgrounds worked his twentieth fair this summer. Throughout the last two decades he has heard many strange tales, from police searching for invisible cows to a rare bird that makes annual visits to the historic Ye Olde Mill ride, where an employee – who was also a bird fancier – died long ago.

Tahti used to lend a sceptical ear to such tales – until he saw a ghost. Twice.

"Every night, the local fire department crew comes in for the fireworks," Tahti said. "During one grandstand show, I was standing backstage with a police officer when five or six guys in the crew told us there was a man on the roof of the grandstand. They had all seen him. We sent security up to get the guy, but no one was up there. And there's only one set of stairs to the roof.

"Then another police officer said 'there's someone up there.' We checked again and couldn't find the man. We would have known if someone jumped off. It's a long way down?"

Tahti saw the ghost again three years ago. "There's a bunker on the infield of the race track," he said. "I was standing in the doorway to get out of the rain, watching the preparations for that evening's grandstand show. I know everyone who works back there – it's very secure – so I was surprised when I saw a stranger standing there. The guy was about five-foot-ten with sandy hair and a moustache.

"I did a double-take and he was gone. The door is in the middle of a hallway that runs 30 feet without a turn. I stuck my head in the door and looked up and down the hall, but no one was there. To leave, he would have had to go through me."

When Tahti discussed his sightings with other fairground staff, they decided the ghost might have been a driver who died on the track years ago.

Tahti said, "There was one who had a heart attack on the front straight and did a lap of the track, dead. The car came to rest in front of the grandstand."

Tahti said a chill went through him when he saw the man at the bunker disappear. "Suddenly I realized what had happened and my hair stood up. It's definitely changed my views. I was a sceptic on the subject of ghosts. Now I'm a believer. I know what I saw."
– *Craig Miller*

The Maid Who Stayed

"A sceptic visited the restaurant a couple of years ago and demanded, 'If there are any ghosts around here, give me a sign.' At that moment a candle exploded, showering him and a woman next to him with hot wax."

So goes one of the many accounts collected by James Crnkovich, a waiter at Forepaugh's restaurant, a converted Victorian mansion in an old neighbourhood. Crnkovich rattled off several more incidents as quickly as possible – hungry customers were waiting.

"For one special event," he said, "one of our waitresses was wearing a nineteenth-century period dress as a costume. As she was setting up, she saw a woman in a similar dress – but not one supplied for the event – move down the hall and disappear."

The building wasn't always a restaurant. In 1870, Joseph Forepaugh built the elegant home for his wife and two daughters. His life wasn't happy there, however. Even though he was the senior partner in the largest wholesale dry goods firm in the midwest, Forepaugh killed himself at age 58. He was found in a nearby park with a bullet wound in his head and a gun still clasped in his hand. The St Paul *Pioneer Press* ran an article on July 10, 1892, that said Forepaugh had despaired needlessly over his financial affairs. Others have speculated, however, that it was an affair of the heart that depressed him.

A maid named Molly committed suicide when she learned of Forepaugh's death. It was rumoured that the two had had an affair. She hung herself from a chandelier in an upstairs room.

"When our staff closes up at the end of the night," Crnkovich said, "it's understood that whoever turns off the lights upstairs should just walk away if that light turns back on by itself."

"I think there has to be something to the stories," he added. "There have been too many reported instances of people having an unusual experience."

Crnkovich said that earlier this year a woman telephoned to make dinner reservations. During her conversation with the maitre d', he had to excuse himself. When he returned, he apologized for making her wait. "Oh that's all right," she said. "I was having a wonderful conversation with the woman who is working there." The maitre d' said, "I'm sorry, that's impossible. I'm working alone this morning."

– *Craig Miller*

Ghost Summit

When Melissa Stevens moved to Minnesota from Michigan for an advertising job in the fashion industry, she needed a high-profile address to match her high-profile job. She found the ideal home on Saint Paul's historic Summit Avenue; a mansion with apartments on the second floor.

Melissa hosted soirées for the advertising and marketing world. To this day, people talk about the house, both for its beauty and for the incredibly "outspoken" ghosts who lived there.

Jennifer was one of Melissa's guests. She says that she thought the haunting was all just a story to get attention – until she witnessed it herself.

"I went up to Melissa's apartment to use her bathroom and it was hot as anything. I thought 'Oh, my God, I'm so hot.' I went into the bathroom and, when I came out, all her windows were open half a foot. Exactly. And I know that no one came in there since I had locked the outer door and left the bathroom door ajar.

"Sometimes the baby grand piano would start playing out of the blue. A bunch of us stayed up all night to watch the thing. Sure enough, in the small hours, the piano began to play – all by itself. I don't remember the song, but I always tell people it had spirit!"

A local news station took an interest in the house when one of its reporters, who had attended a party there, came back to the newsroom with stories from the mansion. They sent a team to see if they could capture the ghostly goings-on.

"It was Halloween night and they [the news crew] spent the whole night with us. They also brought along Echo Bodine, a well-known psychic from the area. They found spirits of people who had lived there in the past. Echo exorcised all but two: the maid who had killed herself and one of the former owners, a man with red hair and long sideburns. He said it was his duty to stay and protect us."

But things didn't calm down after the exorcism. In fact, Melissa felt that things got all stirred up.

"I never felt afraid in the house, although the library was a difficult room to be in. Most of the activity was mischievous rather than harmful."

All three apartments in the house were located on the second floor. Each had its own "special" tenant. The back apartment, occupied by a lady named Donna, had been the red-haired owner's bedroom. It was there that the china would fly off the shelves and tea cups would be moved around during the night. Donna's bathtub would frequently be filled with water when she got home from work. She began hiding the drain plug, but it would always mysteriously find its way back into the tub.

Melissa's apartment is where the children's rooms were originally located. Melissa remembers talking on the phone and looking up to see her wrought iron coffee table begin to levitate. "I remember that heavy iron table coming up off the floor and the silver candle holder sliding off the edge. At first, I thought we were having an earthquake."

Melissa says she and another friend watched as a 3x5-foot painting flew out from the wall. "The painting didn't just drop, it flew out with force."

Guests at dinner would be treated to silverware sliding across the table, plates shattering as they sat still on the table, food disappearing and freezing breezes. Once one of the tenants heard the front door open and slam shut. When he went to investigate he found no footsteps on the freshly fallen snow.

As for the television reporters, when the crew returned to the studio to edit the tapes, they had no audio, even though they had checked the sound before leaving the house that morning.

– *Susan Omoto*

Ghost U

I attended Concordia University, at that time Concordia College, from 1988–1992. While I was there I took a job with campus security on one of the graveyard shifts. We worked between midnight and 600 a.m.

I had heard stories about ghosts on campus, but I didn't believe them. Most dealt with one particular section of campus: the two-storey classroom building and an annexe above the dining hall.

Routinely I worked my night shifts with the same partner, Tim Dahle. We had to lock and unlock plenty of doors in every building we patrolled, and the classroom building was no exception. One night at around 2.00 a.m. we were heading into the building through an upstairs entrance. Every time we opened a door and went through, we immediately locked it behind us. A routine search of the upper classrooms told us all was fine, so we made our way back – and discovered that two of the doors we had been through only five minutes earlier were unlocked!

The doors were near the faculty offices, so we locked them again, double-checked them and searched the offices. We found no one and heard no noises – but when we returned to these two doors, they were unlocked again.

Feeling we were being watched, we locked the doors once again. This time Tim went downstairs to check for anyone below, and I made another search of the office area. We communicated via our two-way radios the entire time. When we returned to the doors we found them unlocked. We immediately left the area and checked all the other departments that might have had night workers on duty. None did.

While other unexplained things occasionally happened during my shift, it was another experience in the classroom building that finally convinced me the place was haunted.

Tim was sick, so I was working alone. By 3.00 a.m. I had made my way through the offices and checked the entire second floor. Suddenly I felt I was being watched and the hairs on my arms stood upright. As I neared the last doorway with only my torchlight in hand, I saw something out of the corner of my eye. When I turned to look, I thought my legs were going to give out on me. In the door stood a woman who appeared to be floating just inches off the ground. She was dressed in turn-of-the-century clothing and she was staring at me. I ran as fast as I could to our office where I spent the rest of my shift. I never worked alone again.

– *Troy Cohrs*

SPECTRAL VIOLINISTS AND PHANTOM FIDDLERS
by Lee Holloway

The eerie sounds of pipes and drums reverberate through ancient castles, and the midnight silence of old English churches is often disturbed by booming organ music played by unseen hands. The U.S. also has its share of phantom organists, along with a smattering of ghostly harpists, pianists and buglers, but it is the violin (or fiddle) that seems to spawn the most supernatural activity in America, primarily, but not exclusively, in the foothills of Appalachia and the rural South.

As for the difference between a violin and a fiddle, someone once said, "It's a fiddle when you want to buy it and a violin when you want to sell it!" Violins are associated with orchestras and classical music; fiddles conjure images of hillbilly clog dancers. But regardless of the purpose for which it is used, many violinists and fiddlers refuse to part with their instruments – even in death.

Library Serenader
The Julia Ideson Building at 500 McKinney Street in Houston, Texas, houses the Texas Room and archives of the Houston Public Library. The Spanish Renaissance Revival-style building looks haunted, so the fact that there is a resident ghost comes as no surprise.

Mr Cramer, an elderly caretaker, was already working for the library when the new building was dedicated in 1926 and took up residence in a tiny basement room. Although considered somewhat slow, Cramer played the violin flawlessly. He could not read music, but if he heard a tune, the old gentleman could play it note-for-note as though he had practised for weeks. Once he finished his daily duties, Cramer walked the halls serenading library patrons with the most difficult pieces from Chopin, Mozart, Beethoven and other notable composers. There were some who claimed Cramer could play Tchaikovsky's Violin Concerto better than any Julliard-trained musician.

Cramer was a dedicated and reliable employee, and during his many years of service he had always been standing ready to open the staff entrance as other library employees arrived. So, one morning in 1936, when the assistant librarian found the door locked, she knew something was wrong. The lady hurried downstairs and after knocking, entered the sparsely furnished but neat little room and discovered the body of the elderly janitor. He had died peacefully in his sleep. Everyone was saddened; the old man had been a favourite with library staff and patrons alike, and they would all miss his concerts.

A few weeks after Cramer's death, a patron approached the librarian on duty and commented, "The piped in music was a good idea. It's almost as if Mr Cramer was still walking the halls playing his violin."

The lady was too shocked to respond. A few nights later, while shelving books in an area near the basement stairs, she, too, distinctly heard what could only be a violin. At first she surmised some teenagers were hiding in the basement trying to frighten her, but immediately dismissed the thought, asking herself, "What kid could play like that?"

For almost 70 years, employees and patrons of the Houston Public Library have reported hearing the spectral violinist. But no one is frightened. They are just happy that in death, Cramer is doing what he most enjoyed in life – playing the violin.

The Haunted Bridge

Fiddles were the instruments of farmers and mountain people. Because they were often played at dances, barbecues and other social events that involved frolicking and the consumption of alcohol, some fundamentalist religious sects condemned them as instruments of the devil. Appalachian folklore is full of ghostly tales in which fiddles play a major role. Usually, a parent forbids a child to bring the "devil's instrument" into the house or learn to play it. Invariably, the youngster disobeys and his actions result in disaster or death. Years later, on cool, clear nights, when the moon is full, music is still heard emanating from some old house or hollow where a child defied his parents by taking up Satan's fiddle.

But not all phantom fiddlers are the result of parental defiance or devilish intervention. For example, the phantom fiddler of Scott Run Bridge (also known as Fiddler's Bridge) south of St Georges, Delware, met his death at the hands of a group of young ruffians.

Ebenezer was the only child of a poor family who lived in a small house near the river. An elderly neighbour who had no children of his own was very fond of Ebenezer and taught the boy to fiddle.

When he was 14, his parents managed to buy a used instrument which they presented to their son as a Christmas gift.

Ebenezer's father and mother died of influenza the following year and the boy was left alone with no other relatives in the area. Kindly members of the little farming community helped the young man until he could find work and support himself. He kept a few chickens, grew his own vegetables and hired himself out as a farm hand. But no matter how hard he worked during the day, when nightfall came, Ebenezer took down his fiddle from the top of the old clothespress and played for hours.

As he aged, Ebenezer became more withdrawn, and by the time he reached his 70s, many people considered him downright strange. On warm evenings, the now stooped old man would walk down to Scott Run River and sit on the railings of the bridge fiddling the night away.

Elderly eccentrics are often victims of teenage taunting, and Ebenezer was no exception. Early one evening, several boys were tormenting the old fiddler. During the horseplay, one of the youths gave the curmudgeon a slight shove and Ebenezer toppled over the railing. The river, swollen from spring rains, was deep and swift, and the boys watched helplessly as the frail old man was pulled under, still clutching his beloved fiddle.

A few weeks after the incident, a child crossing the bridge with a group of friends stopped, tossed a penny into the river, and made a wish. When the penny hit the water, they heard a few notes of what sounded like fiddle music. Other children threw pennies into the river with the same result.

Word of the haunted bridge spread, and people travelled many miles, hoping to hear the phantom fiddler. One October night in the early 1900s, a lady who lived nearby gave a party and, after dinner, led her guests outside. Under a full, low-hanging moon, they made their way to the bridge. One threw a coin into the river, and sure enough, they were rewarded with the distinct music of a fiddle. Another followed suit and, before long, a veritable concert arose from the dark, eerie waters of Scott Run River.

By the time they returned to the house, the lady's conscience had gotten the better of her and she timidly confessed that her nephew had been situated in a boat beneath the bridge playing his violin. As her guests laughed at how they had been fooled by their hostess, the nephew came into the room with a sheepish look on his face. "It's all right, I admitted our trick," his aunt announced.

Looking relieved, the young man replied, "Oh, good. I thought you'd be disappointed. I dropped my bow in the river as I was getting in the boat. I hope I didn't ruin your party."

To this day, people claim to hear the merry strains of old-fashioned fiddle tunes drifting from beneath Fiddler's Bridge.

Playing for Snakes

Another location named for a phantom fiddler is Fiddler's Rock near the top of Stone Mountain in Johnson County, Tennessee. It seems a fiddler by the name of Martin Stone heard about Indian snake charmers and wondered if he could charm rattlesnakes in the same manner. One day, he climbed the mountain where he knew there was a proliferation of rattlesnakes, sat down on a rock, and began fiddling. Sure enough, the snakes began slithering from between the crevices in the stones, charmed by the music.

After that, every few days, Stone hiked up the mountain trail with his fiddle in one hand and his shotgun in the other. He would play for the snakes and shoot a few once the concert was over. There were always several rattlesnake skins drying on the side of his barn. Tourists paid high prices for belts and other items made from snake-skin, and many fiddlers purchased snake rattles to place inside their instruments, believing – as did Stone himself – that it improved the tone. Fiddling for the snakes was proving profitable and Stone couldn't resist bragging about his success.

Growing evermore cocky, Stone decided he would try charming the snakes at night. His buddies warned him not to climb the mountain after dark, arguing that if the snakes came out, he wouldn't be able to see them. Stone just laughed. "I'm wearing knee-high boots. There's not a snake alive that can bite through this leather!" he declared, slapping his bow against the side of his right boot for emphasis.

So one warm Indian summer afternoon, as a blood-red sun slowly disappeared behind the distant western peaks, Stone hiked up the narrow path. As the sky darkened, people in the valley heard him playing a lively tune. Apparently the snakes came out, because the following day a group of men found Martin Stone lying dead on Fiddler's Rock. His back, arms, chest and even his face were covered by ugly purple bruises and streaks of congealed blood, the results of numerous snake bites. Stone was right about the boots though; they had protected his legs. He just hadn't counted on the wily reptiles silently slithering up from behind as he perched on his favourite rock.

Getting Stone off the mountain presented a problem for his friends. He had been dead several hours, rigor mortis was setting in, and his left fist was clenched tightly around the fingerboard of his fiddle. The right was just as tightly clutching the bow. Unable to pry loose his fingers, the men placed their coats over Stone's face and grotesquely positioned arms and transported the corpse – still gripping the bow and fiddle – down the mountain. To circumvent the curious, the men discreetly entered the undertaker's shop through the back door.

It has been more than a hundred years since Stone charmed the snakes on Fiddler's Rock, but on clear autumn nights, close to the end of camping season when the campsites are almost empty, tourists sometimes hear fiddle music wafting down from the top of the mountain. One family holidaying in the Cherokee National Forest mentioned the phenomenon to a park ranger. Before the ranger could answer, a local man of advanced years, standing nearby, shrugged and said, "Ah, that's just Ol' Martin up there, charmin' the snakes."

The Dancing Ghost
One of the most intriguing tales of phantom fiddlers comes from southern Alabama, where the dancing ghost of Grancer Harrison still parties near his tomb in the old Harrison Cemetery just west of Kinston.

William L. Harrison was born around 1789 in South Carolina. He relocated to Alabama in the 1820s with his father and other family members. The Harrisons arrived in what is now Coffee County with purebred horses, a champion herd of cattle and wagonloads of fine furniture. William immediately married a lovely girl named Nancy and began construction of an impressive house on an elevation where Cripple Creek enters the Pea River. William and Nancy produced 12 children, 10 of whom lived to adulthood.

Harrison truly possessed the golden touch. He was successful at everything he did. His plantation produced superior cotton, people paid high prices for his livestock and his children were robust and high-spirited. But even though Harrison had it all, so to speak, it was not his success as a farmer, stock breeder and father that set him apart from his neighbours – it was his love of dancing.

Almost every Saturday, weather permitting, Harrison sponsored a horse race or held a fish-fry or barbecue, and people from three counties travelled great distances to partake of his hospitality. For Harrison, daylight was a time to mix and mingle with family and friends and enjoy the best food and drink in southeastern Alabama – but the night was made for dancing. As the day dropped slowly into night, Harrison guided his guests to a specially constructed pavilion where skilled musicians played sprightly tunes, and the dancing began.

As Harrison's sons reached manhood and built nearby homes of their own, they acquired the privilege of being addressed as "Sir." This was confusing to the servants, so they began calling the Harrison sons "Sir" and William L. became "Grand Sir". As the years passed, "Gran' Sir", as it was pronounced in the lazy Alabama drawl, slowly evolved into "Grancer" and for about the last 25 years of his life William L. Harrison was known as Grancer Harrison.

As his 70th year approached, Grancer began to contemplate the hereafter and, one might say, prepare for his last dance. He picked a spot for his grave just a few yards from the dance pavilion and decreed that a special tomb was to be constructed (one large enough to accommodate his feather bed) and that he should be buried in his dancing suit with his dancing shoes on his feet. To shade his final resting place from the hot Alabama sun, he also ordered the construction of a large pavilion – a smaller version of the dance hall – to shelter his grave, and gave instructions that the hatchet used to notch the timber be placed above the entrance. (No one has ever been able to explain Harrison's request regarding the hatchet.)

Death claimed Grancer Harrison one warm spring night in May 1860. Some family members were less than enthusiastic about carrying out the wishes of the dead patriarch, but the servants insisted, fearing their master would "walk" if they failed to do so. Thus Grancer Harrison was laid to rest on his feather bed, attired in his dancing clothes and shoes. Another of Harrison's instructions was that the dances were to continue. He had declared he would never rest in peace unless he could hear the sounds of feet tapping the hardwood floors of the dance pavilion in time to his favourite fiddle tunes.

For a while, the Harrisons continued the barbecues and dances, but things just weren't the same without Grancer calling the sets and teaching everyone new steps. Attendance was sporadic at best. Finally, the events were suspended altogether and the once grand affairs faded into memory, as did Grancer himself.

Shortly after the cessation of the dances, the servants began mumbling among themselves that Ol' Grancer was restless. After two young boys insisted they heard the sounds of unseen feet tapping in time to the music of a fiddler, no servant on the place would go near their dead master's tomb – or the dance pavilion – after dark. Initially, family members dismissed the servant's tales as superstitious fantasies. Then, a neighbouring farmer, passing the cemetery one Saturday night, declared that he, too, heard what sounded like a party. At first, he thought the Harrisons were entertaining – but the dance hall was dark.

The reports became so numerous that Harrison's family ultimately accepted the fact that Grancer, displeased by the discontinuation of the parties, had found a way to continue his love of dancing from beyond the grave.

The Harrison Cemetery very quickly became a favourite spot for young thrill seekers, but for the most part they were respectful. That is until one night in 1964 when someone, having heard rumours of buried treasure, dynamited the tomb. The following morning, feathers – and Grancer's bones – were scattered all over the little graveyard. Although the bones were replaced and the tomb repaired, the disturbance caused a flurry of supernatural activity, with some of the most sobre and serious members of the community claiming to have heard the phantom fiddler.

The pavilion covering the grave, slightly damaged in the explosion, finally rotted away. However, for several years after that, Grancer seemed to be at peace as he lay undisturbed in his splendid tomb, now warmed by the summer sun, cooled by the gentle rain and open to a canopy of stars twinkling in an ebony sky.

Then, in the early 1990s, several men, or teenaged boys, entered the remote little cemetery one night and, using sledge-hammers, vandalized Grancer's tomb once again. Huge chunks of white stucco and brick were broken away, leaving the contents of the tomb open to the elements. It was rumoured the grave was desecrated by a group of people who considered all paranormal activity demonic in nature; however, nothing was ever proved. But regardless of the motives for the vandalism, this time the Harrison family did not repair the damage, although Ms Jewell Harrison Johnson is presently collecting money for its restoration.

The Harrison house, barns and other buildings are gone now and the forest has reclaimed much of the area where they once stood along the banks of Cripple Creek and the Pea River. No-one living today remembers the wooden dance pavilion, but they know it was located near the edge of what is now the cemetery. Nevertheless, people from far and wide still visit the isolated little country graveyard, even though after more than 140 years, few hear the phantom fiddler or encounter the dancing ghost.

But as recently as the late 1990s, a local farmer, his son and nephew, toiling well into the night in one of the peanut fields bordering the cemetery, heard what they later described as "old-time fiddle music". It was mid-September, rain was forecast and clouds were already partially obscuring the heavy, gibbous moon. The farmer's brother and another nephew had just left with the last load of peanuts, leaving the remaining three to retrieve the other items of equipment. It was while they were hurrying to get everything together that the fiddling began.

Thinking someone was playing a joke on them, and tired from working since sunrise, the three decided to teach the pranksters a lesson. One of the teenagers grabbed a torch, the other a shotgun, and they all headed toward the direction of the music. As they approached, the fiddling seemed to get louder, then abruptly stopped. A shot was fired into the air to scare off the rascals, but there were no cries of "Don't shoot!" or sounds of scurrying feet.

While the farmer attempted to rationalize the situation to the pair of clearly frightened teenagers, a dark cloud enshrouded the moon, turning the night pitch black, and a sudden, chill wind made them shiver. Finally, the farmer broke the silence, "We need to get out of here before the rain starts," he declared. "Shine that torch around and let's see where we are." And there, just a few feet away, clearly visible in the pale beams of light, stood the once magnificent tomb of Grancer Harrison.

Lee Holloway is a writer and researcher living and working in Florida. In addition to articles, she has contributed to several books and has conducted research for television specials.

THE FIERY HAND
by Ervin Bonkalo, Ph.D.

The book showed the burned imprint of a hand on the first 100 pages – yet page 101 was not even yellowed.

EARLY in 1952 a fire swept through the ancient convent of Cinta, Portugal, and destroyed what was perhaps the world's most curious book. Printed in 1620 at Pozsony, Hungary, this book, a collection of Bibilcal stories, was known as the *Kada Codex*. The book was exceptional not because of its contents or its antiquity but because of the mark which appeared on the cover and the first 100 pages.

This strange mark looked as if a man had placed his right hand on the closed book and left a burned imprint. The heavy leather cover and first seven pages showed the entire outline of the hand. The following sheets were successively less burned. Page 100 was heavily scorched. The remaining pages of the *Codex* remained intact. Strangely page 101 – opposite page 100 – was not even yellowed.

The *Kada Codex* was discovered in 1902 among books of the Calasantine convent of Privigye in North Hungary and was sent to Budapest for examination. Until 1947 the book was in the custody of the Calasantine Fathers of Budapest. During those 45 years the *Codex* was inspected by individual experts from various countries and by many special scientific groups.

The first official investigation took place in 1903 when an attempt was made to trace the book's history. The only information unearthed was that the *Codex* was presented by Leopold Kollonits of Vienna, in the year 1667, to the Calasantine Fathers in Privigye for use in their school which had opened the previous year. The volume was described by an ancient letter as "brand new".

One member of the 1903 group, Dr E. Friedreich, a professor of history, started a methodical investigation of his own. After 10 years of digging in old documents, he presented his findings to a committee composed of clergymen, library experts and historians.

Friedreich's most important discovery was a letter which a monk named Matheus Ursinus wrote in 1710. This letter dealt with the death of another monk of Privigye, Franciscus Hanacius. "Many people got together after we came back from the cemetery," Ursinus wrote, "and wanted to see the book which was touched in his presence by the soul of Stephen Kada but we were not able to find it."

Dr Friedreich explored the life of Stephen Kada. He was born in 1617, became the Roman Catholic Bishop of Erdley and North Hungary in 1690 and died in 1695 at Pozsony. On official travels through his territory Bishop Kada frequently spent the night at the comfortable convent of the Calasantine monks in Privigye.

The committee could not understand how one side of a sheet of paper could be scorched without damage to the other side, as happened on page 100 of the *Kada Codex*. Because the committee was not satisfied with the theory that a supernatural force burned the hand-mark on the book it was proposed that an extended search be made in the libraries of all Calasantine convents and in municipal documents. Any historical material which dealt with the affairs of North Hungary and Erdely, between the death of Bishop Kada in 1695 and the death of Hanacius in 1710, was to be reported to Dr Friedreich.

Shortly after this decision World War I postponed the investigation. At the end of the war the state of Hungary was dismembered; North Hungary became part of Czechoslovakia, Erdely went to Romania and South Hungary to Yugoslavia. Due to the new borders, two-thirds of the Calasantine convents and Episcopal territories joined foreign countries. And, because of the political chaos and the destruction of many municipal documents, the official search into the circumstances behind the marking of the *Kada Codex* sank into oblivion.

Dr Friedreich, however, continued his personal investigation during the next 25 years. And he pieced together the full story behind the strange marking of the *Kada Codex*.

The year 1938 was the Holy Year of Hungary. Festivals and a Eucharistic World Congress were held on the 1,000[th] anniversary of the death of St Stephen, the first king of Hungary, who Christianized the nation. Foreign church dignitaries, scientists and members of the Middle European Archaeological Institute, which held their annual convention that year in Budapest, visited the famous museum of the Calasantine Fathers. Many of them became interested in the *Kada Codex*. Dr Friedreich, now director of the museum, invited guests to a meeting at which he told the story of the mysterious hand-mark. Some members of the old committee of 1903, an anthropologist, a paper expert, members of the Middle European Archaeological Institute and editors of magazines were present. I was among the persons invited.

Dr Friedreich's story, based on history as found in old documents, is as follows:

Bent over a book late on the night of April 1, 1696, Father Franciscus Hanacius heard a knock at his study door. Wondering who wanted to see him at this late hour he picked up his oil lamp and opened the door. In the flickering light from the lamp the pale faces of other monks stared at him from down the corridor. All had heard knocks at their doors – all had opened their doors at the very same time!

The following night, at midnight, the mysterious knocks were heard again and with such violence that the thick wooden doors rattled. The prior ordered the startled monks into the chapel where they prayed and sang hymns until sunrise. They returned to their cells to find cupboards and drawers opened and everything in wild disorder. Ink bottles and oil lamps lay overturned, their contents spilled.

On April 3, steps, clicks and cracklings were heard all through the night in the rooms and hallways. The noises could not be stopped by prayer or the sprinkling of holy water. The next night they were repeated.

The rumour that ghosts inhabited the Calasantine monastery spread quickly through the city of Privigye. Adam Borsanyi, the mayor, was anxious to know the truth. He was a courageous man and decided to spend a night in the monastery.

What actually happened on the night of April 5, 1696, is not known. The only facts, revealed in a letter written by a member of the city council and now in the archives of the monastery, are that towards morning the mayor was found sprawled in the street not far from the monastery. He wore his night cap and night gown and was trembling but sober. Apparently he had departed from the monastery in an enormous hurry because he held his slippers.

Father Hanacius was deeply troubled by the strange happenings at the monastery and determined to solve the problem. On April 6 he asked the other monks to go into the chapel and to stay there until sunrise. He remained in his cell. On the little table in the middle of his room he placed a valuable book of Biblical stories, a burning candle, salt, wine, bread and oil in small dishes.

At midnight heavy steps were heard. The cell door swung open and slammed shut. The sound of heavy boots approached the table. Father Hanacius could see no one.

"Take a seat and tell me who you are and what you want," said Father Hanacius, speaking evenly despite his fear.

The empty chair beside the table creaked under an invisible weight. The dishes were pushed around, the pages of the book were turned. The unseen hand stopped turning at page 100. The chair creaked again and there was again the sound of footsteps. The door opened and closed.

Father Hanacius was deeply impressed. He felt that his unseen visitor was not an evil spirit or he would not have touched the holy book. He was confident that sooner or later he would communicate with the restless soul; he need only to be patient.

During the next three nights the invisible being did not appear. On the night of April 10 Father Hanacius sat reading his breviary at his table. The night watchman's steps sounded hollowly on the empty street outside as, with his lantern and halberd, he made his usual tour around the monastery.

At this moment Father Hanacius heard the heavy boots of the ghost approaching – right through the closed door of his room. A voice thundered suddenly from the opposite side of the table.

"Listen, Franciscus! I am Bishop Kada," said the unseen visitor in Latin. "I want you to go on a pilgrimage to the town of Nagyszombat and celebrate a Holy Mass over my grave and to pray for the release of my poor soul from Purgatory where it has been burning for 100 days."

The startled monk recognized the voice of the deceased bishop. He had heard it several times when Kada came to Privigye to celebrate Mass in the chapel.

But Father Hanacius decided to make a test. "I do not believe you," he said. "Evil spirits are able to simulate anyone's speech. I want you to prove that you are the person you claim to be."

Again the invisible spoke. "The Devil has not the power over sacred books. Look here."

The book of Biblical stories lay on the table. Suddenly smoke and the smell of burning leather and paper filled the room. The mark of a man's right hand appeared on the cover and on the first 100 pages of the book.

Shouting excitedly, "A miracle has happened, brothers, a miracle!" Father Hanacius rushed from his cell.

At this moment the night watchman saw smoke coming from the monastery window where the light burned. He rattled the main door. The excited shouts of Father Hanacius and the knocking sounds from outside terrorized the monks. They were convinced that a horde of ghosts was attacking. The watchman heard the noise of running feet and the yells from within. Believing that the monastery was burning he sounded the alarm.

A crowd of citizens rushed to the scene with water pails, ladders and ropes. It was hours before the confusion subsided. Startled townspeople demanded that the mayor investigate this strange incident and the monks were unable to keep secret the ghostly visit, as they had intended until the church investigated. The city magistrate conducted hearings and the affair was reported in the city annals. A duplicate of the report went to the monastery. A triplicate went to the king's archives in Buda, at this time the capital of Hungary. This last copy, in poor condition, is preserved to the present time.

Father Hanacius wished to fulfil the request of the deceased Bishop Kada as soon as possible. He took the book and the duplicate of the report and, accompanied by Father Herchl, set out on the long walk to Nagyszombat.

During the journey a thunderstorm made the two monks seek refuge at the castle of Count Hunyady, where they spent a night. The count greatly admired the miraculous *Codex*. His diary, with notes concerning the visit of the two Fathers, is preserved in the archives of the castle.

The next existing document, in which the two monks are mentioned, reports that they appeared before the city council of Nagyszombat on April 13, 1696. Father Hanacius celebrated a Holy Mass in the St Dorothea chapel, over the grave of Bishop Stephen Kada, on which occasion members of the city council, "monks, nuns, priests and hundreds of the common folk were present, all hoping that something extraordinary would happen".

Although nothing happened at the St Dorothea chapel, 60 miles southward in the city of Pozsony at the bishop's palace an excited man was giving orders to his secretary. Bishop Illyes, the successor of Kada, had received the news of the supernatural happenings at Privigye and of Father Hanacius' pilgrimage. Since he did not believe in the "miracle" he issued a command to "hinder the eccentric monk in the spreading of his imagination."

Next day the command was withdrawn. The secretary hurried a letter to Father Hanacius in which Bishop Illyes apologized for his action, stating that Bishop Kada had appeared to him in a dream and reprimanded him for his disbelief.

This was the last known appearance of Stephen Kada.

The scientists at the 1938 meeting which I attended could not find a natural explanation for the burning of one side of a book page without damage to the opposite side. But the Catholic Church refused to proclaim the event a miracle.

The *Kada Codex* was returned to its case in the museum of the Calasantine monks in 1938 and then was taken with other relics to Cinta, Portugal, in 1947.

The fire that eventually destroyed the book in early 1952 also destroyed any hope of explaining the mystery of the burned handmark.

THE FLYING ROCKS

By Antonio J. Lopez Baez

HAVING lived peacefully for five years at Avenida Ocampo No 52 Poniente, Torreón, Coahuila, México, my friend, Augustín Vázquez Puga, was surprised when told on the afternoon of November 15, 1932, that somebody was throwing rocks over his garden wall into his yard.

He went home right away and was shocked to find about 40 persons gathering there watching the rocks fly in by hundreds. He had some trouble making his way into his house but finally got in and immediately started to look for his aunt, Mrs Santos Puga de Moreno. He found her in one of the rooms with the maid and his cousin, Miss Tomasa Rivera. Their lips were moving as if they were praying but he paid no attention.

He walked out again to the place where the rocks were falling and was followed by some of the neighbours. They noticed that the rocks came from a plot of land separated from his house by a wall. No rocks could be found near that area and yet they saw the rocks come from that direction. The rocks were ordinary pebbles like those found near a river.

Alarmed by this situation Augustín called the police but was told there was nothing they could do about it. He became angry, fired the maid and took his cousin back to her family. He returned home and with great pleasure noticed that the rocks were no longer falling. Next day the rocks had to be carried out in wheelbarrows. The furniture in the house was greatly damaged by this phenomenon.

A few days after this happened my friend was talking to his cousin's grandmother, telling her all that had happened while Tomasa was spending a few days at his home and the old lady told him that next to where they lived there was a church where many pigeons nestled and every time the girl looked up at them, the pigeons fell dead at her feet.

– Torreon, Coahuila, Mex.

169

FOOTSTEPS TO NOWHERE

This mysterious story happened a few days before Christmas Eve 1996 in the small, cozy village of Plumlov in the east of the Czech Republic.

An older woman named Jane Prochazkova was watching television in the family house. She was alone, and the house was empty. When her film ended, she came over to the window, enjoying the beauty of the falling snow.

Suddenly Jane caught sight of footsteps in the fresh snow leading up to the door. She thought it must be her husband getting back from work. She listened attentively for the sound of the opening door. A long time passed, however, and Jane did not hear the sound of keys in the lock, nor the sound of the doorbell signalling that her husband was locked out. It was strange. She approached the door hesitantly and opened it. There was nobody in the doorway. Jane saw only the footsteps leading up to the house, ending right at the door. She observed that the footprints were those of a man.

A stark terror seized her at the thought that someone unknown had come to her house – except that this person had neither entered nor left. Jane closed the door, returned to the window, and opened it. She strained her ears to hear any queer noise. If there had been a thief in the house, she would surely have jumped out of the window. It was on the first floor, so there was no danger of hurting herself.

Ten minutes later, when nothing strange had happened, Jane saw her husband coming home. She called his name through the open window. "John! Look at the footsteps! They lead up to our house!"

Of course, John didn't see anything strange in that. Jane explained to him excitedly what she had seen. Apparently it caught his attention. They decided to search the house together from top to bottom to see if someone unknown had entered unnoticed. They armed themselves with kitchen knives and started to search. After half an hour of ransacking, they found nothing.

Whose footsteps could they be? Why had no one entered? How had he got back? The footsteps led in one direction only.

The great suspense led them to put their coats on and go outside to follow the footsteps to their source. The trail led to a pond close to the field. The surface had frozen, so they followed the path on to the pond.

Suddenly Jane and John stood in great astonishment. The footsteps ended in the middle of the frozen pond! No other tracks around – footsteps from nowhere to nowhere.

They thought perhaps a ghost had visited, but there had never been anyone who had died in their family house. The story of the Prochazkas has never been explained.

– *Prague, Czech Republic*

MY FRIENDLY GHOST
By Joyce Erickson

A friendly ghost fluttered into my life on October 1, 1994. For me, it was as delicious an experience as my first discovery of Father Christmas. Indeed, I was like a child again, clapping my hands, laughing and running from room to room urging him on. I knew from the first that my ghost was a friendly, funny, playful and teasing being. Not once – even when he left a streak of blood on the arm of our bathtub – was I remotely afraid.

At the time, I was working as a writer with a friend, whom I'll call Keith, in a one-bedroom apartment in North Hollywood, California. We had lived there for more than a year without mishap. Keith had had earlier run-ins with a spiritual presence, but I had never experienced such a wonder in my life. Then one day strange things began to occur. The only conclusion we could draw was that we had a male ghostly visitor.

One of the earliest witnesses was my son, Lance, who was visiting us for a weekend in early October. Lance and I had just returned from a day's excursion. We found Keith seated on the living room sofa with a wary expression on his face.

Sounding disgruntled, he said, "We've had a visitor. When I came home from work the coffee pot was plugged in, the fan was on, and that poster was cut clean in half!" He pointed to the far wall. A film poster taped to the wall was slit diagonally as with a knife or a razor.

I could feel my adrenaline rushing, realizing Keith meant the ghost had dropped by. I, too, was sure the ghost had been active, since I always double-check the coffee pot and fans before leaving home.

The following morning, the three of us were sipping coffee and discussing our work while Lance prepared to leave for his home in the Bay Area. No one had come by, and we hadn't left the apartment since early the previous evening.

Lance came out of the bathroom and stood dramatically in the hallway, looking as though his life had been altered. In a cautious, drawn-out voice, he called, "Mum," and crooked a finger at me.

Puzzled, I followed him back into the bathroom and stopped in my tracks. A picture on the wall was turned upside down, and a rose-shaped knick-knack that usually sat on the windowsill was gone.

I felt myself swelling up inside with anticipation. A tingly feeling started at my head and travelled down my spine. I knew! I just knew! My ghost was finally performing for me! My thoughts swirled, and I remember saying, "At last!" My feelings were overwhelming and I hugged them, absorbed them, like a high I had never felt before.

I yelled for Keith to come and look.

Space doesn't allow me to list the day-by-day mischief my ghost got into, so the easiest way to convey his actions is to point out the most dramatic ones. Mind you, I have pages and pages in my journal from October 1, 1994, to February 1995, when Keith and I were forced to vacate the apartment when it was put up for sale.

The ghost was constantly active throughout October and November. He then tapered off and acted only sporadically. But he was always there; we could feel him, and some of our visiting friends were aware of a presence. Some left in terror. Some left shaking their heads. Others simply didn't believe it. I am the only person who enjoyed the ghost.

Even my son was more befuddled than entertained. In fact, as he was leaving the weekend I mentioned earlier he found the missing rose knick-knack in his overnight bag. He held it up gingerly between thumb and forefinger and said, "What's this doing in my bag?"

I laughed. Keith sighed. Lance said, "I'm outta here!"

I happily dug out my journal and wrote down everything my ghost did from that day on. I'd wake up in the morning and go from room to room looking for the ghost's leftovers, and I'd rush home from work at night to see what awaited me. Things would move around and appear and disappear continuously.

Few items disappeared completely, but knick-knacks and utensils were moved to different areas or placed in the refrigerator! (It's startling to open the refrigerator and see a photo of yourself staring at you!) Pictures, posters and our writings would disappear for one or two days, until we asked for them to be returned.

Sometimes the ghost did even more annoying things, like dump bath salts and coffee grounds in the sinks or turn the radio and electric fans on.

I would laugh and scold him for making so much work for me to clean up. Occasionally he was more helpful. One time the ghost actually cleaned up a messy cabinet we used to dump stuff. At other times my coffee, creamer, cup and spoon (usually put away) were set up next to the coffee pot ready for me when I returned from work.

The ghost seemed to be most attracted to the bathroom, kitchen and living room. He occasionally appeared in the dining room and bedroom.

At times the ghost's actions seemed more directed, almost like attempts to communicate. The ghost often moved books and videos in interesting combinations. Returning home from work one night, I opened the front door and at my feet lying side-by-side were two novels – *Pretty Women* and *No Time For Tears*. We have no idea where these novels came from. Did the ghost steal them from someone else?

On the coffee table one evening we found the book *Necessary Losses* opened to a page that had no apparent relation to either of us. Our Bible was once bookmarked to the Book of Luke. Again, the opened page seemed to bear no relation to us.

A video, *Invisible Stranger*, was placed on the dining room table (we didn't know we had this video), and we found two more videos, *To Live and Die in L.A.* and *The Hard Way*, lying on the living room floor. Interesting connection, we thought.

In addition to moving books and videos, the ghost made other dramatic gestures. Once I went to the linen cupboard for a towel. Sitting on top of the sheets was a fake rose. Lined up side-by-side were the Queen of Hearts and the 8, 10 and Jack of Diamonds.

The ghost once used a soap bar to write initials on the bathroom mirror.

(We weren't positive what the initials were, or if there was meaning to them.) On another occasion the ghost rummaged through my makeup, took my foundation and wrote on the linen cupboard door, "I'm Here Find Me." I have to admit this stunned me for a few seconds, then I said aloud that I would love to.

The ghost lit a candle and left it burning until we arrived home one day. Beside the candle he had dumped my pen and pencil holder all over the dining room table and had written my daughter's name in pencil on the reverse of a business card.

I must emphasize that I loved every minute of my ghost's presence and was sad to leave him.

GUARDIAN FROM THE GRAVE

The Ghost of Marsalee Bishop
by Chris Brethwaite

On a sleepy residential street in a small central Missouri town stands a picturesque stone house, known locally as the Bishop House. Currently, it is empty – empty, that is, except for the spirit of Marsalee Bishop, who died there in 1939 at the age of 19, a victim of scarlet fever.

Dreams and Apparitions

In May 1997, Becky Ray, a recent divorcee, moved into the Bishop House with her teenage daughter Dusty to start a new life. Shortly after moving in, Dusty had a series of unusual dreams on nights when she had fallen asleep on the couch in the living room. In the dreams, she was asleep on that same couch. She opened her eyes and saw a shadowy figure walk past her. She couldn't tell if the figure was male or female. Dusty didn't know what to make of the dreams. In time, she dismissed them.

A short time after this, Becky was working in the kitchen one day when she saw something out of the corner of her eye. She turned just in time to see the image of a young woman in her late teens or early twenties, with short dark hair walk past the doorway in the direction of Dusty's room. The woman resembled Dusty in general appearance. Because of this, Becky assumed that it must have been her daughter. But having just seen Dusty asleep, she was curious as to why she was up. Becky walked to the doorway, but when she looked down the hallway, she didn't see anyone.

She thought it was odd that she hadn't heard Dusty's bedroom door open or close. She went down the hall and looked in the room, but no-one was there. She then went to her own room where she found Dusty still asleep on the bed, right where she had last seen her. Becky kept the sighting to herself, but it wouldn't be long before Dusty, too, encountered Marsalee.

One day when Dusty was in the kitchen, she had a strange feeling: "You know when you get the feeling that someone's watching you? I could feel it, like a tingly feeling."

She turned and saw the translucent figure of a petite young woman with short brown hair looking at her. The figure calmly turned and walked away.

About a month later, Dusty was in the kitchen again, when she got a feeling that someone was watching her. The feeling was so strong that she said aloud, "Please just leave me alone!"

She then turned and saw the apparition of Marsalee standing in the doorway, slightly bent forward with her hands on her hips, as though she was about to scold a young child. Dusty was so taken by the sight that she can't recall what happened next. The experience upset her so much that she slept with her mum that night.

Sceptical Sister

The next person to see Marsalee was Becky's oldest daughter, Deanna, who was 20 at the time. She was living in Kansas City and had come to visit. She was in the living room one morning folding a quilt when, like Dusty, she felt that someone was watching her. She turned around, and there next to the kitchen doorway was the translucent figure of Marsalee. She was standing with her face cradled in her hands and her elbows resting on top of the counter. Marsalee appeared to be simply watching Deanna fold the comforter.

Deanna stood in awe for what she estimated to be 30 seconds. She then watched Marsalee step back and run into the kitchen. Deanna walked over to the doorway and peered in the kitchen, but she was gone.

Before her own sighting, Deanna was aware that both Becky and Dusty believed they had seen a ghost in the house. She had been somewhat sceptical of their claims; but now, of course, she was a believer. Upon reflection, Deanna was surprised that she hadn't been scared during the sighting. (This probably explains why she stood for half a minute looking at Marsalee.) However, like Dusty, she was fearful afterwards.

The next person to experience Marsalee was a friend of Dusty's, Steve Whitlock. One night, Dusty had some friends over. They were in her room, talking and hanging out. Steve left to use the bathroom. When he approached the kitchen, he saw a young woman with short brown hair sitting on a bench to the right of the kitchen doorway. Thinking that it might be Dusty – but not knowing how that could be – he glanced back toward Dusty's room. When he turned back again, the figure was gone. He told Dusty about the experience the next day.

Dusty saw Marsalee on two more occasions. On one occasion she was sitting on the couch and saw Marsalee walk from the direction of the kitchen toward her room. Another time Dusty was on her way into the kitchen when she saw Marsalee come around the corner as though she had come from the guest room.

Psychokinetic Displays

Though all the sightings took place close to the kitchen doorway, in an area approximately four feet by ten feet, Marsalee's presence was made known in other parts of the house.

One night, after Dusty's second sighting of Marsalee, she was sitting in the living room with an acquaintance named John. They had just finished watching a film and were rewinding the tape. John got up, put the videotape case on the mantlepiece, and went into the kitchen. When he came back, he started pacing back and forth in front of the mantle waiting for the tape to finish rewinding. Suddenly, the tape case flew violently off the mantlepiece, landing several feet away on the floor. The Rays believe this was Marsalee's way of expressing disapproval of the young man.

About three or four weeks after Dusty's final sighting, she came home from school to find four of her candles sitting in the middle of her bedroom floor. These candles had been on her dresser when she had left the house that morning. She was the last to leave the house and the first to arrive home. The incident made Dusty think that Marsalee didn't want her in that bedroom, so she moved into the guest room.

One day Becky came home from work and noticed that she couldn't find her sandals, which she usually wore every day. Her first thought was that maybe her dog Molly had made off with them, but she didn't think that was likely as Molly would usually just play with one shoe, not both. She and Dusty tore the house apart looking for the missing sandals, to no avail. Dusty jokingly suggested that maybe the ghost took them.

That night when Becky went to bed, she said aloud, "If you took my sandals, please put them back because I wear them a lot." The next morning when she awoke, the sandals were next to her bed.

On another occasion Becky and her girlfriend Diane were

sitting on the bed in her room when they both observed one of the bedroom windows opening on its own. The windows opened inward like French doors, and had been latched. According to Becky it took quite a bit of strength to unlatch the windows. Though neither Becky nor Diane heard the window being unlatched, they both definitely saw it opening on its own.

There were other times when Becky and Dusty heard footsteps in the living room when nobody was in there. Another thing that caught their attention was the behaviour of their dog Molly. Sometimes Molly would be sitting on the couch with Becky and suddenly whip her head around and stare in the direction of the kitchen doorway.

Dusty had a similar experience. She was sitting on the couch in the living room one time when she noticed Molly's head going back and forth as though she was watching someone pace in front of the kitchen doorway. Dusty was home alone, and was so frightened that she had to call a friend to help calm her nerves.

Marsalee's Story

After seeing the apparition and experiencing some of the odd events that were taking place in the house, Becky was able to discern what she described as a "sense of loneliness" that she felt was connected to whoever was "residing" in her house. This feeling made her want to know who this individual was, and so she started researching the history of the house. She found some information in a local museum, and later was able to track down a descendent of the original owners.

Given a description of the young woman the Rays had seen, he replied that it matched the description of his cousin Marsalee, who had died from scarlet fever at the age of 19. Her death had been very tragic and very sudden. The "Bishop House" was her grandparents' residence; Marsalee was staying with them because her parents were out of town on business when she became ill. He also confirmed that Dusty's bedroom – the one with the moving candles – had been Marsalee's room during her stay there.

In the summer of 2000, Becky lost her job. With opportunities limited in a small town, she decided to move to Kansas City, where she soon found employment and rented an apartment in Independence. She and Dusty hadn't lived in their new place long when they again started experiencing things they couldn't explain.

Not Left Behind

One evening while they were both sitting in the living room, they noticed a lamp dim on its own, as though being turned down by an invisible hand. Some time later, Dusty was in her bedroom with her four-year-old cousin Skyla, who threw a small key chain behind Dusty's bed. Because there was a box stored under the bed, there was no easy way to reach the key chain, so they just left it. A couple of weeks later, Dusty found the key chain lying in plain view in the middle of her floor. She and Becky had no idea how it could have got there. They considered the possibility that Molly had retrieved it but she was too big to have squeezed between the box and the wall. Besides, Molly was seldom ever allowed in Dusty's room.

There were other things that took place in Dusty's room that defied an easy explanation. On her bookcase was displayed an angel book with the cover facing forwards. On several occasions, she went in her room and noticed that the book had been turned so that the spine was facing out. She asked Becky if she had moved it; Becky said she hadn't. Later, Dusty noticed that another book of hers had been taken off the shelf and displayed so that one could read the cover – just the opposite of what had happened to the angel book.

Probably the most incredible event took place in Becky's room. Against the wall she has a small piece of furniture called a coffee cabinet. The two doors are held closed by a piece of wood that revolves on a screw. When the piece of wood is in the horizontal position, the doors are latched shut. When it is turned vertically, the doors are unlatched. Two days in a row Becky came home from work and found the left door unlatched. Someone had to have unlatched the doors, and then, holding the right door closed, moved the piece of wood back down to a horizontal position. There was no way that Molly could have been responsible for this – this was a deliberate act that showed an intelligence at work.

Why Marsalee followed them to Independence is anyone's guess. The Rays believe that Marsalee has taken an interest in them – particularly in Dusty. Part of this belief is based on the fact that most of the paranormal activity they've experienced has centred on her. It was Dusty who had the most sightings of Marsalee, and it was Dusty's bedrooms where the majority of unexplained events took place. Additionally, Dusty has a strong physical resemblance to Marsalee.

But there is another, stronger reason for their belief. There is evidence to suggest that Marsalee saved Dusty's life.

Guardian Angel?

On April 29, 2000, Dusty and her then boyfriend Daniel decided to drive to Columbia, Missouri. Daniel had wanted to leave around noon, but Dusty and Becky were hosting a wedding shower that wouldn't be over until around three in the afternoon. Daniel was tempted to go by himself, but decided to wait for Dusty.

Shortly after he picked her up, a strange feeling came over Becky that she hadn't told Dusty that she loved her often enough. Unknown to Becky, Dusty was experiencing a similar feeling. It was so strong that she almost asked Daniel to turn around and take her back home.

About an hour later, Daniel and Dusty were run into by a drunk driver travelling at a high rate of speed. Daniel's Mitsubishi was demolished, but they both survived with only minor cuts and scrapes. The Rays can't help but feel that someone was looking out for Dusty that day, and they believe that person was Marsalee.

On the day I finished working on this article, I debated whether or not to write about the car accident. I knew that Becky and Dusty were convinced that Marsalee looks out for them; judging by the photos of Daniel's car, it *did* seem miraculous that neither she nor Daniel had been seriously injured or killed, but I had no evidence that Marsalee had intervened…until a few days later.

That Sunday I called Becky to get some answers to questions I had about the accident. Before we got talking about that, I inquired if anything out of the ordinary had happened to her or Dusty since we had spoken last. Becky told me that when she went in the kitchen Saturday morning, the doors on the small cabinets over the stove were wide open. Later that day she asked Dusty if she had got anything from the cabinets, to which Dusty replied "No."

The blame then fell to Marsalee. However, Becky couldn't understand what Marsalee's purpose was in opening those cabinets as they only contained paper plates. It then struck her. Those paper plates were last used at the wedding shower – the same wedding shower that took place on the day of the accident. We could only conclude that Marsalee opened those cabinet doors as a way of letting us know that she had a hand in saving Dusty from death or serious injury that day.

It is also our belief that Marsalee knew of my reluctance to include the car accident in the story, and that this was her way of encouraging me to use it.

Lingering Presence
I don't think this was the only thing Marsalee did for my benefit. I first met Becky and Dusty at the Bishop House just before to the holidays. Though they were living in Independence, they had been invited to a wedding in their old town and had asked the owner of the house if they could show it to me. He gave them permission on the condition that I not reveal its exact location.

During the hour or so that I spent with them at the house, I took video and photos of the premises and tape-recorded an interview with them. Though nothing unusual was present in any of the pictures or video, there was an intermittent, rhythmic clicking sound on portions of the audio tape. Dusty had to leave on an errand shortly after I arrived, and was not there when I started the interview. Interestingly, the clicking doesn't start until about the time she returns.

None of us could recall hearing anything in the house that may have been responsible for the sound. I checked a tape that I had made before their interview and there was nothing unusual on it. There are no unusual sounds on any subsequent tapes I have made on that machine. At the time of the interview, the house was completely empty. We had turned on a ceiling light in the kitchen, but nothing else. I will make this tape available to any serious investigator who would like to analyse it.

As you can see, this is a story that has no end. There is no way to know exactly why Marsalee has chosen to look after Dusty, or how long she will continue to do so. In any event, Dusty can go through life with the added confidence of knowing that she has a very special guardian angel looking out for her.

Chris Brethwaite has had a lifelong interest in the paranormal. He teaches a class on "The Haunted Heartland" in Kansas City and is currently working on a book entitled Evidence For Life After Death. *He works as a full-time writer for Hallmark Cards.*

FRONTIER PHANTOMS
by W. Ritchie Benedict

Canadian ghosts are subtly different from those that haunt the United States. They are a reflection of the cultural differences between the two countries. The American West has a tradition of wagon trains, Indian massacres, gunfights, claim jumpers and stagecoach robberies. In Canada, it was more often a case of a lone Mounted Police officer staring down hostile Indians by force of will alone. Canadian ghosts tend to be low key.

Names With a Reason

In the beginning, there were the native Americans, who often labelled places with names that were indicators of strange events. One such is Ghost River, Alberta, which appears to have come by its name honestly. There seems to be a long-standing curse hovering over the area as well. An unusual number of deaths has been associated with this remote area, going well back into the 1920s and before.

A century earlier, long before Alberta became a province, Ghost River already had a bad reputation. The traders from the Hudson's Bay post at Rocky Mountain House referred to Ghost River as *Riviere de Mort*, the River of Death.

The Ghostly Hunt

In September 1935, the *Albertan* headlined a story by James McCook that read, "Mysterious Hunters Gave Ghost River Name: Stony Indian Recounts Story of Buffalo Hunt by Ghosts of Dead Men."

An old Stony man at Morely recalled a tale told by his father that dated back to the days when the Stonies were so numerous that their tepees extended from the mouth of the Ghost River to the Rocky Mountains. One year when the tribesmen were gathered together, a great sickness struck and hundreds died. Months went by, and a group of tribesmen camped on the south side of the Bow River, east of what is now Morley. To their utter astonishment, they saw a large band of tribesmen to the north chasing a herd of buffalo with the animals dashing over the foothills in terror. The Stonies were afraid. They knew none of their tribe was hunting on the north side of the river, and the visitors must be either hostile Blackfoot or Crees. Cautiously, they crossed the river and made their way up to the buffalo herd, which continued to dash back and forth, as if being pursued by hunters. And yet there was no sign of any hunters.

The ghostly hunt continued until the harried animals were on the verge of total exhaustion, then suddenly everything went quiet and the herd grazed peacefully. The Stonies came to the conclusion that the spirits of those who died of the "great sickness" had come back to visit their old hunting grounds and so the river became known as the River of the Spirits. The age of the old man who told the story would place the event at approximately 1870. The "great sickness" may have been the smallpox epidemic which took thousands of lives among the native Americans and early settlers that same year.

Although these ghosts were the result of an epidemic, the ones that lurk on the site of the Custer massacre at the Little Big Horn, just over the border in Montana, were the result of violent death. In the late 1970s, the battlefield's former Plains Indian historian Mardell Plainfeather, a Crow who lived in the government housing at the site, said she saw two warriors on horseback, high on the bluff. The apparition even featured one of the warriors lifting himself up on his horse to get a better look at her! Plainfeather's daughter was with her and also saw the figures on horseback. One warrior had long, flowing hair, while the other wore braids. One carried a spear and bow and quiver, while the other had a shield.

Swamp Gas?
Another, lesser known story was published in the *Toronto News* for March 20, 1885, and was titled: "IN THE LOST CANYON/Terrified by the Antics of Will of the Wisps/The Strange Adventures of Two Related Fishermen in Montana." Dated Butte, Montana, March 15, 1885, it cited the experience of a man named Penrose and his companion, who decided to go fishing on a clear summer morning. The two men took the Utah and Northern narrow-gauge railway from Butte to a scenic fishing spot about 30 miles away near a ranch owned by a man named Forest. When they left the train, they made arrangements to be picked up by the "up" train after the day's fishing was done. As twilight approached the fishpails were full and the two men began to think about making their way back to the railhead for the journey home.

At around 10:00 p.m., the distant light of the engine

appeared. Penrose set fire to a newspaper and both men yelled at the top of their lungs, all to no avail, as the train roared past them into the darkness. It looked like they were in for a very long, dark walk. After some discussion, they decided to try the canyon to their rear, which led directly toward the camp in the northeast, their only hope of food or shelter that night.

Encouraged by a full moon, they began the long trek. Soon the moon sank out of sight and a yellow fog, which condensed into a warm rain, settled over the canyon. For over an hour they trudged along, with a range of hills just visible several hundreds of yards on either side. Suddenly, without warning, a light appeared to their left about 100 yards in front. It seemed that it was a lantern carried by a man. Both were overjoyed by the sight and called out repeatedly. The light bounced along, about three feet from the ground, and it gave off a yellow glow. Suddenly, it shot high Into the air, fell to ground with a crackling sound, and went out with a flash. Dumfounded, the pair stared at each other and then were chilled by the sight of faint, luminescent patches of light hovering over the mounds and in the hollows. A chill wind swept into the valley and the lights all went out simultaneously.

Immediately ahead, some 150 yards away, another great, glaring light like the headlight of a locomotive came into view. With an audible whiz, it headed straight for them, causing both to dive out of the path. It got within ten feet, then went out again, leaving them in the dark, until the glow over the mounds started again. To the right on the crest of the ridge, a gigantic mass of whitish flame went on and moved with incredible swiftness.

The light illuminated the trees at the top of the ridge. It seemed to hover in the bare branches of a blasted tree at an elevation of 20 feet above the ground. It shot up another 60 or 70 feet, then descended. The men watched the antics for more than half an hour. The mass eventually took on a superficial resemblance to a horse. It would flit along the ridge for several hundred yards, then return to the burned-out pine. After two hours, the horse-like flame finally vanished, having paced them for eight miles.

Much relieved, the men finally arrived back at the Forest ranch. They decided to say little or nothing about their strange experience. There had been 67 distinct lights. None of the old-timers had ever spoken about the mound valley.

Although we may never know today what the two fishermen experienced on that night 117 years ago, the most common explanation today would be that it was merely swamp gas caused by rotting vegetation. The late Dr J. Allen Hynek got himself into much controversy back in 1966 by suggesting that the Hillsdale, Michigan, UFO sightings were due to such a phenomenon. Nevertheless, something else may have been at work in 1885, judging by the remark made by the foreman Ike to the fishermen before they left. He said that one of the native Americans left the ranch early in the morning to smoke a pipe on Big Horse's grave beyond the ridge, as the previous day was "Injun All Souls Day".

This fits into the many instances where "spook lights" give every indication of being under some sort of intelligent control.

Animal Ghosts
Animal ghosts, while sometimes reported, are a relative rarity. The Cache Lake spectre, observed near Spedden, Alberta, is said to appear once every 50 years (which means it will not turn up again until 2033) at the time of the harvest moon. Back in 1933, several well respected people were said to have seen it.

The newspaper of the day, the *St Paul Journal*, was quoted as follows:

"A farmer, crossing the lake in a small boat saw quite clearly the head of a white horse emerge from the water with glaring eyes and gaping jaws. It uttered a long rollicking laugh more than equine, lashed a long white tail in the air and disappeared beneath the surface. The horse or whatever it was cracked its tail louder than a rifle shot. The next night, the same unbelievable sight was witnessed by three men who were swimming in the lake, all good honest fellows. It is not on record that any disastrous effects followed, but it is certainly a strange, eerie, inexplicable thing."

Press coverage, which extended to other regional newspapers either confused the ghostly horse with a lake monster or regarded it as a hoax.

American ghosts are usually far more terrifying, as shown by a story that appeared in the Quebec newspaper *The Stanstead Journal* for January 6, 1898. Headlined "Headless Woman's Ghost," it mentioned the appearance of a phantom that bothered railwaymen on the Baltimore and Ohio West Virginia Central railway. The location was a spot known as Greenwade's Siding, between Cumberland and Keyser, West Virginia, where freight trains were stored. While the railwaymen waited, a headless woman emerged from an old culvert or bridge and walked up and down the track. Whenever anyone attempted to follow her, she disappeared. One man became so frightened that he left his job, and several other employees were also thinking about doing so if the materializations did not come to a halt. Another railwayman was so horrified he actually crawled under the locomotive to avoid seeing the headless object. The ghost was reported to appear almost nightly.

Trader King's Ghost

Likely the earliest ghost story in the Canadian West was that of King's ghost. However, this was more in the nature of a deathbed or crisis apparition. In 1803, there were only a handful of people on the Canadian plains – trappers and traders and some tribesmen. Fort Augustus was one of the few points of civilization, and, in January of 1803, a tough-minded Scottish trader was compelled to record some unusual events in his diary.

After receiving word from an local camp that they would be open to trade, a trader named King was sent out by the North West Company, not realizing that another bad-tempered trader named La Mothe, who was employed by the rival XY Company, would also be on the scene. As he fitted out his sleighs for the journey to the encampment a day away, the agent at the fort came over to warn, "Take care, King. Be careful of La Mothe. La Mothe may shoot you." King replied laughingly, "To be shot by La Mothe...that would be a good joke indeed."

Several days later, King's wife, a Native American girl, was sleeping in their tent at Fort Augustus along with their six-year-old daughter. A strong fire was burning to keep out the cold, when suddenly Mrs King was awakened by a whimper from the little girl, who said, "Mother, there is father at the foot of the bed...his neck is all red." Mrs. King assumed it was all just a dream and told the girl to go back to sleep. Then it happened a second time – the same vision of her father with an injury to his neck. The following morning, the mother was so disturbed by the dream that she told it to many inside the fort, including John McDonald. Nothing was thought of it until the following afternoon, when King's party was spotted returning back to the fort. Oddly, there was no sign of King himself, but as they drew nearer, the reason became clear. He was dead, shot through the throat by La Mothe after a violent argument. La Mothe was arrested and sent to Montreal for trial, where he was acquitted. King was buried on Edmonton's Rossdale flat with the full military honors of the North West Company.

Holding Up the Stage

Many miles to the south and nearly a century later, on September 4, 1897, some different ghosts were on the prowl, although the causes (human propensity for violent acts) were the same. As reported in the *Sherbrooke* (Quebec) *Daily Record*: "GHOSTS IN ARIZONA Said to Appear Annually Near Skull Creek," the story was related by a local resident, Col Ham Spingett. He claimed that there was a gully about ten miles out of Boneville on Skull Creek, inhabited by bandit ghosts who rode in once a year on the anniversary of their deaths. The district had been plagued by a series of stagecoach robberies until finally Judge Smith, a leading businessman, determined that something had to be done to halt the depredations. He called a meeting and a plan was mapped out whereby 20 or so men with rifles would go out to Skull Creek and wait in ambush at the end of a long bridge. It was at this point that the stage was usually held up, and a row of crosses near the creek bank testified to the bloodshed.

Eventually the inbound stage appeared. As it rolled onto the bridge, there was a volley of shots and six men on horseback came roaring onto the bridge, following the stage. Just before the stage reached the ambush, the driver fell off the box, hit by a shot, whereupon the horses swerved and went into the creek carrying the stage and the passengers. The gang on horseback reined in just as they reached the ambush, and shots rang out. When the smoke cleared away, there were six dead men and six dead horses. The stage was retrieved from the creek, but the horses pulling it were so badly injured they had to be killed. One of the passengers, a woman coming out to join her husband, was found to be dead along with the stage driver. Both of their bodies were brought into town, but the dead robbers were dumped unceremoniously into a deep cut near the creek and covered up.

A year passed, and the extermination of the gang was largely forgotten. A man from the town decided to go out hunting near Skull

Creek. It took longer than he expected and dusk caught him near the bridge. Suddenly he heard a rattle of wheels, and looking back at the bridge, he saw a stagecoach coming at a terrific rate of speed.

The Phantom Stagecoach

This was particularly astonishing, because he knew the stage wasn't due to arrive until the following day. Then he saw six men on horseback tearing along behind the stage, firing guns. Too frightened to run, he watched as the driver was hit and tumbled off the box. The horses and stage went into the creek, and the next minute, a cloud seemed to hide all the light. When it cleared, there wasn't anything in sight except the trees, the bridge and the creek. Puzzled, he suddenly came to the realization that he was seeing something supernatural when he spotted the crosses on the creek bank. He ran into town and never went back.

Every year subsequently, when the date of the massacre came around, anyone near the bridge would see the reenactment. Colonel Spingett claimed to have seen it twice himself and confessed he would not have stayed for the whole show had he been alone. He said: "It's awful ter see the sight. You can hear the roll of the wheels, heavy like the rattle of a smothered drum beating the funeral march, and the pounding of the animals' hooves upon the boards seems deadened, jest for the world like you hear them a long way off, and then, too, the shots come in your ear like you done heard them in a dream. You see it all, and then a cloud 'pears to hide everything, and when it clears away thar ain't a thing in sight 'cept yourselves."

This case, which was also reported in the New Orleans *Times Democrat* of the day, has some very modern implications. It has been noted with regularity that place names are often an indicator of weird events. Skull Creek in the U.S. and Ghost River in Canada are but a few of many examples.

Isabella Brown

There are phantoms who communicate on a personal level, which seems to indicate a surviving personality. One such resides in Canada's Kilmorey Lodge in Waterton National Park The ghost is believed to be Isabella Brown, the Cree wife of Kootenai Brown, the famous mountain man, guide and explorer. Several guests in the lodge have seen an elderly woman wearing a light blue and white dress in their rooms, generally in the middle of the night. A spiritualist brought in by the owner says the ghost is a friendly entity who likes to sit in a comfortable chair covered by red velvet near the main entrance. The ghost never bothers guests or creates any problems whatsoever. In short, it is the typical Canadian spirit: quiet and polite, with a reputation for bringing good luck. The owner of the lodge, Gerry Muza, says that about three guests have seen the ghost in the time he has been running the business. "I've never seen it myself. Maybe I'm not sensitive enough."

Isabella Brown died on April 1, 1935, and is buried next to her husband and his first wife.

It may be that such ghosts who can and do communicate with the living exist in a higher dimension, one that is vertical rather than horizontal, such as the repetitive stagecoach robbery. This implies that there are at least two different types of hauntings, and the structure of space-time is much different than we suppose.

Certainly, we can learn much from these old stories regarding our respective national characteristics, and even how the nature of reality works, providing we pay attention to what may seem to be inconsequential details.

W. Ritchie Benedict *is a freelance writer, researcher, and lecturer residing in Calgary, Alberta, Canada.*

THE GAY PHANTOMS IN OUR LIVING ROOM
By William H. Runk

"There may be a rational explanation for our pixilated prewar Danish spooks – but if there is, we should be pleased not to know about it."

During the years 1938 and 1939, just prior to the invasion of Denmark by the Germans, William H. Runk and his wife Ruth occupied a pleasant and entirely satisfactory house at Kastelsvej 36, next to the embassy in Copenhagen. They came to believe, with good reason apparently, that they were sharing the premises with unknown and inexplicable company. However, the Runks' feelings towards whoever or whatever it was that visited them remained cordial and friendly and they managed not to feel the slightest uneasiness about the matter. However, performances were put on regularly for them and occasionally for friends and visitors in a most insistent and convincing manner and Mr. Runk considered them significant enough to record. He left the following written description of their experiences to his step-daughter Barbara Darr who attests that they are true. Miss Darr gave the manuscript to her friend Yolana Lux who, finding the original in poor condition after all these years, retyped and edited it.

The house we rented in Copenhagen is one of three, built a good many years ago on a secluded and tree-studded patch of ground which lies a bit back from the street. It was in the gold and lavender glow of spring that we moved into our house. The chores connected with getting settled were about complete and I was alone one Saturday afternoon and comfortably reading in the living room when I became conscious of a light tapping noise. The living room measured eight by nine metres (approximately 26 feet by 30 feet) with a ceiling four metres (13 feet) high. The sound seemed to issue from one of the walls and came with varying intensity but at regular intervals.

After listening to it for a while I shut the sound from my mind and continued reading but each time I inadvertently stopped to listen there it was again – a steady tap, tap, tapping. Finally I left the room and asked Elizabeth, our maid, to listen and to assure me I was not imagining things.

Elizabeth immediately said, "Yes, I have heard that sound

many times. I have been watching for signs of a water leak because I thought there must be water dripping somewhere within the wall but it seemed to me to be in the wall in the hall."

We returned to the room where I had heard the sound but it had stopped there and now, strangely enough, apparently came from the hall leading to the living room where the maid said she had heard it. In order to check on the possibility of a water leak we explored the ceiling of the cellar but found no damp spots. Elizabeth then looked up the caretaker of the property to consult him about a possible water drip in the walls but he stated positively there could not be one as there was no built-in piping.

Our next and obvious thought was that we were dealing with one of the various types of beetles which often inhabit the beams and woodwork of old houses and make life miserable for the superstitious. Elizabeth and I therefore set out in earnest to locate the exact spot where the beetles might be working so that the proper steps might be taken to get rid of it. We spent considerable time on that hunt and finally had to give it up. At times we thought we definitely had located the worker in the walls of the living room but when we approached the spot the tapping would cease, to be resumed almost immediately under the flooring. Then as soon as we got right up to the spot where we were sure it must be the tap, tap, tapping would seem to come from the wall of the room again.

We did determine that the sounds never came simultaneously from two locations at the same time. We tried investigating the walls and the floor simultaneously but when we did this, we found that the tapping would begin in an entirely different spot, where neither of us had heard it previously. We would move to the suspected spot ever so stealthily and set up all manner of scaffolding to take our weight from floorboards and joists so that no slight sound would betray our approach and thus cause the elusive bug to transfer himself quickly to another spot. These methods brought no success.

While these "scientific" investigations were going on my wife returned and was not to be dissuaded from laughing and speaking with considerable sarcasm about all the trouble I had been to in order to locate a harmless little beetle. But after she had listened a while and convinced herself that the tapping was not imaginary we started on a three-man hunt, adding further ingenuities to the chase.

At last we looked at one another and the same thought was in our minds: there was nothing to be done about the business and if we were dealing with a beetle it surely was an active one and either endowed with powers of ventriloquism or possessing a well-developed subway system and some means of rapid transit, because no bug ever had legs that enabled him to move with the speed this one showed!

So we lived with the tap. And it seemed to be going on as often as we stopped to listen for it. We even developed a liking for it and as time went on we endowed it with a personality. However, our friends did not feel friendly towards it. At first, when one or two visitors were present and conversation quieted down as it sometimes will, one of them would stir uneasily and finally ask, "I say, what is this? Am I hearing things or have you a little spook about the house? I don't feel comfortable."

Then we would explain and the visitor would try to locate the sound only to give it up as we had. But eventually our friends also stopped worrying about the business and referred to it as our "spook." Only one or two said, "How can you live here? Doesn't that worry you?"

Well, no, it did not worry us. But there were other things to come.

Our bedroom was connected with the living room by a French door, which means that the seal between the two rooms was not very tight and what went on in the living room could readily be heard in the bedroom. Nevertheless, the sound of the tapping was not audible in the bedroom when the door was closed.

One night I was awakened suddenly from a sound sleep and found myself sitting bolt upright, listening. Something had disturbed me and there was no mistake about it for the same thing had happened to my wife. We knew there was someone moving about in the living room! I reached for a torch, went quietly to the door and flung it open wide, snapping on the torch at the same time. I felt certain that I should see a startled burglar dive out of a window. But there was no-one in the room and no one had been there.

My wife and I both were absolutely certain that some sound or commotion in the living room had awakened us. We both sleep soundly and do not awaken readily; neither are we easily unsettled and therefore we were soon asleep again.

One night, shortly after this unusual but possibly not inexplicable experience, we had retired late when my wife remembered something she wanted to arrange for the next day. She went to the front part of the house, leaving the door to the living room open. After she had left the room I noticed that the tapping was going on at a great rate. When my wife returned I heard or thought I heard, tramp, tramp, tramp, someone's footsteps walking along with her or following her through the living room. The sounds were unmistakable but as I have tried to explain there was nothing of menace, fright or uneasiness conveyed to us by this happening.

I simply said, "Who's your friend out there?"

And I recall her answer, "Just the spook. Clubby, isn't he?"

We felt that this rather intimate demonstration of friendliness was due to our having taken the previous experiences calmly and as something that could happen to us only in Denmark.

Naturally we were interested and listened attentively after my wife had closed the door. There were a few moments of silence and then we both heard something or felt something that only the presence of people can bring or give. It was not that we could distinguish voices, words or phrases, nor could we hear laughter, but we felt unquestionably the presence of a group of people. Just for the sake of formality I opened the door and swung the torch beam around the room. Nothing unusual was to be seen and except for the tapping the room was silent. (No, there was no party going on in a neighbour's house.)

This same experience was repeated many times after that and if we did not burst into the room it would continue for some time. With the exception of the one occasion I have described we were not again disturbed in our sleep again. With careful choice of words I must state that we rather enjoyed these goings-on. This is not stated in bravado but things were generally so pleasant for us in Denmark that we never doubted that whatever spook or spooks were favouring that house and us with their attentions would not do us harm. Further indication of our attitude can be taken from the fact that I frequently was away in Norway and Sweden and my wife would be alone at such times. She never minded this in the least. When I returned after several days' absence I frequently would include in my usual questions about how things had gone, "And how was the spook? Were there any more parties?" My wife would reply matter-of-factly and never expressed uneasiness – although she might remark, "The other night they did carry on a bit."

Elizabeth also took these mild demonstrations with typical Danish calm. She would sometimes smile and say, "Yes, I guess we have *spogelse* here." But she never showed any alarm.

Our friends thought our accounts of these occurrences rather strange. Once a friend of my wife had occasion to check them. My wife had a broken collarbone and was forced to remain in bed for a few days. One evening a Danish friend, Toby Eirhleshon, and Bine, her personable little wirehaired terrier, came to see her. Bine often had visited us and knew all about the tap. She had expressed interest the first time she heard it and indicated her willingness to tear down the wall or dig up the floor to locate the sound but then she had backed off with her hair standing on end. She had growled slightly, looked up at us in a puzzled manner and never again showed any interest in the tapping – other than to give a wide berth to the spot where she imagined it to be.

On this particular evening we were seated in the bedroom. The door to the living room was partly open and Toby was talking to my wife. Bine, who had been lying quietly nearby, suddenly jumped to her feet, cocked her head and walked to the door to stare into the darkness of the living room. The presence or consciousness of people in the living room which we knew so well by that time was evident. Bine listened a moment, the hair on her back rose, she whined a little and backed away.

Toby was mystified and said, "Look, Bine is frightened at something."

We told her to listen and she said, "That's what you have been talking about! I feel it too. It's a shame that this nice house should have this and of course you don't want to move."

I went into the living room and turned on the light. Bine quieted right down. The tapping then started ever so softly but Bine paid no attention to it and offered no objections to passing through the living room on her way to the front door when it was time to go home. She did, however, make a wide circle around the section of the room where she imagined the tapping to be.

We did not think of moving from these pleasant quarters and by and by none of our friends thought we should so long as we could take the queer phenomena so easily.

We lived there happily until we were awakened by a cannon shot and the sound of low-flying planes a little before six o'clock on the morning of April 9, 1940. Unfortunately for Denmark and for us it was not the spook this time.

It was a month before we were permitted to leave Denmark. After the enemy came we did not once hear the tapping, the footsteps or entertain the strange impression that a group of people were in the living room. The enemy had driven even our spooks from their accustomed haunts.

All this seems queer and unreal as I write it thousands of miles from Denmark. But the manifestations or whatever one wants to call them made such an impression on us that even here and now we find ourselves listening for our friendly tap and the gay phantom crowd which visited our living room in Kastelsvej.

Possibly there is an explanation for these matters which ties up with well known physical laws; if so we should be pleased not to know of it. In a world where everything is being reduced to mathematical formulae we are happy to have had an experience which to us still has the mystery that can come only from the visitation of a spook.

THE GHOSTLY GENERAL WAYNE
by Guy Arseneau

For almost three hundred years, the General Wayne Inn has greeted travellers and townsfolk in the Philadelphia suburb of Merion, Pennsylvania. The colonial edifice has sheltered a number of remarkable figures.

Benjamin Franklin regularly conducted postal business from the inn's present-day banqueting hall. In the course of winning America's independence, George Washington and the Marquis de Lafayette took advantage of the inn's comfortable accommodation. Initially called the Wayside Inn and later known as the Tunis Ordinary, the establishment's current name stuck after a lavish celebration honoring local military veteran "Mad" Anthony Wayne in 1795. The inn, where a night's lodging could be had for a quarter, was a favourite meeting place for affluent eighteenth-century travellers.

Some of those guests may never have left.

Said to be America's oldest restaurant, the General Wayne survived the invasion of British and Colonial troops, a one-year closure during Prohibition, and a fire in the 1960s. The establishment also faces an enduring challenge – ghosts. Even confirmed sceptics who have experienced the General Wayne's paranormal activity swear the inn is haunted.

Sitting in his long, narrow office, a room dominated by a modern computer and a fax machine, current owner Barton Johnson related his own nerve-shaking experience in this most peculiar inn.

"A couple of years ago I was sitting at the corner of the bar. It was a little after midnight and the cloakroom girl, the piano player, and I were having a conversation – though not about ghosts, I can assure you. Now bear in mind, nobody was drunk or anywhere near it, so don't write this off as a story from someone with too much bubbly in them. I heard a noise above my head and looked up to the ceiling over the bar. A large metal ball emerged from the panel and dropped to the floor. After sitting there a few seconds it began to roll by itself and it stopped right in front of me. That was weird enough, but what happened next I swear is true. I picked it up to get a good look at the thing and it just disappeared. I mean, one moment a solid metal object was in my hands and the next second it dematerialized. Believe me, all three of us were speechless."

Bizarre as the experience was for Johnson and his companions, it represents just one link in a chain of inexplicable events now considered commonplace at the General Wayne. In the late 1980s, a young kitchen helper was terrified when a human head mysteriously appeared on a kitchen counter. He resigned on the spot and hasn't been back since.

Drew Johnson, Barton's son and the inn's daytime manager, said, "It's impossible to tell who will or won't have an unusual experience here. Among our employees we've had people who have worked here for twenty years and seen nothing. Others have been here twenty minutes and had a paranormal encounter."

Supernatural happenings are common throughout the building. The first floor serves as a private banquet area. From time to time people dining in these rooms ask about the waiter dressed up in colonial costume. One woman reported that just such a waiter emerged from the upstairs men's room, passed out menus to the woman and her companions and walked out of the room. When he failed to return to take their orders, she asked about the man "dressed up for a Fourth of July parade". She was informed that no staff member of the General Wayne ever wears early American attire.

Other stories from the inn suggest that two soldiers haunt the inn. Reportedly, the Hessian hired guns complained about how the English officers treated them. On occasion, a colonial barmaid has been seen with the soldiers or by herself in a nearby graveyard.

The Raven's Roost
Along with its role in America's developing political identity, the General Wayne was a favourite hangout for Edgar Allen Poe, the dark genius who penned "The Pit and the Pendulum", "Masque of the Red Death" and "The Raven". Addicted to an opium deriviative, the writer travelled by stagecoach from Philadelphia to the inn, where he would meet his drug supplier, a blacksmith who worked directly across the street.

Poe's ghost has been spotted in the room known as the Franklin Post Office. Visitors also can see the spot where Poe used a diamond to etch his initials into a window pane. Dressed in either a nineteenth-century suit or a military uniform, he has appeared wandering through the room, on at least one occasion mocking his own portrait.

The inn is the centre of local media attention every Halloween. Spirits indulge in mischievous antics at the General Wayne, much to the puzzlement of the Johnsons and their customers. Barton Johnson recalled an incident several years ago. "A local TV station came out here to do a story on the place. When it was broadcast a couple of days later we had the set on in the bar area. As our segment came up, the picture began slowly rotating until it was completely upside down. Nobody else in the neighbourhood experienced this problem. Our TV was in perfect working order, and the television people assured us there was no problem with their equipment."

When asked if he believed in ghosts, the elder Johnson sighed. "Yes," he said, "but not by choice. When I think of everything I've seen around here, along with what others have told me, I don't have much choice but to believe in them.

"I can't say, though, that I think very much of their sense of humour, and here's why. For a long time Pennsylvania had in effect what are called 'Blue Laws'. Simply put, it meant you couldn't sell liquor on Sunday. When the law changed so did we, like a lot of other places. The first Monday after we started this I came in early, and frankly, I didn't like what I saw.

"Like most businesses that deal in cash, we leave our cash register drawer open so would-be robbers don't break it. On that particular day the cash drawer was full of water, the rack that runs around the base of the bar was full of water, and about forty carafes that I know for a fact were empty the night before were all filled with water. I was the last one out the night before, the first person in that morning, and yes, the plumbing was checked and there were no problems. If there's a reason they pulled this, I'm still waiting to find out what it is."

For some of the employees, frayed nerves are just part of the job. Employee George Silli related his own encounter with things unseen. 'That secret room they discovered a few years ago, down in the basement? Well, for a while we used to store wine in there. I was down there once looking for a particular bottle and all of a sudden it happened. The light bulb went out and the door slammed shut. Nobody else was in that basement, and there was certainly no wind coming in to slam the door. Other people have told me the same thing has happened to them and that they felt a sudden drop in temperature. To this day, I hate going down there."

Off to one side of the inn's dark, intimate bar, an ornate iron grille resembling a baroque church confessional houses the more expensive brands of champagne. Running the length of the bar and firmly attached to sturdy overhead beams, a wooden rack provides a storage area for hundreds of glasses.

Periodically the glasses begin to dance. "There's no rhyme or reason to it, at least as far as we can see," said Drew Johnson. "Sometimes the whole thing just starts to shake violently. The noise is bad enough, but when you step back a couple of feet and realize you're the only one in the room, it brings up the goosepimples. Once it got really bad. Once a day for six in a row straight the whole thing just started to shake. We checked with the earthquake centres and they told us there wasn't even a tremor in the area."

Reports of the inn's strange happenings serve as a magnet for the curious, psychic wannabes and a wide assortment of no-frills weirdos. Drew Johnson remembers one man who drove all the way from Iowa after seeing the General Wayne featured on television's *Unsolved Mysteries*. While the Johnsons are wary of seers, one local man's paranormal abilities have earned their attention and respect.

The Psychic Connection

Walt Bauer, a thirty-one-year-old lorry driver, was an average bloke until February 1991, when he almost died in a freak accident. Bauer's brush with death brought him into contact with what he believes is another dimension of existence.

"As I remember it," he said, "I was helping with a load of phone cable. We had a manhole cover off and had started feeding cable underground, when I raised my head and was struck full force by a crane." The impact of the blow was so great the words "patent pending" were embedded in Bauer's forehead for several days.

"I saw my grandfather, and he said to me, 'What are you doing here?' I asked him the same thing and he said, 'Walt, if you can see me that means you're dead, but it's not your time yet.' With that he raised his hand toward me and the next thing I knew I was tumbling head over heels back into my physical body."

Although he still has no conscious memory of it, Bauer says co-workers later told him that moments after he was pronounced dead he sat upright and said, "Grandpa, I want to stay with you."

His nearly year-long recovery was punctuated by severe migraine headaches and partial paralysis on the left side of his body. Adding to his physical distress was the disturbing new ability to see people and entities no-one else could see or hear. At the urging of his family he sought psychiatric help, but emotional disturbance and organic brain damage were quickly ruled out.

His contact with the spirit world was growing routine, but it was a point of contention between him and his wife, who was convinced he was under satanic influences. Unable to accept his strange new powers, the couple divorced. Confused and often unsure of what his abilities meant, Bauer decided to learn more about them.

"One night I woke up around 3.00 a.m. and saw the walls of my bedroom just disappear. In their place was a large glass-like tunnel with stars all around the sides. A man came walking down this tunnel and told me his name was Joe. He asked me to tell my neighbours that he was around them and always watched out for their safety.

"When he turned to walk away, I said goodbye and he became very irate. 'No, not goodbye, just so long for now. There is no such thing as goodbye.' The next morning I told my neighbours about the experience. They brought out an armload of photos, none of which had any names on them. Right away I spotted the man among their photo collection.

"'That's my father,' my neighbour said, 'but he's been dead since 1965.' When I told them what the man had said about saying goodbye, my neighbour confirmed that that had always been a sticking point with his father, whose name was indeed Joe."

Bauer's unusual powers soon came to the attention of David O'Reilly, a reporter for the *Philadelphia Inquirer*. Struck by the lorry driver's reputation for supernatural insights, he suggested he and Bauer visit the General Wayne to see what, if anything, might happen.

"The moment I walked in there it was like being hit over the head," Bauer said. "In all, I felt the presence of eighteen different spirits inhabiting the place."

Drew Johnson vividly recalls his first meeting with Bauer. "Walt's intimate knowledge of the place and details he provided about each room caught us by surprise. He'd never been here before, yet he walked around and pointed out things and facts to us that he would have no way of knowing. This guy is no average lorry driver.

I walked with Walt from room to room. Before entering a doorway, he would stop, fall silent, and appear to be straining to hear someone. After a few moments he'd tell us what was in the room, describe in detail a certain painting and where it was hanging, tell us where a vase or other object would be and then tell us if any spirits were present."

Just over six feet tall and sporting an extensive beard, Walt Bauer is anything but the proverbial sunken eyed, frail mystic. Unlike some professional seers, Bauer acknowledges the doubts some people have about his gifts. "To tell you the truth, if nothing had ever happened to me and someone told me they could see and talk to people I couldn't see, I think I'd have some trouble believing that, too. But for a lot of people I think it's fear that keeps them from accepting anything they can't see or touch. I don't judge them. Hell, I have plenty of fears of my own."

Sceptics aside, Bauer's abilities carry considerable weight with a surprising number of people in the public eye, including comedienne and talk show host Joan Rivers. Intrigued by the idea of doing her show from a haunted house, she sought Walt Bauer as a guide. The two of them, along with her production staff, decided to peer into the Great Beyond at the General Wayne.

Joan Rivers at the General Wayne Inn

Joan Rivers has more than a theatrical interest in the occult. A strong believer in the paranormal, she was convinced that her luxurious New York apartment was haunted by the spirit of the previous tenant. In an effort to give the soul some rest, she had her residence blessed by a rabbi and a Catholic priest. "Sometimes I think Joan has some psychic ability herself," said Suzie Pileggi, a long-time staffer and producer for Rivers. "Her hunches are too right too often to be just coincidence."

During an overnight stay at the General Wayne, Joan Rivers and company journeyed into a reality all have heard about but few understand. "There were some weird things going on at that place," Pileggi said. "For instance, Joan always likes to travel with her dogs. On this trip she brought her Yorkie Spike with her as she toured the inn. In one of the upstairs rooms Joan didn't see anything, but her dog did. Spike started barking wildly, jumped out of Joan's arms, and ran all over the place trying to find a way out of there.

"Joan later complained that someone had pinched her while

she was standing on the staircase leading to the private dining rooms. When it happened, there was no-one we could see within twenty feet of her. Walt kept telling us that one of the spirits, Alexander, was going to play a trick on everyone.

"For myself, I believe in the supernatural. I brought two cameras along and took pictures in the basement using a 35mm camera and a Polaroid. The 35mm shots were normal but the Polaroid shots revealed a skull in some of the pictures. The whole experience was a strain on everyone."

Bauer's prediction that Alexander would play a trick on the crew seemed to be fulfilled once the videotape was back in the New York studios. "We use a state-of-the-art Beta tape machine to make duplicate copies of the master," Pileggi said.

"This way we have three tapes we can edit in and out from. When we put the General Wayne tapes in the machine things got crazy – the machine literally spit them out. An engineer told me the chances of this happening were about the same as someone winning a state lottery three weeks in a row, using the same numbers each week.

We offer viewers transcripts of our show and on this particular programme we had three segments altogether. The first two transcripts were perfect, but the thirteen pages dealing with the inn were just gibberish. The typist is a professional, the printer was in working order, and the word processor was normal. I can't help but believe that whoever or whatever Alexander is or was, he kept his promise to play a trick on us."

The workers at the General Wayne view the spirits there as mysterious but generally harmless – even when they play tricks. Dan Friedman related an experience he had his first night. "The inn was closed and I had just finished setting up the tables for the following day. I turned away for a few moments, and when I looked back, one table had been messed up and stripped of the tablecloth. Kind of weird since I was the only one there."

Porter Sean Halpin agreed. "Nothing's happened to me yet, but from what I hear, it's only a matter of time.

A GHOST AT RELAIS DE L'EMPEREUR

The Relais de l'Empereur is an imposing structure in the small city of Petit Goave, on the southern peninsula of Haiti. The large edifice was originally the home of Faustin I, Haiti's first and only Emperor. It was later converted into a hotel, and a pretty creepy one at that.

I had decided to visit the hotel because of its historical connections and exotic atmosphere. The building takes up a whole city block. Inside is a courtyard with a cage that once housed a jaguar. These days it is empty and sad.

The rooms are incredible – literally fit for an emperor. There is a gigantic bathtub on a dais in the middle of the room. It looks more like a ship or a swan. The windows are actually French doors which open onto a balcony.

Before I went to bed I made sure the French doors were shut. I woke up in the middle of the night and saw a young boy standing in our room. He was wet and shivering, as if he had come in from the rain. All the doors were shut, and it was not raining. I said to my boyfriend, who was sleeping next to me, "There's someone here!" I did not realize at the time that it was a ghost. My boyfriend threw a pillow in the direction that I was pointing (he never saw the boy). The apparition disappeared. The boy was gone.

The next day I asked the man at the front desk if anyone had ever reported seeing a ghost. He told me no, and I told him about my experience. Later, when I told my Haitian friends about what happened, they said that the Relais de L'Empereur was known to be haunted. I realized then that of course the man at the front desk wouldn't admit that there were ghosts at the hotel – it might hurt his business. But after learning that the hotel is no longer open, maybe it already has.

– *Rebecca Day, Harlingen, Texas*

THE GHOST OF LEBUFFET
by P. Walker Hastings

Opening a new business in an unfamiliar setting can be an unnerving experience for even the pluckiest of entrepreneurs. But when the ring of the cash register far exceeds expectations, few ever claim the event to be hair-raising.

Rumours that yet another restaurant had opened at a former veterans welfare organization hall spread like wildfire through the quaint hill country village of Wimberley, Texas. The new owners, however, were disheartened by comments made by residents they talked with.

Backhanded well-wishers said, "I wish him luck. He's gonna need it." Others proclaimed, "There's something about that place that just isn't right." To bolster their claims they listed the five restaurants that had come and gone in as many years, some lasting only a few months.

Disregarding these observations, restaurateur Mike Poston plunged ahead, and LeBuffet Restaurant's opening day exceeded his expectations. Hungry residents arrived to relish his culinary preparations, and for a while Poston was a happy man.

After a few weeks, his enthusiasm began to ebb, and he started to feel that something was definitely amiss. He had been open about two months when he called and asked if I would come to the restaurant, saying, "I've got a little investigation I'd like done."

I had first met Mike about 10 years before in the neighbouring town, Dripping Springs, where he owns a successful cafe. I was just beginning a career in journalism and Mike served the best coffee in town. His place became a regular haunt for our staff. After leaving the paper to become a freelance writer for a crime magazine, I continued to visit Mike, sharing the latest gossip. Mike's call piqued my curiosity, and I arrived the next day, several hours before the restaurant opened. Mike poured each of us a fresh cup of coffee. There was strain on his face that I'd never seen before.

He stirred his coffee slowly and stared into the steaming brew before speaking. "I don't know where to start," he sighed. "At first it was just a feeling, like someone was in the building when I knew it was empty. Even though business was great, I dreaded coming in the doors and I just couldn't figure out why. It was just a feeling, depressing, I guess you'd say. I began to wish I'd never opened up. Then," he added, while glancing toward the kitchen, "the pans began flying off the shelves."

I stared at him for several seconds, not knowing exactly what to say. I'd known Mike long enough to know he was a level-headed, no-nonsense type, but what he was saying didn't quite register.

Finally finding my voice, I asked, "What exactly are you saying, Mike?"

"Well," he replied, "I guess I'm saying this place is haunted. I want you to find out everything you can about it. How it was bought and sold, and as much as you can about the original owner. I've got a feeling it's him."

The investigation

I began my investigation by interviewing the people who worked in the restaurant. Several of the 15 employees had tales to tell. Debbie French, a waitress, and Phillip Sellstrom, the assistant cook, told me how one evening the volume on the entertainment centre rose to blast out the strains of Willie Nelson's "Red Headed Stranger".

Phillip, who had witnessed the flying pans on more than one occasion, had had his hands full with a pot of boiling potatoes when Debbie burst through the swinging doors.

"I reached over and turned the dial back down," she told me. "There was no way anybody could have turned that dial up and moved away without me seeing them through the glass in the door."

During the next several weeks of my investigation, all the employees reported that the hood lights over the kitchen cooker would flicker off, though the fuses were not thrown and a professional inspection of the electrical system revealed nothing out of order. The same was true of the floodlight that illuminates the car park. On occasion it would turn off for several hours.

Another anomaly is the music box which Poston proudly displays on the restaurants mantleplace. It plays "Happy Days Are Here Again". Several staff members, including Poston, have heard the music playing when no-one is near the box on the mantlepiece.

While these events left Poston and his staff unnerved, nothing compared with what Poston experienced as he began his kitchen chores one morning:

"I was lighting the burners on the cooker when I felt like someone was watching me. I thought Phillip had come in early, and I turned, expecting to see him." Instead, what Poston saw made the hair on the back of his neck stand on end. "For a brief second I saw a man, 5 feet 11 inches or 6 feet tall, standing by the door. He just vanished into thin air. It scared the...well, it scared me pretty bad."

Poston told his staff and several regular customers about the occurrence. Finally, the rumours that had been flying around came home to roost, and Poston learned from local residents that many believed the location to be jinxed.

The jinx, they said, began when the original owner sold the property to the veterans' organization. Upon the original owner's death, the veteran's group sold the property to finance a larger facility at a new location. The original owner had been Edward James, a Houstonian who had developed the Eagle Rock Ranch Club and Resort, now known as Woodcreek Resort.

Poston was still mulling this information over when one night he awoke to find the car park floodlight off again. Looking out into the darkness from the small window of his caravan parked at the rear of the restaurant, Poston said, "Okay, Mr James, I know it's you." The light immediately came back on.

Since that day Poston has opened his business doors, saying, "Good morning, Mr James," and closed the restaurant with, "Good night, Mr James."

"The depressing feeling left as soon as I began calling him by name," reports Poston. "I think he wants me here. I think he likes me. I just wish I understood more about why this is happening. I am a God-fearing man, raised in the Catholic church. I never believed in all this mumbo jumbo ghost business. But I have to admit, I do now.

Though I attempted to contact all of the former restaurant owners at this location, only one would allow himself to be quoted. Local resident Robert Chaney operated the Park Restaurant in the old veterans' hall for several months before closing its doors. "I think a lot of the locals just take it for granted that the place is jinxed. Some say the veterans' welfare organization should never have moved. I had some of my staff members tell me about things that happened there that they thought were brought on by bad energy. I don't know. I just walked in one day and said to myself, 'This is not what I want to be doing.'"

Psychic readings

Two psychics were contacted in hope of shedding light on the situation. Local psychic Judith Black, who has written several books, asked her spirit contact, master Tai Won Chu One, about the spirit entity at the restaurant. She received a lengthy message that said the entity was Edward C. James and that he is pleased that Poston has opened the business, but he was not pleased with the former operators. The medium also revealed that it would please Edward James to have his portrait hung in the establishment as benefactor of the property.

Next, we contacted Susan James, the only child of Edward and Evelyn Davis James. Susan shared her insights into her father's personality and the sale of the property to the veterans' organization:

"My father," she said, "died at age 68 in Huntington Beach, California, on September 1, 1970, of liver failure. He was a man who loved to party, and I guess it finally killed him. He bought the Wimberley property in 1946 and lived there until 1955. He loved Wimberley; he was like a kid about it. He's the one who had the steps built up Mt Baldy. He ran an electricity cable all the way up that mountain to run a jukebox so people could dance up there on top. He just wanted people to have fun."

Edward C. James was a millionaire who made his money in the tool and die business. He was also known worldwide as the king of the venetian blind industry. The family moved to Wimberley from Houston. Edward dreamed of raising cattle and building a first-class resort where the land was free for all to roam and enjoy. Within a few years the family had built one of the finest resorts in the state, sporting one of the first air-conditioned buildings in the nation.

With the passing of several seasons, requests from visitors to buy land became so numerous that the Jameses decided to expand their venture into a community, with the stipulation that the land would still be open for all to enjoy.

After nearly 30 years, his Houston-based businesses began to go sour and James decided to move his family to California, where he hoped to cash in on better times. He didn't. Within a few years, he was forced to sell the property in Wimberley, but not without one last fight to preserve his dream.

In a case that is still reported to be the longest in Hays County history, James fought from 1958 until late 1959 to retain the rights of the neighbouring property owners to roam the land at will. Though he lost the case, his opponent and new owner of the land, C. B. Smith, stated during an interview, "Edward James is the fairest man I've ever done business with."

Armed with documents provided by Susan James, I researched the sale of the property to the veterans, and found that though Edward James had originally designated the property for their sole use, he later sold the property to the group for the sum of one dollar and removed the previous stipulation concerning its future use or sale.

His daughter recalls, "I remember the day my father died. We were going to the hospital, and when I passed by the dining room table, there were three yellow roses in a vase. They were wilted and I was about to toss them out when my mother called for me to hurry up. He died later that day, and when we got home, I passed that table again and the roses were fresh. That night the lights kept flickering on and off, and we were all convinced it was Daddy. I put those yellow roses on his casket."

Susan had just finished relating this information when Phillip, who did not know she was present, popped into the restaurant's dining room to state, "The lights on the cooker hood are going off and on again."

"Do you remember your father's favorite song?" Poston asked.

"Yes, how could I forget?" Susan replied. "He had two [favourites] and he played them over and over: 'You Are My Sunshine' and 'Happy Days Are Here Again'."

An oil portrait of Edward C. James now hangs over the fireplace at the LeBuffet.

"Business is good," says Poston, "and the oppressive, negative feeling that used to be here is completely gone now. Every once in awhile something extraordinary will happen. When it does, we just smile and know it's our friend, Mr. James."

My mother's dear friend Phyllis Jenkins lived in Mount Martha, Victoria, not far from my parents' house. Phyllis had been widowed for many years and Mother used to visit her weekly for a friendly Bible reading. Over the years they had grown very close, and it was shortly after they met that Phyllis told Mum her true ghost story.

When Phyllis had been a young newlywed, shortly after World War II, she had stayed in a friend's house in Queensland with her husband and their small son. After a stay of a few months the friends moved out, but Phyllis and her family stayed on for several years as tenants. The house was a typical Queensland home, weatherboarded and on stilts. But there was something atypical about its atmosphere.

Apparently, one night as Phyllis was in the bathroom, she was startled when a large man walked past the open doorway – because other than her sleeping son, she was the only occupant in the house at the time. Phyllis searched all the rooms, but she could find no trace of the man.

When her husband and friends returned later that evening, she told them about her encounter. "So you've met our captain," her girlfriend said. She then went on to explain that apparently the house was haunted by the ghost of a sea captain. He was not seen very often, and then only when passing the bathroom when the door was open. At the time, Phyllis didn't know whether to join in the laughter about her encounter or to be frightened about the ghost. After some time had passed, however, having not seen the ghost again, she put the episode out of her mind.

A few months later, Phyllis took her son to the beach for a swim. The tide was a long way out, and they merrily splashed their way from one sandbank to another until they were quite a distance from shore. Suddenly, the sand beneath their feet gave way and they began to sink. Somehow they had found a small stretch of quicksand, and before they could move, their ankles were firmly grasped by the slippery substance, which was pulling them down further. Panicking, Phyllis tried to pull her son out of the quicksand, but her struggles only sank them deeper.

Suddenly, from nowhere, two strong arms ripped them from

the sand sucking around their calves and carried them away from danger. Shocked by the horror of the quicksand, Phyllis barely registered that the strong arms belonged to the sea captain! After a short distance, Phyllis and her son were abruptly set on their feet, standing on a firm sandbank closer to shore. Phyllis turned around to thank their saviour, but found no-one. Turning wildly from side to side, she could not see anyone – they were surrounded by open sand and water. Nobody could have disappeared so quickly. Puzzled but grateful, Phyllis sent a swift prayer of thanks to heaven and quickly made her way back to the beach and home.

From that time until they moved to Victoria, Phyllis and her family saw the ghost of the sea captain on a number of occasions, always passing the bathroom door. She always said, "Thank you," when he passed, although he never acknowledged her. The house took on a feeling of security, one that she missed greatly when she finally moved away.

– *Karin Dallas, Mornington, Victoria, Australia*

GHOST OF JOE'S RIVER
By Edward A. Stoute

It took a destructive hurricane to reveal the reason why the old Barbados manor house was haunted.

ABOUT 175 years ago the plantation called Joe's River, situated in the parish of St Joseph in Barbados belonged to a Mr Holder, who died and left an infant son. His wife had predeceased him and his brother became trustee on behalf of the orphan. The uncle, the child and his nurse, a faithful old African slave, lived in the manor, or "Great House", on the estate.

Sugar was then bringing about $4.40 per hundredweight and the plantation was clear of debt. It was a valuable and desirable property. The uncle, realizing that this delicate child was all that stood between him and ownership suggested to the old nurse that they get rid of the child. The old woman, who had cared for the child since his birth, loved him as her own and refused to be party to any such wicked scheme. She now guarded the child so that he was never out of her sight.

Nevertheless, one morning the whole neighbourhood was appalled to hear of the disappearance of both nurse and child. An intensive search was made for them but no trace could be found. The uncle assumed mourning and made a great show of lamenting the child's death. He now inherited the estate and as the years passed, the incident was almost forgotten. It was forcefully recalled only on the uncle's death.

It is claimed that when the coffin containing the body of the uncle was put into the hearse to be taken to its grave at the nearby parish church, then situated on the lands of the Joe's River plantation, the horses refused to pull the vehicle. They kicked and plunged to such an extent that it was considered advisable to unharness them and substitute another pair of animals. The second pair also refused to move. Under the lash of the whip the horses pranced and reared and the hearse nearly overturned.

The coffin was removed from the hearse and buried in a grave hastily dug on the plantation itself. This was not unusual as in those days the owners of plantations often wished to be buried on their own

211

lands. Many vaults and graves remain standing, well preserved to this day upon the plantations in Barbados.

The peculiar behaviour of the horses reminded the audience that something mysterious had happened to the nurse and child at this same spot years before.

The uncle had ordered a thick wall built across one of the largest rooms in the house, completely dividing it. After his death the plantation house became a sea-side hotel and many of the transient occupants of the divided room were frightened by the spectral appearance of a nurse and child. The house got the reputation of being haunted and was abandoned.

It remained unoccupied and fell into disrepair. The hurricane of 1898 completed the destruction. The wall between the two rooms fell and the skeletons of an infant and a female adult were discovered. These poor remains were reverently interred and it is said that from that time the nurse and child ceased to haunt the house.

The old house has gradually disappeared under the encroaching cane fields. Today all that remains is the old entrance road which is used as a "cart road" for the removal of cut canes but the haunting is remembered.

THE GHOST OF THE MUSICAL MARINER
By Michael Tatlow

What occurred in this house long ago remains only rumour, but four intrepid young men today have evidence of their own senses: whatever happened left its mark.

Near a cliff overlooking the Pacific Ocean in Sydney, Australia, is a lonely pile of charred timber and sandstone. Today it is all that remains of the house where I met the ghost of the musical mariner.

I first heard of this ghost in July, 1964. A friend of mine, who wants to remain anonymous, rang me at my newspaper office and self-consciously reported that a week before he had begun renting a rather ugly sandstone house at 69 Undercliffe Road in Sydney's fashionable northern seaside suburb of Harbord.

"It's nearly 100 years old," my friend said, "but it's comfortable, has two storeys and gives a marvelous view of the sea. And they wanted only twelve dollars a week for it.

"It seemed strange that it was so cheap but I snapped it up. It even has a piano. Strange, that is, until my first night there. So help me, about two in the morning I was in the upstairs bedroom when I was a woken by the sound of a piano playing.

I went to the window wondering what stupid neighbour would be playing at that unearthly hour. Then suddenly I realized that the noise was coming from downstairs, faint but distinct. Beethoven, it was. I recognized snippets from *Moonlight Sonata*.

I switched on the light and ran to the head of the stairs but as soon as I reached there the music stopped."

My friend went on to say he had found the downstairs lounge deserted; the quiet piano stood at the foot of the stairs. Finally, wondering if he had been hallucinating, he had gone back to bed only to be woken again at about 5.00 a.m. by a hissing sound emanating from the bedroom across the small landing at the head of the stairs.

But again as soon as he turned on the light and went to his door the sound stopped. He could find nothing to account for the noise.

"Well, I'm not superstitious," he continued, "but after that I'd had enough. I didn't go back to bed and at nine that morning I packed my things and left for good."

Later that day my friend returned the house key to the property agent and, not wishing to seem a fool, simply told the agent he had received an unexpected transfer in his work.

"Oh, not another one!" the agent, Mr Ken Baynes, of 497 Pittwater Rd., Brookvale, Sydney, had groaned. "I can't get anyone to stay there for long. So you think it's haunted too do you?"

My friend described what had happened.

"In the last few months since the owner vacated it four different tenants have left there telling me similar stories," the agent admitted. "The word is getting around. That's why the rent is so cheap. The owner won't live there either. He's trying to sell the place."

Frankly, the story sounded too unlikely even to justify an investigation – especially by a sceptic like me.

Two weeks later I learned that the popular Sydney bandleader Roland Storm, his mother and three of his musicians had rented the house. Later when I met Roland at a party I casually asked how he had settled into his new residence.

"We didn't settle in at all," he said bluntly. "We spent one week there. Didn't like the location."

"Strange noises in the night by any chance?" I asked.

"How did *you* know?" he replied.

Roland had a fascinating tale to tell. All five of them had heard inexplicable hissings and groanings; doors he and others had locked evidently opened by themselves; certain rooms sometimes took on a cold eerie atmosphere and, yes, they had heard the piano play Beethoven.

I decided to solve this mystery. No doubt there was a logical explanation which, if they had not been so terrified or so superstitious, the previous occupants of the house would have discovered. And perhaps there was a newspaper story in it.

Property agent Baynes soberly told me the house still was vacant and gave me permission to spend a night there.

So at 10.00 p.m. on Friday, September 14, 1964, carrying torches, food, a tape recorder, a thermometer and several spools of black cotton thread, three other investigators and I arrived at the house.

John Heel, of Thornton St, Randwick, a suburb of Sydney. John, who migrated to Australia from Britain several years ago, has

investigated psychic phenomena in Europe and Australia for the past
25 years and admits he believes in ghosts. Geoffrey Kearns of Wingate
Ave, Eastwood, another suburb of Sydney, was to act as John's
assistant. Sydney psychologist Mac Vagg, like me, was intrigued but
confident we would find a logical explanation.

The sky was overcast and despite a slight breeze it was
unnervingly quiet. The only outside sound came from the waves hitting
the nearby beach and the rocks below the cliff. I had to admit the
house looked sinister. It was sited well back from the road on an
overgrown bank. Built of big sandstone blocks, it had ugly upstairs and
downstairs verandas across the front and on one side. It was not a big
house. Upstairs there were just two bedrooms with French windows
opening onto the verandah. The stairs to these bedrooms rose from a
big lounge room which was sparsely furnished with a few comfortable
chairs, some cabinets and an old German piano and there was a
fireplace. A door led into a smaller games room. At the rear of the main
building a single-storey addition, also of sandstone, contained a pantry,
kitchen, laundry and bathroom.

John Heel had learned that the house initially was the home
of a Captain James Albert O'Reilly from San Francisco, formerly the
master of a whaling clipper that sailed the Pacific in the late 1870s.
Local legend had it that O'Reilly, a keen pianist, had murdered his wife
in the bedroom upstairs to the left of the stairs. But, alas, John could
find no documentation. Several old residents of Harbord had told him
the story but he could find no records.

Recently I have learned much more of the legend behind the
ghost of the musical mariner by searching through a Harbord lawyer's
old property records, which, although far from complete, show that a
Captain J. A. O'Reilly owned the house for 12 years from 1881.

The records carry the cryptic notation that Mrs. O'Reilly, at
the age of 47, had died in February, 1882, "by drowning".

The late father of the lawyer also practised law in the district
and after some prodding the lawyer (who does not wish his name used)
told me his father had told him a strange tale about O'Reilly.

By the time he was well into his 40s, the story goes, the
whaling skipper had saved a considerable amount of money. His wife
accompanied him on short voyages. Nonetheless O'Reilly often called
at Papeete, Tahiti, and there fell in love with a beautiful blonde French
girl named Maria. It was believed she was an entertainer. O'Reilly

lavished expensive gifts on her and finally obtained her promise to marry him if he could get rid of his wife. O'Reilly is said to have told her he would have to kill his wife as he was positive she never would grant him a divorce.

O'Reilly recently had bought the then-new house at Harbord, which was known as Freshwater at that time. He told Maria he had enough money to retire and they would make the house their love nest. He said he would return to Sydney, kill his wife then write to tell Maria to sail into his arms.

O'Reilly gave his mistress sufficient money for the voyage from Tahiti to Australia, plus plenty of extra cash. The lawyer remarked that it certainly seemed as if O'Reilly had carried out his part of the scheme.

A few weeks after he returned from Tahiti and signed off from his ship O'Reilly reported that his wife had been swept off a small rowing boat from which they were fishing at night near their home.

The lawyer has only his father's word for it but the legend says O'Reilly in fact had bludgeoned his wife to death as she slept in her separate bedroom. He then rowed her body a short distance out to sea and fed it to the sharks. There is nothing to dispute this, for Mrs. O'Reilly's body never was found.

O'Reilly duly wrote to Maria. Then he began his long wait – but he never heard from the French beauty. He wrote hopefully several more times and was still waiting at the time of his death 10 years later. In vain he met every ship that came from Tahiti to the Sydney wharves. He spent countless hours pacing the upstairs veranda of his home, watching the horizon for the ship that would bring him his love.

Late into the night, forlornly, alone with his terrible secret, he played his piano – mostly the music of Beethoven. O'Reilly had no friends and eventually died a lonely heartbroken death.

No one seems to know what happened to Maria. She may have died soon after O'Reilly sailed away from Tahiti for the last time. But it seems more likely she was stringing the old boy along, getting all the money from him she could. She well may have caught a boat home to France.

On arriving at O'Reilly's former home that September evening three years ago we four intrepid investigators spent nearly an hour painstakingly searching the building, including the attic, inside and out, for loose fittings or anything movable that could explain strange noises. We found nothing.

Then we locked every door and window through which anyone – that is any earthly entity larger than a mouse – could enter the house. In addition we bound every door lock and window latch with several thicknesses of our black cotton thread so that if somehow someone or something sneaked inside and relocked the door or window we would know it.

John Heel hung the thermometer on the lounge wall. "Often when there is a supernatural presence in a room the temperature drops sharply," he explained.

Nearby we placed the portable tape recorder, set up ready to be turned on if we heard anything unusual.

I admit I was privately amused.

At 11.00 p.m. we switched off the lights in all the other rooms and the four of us quietly settled into chairs in the lounge to wait. By midnight we had heard nothing untoward. The wind had gone down; the thermometer registered a steady 68 degrees. Occasionally, walking softly, using torchlight and keeping conversation to a minimum we checked every room in the house but found nothing disturbed or disturbing.

When by 2.00 a.m. nothing notable had happened we all relaxed and I felt convinced the legend was another tall tale. I fell asleep on the floor.

I woke with a start at 2.50. Mac Vagg, sitting nearby, was looking uneasy. The atmosphere in the room had become electric. John Heel and Geoffrey Kearns were sitting bolt upright.

"I just heard a slight tapping sound upstairs," Mac Vagg said.

After waiting a few minutes Mac and I cautiously searched the house again but found nothing changed. All the threads were still in place, intact.

We had been back in the lounge some 15 minutes when we all heard a high-pitched hissing sound coming from inside the house. It faded for a few seconds, then resumed, sounding like a thin stream of water falling into an empty tub. The sound lasted about a minute, until Mac crossed the room to turn on the tape recorder. It had seemed to come from several different directions at the same time. All of us searched the house again and this time we turned on several lights.

We discovered there was no thread on the French window

leading from the downstairs balcony to the games room. John Heel and Geoffrey Kearns swore they had threaded the window with about six thicknesses of thread. But now there was no sign of it.

Throughout the night Mac Vagg and I had been sitting no more than 15 feet from this French window. Not even the sneakiest cat burglar could have opened the window without our hearing him. The only other entrance to the room was through the door beside my chair.

"It's impossible for cotton to vanish like that," I observed superfluously.

All of us together then rethreaded the window and at 4.30 a.m. we were again sitting quietly in the lounge. The temperature had dropped only one degree.

Now began the weirdest hour of my life!

At 4.40 a quite audible noise began in the room directly above us. Even John Heel, who has defective hearing, picked it up plainly. "It sounds like escaping gas," he said switching on the tape recorder.

Mac Vagg and I thought it sounded more like running water although there was not one pipe up there and it had not rained for days.

We ran upstairs but the noise stopped as soon as we reached the staircase. But as we entered the room from which we thought the sound had originated another noise stopped us in our tracks. A high-pitched whistle was coming from the bedroom behind us. This was the room in which Captain O'Reilly was said to have murdered his wife. This sound stopped as we opened the door.

At 4.45 we had returned to the lounge in time to hear three distinct but muffled thuds, like heavy footfalls. They made the house vibrate slightly and seemed to come from upstairs, possibly from the rickety old verandah which no man could reach quietly without climbing the stairs. The noises stopped as soon as we spoke.

At 4.50 Mac Vagg set the transistor tape recorder at the top of the stairs and turned it on.

At 5.08 we heard four muffled footsteps upstairs. At 5.16 there were three more steps. At 5.18 there was one loud stamp in the room above us. It made the house quiver. At 5.30 we heard two more loud stamps in quick succession. These were followed in a few seconds by softer thuds. At 5.31 we heard one distant thud. And at 5.39 we again heard the sound of hissing or running water for about minute. At 5.45 we heard two more steps.

By 5.45 it was beginning to get light and we made a careful search inside and outside the house. We could find nothing to account for the noises. The tape recorder had picked up nothing but it was not a sensitive machine and its tape had surface noise.

John Heel later told us the sound of a ghost has been recorded on tape only once so far as he knew.

"There is something very weird in that house," he said. "The only explanation I can offer is that it is a ghost. The noises could not possibly have been made by an underwater stream, faulty plumbing, mice, rats or possums."

Because the tape was bare of sound I wondered if we had heard the noises as a result of some sort of auto-suggestion. We certainly had been keyed up during those early morning hours.

So the following Wednesday night, September 19, seven of us went to the house. Heel, Vagg, Kearns and I were accompanied by: Patricia Jensen, 25, of Henry Street, Guildford, Sydney; Patricia Sutherland, 20, of Binburra Avenue, Avalon Beach, Sydney; and Brian Welsh, of Stoney Creek Road, Kingsgrove, Sydney.

During the afternoon Mac Vagg and Brian Welsh again had examined the house in the sober light of day. They had paid especial attention to the small empty attic. The seven of us rechecked the house and sealed it with thread as we had before.

We had another companion – one who is inquisitive, intelligent and friendly and who has very sharp hearing – Prince, my collie. Prince trotted around the house like the regular investigator he is, looking under the beds and in dark corners. We felt if he picked up any strange noises they could not be attributed to human auto-suggestion.

For our base this time we took the downstairs games room where the cotton had vanished. At the top of the stairs we placed a larger, more sensitive tape recorder with a lead enabling us to turn it on and off from the games room. It ran for three hours that night without recording one noise.

We did not hear or see anything unusual until 1.50 a.m. on the Thursday. Then five of us, including me, picked up the high-pitched hissing whistle we had heard before. It lasted about three minutes. Prince did not seem to hear it.

A few minutes later all of us heard three faint thuds upstairs. Prince immediately pricked up his ears and began to walk uneasily about the room whining.

At 2.00 a.m. John Heel, Geoffrey Kearns, Prince and I made the usual hourly torchlight search. A shock awaited us at the top of the stairs. Earlier we had shot home the latches on every door in the house. Yet the door on the left, leading to the bedroom over our base room and in which O'Reilly's wife is said to have been slain, was wide open! It was pushed right back against the wall.

There had been no key for us actually to lock the door but three of us had watched Geoffrey close it firmly an hour before. It could not be opened without turning the fairly stiff handle.

I held the door half open to see whether, if by some chance the lock had undone itself, the door would swing open. The door slowly swung *shut!*

Back in the base room some 20 minutes later Mac Vagg and Patricia Sutherland said they thought they heard a distant clock chiming. All of us, including the dog, heard two more slight thuds at 2.45 a.m.

We made another torchlight search of the premises at 3.00 a.m. and as we gingerly approached the top of the stairs we found the *other* door wide open! It too had been pushed right back – over the edge of a big carpet. I myself had made certain the door was securely closed and no one had left the base room between searches. Because they did not afford entrance to the premises none of the inside doors had been threaded with cotton.

I reclosed the door then pushed it open again to where it had been when we discovered it. It took quite an effort to push it over the carpet although the door did not squeak. No draught could have opened it that far.

After examining both bedrooms and finding nothing amiss we turned to go back downstairs. We were at a loss to explain the opening doors, one of the things the house's previous occupants had complained of.

In his usual eager manner Prince rushed ahead to lead us down. But when he reached the top of the stairs he froze. Staring down into the darkness he took several steps backward, then ran back along the landing.

By this time I was standing at the head of the stairs. I called Prince three times. Each time he came back to my side at the head of the stairs, stopped and ran back to the far wall. He began to whine mournfully.

Prince refused to go down the stairs until I started off ahead of him. I never had seen him act this way before. Nor has he acted this way since. He seemed strangely subdued for the remainder of our "ghost watch". Did he hear or sense some sinister presence not detected by the rest of us?

From 3.10 to 3.25 a.m. Mac Vagg, Brian Welsh, Prince and I sat quietly in the dark in the upstairs bedroom in which the old captain is said to have killed his wife.

We had been there only five minutes when Mac said, "Ah, now I know what it is." He walked over to the French window then added, "That's strange. I don't know after all. I heard that chiming sound again and thought it was a bell ringing in the distance. But there's no bell ringing out there. It beats me."

We ended our "watch" in the early daylight at 6.00 a.m. without hearing anything else strange.

We found no explanations for anything that occurred during the two nights we spent in that house and those of us who went there believing there are no such things as ghosts now are not so sure.

We did not hear the piano play. But those persons who claimed the piano played Beethoven by itself in the middle of the night had not previously heard the legend of the musical mariner. Did the chiming we heard explain the mysterious piano playing? And if so then what explains the chiming?

Did the high-pitched whistle from Mrs O'Reilly's bedroom have some connection with her death? Are the footsteps those of the mariner's ghost still pacing the veranda and awaiting the arrival of a long-lost love?

I am quite certain none of these questions ever will be answered for . . .

Two weeks after we spent our second night in the "haunted" house it suddenly burst into flames and burned to the ground. The old building was unoccupied and authorities could find no cause for the fire. Even the end of the strange house is a mystery.

The property is now owned by agent Ken Baynes and it is still for sale. If you do not believe in ghosts you may have a bargain.

THE GHOST BELONGED TO THE ROSES
By W. J. Brands

*The Indian gardener died – but not even death, it seemed,
could separate him from his beloved flowers.*

IN 1928 I was appointed Chief Engineer in charge of the construction
of the Lyallpur–Jaranwallah Railway in the Punjab. My first problem
was to find suitable living quarters and offices and after a few days' stay
in the Lyallpur Dhak bungalow, I was lucky enough to discover what I
wanted through Mr S., the Parsee jute buyer for the well-known firm
of Ralli Bros. He occupied a bungalow on the outskirts of the town; it
was in fact the last one on the street, adjoined by fields, and Mr S.
offered me half of the premises. I told him that my wife intended to
join me in a few months but he said this would fit his plans splendidly,
as by then the jute season would be over and he would be returning to
Bombay Mumbai until the next season. While he was gone I could
have the entire house at my disposal.

The rectangular building was divided lengthwise into two
parts, separated by an inner wall. Only two doors in this wall connected
the halves; one opening being in the front room and the other in the
room behind it. Each half consisted of a large front room with windows
and French doors, behind this another large room was ventilated by
fanlights in the roof. There was a bathroom, a dressing room and a
store at the back.

Some steps led to the roof which was flat except for the raised
fanlights in the centre. Surrounding the house was a garden in which
grew some mango trees, although its principal attraction was some
magnificent rose bushes which appeared to be ever-blooming. This
was because this part of the town was irrigated. Every week the entire
garden was flooded with only a broad path and the space in front of the
house remaining dry. The flood lasted 24 hours and was most efficient.

I decided to make the front room an office and use the second
room as bedroom and sitting room. After installing my camp furniture
and engaging domestic servants, my next task was to find workers for
the new line. I was rather lucky in this also as the jute season was
ending and in a few days we made a start. The flat line was staked out
and some hundreds of workers were soon busy building up the new

railway embankment and digging foundations for the culverts and bridges.

A week had gone by when my men approached me and told me that they were hungry. They asked for an advance payment on the work they had done so far. I agreed to this and measured what had been completed. The following day I collected 8000 rupees in notes and cash from the local bank and went down the line paying the gangs. This took me the morning and most of the afternoon. To my astonishment the men I had paid ran down the line ahead of me and after a while all of them, paid and unpaid, disappeared.

It occurred to me that the entire request was simply a scheme to find out if I really had the money to pay them and, having satisfied themselves that I did, they went home, calling it a day.

As a result I found myself with some 500 rupees in my possession. The bank was closed by then and I had no safe. There was nothing to do but keep the money overnight in my bungalow. Worse still, I found on my return that my landlord had left on a jute buying trip so that I would be quite alone with the treasure.

I placed it under a packing case in the front room and piled tins on the top of the case. After carefully securing the windows and doors of the office I lit a strong petrol lamp and, leaving the doors between the rooms open, I retired into my living quarters where only a small oil lamp provided illumination. Thus I sat almost in the dark and could see what went on in the brighter front room.

After reading for a while I turned out my lamp and settled down to sleep. The banging of the two heavy doors leading to the front room woke me with a start. I raised myself. Both doors were shut. My first thought was that a heavy gust of wind had blown them shut but then I remembered that it was impossible for a draught through the fanlights to close those heavy doors. I got up, searching in the dark for my shoes. I could hear somebody walking in the next room. Armed with my only weapon, a Mexican knife, I rushed to the doors. But when I opened them I found the front room empty; the pile of tins on the packing case untouched. I tested the doors and windows. They were all locked. Then I heard whispering outside the house. So my callers were in the garden! I opened the French doors and stepped out. Swirling fog surrounded me; nobody was in sight but the whispering came now from another direction. Stealthily I crept towards it. In the fog no human being was discernible and the whispering stopped. Being afraid that the entire matter was an attempt to lure me out of the office, away from the money, I returned to the house. I locked the doors and, leaving the intermediate doors wide open again went to the inner room to bed. Everything was silent; apparently the night prowlers had left.

Hardly had I settled down when the doors slammed again and now the whispering seemed to come from the roof. I got a black cotton thread and some glue and went out to investigate. In the fog the roof seemed empty. To make certain that nobody was hiding, I glued the thread across the steps. To a man descending it was quite invisible and if broken would prove that somebody had been in ambush upstairs. I shouted for the night-watchman but nobody came.

It was one o'clock in the morning but I was allowed no rest. The doors kept closing, until I jammed them open with my trunks.

Still persons seemed to walk in the front room and to whisper. At last dawn brought peace.

When my boy brought my breakfast I looked suspiciously at him. His face was blank. I did not tell him my night's adventure. Any word of a "bhud" (ghost) probably would precipitate the departure of the entire staff.

That day I had some business in the bazaar. When I told the shopkeeper where to send my purchases he shook his head saying, "Sahib, that is a very bad house."

I pressed him to tell me more but he refused to answer, acting as if he did not understand me.

Later in the day my landlord returned. I told him of my night's adventures and reported the absence of the night-watchman.

He did not seem surprised. He said, "So you have the same trouble I had. It seems only your side of the house is affected. For this reason I moved to the side where I am now. Nothing happens there. As for the watchman, my servants have reported that he took a holiday knowing that I was away. I have dismissed him."

In the nights following I was not disturbed. However, when my wife joined me I took the other half of the bungalow – now that the landlord had left – as living quarters, still using the other part for offices. As the new rooms appeared to be immune I did not tell her of my experience.

We settled down happily. Early in the mornings I drove out to work while my wife stayed in the bungalow. Within a few days the neighbours learned that she had been a nurse and often I waited outside the sitting room while a purdah lady told her of her ailments.

Then one day I had to drive to Lahore and was, unfortunately, obliged to spend the night there. I was quite unworried about my wife's safety. The servants loved her and the new night-watchman, a huge Pathan, was her abject slave since she had cured a big abscess on his foot which the Hindu doctors in the town refused to touch because he was a Muslim.

On my return from Lahore my wife greeted me with a smile. She said, "I had a funny night because first Mahomed Ali, the watchman, shut all the doors so that it became stifling hot in the house. When I opened them again he told me that he was responsible for me and "what will the Sahib say if he comes back and finds that something has happened to you." So to get some air I left the inner doors to the office open. In spite of the heat I dozed off. Suddenly somebody was close to the mosquito net, near my head, and a plaintive voice whispered, "Sahib, Sahib."

Being still drowsy I answered: "Sahib nay hai, memsahib hai." (The master is not here, the lady is here.)

When I raised myself in the bed and opened the mosquito net there was nobody in the room. Your advice to always leave a tiny lamp burning was a boon. Had it been pitch dark I would certainly have been frightened. The only strange thing was that the doors to the inner room were closed. I opened them again and went to bed. Hardly had I laid myself down when the doors swung shut again and I could see the heavy brass bolts slide down and lock them. I thought that an earthquake might be the cause so I did not worry about it any more and went to sleep. But this morning everybody tells me there was no earthquake. What could it have been?"

Now I was forced to confess what had happened to me on my arrival. We decided not to open the inner doors to the office any more at night and there was no further disturbance.

But unfortunately my wife told the story at the club. This split its membership into two parties one of which thought us mentally affected while the other believed us to be liars. Only in chafing us about our *ghost* were both united.

One evening we sat down to dinner as usual. The clerks had gone home; the office was locked. It was still daylight and we decided to leave the door to the office open to get more air. My wife sat with her back to the open door which I was facing. We were chatting quietly over our meal when, on looking up, I saw a man walk through the office and pass through the inner door to the room behind. I jumped up. My wife asked, "What is the matter?"

I replied, "I cannot understand it. I am sure I locked the office doors but just now a man walked through the office into the back room. I didn't recognize him."

Before going to investigate I described the visitor as a small man, dressed in a black jacket and white trousers. He had a white beard.

I found everything locked and no visitor anywhere.

I returned to the table and we continued with our dinner.

A few nights later at the club we were introduced to Mr and Mrs C. who had just arrived from Peshawar. Someone insisted that we tell them our *ghost* story.

I could see that my wife was very annoyed; the joke was beginning to be stale; but there was nothing left but to answer the questions of the newcomers.

Mr C. asked, "What did he mean by ghosts? We used to live in Lyallpur but never heard of one. Where do you live?"

We described our bungalow.

"Oh," said Mrs. C., "we lived there before our transfer. Are those beautiful roses still in the compound? There was quite a tragedy about them," she continued. "Our gardener planted those bushes. He was very proud of them and called them his children. He had no other relatives in the world. Such a nice little man, always spick and span in spite of his work, dressed in a black jacket and white trousers. Visitors often mistook him for our butler . . ."

"Did he have a white beard?" I asked uncautiously.

Mrs C. looked at me with surprise, "Yes, how did you know?"

"Just a guess," I stammered, blushing to the roots of my hair.

"What was the tragedy?" asked my wife to cover my confusion.

"We heard that after we left Lyallpur our gardener continued to go to the bungalow to tend the roses. For some reason the bungalow stood empty for months. Then came the terrible influenza epidemic of 1919 which decimated the country. During that time the little man vanished. As he had no relatives and people were busy with their own tragedies; nobody worried about it. Months later when someone wished to rent the bungalow they found the front door open. The body of our gardener was discovered lying on the floor. He apparently fell ill on his last visit, entered the bungalow to rest and died there, abandoned by everybody. Somebody wrote to tell us the story. I cried when I heard it."

We excused ourselves to go to the card room for bridge.

THE GHOST WHO SMOKED

By Zosimo Venecia

WHEN the Sixth Army reached Manila I was fortunate enough to get a pass to go into the provinces to look for my father. The sights were sad and desolate as you can imagine. I found my father in an amazingly fine house on the edge of a small village. I was astonished that he had found such luxurious living quarters for himself when most of the homes about were impoverished shambles. My father laughed, "No, I have not been dishonest nor a collaborator. I have this fine house because the rest of the village will not live here. It is haunted."

Knowing how realistic my father is, I laughed and asked, "Is it really?"

"Oh, yes," my father nodded, then shrugged his shoulders. "It is impossible and unreasonable – but there is a ghost. He comes in from the porch and would enter this room if I did not keep a lighted candle at the door. He agreeably does not cross the light. He stands at the threshold and smokes his cigarette each evening."

"Smokes a cigarette," I asked in surprise.

With disapproval in his voice my father answered, "It is true. He smokes a cigarette each evening when he comes. It is time for him now."

There were no groans, nor any unpleasant phenomena, but in a short while I heard footsteps in the empty house and soon, at the threshold of the room, stood the misty figure of a man. At intervals his arm was raised to his mouth and equally misty puffs of smoke came from his lips. His features were not distinct. It was rather like looking at a man through a dense fog. The manner of the spectre seemed decidedly melancholy but there was nothing vicious about him.

My father said he had learned that it was the ghost of a man who had killed himself for love in the house of his sweetheart. Each night he returned and smoked a cigarette by the door of her room, which was the room where my father and I had waited. The next evening I lit a cigarette at the moment of the visitor's appearance before the door in front of us and at the moment I had smoked it quite down to the end our ghostly visitor vanished. Each night it remained only the length of time it takes to smoke a cigarette slowly.

– *Dagupan City, Philippine Islands.*

GHOSTLY EXPERIENCES ON HILL STREET

by Marilyn Broad

My husband and I had spent most of our lives in New Jersey, but we felt that it had become too crowded, hectic and noisy for our taste. So, we moved to Biddleford, Maine. We made arrangements to view a very large, New Englander style home, which the agent said dated back to 1893.

Before the agent ever took us inside the house, I could sense a presence within. I told my husband I had a feeling the house contained at least one male spirit. But he is a sceptic, and he laughed at me, saying I had an overactive imagination.

The agent met us at the house and we went inside. My feelings became even stronger, especially as I walked up the long staircase to the bedrooms. We were first taken to the master bedroom, which contained a large dressing room and separate sleeping quarters. As I entered the dressing room, I felt a very cold wind, even though all the windows in the room were closed.

There were two walk-in wardrobes in the dressing room. Standing between them I saw the ghostly figure of a small, thin, elderly man with white hair and piercing blue eyes. He wore an old-fashioned suit with a bow tie and carried a straw hat. Clenched between his teeth was a rather large cigar. He smiled as if he were happy to see me.

I was quite stunned, but I quickly regained my composure. I didn't want the agent to know what I had just seen. Since the ghost didn't seem to be a threat, I accepted him and continued to tour the house with my husband.

Moving in with Ghosts

My husband and I talked it over and decided to move into the house on a rent with option to buy basis. That's when the real fun began!

Almost every evening I walked up to the bedroom alone with our youngest dog ahead of me. Our oldest dog followed close behind me. It surprised me to see our oldest dog, Muffett, walk into the guest bedroom across from our bedroom one evening, her hair standing on end, staring as if something were in the room that she could see but could not understand.

It was then that I saw an elderly woman in a long, flowing white gown sitting on the bed in the guest room. She motioned for me to come into the room, but feeling very uncomfortable, I ignored her and went to bed.

This occurrence was repeated regularly for over a month. Each time the old woman would become more insistent that I visit her. The more insistent she became, the more frightened I was.

Every night after first seeing her I was awakened by a female voice at the side of our bed saying, "Hello! Hello! I want you two out of our house! I want to be left alone." I became increasingly frightened by these encounters, but we continued to live there, hoping that the female ghost, whom I named Agatha, would cease her protests.

We had been attempting to obtain a mortgage on the house, but we were refused four times because of our short time of residence. We decided to give it one last try; if this proved unsuccessful, we would give up.

On the night before the decision was to be made on our final mortgage attempt, I went upstairs and found the guest bedroom illuminated by candlelight. I peered in and saw a party was in progress, with a great many spirits standing around the room laughing. Agatha held a cake topped with candles and once again beckoned me into the room.

I hurried into our bedroom and closed the door. When I told my husband about the incident that night, he said that my imagination must really be working overtime.

The next day we were denied our final mortgage on the house. We decided not to rent there any longer and moved to another house close by.

As for the ghostly house, it remained empty for quite some time, but now it has new owners. Do they have experiences like I had? It's hard to say. I'm just glad that my husband and I are no longer there. Agatha has her house back. I hope she's happy.

GHOSTLY FISHERMAN

*In 1967 my first husband, Donald Alfred Victor Ellis,
and I had been married for four months without
encountering any problems.*

One night as I was settling down to sleep in my room, which was lit by a full moon, I felt someone watching me. I looked up and saw the head and shoulders of a man in his late 30s or early 40s, who had a red complexion. He had a crew cut and full grey beard. He wore a Fair Isle jumper beneath what appeared to be a donkey jacket. He looked like a fisherman from his dress and fresh complexion.

Knowing my husband did not believe in the supernatural, I said nothing. I stared eye-to-eye with this man for a few seconds. In my mind I said, "You are not really there, you are a figment of my imagination."

Suddenly his head and shoulders leaned toward me. I screamed. My husband said that I was being stupid. He said if someone was there, he would have been standing in the middle of the bed. I replied, "He had no lower body, so he couldn't have been standing."

Eighteen months passed and I was expecting my first child. I could feel the fisherman still around me, but I never saw him. The flat we lived in was too small for our family, so we moved to a larger one in a different area of town. The fisherman moved too.

Another year went by and my second child was born, a little girl. She was nearly 11 months old and just starting to walk. Her inquisitive fingers were into everything. One day both children were taking a 4.00 p.m. nap. Knowing they would soon wake, I made tea and read the paper. No sooner had I started reading when I felt that I was being watched. I looked up to see the fisherman, full length this time, standing in front of me. Both of his outstretched hands clasped a large heart-shaped knife. I stood up and left the room. He had never seemed a danger the way a poltergeist might, but I was becoming paranoid about knives. Although I didn't know much about the supernatural, I was convinced he was trying to warn me. Perhaps one of the children would have an accident with a knife. For a month I kept all our knives on top of the wall cabinets, out of the children's reach, even the bread knife.

It was not until an old school friend came to visit that I was able to resolve this. She saw me climb on a chair to retrieve some knives from the top of a wall cabinet so we could eat, and she asked me why they were up there. I told her about the fisherman, afraid that she would laugh and ridicule me, but she was understanding. She said, "I always keep an open mind on such matters. My father sees a genuine spiritualist who doesn't charge, but who has a donation box for registered charities only."

My friend suggested I should visit the same spiritualist and explain what I had experienced. I did. The spiritualist was a lovely lady in her late 40s. We sat in her parlour. She listened to my story, saying nothing until I finished. She told me some people pass over, not realizing they have died. Maybe he was trying to tell me how he met a violent death. She told me I would probably never see him again because of my visit to her and that he would have come with me if he were still around. If he appeared again I was supposed to tell him, "Go over there, your friends are waiting for you."

I often wonder if he was trying to warn me of my first husband's violent temper and the pain and heartbreak he would cause me. From that day on I never saw him again or felt his presence. I still think of him and feel sorry for him. He may have come to me for help, but I was unable to aid him because of my fear.

– *Patricia Smyth, Malaga, Spain*

Guardian Angel

I have been having out-of-body experiences since I was five and I am fairly comfortable on the astral plane. One afternoon I fell asleep and found myself in another country (I got the feeling that perhaps it was Tibet because of the dirt roads and simple buildings). I decided to fly through the walls of these structures and I was having a pretty good time.

Suddenly I entered a room where a man wearing a white turban and white clothing was sitting on a dirt floor in Zen position. I became frightened. He seemed to be expecting me, which scared me even more. Telepathically I said, "I know you, don't I?" Before he could reply I slipped back into my body and awoke.

A few days later I told my psychic about the incident and she informed me it was one of my spiritual guides. I then mentally asked if he would appear to me again. He did. This time he wore a suit and tie (so as not to frighten me). He embraced me, giving the feeling that I was being taken care of.

I realized that he looked just like a man (also in a suit) whom I had never forgotten. He helped me one afternoon when I was stranded on the motorway several years ago. He seemed to know the problem, bought the parts, fixed the car and then was gone just as suddenly as he had appeared. I remember thinking what an angel that man was.

Whether we choose to call them guides or guardian angels, I realize now more than ever that they are always with us, watching over us.

– Christy Sheehan, Montclair, CA

GHOSTLY RIVERSIDE
by Raymond M. Kelly

Most ancient ports are haunted, and Newcastle-Upon-Tyne is no exception. One of the spirits there is the traditional Northumbrian *silky*. This type of apparition takes its name from the silken rustle of clothing that heralds its appearance. The Newcastle silky haunted the Broad Chare area of the quayside and was believed to be the spirit of a woman who had hanged herself in Trinity House, the local mariners' establishment. The body was interred next to the local crossroads in accordance with local custom.

A short while later, people walking through Broad Chare began to hear a silken rustle and a woman's throaty chuckle. She appeared in a more direct form to a keelman (a Tyne boatman). The keelman had been drinking with his crew and was making his way home. A woman was going in his direction on the other side of the road. Suddenly, she stopped and turned. Lifting her veil, she raised her right hand and beckoned him to approach her. He couldn't make out her features because she was in the shadows. As he got closer to her, the effects of his drinking left him. She had no features because she had no head.

There used to be a fountain at the west end of the quayside. Passers-by would hear a woman's voice make the following street call out of thin air: "Fine Chinese oranges, four for a penny. Cherry ripe, cornberries, try them and see." After finishing its sales pitch, the voice would change and plead for the listener to bring Billy Ellison to her. It was believed that the voice was that of Jane Jameson, known locally as Wor Jin. She was a 30-year-old seller of rags and fruit at the Sandgate in the early part of the nineteenth century. She and her widowed mother lived in the Newcastle Keelman's Hospital. Jin started keeping company with Billy Ellison, and in 1828 he joined the two women in their single room.

One night, Jin and Billy ran out of drinking money and returned home to get more from Mrs Jameson. She refused to provide it and a fight broke out. Mrs Jameson accused her daughter of murdering her two children. Jin plunged a red-hot poker through her mother's heart. It took Mrs Jameson two days to die. Jin accused

Ellison of having killed her mother by kicking her with steel-capped boots. The jury did not believe this story and Jin was hanged on the Town Moor on July 3, 1829. Her body was taken to the local hospital for dissection.

This story gives no explanation for why her restless spirit is trying to join the man she tried to frame. Maybe love is strong, or she wishes to apologize.

GHOSTLY LOVERS: LOVE THAT PIERCES THE VEIL OF TIME

Dennis William Hauck

Riding down old Highway 66 east of Kingman, Arizona, is like travelling backwards in time. Not much has changed along the twisting two-lane blacktop since the 1930s, and by the time you reach the town of Oatman, you really start to think you've left the modern world. Wild cattle roam freely on Main Street, prospectors line up on barstools in the saloons, and most of the tattered wooden buildings have been standing there since the early 1900s.

But one building on Main Street has a different look and feel to it. In fact, the Oatman Hotel is the only two-storey adobe building in all of Mohave County. The hotel's other claim to fame is that it is where Clark Gable and Carole Lombard spent their wedding night after being married in Kingman on March 29, 1939.

Gable visited Oatman whenever he had the opportunity. He liked the town. Nobody treated him like a star there, and he often played poker with the townsfolk until the wee hours of the morning. On the evening of their wedding day, he and his new bride checked into room 15 and spent two days making passionate love.

In fact, the sounds of their low whispering and blissful laughter still drift down the halls, and the inexplicable noises of water running and people walking around still emanate from room 15, although today the room is sealed off. The hotel no longer rents its rooms. It has been turned into a museum and bar. Nonetheless, the lights continue to go on and off, toilets flush and footsteps are heard coming from the deserted first floor. The outline of an invisible human body has appeared on one of the beds, and ghostly manifestations have been reported in the Theater Room on the same floor.

While it has been suggested that the ghost is a former maid, most of the townspeople think the first floor is haunted by Gable and Lombard, who have returned to Oatman to relive their happiest days together. The current owner of the Oatman Hotel, Billie Jo Trammel, keeps the room in its original condition and has even laid out a blue satin dress on the bed – just the way Carole would were she still alive.

"There is no doubt in my mind that the hotel is haunted", says former Oatman Hotel owner Dolly Miller. "Clark and Carole didn't have much time together, and I believe their ghosts brought them back together."

Former manager Tom Brown agrees: "I never believed in ghosts before…but now I've changed my mind."

A Mate in Paradise

No-one denies that the two film stars were madly in love, but they were together only a short time before Lombard was killed in a plane crash in January 1942. Just before she left California on a U.S. War Bond tour to the Midwest, Gable had a premonition of disaster and begged her not to go. They got into a heated argument, and Lombard stormed out of the house. As she left, she took off one of the gold topaz earrings Gable had given her and threw it at him.

When he heard of the plane crash, Gable flew to the crash site and sifted through the debris, looking desperately for Caroles other earring. He felt the missing earring would be a symbol of their reunited love. He never found it.

Gable's life was never the same. According to his friends, his spirit was crushed, and he never got over Lombard. Soon after the funeral, he joined the air force and flew several dangerous missions over Germany. When the war was over, his career fizzled out after he made several bad films. He had taken to drinking heavily and was frequently seen shaking in front of the cameras. Gable eventually married twice more, to former actresses who bore striking resemblances to Lombard. Both marriages lasted only a few years. In 1960, the strain of making his comeback film, *The Misfits*, proved too much. He insisted on doing his own stunts and died of a heart attack on the set.

According to his lifelong friend Louella Parsons, Gable's marriage to Lombard was "a match made in heaven". Everyone agreed that it was one of the happiest and deepest loves Hollywood has ever known, According to psychic-to-the-stars Kenny Kingston, Gable's spirit has confided to him that the missing earring has now found "a mate in paradise".

Another famous Hollywood love affair involved Robert Taylor, who vied with Gable as the screen's top romantic star. Taylor's passionate affair and marriage with Barbara Stanwyck are legend in Tinsel Town. After Taylor died of lung cancer in 1969, Stanwyck continued to see and talk to his presence in her home. After she passed away in January 1990 at the of age 82, there were rumours that both their ghosts stalked the home.

Even Taylor and Stanwyck's former love nest, where the two stars met secretly before they were married, carries the psychic impression of their passion. The house, just off Sunset Boulevard in Beverly Hills, became the site of violent poltergeist activity even before Stanwyck died. In 1976, parapsychologist Barry Taff witnessed objects tossed through the air by some unseen hand. A Los Angeles newscaster was chased down a hall by a heavy flying book, and coins rained onto UCLA investigators. A servant quit because flying cabbages chased him through the house one day!

Sealed in a Glass Coffin

It is not the notoriety but the intensity of a love affair that leaves the psychic residue that we associate with a haunting, and one does not have to be a film star to be deeply in love. The ghost of an unknown Indian girl haunts the old Mulls House on Highway 49, halfway between Hollygrove and Helena in Arkansas. The house originally stood in St Petersburg, Florida, but it was moved to Hollygrove by a retired sea captain named Captain Mulls. He lived there with an Indian woman whom he loved deeply, although they never married. Almost every evening, the girl played romantic melodies on a fine piano the captain had bought her.

When his lover died, Mulls was devastated. He had her body embalmed and sealed in a glass casket, which he kept in the house. The poor man spent lonely hours pining over her lifeless corpse and many people believe he succeeded in bringing her back. After Mull's death in 1935, the woman was interred in a local cemetery, but her spirit stayed on in the house. Even today, the sounds of the piano can be heard coming from the deserted house, and locals believe the place is haunted by her spirit.

Sharon Inebrit of Hollygrove heard ghostly piano music coming from the house whenever she drove by the place. Her experiences prompted Sharon to contact Mulls' relatives in Little Rock and tell them what was going on. Then, with the help of antiques dealer Tom Kameron, she discovered that many of Mulls' original furnishings were still in the house – with the notable exception of the old grand piano.

An Eternal Wait

Not every lover has the luxury of embalming their significant other and displaying the body in a glass coffin, but in the case of Florence Martus, a corpse would have been a blessing. Before her fiancé departed on a ship bound for Europe, the faithful woman made a vow that she would greet every ship entering Savannah until he returned to her. Unfortunately, he never came home and for the next 44 years, Florence dutifully greeted every ship coming into Savannah.

She lived with her brother, a lighthouse keeper, on Elba Island at the southern edge of the harbour. Each day Florence stood on the lawn in front of her house and greeted the ships as they came in hoping against hope that her long-gone lover might be aboard one. During the day, she flapped her white apron in the breeze; at night, she waved a lantern. Florence never married, and she never found out what happened to her fiancé.

After her death in 1943, Florence's apparition was seen many times by people in fishing boats, yachts and cruise ships passing Elba Island. Before long, it became tradition to honour Florence's spirit by sounding two perky toots of the horn as boats passed Elba Island. She is said to still appear on the lawn in front of the white house, waving her apron, waiting patiently – and eternally – for her lover's promised return.

The apparition of another woman, also separated from her lover, walks a path that has become known as the "Ghost Walk" on the grounds of Chatham Manor in Fredericksburg, Virginia. Called the Lady in White, she is the ghost of a young English woman who was brought to the estate by her father in 1774. He disapproved of her romance with a commoner and took her across the ocean to put a stop to it.

Chatham was built in 1771 by William Fitzhugh, who named his great house in honour of William Pitt, the Earl of Chatham. Fitzhugh's home became a well-known stopover for sophisticated gentry, and the Englishman, a friend of Fitzhugh's, believed that his daughter would meet someone more suitable there.

But the girl's young lover followed her to the American colonies, and the two met secretly and made plans to elope. With the help of a servant, a rope ladder was smuggled into the house. The girl planned to climb out her window late at night and go to the banks of the Rappahannock River, where her lover would wait in a small boat.

Unfortunately, George Washington, another close friend of Fitzhugh's, was staying at the house at the same time. Fitzhugh had enlisted Washington's aid in watching over the lass, and when Washington's manservant told him about the couple's plans, the man-who-could-tell-no-lies had no choice but to inform his host. Washington waited outside the girl's window, and at the appointed hour, snatched her from the ladder and carried the struggling girl to her father's room. He even had his men arrest her hapless suitor and hold him until the girl could be returned to England.

Though forced to return with her father and marry a nobleman, the girl vowed to return to Chatham and search for her lover. She never made it back to America while alive, but her ghost was sighted at Chatham on the day she died, June 21, 1790. Thereafter, her white apparition was sighted regularly every seven years on the anniversary of her death. The sightings always occurred between noon and midnight.

Many visitors and residents of Chatham have encountered the Lady in White over the years. One former owner admitted seeing the ghost. Mrs Randolph Howard, who resided on the estate from 1909 to 1914 reported that one afternoon, as she was looking out a window on the west side of the building, she saw "a flowing white figure walking up and down the front lawn in the colonial carriage lane." Though reluctant to talk about the sighting with servants and family members, Howard was convinced she had seen a ghost.

Since the Park Service took over the estate in 1977, there have been fewer sightings reported, and the Lady in White wasn't seen at all in 1986 and 1993. Some say she refuses to walk on grounds owned by representatives of George Washington's government, or perhaps she has found the spirit of her lost lover. Others insist she still returns to wander along the path that leads to a high bluff overlooking the Rappahannock River, where she scours the banks looking for the love of her life.

Cases like these tell us that if love is the tie that binds, it is also the tie that survives. When we give our love, we share our essence with another, creating a link that lasts forever. According to people who have experienced the Other Side, love is the only thing that matters, and those who have had near-death experiences say that we cannot appreciate the power of love until we die. They tell us that long-departed loved ones greet and guide us after we have passed on. And, of course, there are those spirits that never pass over to the Other Side – tied to the earthly plane by the same power of love.

Dennis William Hauck *is the author of* The National Directory of Haunted Places *and several other books on the paranormal.*

GHOSTLY USHER
by Kathryn Froehlich

On February 5, 1967, Richard Douglas Miler borrowed money from his mother and drove her car to Sears in St Paul, Minnesota. He purchased a cheap rifle and shells. Then he went back to his mother's car and shot himself.

Often overlooked during his 18 years of life, he faced the same problem in death. His corpse went undetected for two days. When a Sears employee finally found his body, it was clad in his Guthrie Theater usher uniform.

Miler had quit his job as an usher at his parents' request – they had wanted him to concentrate on his college studies. He left a note saying that ushering had been the best thing he'd ever done. He also requested that he buried in his usher's uniform. Miler's note was honoured and he was cremated in his uniform.

Then, almost a year later, in November 1968, Miler's ghost suddenly started appearing. It all started when a Guthrie patron complained about an usher walking up and down aisle 18 during a performance. When asked to describe the usher, the patron gave a description that matched Miler, including the previous season's uniform and a mole on the cheek. There had been no ushers in the house during the performance.

Another incident occurred when three ushers – Herner, Dan, and Bruce – were using a Ouija board one night after everyone else had left. The guys didn't really expect anything to happen. After receiving gibberish answers to several questions, they finally had a comprehensible response. The board told the ushers to look up at the lighting booth for a ghost named "DIKMILER".

Dan suddenly went pale, because he had known Miler. The ushers looked at the booth and asked each other to describe what each was seeing. They all described the same thing: A man standing behind the lighting board in a blue jacket with something red on the breast pocket.

After that, there were still more sightings. Herner became accustomed to seeing the apparition, usually from a distance of 40 feet or so. He reported that he often saw it on the catwalks and would call up to it, "Hey Dick, how are you doing?" The ghost would follow him with his eyes and head, but never spoke or made a sound.

A lighting technician named Don also saw the spirit. Don got out of the lift one night and saw an usher. He thought, nothing of it until he realized that he could see through the figure. He then panicked and got back into the lift.

In 1993, just before the Guthrie held a grand reopening, theatre officials called in Little Porcupine White, an Anishinabe Indian who performs spiritual cleansings. Officials wanted to dismiss the ghostly usher if possible, just to be sure the reopening was a success.

When White entered the Guthrie he said that he "felt some bad stuff at first", and he attributes this to a spirit. But he says the ghost isn't an evil one. "I thoughalthought he was all right, but I didn't want him to hang around and ruin things," White says. White performed his ceremony to send the ghost to the spirit world, which White describes as a positive and proper place for a ghost.

GHOSTLY WAGON

In the early '90s, I was married to a French farmer and lived in (Brittany) on the edge of the Broceliande Forest. It was a beautiful, mystical place, and supposedly Merlin's grave is nearby. Most of the farmhouses there faced the forest. In the afternoons, I would sit outside admiring the trees and scenery.

During one summer, every eight or nine days, I would clearly hear a horse-drawn wagon come rumbling down the road. It would appear out of nowhere and go past by my house. I could hear horses' hooves pounding on the dirt, the wooden wagon creaking, and the harnesses jingling. It sounded like there were gypsies on board. I could hear conversation but it was "German" to me. Then as quickly as it came, the sounds of the wagon would disappear.

No one else ever saw it – of course there never was anything visible.

– *Melissa Mierva, Llewellyn Customer Service, Saint Paul, Minnesota*

THE GHOSTS AND DRAGONS OF SCOTLAND

by Trish Telesco

Scotland's mysterious past and present merged to provide a truly haunted honeymoon.

Ten years ago, my husband and I travelled to Scotland for our honeymoon. Since I had never been there before, I didn't know what to expect. When I stepped from the plane, an odd sensation hit me – it felt like I was returning home. As we travelled, the hospitality of the Scottish people was overwhelming. Everywhere we went, clouds moved away and the sun appeared, as if to welcome us as warmly as the townspeople. Many places had lingering spirits, most of which were content to remain a mystery until our film was developed. Nature spirits rested there, too, happy with the land's beauty and the respect the natives showed it. People there still build roads around the trees.

We only had a week, so we spent no more than a day in each town. Our first two unusual experiences occurred in Inverness. It was a glorious day until we reached the boat that crosses the loch. Half an hour into the trip, a light mist began to form in the air. While listening to the guide tell the history of the loch, I thought I saw something odd in the water. Being a typical sceptic, I tugged my husband's sleeve to get him to confirm what I saw.

To our left was a large hump, blackish and sleek, moving easily against the waves. It came up once, twice, three times, and then was gone. We looked at each other in awe and decided it was best not to say anything. Who would believe us?

Haunted Lodgings

The Inverness home we stayed in was the only place in the country where we felt uncomfortable. At one point, when I got up during the night to get a drink, the door opened into my hand, seemingly of its own volition, then slammed shut behind me. This door-slamming activity went on all night, so we got up early and left the house hurriedly. We believe the spirits of the home did not like the owners and wanted them to move. The best way to accomplish this was to scare away clients. Sure enough, when we called a year later to see if

245

the same owners were still there, the house had been sold.

Next, we went castle touring. Blair Castle stands out, thanks to one little boy with an open mind. While we were taking the conducted tour of the castle, this boy raced into one room set aside as a sanctuary and said, "Oh, hello." No one was visible in the room. The last group of people were already through another door that they had closed behind them. The tour guide didn't seem to notice this disruption and continued with her work. I found it wonderfully amusing, however, that the same boy felt it necessary before he left to also say, "Goodbye now," to whomever he was seeing.

Finally, we arrived at Stornoway and took the ferry to Callanish. This megalithic site was one place we'd wanted to reach all along. Callanish, unlike Stonehenge, is not walled off. You can touch the stones, sit among them, and listen to the voices of the ages.

When my husband and I reached the site other tourists were chatting merrily. We both felt uncomfortable. This was a sacred spot and loud noise seemed out of place. So we went to our host's cottage and waited until sunset.

That evening the area was silent. There was only the land, the stones and the sky. Standing in the circle, everything seemed untouched and timeless. It was like having all clocks stop for a moment. Out of the corner of my eye I thought I saw one of the rocks move, but of course it must have been my imagination.

I took a picture of that stone. When developed, two lines of pink and blue light that look much like the outline of a woman in profile were visible. Maybe someone was trying to say hello.

It had been raining and the clouds covered the heavens like a giant grey sheet. As we walked through the circle, there was a small break in the billowing clouds. Beams of light poured through, touching each stone. It was like seeing music being made.

We moved to a knoll dotted with heather, just beyond the circle. Here, we could look out across the ocean into the mist and feel like we were peering into eternity. The winds grew silent. Birds stopped singing and even the sheep were quiet.

My husband whispered, "I think we should move. This might be a burial place." Sure enough, once we moved, everything returned to normal.

We went back to the stones and sat together until the sun moved into the clouds again. It was our last night in Scotland and nature itself closed the book on our visit. Walking toward the cottage, both of us felt a loss we couldn't quite put into words. Departing would be like leaving behind a good friend.

That night I awoke with a start. I could hear our hosts whispering excitedly in an ancient tongue. Upon the hill, in the centre of the stones, a fire blazed high into the sky. Not knowing anything about local customs, I went back to sleep.

My husband also woke shortly afterwards. As he looked out the window, a silhouette fell across the fires and seemed to alight on top of the circle's headstone. He couldn't quite make out the shape, but it was big. The shadow made him uneasy. He returned to bed, resisting the temptation to look further.

Neither one of us spoke much on the drive to the ferry. We boarded and sat down near an elderly man and a child who appeared to be his grandson, and watched as Lewis Island receded.

The Island's Dragon
The old man began to tell the boy a story. He said that the Dragon of Myrddin protects the islands and watches over all the standing stones in Europe. Once a year it comes out of its resting place on a northern knoll of Lewis and flies to each megalith, checking on them as a mother might check on her children. The only ones able to see this great beast are those considered its kin.

Both my husband and I felt chills go up our backs. The man's story was too close to what we'd experienced the previous day on the hillside and that night. When we docked back at Stornoway, we decided to take a little extra time to see if we could talk to the old man and learn the source of his tale. We disembarked and waited for the old man and the boy to follow.

They never disembarked, and no-one on board remembered seeing them. Were they ghosts sharing old stories of Scotland, hoping someone would listen?

THE GHOSTS OF ANCIENT ROME
By Eugene Grossenheider

Was the biographer, Plutarch, the first psychic researcher?
He did record many interesting cases of psychic phenomena.

As the astronomer, having learned the laws of the moon's eclipses, can calculate the exact dates of past eclipses back through the centuries, so the student of psychic science can see a new significance in the so-called miracles and supernatural occurrences in ancient writings. The woman of En-dor calling up the spirit of Samuel in the presence of King Saul takes on a new probability. The apparition of Hamlet's father may well have been more subjective hallucinations described by Freud.

Such thoughts come when one reads Plutarch's magnificent old classic, *Parallel Lives of Greeks And Romans*. Proceeding through the book one sees proof of a superior mind, of the careful precision of the true scientist. Plutarch strikes a happy compromise between easy gullibility and hard-boiled scepticism. He weighs every report before putting it onto his pages. Untouched by the general hedonism and brutality of his time, he has pity and compassion for the slave and for the beast of burden. He is a civilized man, with an educated heart.

To such a writer we may listen with profit.

As psychic science becomes better understood the portents, visions and other events recorded by Plutarch drop into their right places.

In his *Life Of Theseus*, the first of the series, he says:
"In succeeding ages the Athenians honoured Theseus as a demigod, induced to it as well by other reasons, as because, when they were fighting the Medes at Marathon, a considerable part of the army thought they saw the apparition of Theseus completely armed and bearing down before them on the barbarians."

Doesn't this remind you of the vision of the Angels of Mons in World War I? When, in a supreme crisis, the soldiers of England saw the spirits of the bowmen of Agincourt fighting on their side!

In his *Life of Romulus* Plutarch says:
"While things were in this disorder, a senator of great distinction, and

famed for sanctity of manners, Julius Proculus by name, went into the Forum, and declared on the most solemn oaths, before all the people, that as he was travelling on the road, Romulus met him, in a form more noble and august than ever, and clad in dazzling armour. Astonished at the sight, he said to him, 'For what misdemeanor of ours, O king, have you so untimely left us?' To which he answered, 'It pleased the gods, my good Proculus, that we should dwell with men for a time, and having founded a city the most powerful in the world, return to heaven, whence we came! This is very like the Grecian account concerning Aristeas, the Proconnesian. For Aristeas, as they tell us, expired in a fuller's shop; and when his friends came to take away the body, it could not be found. Soon after some persons coming in from a journey said, they met Aristeas travelling toward Croton."

How like the account of the Disciples meeting Jesus on the road to Emmaus!

In the *Life Of Themistocles*, Plutarch speaks of the battle of Salamis, one of the decisive naval fights of history:
"While the fight was thus raging, a great light appeared, as from Eleusis; and loud sounds and voices were heard through all the plain of Thriasia to the sea, as of a great number of people carrying the mystic symbols of Bacchus in procession. A cloud, too, seemed to rise from among the crowd that made this noise, and to ascend by degrees, until it fell upon the galleys. Other phantoms also, and apparitions of armed men, they saw, stretching out their hands from Aegina before the Grecian fleet. These they conjectured to be the Eacidae, to whom, before the battle, they had addressed their prayers for succour."

Herodotus too, in his *History*, makes mention of these voices and visions at Salamis.

In the *Life Of Camillus* we read:
"Camillus, in offering up his petition, touched the image of the goddess Juno, and entreated her to go with them and she consented. Those that support and defend the miracle, have the fortune of Rome on their side, which could never have risen from such small and contemptible beginnings to that height of empire, without the assistance of some god. Several miracles of a similar nature are also alleged; as, when images have often sweated; that they have been heard to groan; and that sometimes they have turned from their

votaries and shut their eyes. Many such accounts we have from our ancients; and not a few persons of our own time have given us wonderful relations, not unworthy of notice. But to give entire credit to them, or altogether to disbelieve them, is equally dangerous. It is best to be cautious, and to avoid extremes."

Again, in the same *Life*, Plutarch writes:
"The first token of the approaching calamities was the death of Julius the Censor. A second token happened a little before the exile of Camillus. Marcus Ceditius, a person of great probity and virtue, informed the military tribunes of a matter which deserved attention. As he was going the night before along what is called the New Road, he was addressed by a loud voice. Turning about he saw nobody, but heard these words in an accent more than human, 'Go, Marcus Ceditius, and early in the morning acquaint the magistrates that they must shortly expect the Gauls.' But the tribunes made a jest of the information, and soon after followed the disgrace of Camillus."

Then he tells the sequel, after the return of Camillus from exile:
"Next, Camillus sacrificed to the gods, and purified the city, in a form dictated by the pontiffs. He rebuilt the former temples, and created a new one to Aius Loquutius, the *speaker*, or *warner*, upon the very spot where the voice from heaven announced in the night to Marcus Ceditius the coming of the barbarians."

In the same *Life* Plutarch writes:
"The persons appointed to search for the holy places found all in confusion. As they came to the court of Mars, where the buildings, like the rest, were burned by the barbarians, they discovered under a great heap of ashes the augural staff of Romulus. When he was taken out of the world, the priests carefully preserved it from defilement, like other holy relics; and this having escaped the fire when the rest were consumed, they considered it a presage that Rome would last for ever."

The staff of Romulus, regarded with veneration for centuries, had acquired an immunity from destruction. This strongly reminds us of the many instances of Bibles and Crucifixes surviving untouched in buildings reduced to ashes.

In the *Life of Pericles* we read:
"In the building of the vestibule of the Citadel, one of the best workmen, missing his step, fell from the top to the bottom, and his life was despaired of by the physicians. Pericles was greatly concerned at this accident, but in the midst of his anxiety the goddess appeared to him in a dream, and informed him of a remedy, which was applied, and thereby soon recovered the patient. In memory of this cure, he placed in the Citadel, near the altar, a brazen statue of the Minerva of Health."

A little later Plutarch writes:
"About this time Pericles was seized with the plague, but not with such symptoms as it generally shows. Theophrastus relates, that Pericles showed to a friend, who came to visit him in his sickness, an amulet which the women had hung about his neck, intimating that he must be sick indeed, since he submitted to such a thing!"
It appears that the use of talismans and religious models is not exactly of recent origin! Possibly this "superstition" has some basis in fact, and the long experience of humanity has shown some connection between consecrated amulets and good fortune.

In the *Life of Fabius Maximus* we find:
"Hannibal, invading Italy, gained the battle of Trebia, laying waste the country, and striking Rome itself with terror. This desolation was announced by signs and prodigies, some quite strange and unaccountable. For it was said that certain shields sweated blood; that the Falerians saw the heavens open and billets fell."
These bleeding shields may have been the 12 sacred Anciles, which had hung in the temple of Vesta since the time of Numa. The bleeding image of St Ann, as related in FATE for May, 1954, lends credibility to the account of the bleeding shields.
In the *Life of Coriolanus*, Plutarch has an interesting passage in which his incredulity and scepticism assert themselves and oppose the testimony of many eye-witnesses. He relates how, after the city was delivered from the imminent threat of the Volscians, largely by the heroism of the women, a new temple was built and the image of the goddess (whom he does not name), uttered these words: "O Women! Most acceptable to the gods is this your pious gift!"
Then he adds: "They report that this voice was repeated

twice, thus offering to our faith things that appear impossible. Indeed, we will not deny that images may have sweated, may have been covered with tears, and emitted drops like blood, for wood and stone often contract a scurf and moldiness that produce moisture. They do not exhibit many different colours themselves, but receive a variety of tinctures from the ambient air; at the same time there is no reason why the Deity may not make use of these signs to announce things to come. It is also very possible that a sound like a sigh or a groan may proceed from a statue, by the rupture or violent separation of some of the interior parts: but that an articulate voice and expression so clear, so full and perfect, should fall from a thing inanimate, is out of all the bounds of possibility. For neither the soul of man, nor even God himself, can utter vocal sounds, and pronounce words without an organized body and parts fitted for utterance. Wherever, then, history asserts such things, and bears us down with the testimony of many credible witnesses, we must conclude that some impression not unlike that of sense, influenced the imagination, and produced the belief of a real sensation; as in sleep we seem to hear what we hear not, and to see what we do not see. As for those persons who are possessed with such a strong sense of religion that they cannot reject anything of this kind, they found their faith on the wonderful and incomprehensible power of God. For there is no manner of resemblance between him and a human being, either in his nature, his wisdom, his power or his operations. If, therefore, he performs something which we cannot effect, and executes what with us is impossible, there is nothing in this contradictory to reason; since, though he far excels us in everything, yet the dissimilitude and distance between him and us, appear most of all in the works which he hath wrought. 'But much knowledge of things divine,' as Heraclitus affirms, 'escapes us through want of faith'."

In the *Life of Timoleon* he says:
"It was in the night that he set sail, and was making his way, when on a sudden the heavens seemed to be rent asunder, and to pour upon his ship a bright and spreading flame, which soon formed itself into a torch, such as is used in the sacred mysteries; and 'having conducted them through their whole course, brought them to that quarter of Italy for which they designed to steer. The soothsayers declared that this appearance perfectly agreed with the dream of the priestesses, and that by this light from heaven the goddesses showed themselves interested

in the success of the expedition. Particularly as Sicily was sacred to Proserpine, and the island was bestowed on her as a nuptial gift."

The brilliant light that guided Timoleon to his destination corresponds strongly to the Pillar of Fire which went before the Israelites.

In the same *Life* we read:
"Upon this the people of Adranum opened their gates to Timoleon, declaring with terror that during the battle the sacred doors of the temple opened of their own accord, the spear of their god was seen to shake to the very point, and his face dropped with sweat."

In the *Life of Pyrrhus* Plutarch writes:
"It was believed that he cured the swelling of the spleen by sacrificing a white cock, and with his right foot gently pressing the part affected, the patients lying upon their backs for that purpose. There was no person, however poor or mean, refused this relief, if requested. He received no reward, except the cock for sacrifice, and this present was very agreeable to him. It is also said that the great toe of that foot had a divine virtue in it; for, after his death, when the rest of the body was consumed, that toe was found untouched by the flame."

Here we have a parallel to the King's Touch for scrofula, as practiced by the royal houses of France and England from the time of Saint Louis to the reign of Queen Anne.

In the *Life of Sylla* (or Sulla), Plutarch relates that the general, being in Asia Minor with his troops, had a vivid dream in which the goddess Bellona appeared to him:
"She seemed to stand by him, and put thunder in his hand, and having called his enemies by name one after another, bade him strike them: they fell and were consumed by it to ashes. Encouraged by this vision, he took his way to Rome."

To this vision, which induced Sylla to break off hostilities with Mithradates and return to Rome, he owed the fact that he became emperor.

Plutarch also tells us:
"In all his battles he wore in his bosom a small golden image of Apollo, which he brought from Delphi. On this occasion he kissed it with

particular devotion, and addressed it in these terms: 'O Pythian Apollo, who hast conducted the fortunate Cornelius Sylla through so many engagements with honour; when thou hast brought him to the threshold of this country, wilt thou let him fall there inglorious by the hands of his own citizens?'"

In the *Life of Cimon*, Plutarch tells an anecdote of a young man, Damon by name, who with some accomplices had killed the whole senate of the town of Cheronca, in revenge for some insult to himself. But under pretense of pardoning him, the citizens lured him back into the city, and immediately after killed him as he was anointing himself in the bathhouse. Plutarch adds:
"For a long time certain spectres appeared on that spot and sad groans were heard; for which reason the doors of the bath were walled up. And to this very day those who live in that neighbourhood say that they see strange sights and are alarmed by doleful voices."
It is possible that in this case Plutarch had direct knowledge of these phenomena, for it was in this town of Cheronea that he lived through all the latter part of his life, and in which he wrote his famous *Lives*.

In the same *Life of Cimon* we read:
"When Pausanias was at Byzantium, he cast his eyes upon a young virgin named Cleonice, of a noble family there, and insisted upon having her for a mistress. The parents, intimidated by his power, were under the hard necessity of giving up their daughter. The young woman begged that the light might be taken out of his apartment, that she might go to his bed in secrecy and silence. When she entered he was asleep, and she unfortunately stumbled upon the candlestick, and threw it down. The noise waked him suddenly, and he, in his confusion, thinking it was an enemy coming to assassinate him, unsheathed a dagger that lay by him, and plunged it into the virgin's heart. After this he could never rest. Her image appeared to him every night and with a menacing tone repeated this heroic verse – 'Go to the fate which pride and lust prepare!'
"The allies, highly incensed at this infamous action, joined Cimon to besiege him. But he escaped; and as he was still haunted by the spectre, he applied to the temple at Heraclea, where the dead were consulted. There he invoked the spirit of Cleonice and entreated her

pardon. She appeared and told him: 'He would soon be delivered from all his troubles, after his return to Sparta,' in which it seems his death was enigmatically foretold. These particulars we have from many historians."

The editors of Plutarch added this note: "Pausanias applied to the necromancers at Heraclea called Psychagogi, whose office it was to call up departed spirits." Apparently, these were mediums.

In the *Life of Lucullus*, Plutarch tells that the goddesses Proserpine and Minerva were seen in dreams by many at the siege of Cyzicus, in Phrugia. A dream of one person only may be explained away as an act of the unmonitored imagination; but when an identical dream appears to a number of persons, it becomes a subject for parapsychology.

In the *Life of Pompey*, Plutarch tells of the mystic omen that appeared in the dawn, on the decisive field of Pharsalia:
"...a panic fear ran through the camp, the noise of which awakened him. And about the morning watch, over Caesar's camp, where everything was perfectly quiet, there suddenly appeared a great light, from which a stream of fire issued in the form of a torch, and fell upon that of Pompey. Caesar himself says he saw it as he was going his rounds."

Here we have, not a subjective impression received by one, but an objective appearance witnessed by many.

In the *Life of Cato the Younger* our author writes:
"Cato had likewise in his train some of the people called Psylli, who deprive the serpents of their ferocity by their charms."

The translators added this note: "Crates Pergamenus says there were a people of this kind at Paros, on the Hellespont, called Ophiogenes, whose touch alone was a cure for the bite of a serpent. Some writers asserted that the Psylli have an innate quality in their constitution that is poisonous to serpents, and that the smell of it throws them into a profound sleep. Pliny maintains that every man has in himself a natural poison for serpents; and that those creatures will shun the human saliva as it comes within their mouths, for it kills them innediately."

With these statements we might compare a passage in John W.

Vandercook's fascinating book *Tom-Tom*, which has a chapter on true Surinam. He tells of snake-cut, a black powder prepared by witchdoctors in the jungles of Guiana, which, rubbed into an open cut or taken by mouth, makes one absolutely immune to the venom of serpents. No snake will strike a person inoculated with it. And any snake coming within a few feet of such a person goes into a coma. Smaller snakes die. Some of this black powder, sent overseas to Dutch chemists, was analysed. Eighty-eight per cent of the ingredients were identifiable; 12 per cent were absolutely unknown. Is it possible that a person in whose bloodstream this potion is mixed, radiates an aura, or vibration, which affects reptiles? And does this in any measure throw light on Plutarch's Psylli?

In the *Life of Cicero* the biographer describes the pathetic last days of that orator's life. Hunted by the hirelings of Antony, "He passed the night in the most perplexing and horrid thoughts; insomuch that he was sometimes inclined to go privately into Caesar's house and stab himself upon the altar of his domestic gods, to bring the divine vengeance upon his betrayer."

This brings to mind the statement of Franz Hartmann, in his book *Magic, White and Black*, that many Chinese commit suicide with the express purpose of haunting an enemy and driving him to insanity. An Associated Press dispatch some five years ago reported that six young Chinese women, whose families had been destroyed and whose property was confiscated by Communists, killed themselves by mutual agreement, in order to take effectual revenge upon their Red persecutors.

Seemingly, this is what Cicero, hunted and desperate, considered doing for a time.

Finally, Plutarch, in his *Life of Antony*, recounts some of the omens that appeared at the opening of the war which Caesar declared on Antony and Cleopatra:
"Pissaurum, a colony of Antony's on the Adriatic, was swallowed up by an earthquake. Antony's statue in Alba was covered with sweat for many days, which returned, though it was frequently wiped off."

We can see that Plutarch did his utmost to be conscientious and cautious before including supernatural events in his history. Moreover, almost every event he did include had been witnessed by a number of persons.

He used such care in sifting the material for his various *Lives* that scholars, checking his statements against earlier writers, find small fault with his accuracy. His few errors are minor ones. No major mis-statement has ever been proved against Plutarch.

WHEN GHOSTS ATTACK
by Marcia Jedd

The belief in possession and attacks from the spirit realm has been with us for centuries. Is sexual assault from the other side possible as well?

While living temporarily in her mother's basement, Mary Klein awoke to the sound of heavy breathing in her right ear. "I tried to get up and I couldn't move. I couldn't talk or scream. It felt like there was a hand over my face," she says.

She was unable to move her spread-apart legs, and her shoulders felt pinned down. Her dog barked repeatedly and backed away from her bed. Her cat escaped into an adjoining room. An innate sense told Mary that she was being accosted by a large male presence without a physical form. "I had to figure out how to convince this entity to leave me alone, and I started to will it to do so in my mind," she says.

During the attack, Mary felt rubbing on her pelvic bone. "I got very angry with the entity and I think he knew it," she says. After several minutes, the presence and the pressing sensation vanished. "There was no actual penetration, but I was sore for two days," she recalls.

This wasn't Mary's first experience with the paranormal. She had witnessed poltergeist-type activity in a childhood residence, hearing noises and seeing a dark presence in a particular room. Later residents of the house reported activity in the same room. But for years Mary was too terrified to talk about her latest experience. She tried to dismiss it until last year, when she noticed a book in the library about ghost attacks.

A few weeks later, she felt bold enough to tell her mother, who admitted similar, less severe experiences. That was more than five years ago. Now, Mary reports no other attacks and remains convinced it was a random incident.

For Carla Moran, a single mother with four children living in California in the mid-1970s, nothing seemed random about the repeated and apparently violent attacks that, like Mary's, felt like rape. Carla sought psychiatric counselling and books on the subject, and while in a bookstore, she happened to meet Kerry Gaynor and Barry

Taff, two parapsychologists specializing in haunted-house and poltergeist cases. Gaynor and Taff volunteered to investigate Carla's case. Her story was overdramatized in the 1982 film *The Entity* and a book of the same name. Neither treatment was completely factual.

Carla was initially accosted by what she perceived as three entities – two holding her down while the third assaulted her. Over the course of nearly a dozen incidents, the number of perpetrators decreased to just one. Carla reported attacks that simulated penetrating rape in some instances.

Her teenage son described a particularly vicious attack in which Carla was thrown by the malevolent force and hit her head. He tried to intervene, but he was also thrown, breaking his arm. ("In the filming of *The Entity*, the actor playing the son broke his arm in that scene, and the curtains tore from top to bottom without explanation," recalls Gaynor.) Carla later moved to Texas and the attacks subsided and eventually stopped.

Despite on-site investigations by Gaynor and Taff, as well as psychics and professional photographers, the attacks on Carla never occurred in the presence of non-family members. Gaynor observed only bite marks on Carla's neck and bruises on her body. But general paranormal phenomena in the house was observed by many.

Strange lights started to appear on the walls. Investigators covered the walls and ceiling with black cardboard and told the light source to move to certain spots. The light obeyed. On several occasions, it floated into the middle of the room, gaining speed and dimension, and formed into a distinct human-like figure before dissolving.

Gaynor remains convinced there was legitimate paranormal activity in the house, but he stresses that there was no evidence of anything paranormal about the attacks. If Carla did experience sexual assault, possible sources could have been a random violent spirit or disturbances in her psyche, such as subconscious childhood abuse memories.

The experiences reported by Carla and Mary are similar to other reports of attacks by unknown forces having sexual or rape-like characteristics. Gaynor speaks from examination of 900 cases over 25 years. "Sexual aspects to cases are not that unusual," he says. "It's far more a part of [paranormal] phenomena than is recognized. These may very well fall into the domain of psychological disturbances."

Demon and Poltergeist Lovers

Reports of phantom sexual attacks go back centuries to the realm of the incubus and classic demon lovers. The incubus is a male demon who lies on sleeping women to have sexual intercourse or otherwise abuse them. The succubus is a female version of this demon, and attacks men. Bruises and cuts might appear on the victim's body following such encounters.

"This is an ancient phenomenon utilizing popular figures in our culture, archetypes and myths," says Brad Steiger, whose many books on the paranormal include *Sex and the Supernatural* and *Haunted Lovers*. According to Steiger, incubi have many modern spins. The intruder may take on the form of a priest, a rock star or other respected or idolized figures. Alternately, a visitation could be triggered by a UFO sighting or alien contact. "Seeing a being seems to open the doorway," says Steiger. "They may not be aliens in the extraterrestrial sense, but other non-physical lifeforms indigenous to this planet."

One of the most commonly accepted explanations for entity attacks, especially when the victim reports pressing sensations, is sleep paralysis or "night heavies", a phenomenon linked to out-of-body experiences. "If your torso hasn't awakened when you come to consciousness, you feel like there's pressure on you," says parapsychologist Loyd Auerbach. But while victim Mary Klein has experienced the related sleep phenomenon of lucid dreaming (dreaming with awareness), she notes that during the attack she was fully awake, felt considerable physical discomfort and heard heavy breathing.

To understand the topic of assault by entities, it's important to differentiate between poltergeists, ghosts and other types of spirits. The word *poltergeist* literally means "noisy ghost". But an accepted theory is that poltergeist activity is actually energy that leaves one's body and has conscious or unconscious effects. Dishes falling off a shelf, loud noises and other poltergeist-associated activity may emanate from a living human – for example, an adolescent with repressed anger, sexual energy or hostility. "That energy *causes* the poltergeist," emphasizes Gaynor, adding that the energy typically manifests within ten feet of the person or "agent" causing the phenomena. "Poltergeist activity can be an externalization from the person himself or someone in the family," adds paranormal observer Bufo Calvin.

Attacks may also be a form of psychokinesis (PK) – the mind's influence on material objects, events and energy. PK energy can bring on self-inflicted wounds such as cuts, bleeding and bruises. The victim could be her own perpetrator, as her unconscious "dark side" manifests. Calvin suggests that mentally unstable adults may fall prey to such self-attacks. When sudden and unexpected violence, noises or other disturbances happen repeatedly in close proximity to a particular person, they are classified as Recurrent Spontaneous Psychokineses, or RSPK. Gaynor and Taff suggest that the case of Carla Moran had all the symptoms of RSPK activity.

This is not to say that sexual assault cannot be the work of actual ghosts – although in the majority of haunting cases, there's nothing to worry about. Most hauntings are simply recorded impressions of an event, and do not interact with the living world. But other types of spirits are akin to concentrations of energy, and the non-human realm can encompass parasites or psychic residues. "These parasites feed off human vibrations and become stronger or energized," says Steiger. Parasites can be found anywhere, often in public spaces such as hotel rooms.

Calvin goes so far as to suggest that a discarnate, nonhuman entity in search of a fix would attack a human sexually to gain energy. "Sexual energy is very strong, powerful energy," says Calvin. Indeed, orgasmic energy is associated with cosmic energy. Sexual energy, as the second chakra, is linked to creativity. That chakra is located in the sexual organs and governs relationships, sex and reproduction.

Meanwhile, lower-level entities could purposely attack a human to inflict pain, says Calvin. Hypnotherapist Dr Bruce Goldberg agrees, arguing that attacks of a sexual nature can fall into the broad arena of "psychic attacks". Psychic attacks, both sexual and non-sexual, may be inflicted by troubled discarnates or ghosts. But the most severe psychic attacks, which may contain sexual overtones and produce physical wounds, make up only a tiny portion of the phenomena, and might derive from true black magic or demonic activity requiring an exorcist, says Goldberg. Another twist is a non-human spirit posing as a human spirit in order to deceive a victim. Furthermore: "What have been perceived in history as incubi and succubi could really be witches or demonic spirits in an astral body," Goldberg adds. Suspected encounters of these types should be treated with caution.

But truly related to the dark side is the notion of *consensual* sex between a human and a discarnate entity, whatever its form. "One can invite this," says Steiger. "It's one of the most dangerous things a human can do – ultimately courting possession."

Marcia Jedd is a Minneapolis, Minnesota, writer who has covered the topics of astral travel, alien contact and the soul-trading "Walk-ins" for FATE.

THE GHOSTS OF GERMANY
by David F. Godwin

"Deep forests, gloomy mountains, limitless morasses, caverned rocks and mysterious springs - all these helped to shape the weird and terrible imagination which may be traced in Teutonic mythology and later in the darker and more repulsive aspects of magic and witchcraft, which first arose in Germany and there obtained ready credence."
– Lewis Spence

Germany, like every other part of the world, has its share of ghosts and ghost lore. One Hessian tale, reported by Jacob Grimm in his monumental work on Teutonic mythology, relates how a farmer named Kurt didn't seem to know that he was dead and continued to work around the farm. In the barn, he helped a worker throw sheaves from the loft. When the worker threw one, Kurt threw another.

But one day a stranger was hired to throw sheaves, and Kurt stopped working. When the man yelled, "Throw, Kurt!" the ghost seized him and threw him to the threshing floor, where he broke both his legs.

This rather minor tale serves to point out the difference between German ghost stories and those of other nations. In England, a ghost will merely scare you silly. In Germany, it will do its best to break your neck. Most German supernatural tales seem to possess an element of violence and deeper horror than those from happier climes.

Take Bishop Hatto, for example.

The Rats in the Walls
In the tenth century, there was a Bishop of Mainz named Hatto. Prior to becoming bishop, he was abbot of Fulda. There was a famine in 970, but Bishop Hatto had plenty of food. The starving poor congregated around his door, begging for food. Being rather a greedy fellow, the bishop refused to share his grain, which he had laid up for himself. In order to get rid of the pests, whom he compared to rats, Hatto invited everyone to his great barn. The hungry and poor flocked into the barn until it could hold no more. Hatto then locked them in and burned down the barn. Quite satisfied with himself for ridding the country of

these freeloaders, Hatto slept peacefully that night. But he never slept again.

In the morning, he found that rats had eaten his portrait out of its frame. Then a servant reported that rats had eaten all the corn in the granaries. Then came a messenger to tell that an army of rats was advancing on the castle.

Bishop Hatto looked out the window and saw the landscape dark with rats, advancing remorselessly toward his palace. In terror, he fled by boat to his tower in the middle of the Rhine. But the rats swam the river, climbed the tower, chewed their way in and ate the bishop.

To this day, tourists are shown the Mäusethurm (Mouse Tower) where the deadly assault took place.

Vivat! Vivat!
Not all German ghost stories are morbid or violent, however. Take the tale of St Cassius and the peasant.

Near Bonn rises the Kreuzberg. There once stood an old convent church on the mountain at the site of the martyrdom of Cassius and his companions, Florentius and Melusius, who died for the Christian faith.

Once, a simple peasant made a pilgrimage to the place to pray to St Cassius because of a bad harvest and his many debts. He visited the chapel and went through the required devotions. On his way back home, he stopped at an ancient Roman tower to spend the night rent-free.

He woke up when somebody tapped him on the shoulder. Standing before him were three Roman soldiers, whom he recognized as the martyrs of Kreuzberg. He followed them into another building, where they showed him a table stacked with gold. They filled his pockets with gold coins and offered him a glass of wine. He toasted them with the only Latin word he knew, from the vicar of his village church: "Vivat!" ("He lives!")

The three warriors smiled and returned his toast, and then the whole building was full of Roman soldiers drinking and shouting, "Vivat! Vivat!"

Startling himself by all the noise he was making by shouting, "Vivat," the peasant awoke on the floor of the Roman tower.

The peasant naturally assumed that he'd had a wonderful dream – until he felt in his pockets. They were filled with ancient gold coins. Elated and celebrating, he wandered the streets shouting, "Vivat! Vivat!" A watchman stopped him, and the peasant told him his story and invited the watchman to share a draught at a nearby inn. The story spread, and the road from the square to the tower was renamed Vivat Lane. It still bears that name to this day.

Other Tales

But these are very far indeed from being the only tales of the supernatural that Germany has to offer. In more modern times, there is the matter of how Adolf Hitler seemed to be protected and at times possessed by some strange spirit determined to propel him to his destiny, and Elie Wiesel's mention of reports of the blood of Jewish victims geysering from the ground for months after a Nazi massacre in the Ukraine.

From the Wild Hunt and the Flying Dutchman to WW II appearances by the Red Baron of WW I and the mysterious happenings surrounding the *Scharnhorst*, Deutschland has abounded in accounts of the unexplained.

GIVING UP THE GHOSTS
by Sue Politella

Gerda Mueller (name has been changed) is a Cleveland nurse whose problems couldn't be solved by logic. She had the sensation of someone riding in the car next to her whenever she drove. Lights would go on by themselves seconds after she had turned them off. Sometimes, in her peripheral vision, she'd catch a glimpse of a man sitting on her living room couch. And she was exhausted beyond belief even after a full night's sleep.

She was in a stressful new job and questioned whether these pressures could be the trigger. But how could they affect her kitchen lights? There had to be something more, and she wondered if she had a ghost.

"You need Mary Ann," said a friend, who gave her a phone number. "If you do have a spirit she'll persuade it to leave and go into the light."

Somewhat reluctantly Gerda called, not knowing what to expect. She explained that she was a nurse with psychic problems. Just from hearing her voice Mary Ann picked up some surprising information.

"You have three ghosts," she told Gerda. "The first, who's been with you longest, was a 20-year-old girl who committed suicide. She latched on to you the first week you started working at the hospital. She never leaves you, and she's the one who rides with you.

"The second is a man who died violently at the hands of one of your immediate neighbours during the past year," she continued. "He goes back and forth between the two places. He's the one who sits in your living room. He'd like revenge against the man who killed him, but no-one in that house is aware of him.

"The third is a Frenchman. He came into the house a few months ago with a medieval manuscript you bought. Does your basement have a small storage room in it?"

"Yes," said Gerda.

"Well, he lives down there."

Gerda had never been too happy about going down into that storage room because there were spiders there, but she'd been even more reluctant for the past few months, for more than spidery reasons. And she was well aware of the man who'd been killed by her neighbour. As Mary Ann told her more about the three spirits, Gerda was impressed by the accuracy of what she heard.

The two women set an appointment, and Mary Ann appeared on a hot, sunny afternoon. Gerda had invited two of her friends to be there.

Mary Ann usually gets rid of ghosts in fewer than ten minutes, but there's a preliminary period when the householder can ask questions of the spirits. That may take a half hour to an hour or more. The questions are usually about who the spirits are and why they are there. Once the ghost moves on, no questions are possible, and after it's too late, many people think of things they wish they'd asked.

The spirits speak
Mary Ann spoke with the spirits separately, because even though all three were in the house and aware of each other, they didn't interact with one another. Each lived in his or her own little world and had no interest in the others.

First Mary Ann spoke with "Dee Dee", a sensitive student nurse who killed herself in the early '60s. She took an overdose of drugs, but was afraid they wouldn't do the job, so she also slashed her wrists. She'd wandered around between the earthly and astral planes, and attached herself to Gerda the week she started working in the hospital. Since she was attached to Gerda personally, she never stayed in the house unless Gerda was also there.

The spirit spoke bitterly of an instructor who took pleasure in dehumanizing and humiliating the students. "It's her fault I did this," said Dee Dee. She mentioned the instructor's name, but no one thought to ask Dee Dee's real name until it was too late.

Bill Melton (name has been changed) was killed while trying to gate crash a party. He wanted revenge against his killer and had settled in the man's house. He moved back and forth to Gerda's house, however, because she was more aware of him. He was there only because of geography. He was the one who kept messing with the light switches.

Angry about a lot of things, he was glad his killer was in jail, but thought the sentence was too light. He was furious about having been buried in southern Ohio in a family plot, to save money, instead of being buried where he lived. He had a lot of grievances, but mostly wanted revenge.

The third spirit was far more complex. He was a French politician who lived in the late 19th and early 20th centuries. He was assassinated just before World War I.

He said his name was Jean Jaures. He was a Socialist and pacifist and had served in the French Parliament, as a member of the Chamber of Deputies, for several terms. He had lectured at the University of

Toulouse and written an eight-volume *Socialist History of the French Revolution*. He was unkempt and told Mary Ann that people had to tell him to take a bath. He was bearded, short and potbellied. He loved to eat and was in a restaurant having a meal when he was shot in the back on July 31, 1914, by a fiery nationalist. "He didn't even let me finish my meal!" complained the ghost.

Jaures had no idea how he ended up in the U.S. He wanted to go to the light but didn't know how to do it. He said he went to churches and even to other religions but couldn't find a way out. He may have been attracted to Gerda's medieval manuscript, which went back to 1450, as part of that same quest.

Sent to the light
When the information session was over, Mary Ann sent the spirits to the light. It was easy to do that with Dee Dee and Jean Jaures, because they both wanted it. Bill Melton was another story. He wasn't interested in light, but revenge. When Mary Ann showed them the light all three started toward it, then Bill stopped. Mary Ann strengthened the vision of the light and suggested to him that if he were to go on, he might find justice there. So after a brief pause he continued by himself. Until that moment, she didn't really know whether or not he would go.

One problem with spirits is that they continue the same way they were in life. If they were liars on this plane, they'll lie on the next level. Mary Ann can only report what they say, and she has no way of knowing whether their statements are true or not. She doesn't have time to investigate the facts in most of her hundreds of encounters, but Gerda and her friends were eager to check for accuracy. Though they didn't get Dee Dee's exact death date or name (she was obviously using a nickname), Gerda knew someone who had recently retired from the nursing school and who would remember the situation.

Bill Melton was easy to check because he'd been in the papers off and on for several months after his death, and all of the witnesses recounted the story. It took only a few hours in the library, though of course there was no way the newspapers could report about his feelings on the burial selection.

Jean Jaures was also easy. Since he was a historical figure, his biography appeared in the 1915 *Encyclopedia Britannica*, and almost everything he said about himself was easily verified. Through modern computer technology interlibrary cooperation, a reference librarian confirmed within minutes that his *Socialist History of the French Revolution* was available in two Ohio university libraries. Several biographies of Jaures have been written.

Psychic potential realized

Mary Ann has been able to see and communicate with spirits all her life. Her Italian grandmother had other psychic skills, and when Mary Ann was three, Grandma realized her potential. She encouraged Mary Ann by asking such questions as, "What does it look like? What is it saying? What is it doing? Is it nice or bad?" Then she'd say, "Make a nice white cloud and send them there." None of her other family members knew she could do these things until a few years ago.

Mary Ann went to Catholic schools throughout. She thought everyone could see what she saw, but she was rudely awakened in her first year.

She saw a decrepit old man attach himself to one of her friends and she mentioned it to her teacher, a nun. "That's just her guardian angel," said the Sister.

There were pictures of guardian angels all over the school building, and Mary Ann knew that old man was no angel. So later on the playground she pointed him out to Sister, who of course saw nothing. The result was to send Mary Ann to Father, which was serious business for a small child. She never again mentioned these things publicly, just to Grandma.

After she got into her teens, Mary Ann didn't like to do psychic work. When she married a few years later she never told her husband about her talents. One night they went to play cards with some friends, and one of them laughed nervously and said, "I think we have ghosts in this house." Neither Mary Ann nor her husband said anything, but on the way home she told him, "She was right. They do have ghosts." Then she told him about her abilities. He was surprisingly sympathetic, and when she began to work as a psychic he often accompanied her.

Mary Ann has much psychic potential, but she doesn't want to become scattered, so she limits herself to working with the spirits. That is not the same as channelling, which concentrates on more advanced spirits and which usually requires a trance state. Mary Ann is fully conscious during all her communications.

"If they've been to the light I can't see them," she says. "My job is to help them go to the light."

Funerals and haunted houses

Her biggest work is with funerals and haunted houses. She is called on to do funerals – about 200 per year, on average – because the family wants last-minute messages from the deceased. As a rule the spirit is present at the funeral service and goes to the cemetery, but it may leave after the priest commends his or her soul to God, or it may wait until the casket is lowered into the ground.

One widow knew her husband had money hidden, but she didn't know where. Mary Ann was able to receive the message that it was located in a stovepipe, and $27,000 in cash was found there. In other cases, Mary Ann obtained information about unknown safety deposit boxes and other valuables. Occasionally, the messages have been personal ones; unfinished business that she was able to clear up, giving the spirit peace.

"Most nursing homes have a lot of male spirits hanging around, waiting for their wives to pass on so they can go to the light together," she said.

In addition to funerals and houses, she has been reluctantly drawn into another area. Doctors and families have asked her to try to communicate mentally with comatose patients, to see whether they'd like to be kept alive or have the life support systems removed so they can leave in peace. She doesn't like doing this, but the patient reactions have been 100 per cent requests to let them go. None of them have wanted to be kept alive artificially. Sometimes they wanted to take care of unfinished business first, and Mary Ann passed on this information to their families, who handled their requests before shutting down the system.

Not all spirit dismissals are easy. It is more difficult to send children to the light. It doesn't work to ask them if they'd like to go see Mummy or Daddy, because sometimes these people were cruel and they're terrified at the thought of facing them. In these cases she has suggested that they could see Grandma, and occasionally this works. In one instance a little girl who had been murdered loved only her dog, so Mary Ann pointed out that if she went to the light her little dog would be waiting there. She left willingly then.

It is also difficult to work with the spirits of people who have had Alzheimer's or mental illness, because they're confused. It takes a lot longer to help them to the light.

Mary Ann has been asked by many people to write a book about her work, and she hopes to start that next year.

She dislikes the term "ghostbusters," and her card simply identifies her as a paranormal investigator. She has been helping displaced spirits for more than 40 years, yet she still learns something on every job.

And what did she learn from Gerda's ghosts? "French history!" she said.

GRAPPLING WITH A GHOST
by Becky Elder

Parapsychologist and professional wrestler Dr Johnny Peebles III comes face to face with a ghost in Birmingham, Alabama's central Public Library.

"From ghoulies and ghosties and three-legged beasties and things that go bump in the night, saints and angels preserve us," goes the old saying. Patrons of the central branch of Birmingham, Alabama's public library need no preservation from its resident ghost, as long as they stay out of non-public areas.

Built in 1927, the original library building is a beautiful stone neoclassical-style structure on the southeastern corner of Linn Park in downtown Birmingham. In the early 1980s, after the library moved most of its operations into its ultra-modern quarters across Twenty-First Street, the building was completely renovated using the original plans. Modern conveniences blend well with traditional style – the building looks very much like it did when it was new. It now houses the archives, government documents and interlibrary loan departments, along with administrative offices. The first floor contains the Southern history department, one of the most extensive historical and genealogical research centres in the South.

In 1953 Fant Hill Thornley became the director of the Birmingham Public Library, and held the position until 1970, when a heart attack ended his life – before the new library building was even on the drawing board. A refined, scholarly gentleman, he was extremely fond of books and learning. He was also a great storyteller. Thornley passionately believed that a library could be more than an educational institution. He is quoted as saying that "As a cultural and moral force, the library is unsurpassed." Believing and teaching that "libraries contribute to peace", Thornley worked tirelessly to provide the Birmingham area with a facility able to meet the needs of the entire community. At the time of his death, the Birmingham Public Library was circulating more than 2.5 million books per year – one of the largest per capita circulation rates in the country. Thornley ran a tight ship and made it his business to be aware of everything that went on in the library. Apparently he still does.

When Smoke Gets in Your Eyes

Although smoking is banned in the library today, one could smoke in certain sections of the building during Thornley's directorship. Library staff members who remember him say that you could always tell when he was coming by the smell of his distinctive cigarette smoke.

This odour is what alerted retired archivist Dr Marvin Whiting to the presence of Thornley's spirit a few years ago. Whiting was working in the stacks after hours one evening. He knew that the security guard was the only other person in the building.

"I heard the lift come up and the doors open and close," Whiting told the *Birmingham News* last year. "I heard the door to the room swing open, and turned to see what the guard wanted."

Nobody was there. Then Dr Whiting noticed the familiar aroma of Thornley's cigarette. Deciding that it was only Fant Thornley checking to see who was in the stacks that late at night, Whiting returned to his work.

Whiting said, "In a few minutes the door swung shut. I heard the lift doors open and close and the lift go down." The door into the area where Whiting was working is made of heavy oak and opens onto an interior corridor, which rules out the possibility that a gust of wind could have caused it to open and close.

When Whiting left the building later that evening, the guard confirmed that nobody else had been inside the library during that time.

Whiting is not the only person who's had a ghostly encounter with Fant Thornley. One day last year an employee who asked for her name not to be used was in the third-floor auditorium setting up refreshments for a meeting. To the left of the refreshment table is a doorway that leads to a modern, spacious kitchen. The only other way into the kitchen is a door to the storage area, which is kept locked at all times and to which only the security and maintenance departments have keys.

According to Jim Baggett, who succeeded Whiting as the library's archivist, "She saw a man who looked like someone from the 1950s walk through that door from the kitchen. It frightened her so badly that she simply ran out of the room. She had been in and out of the kitchen for the past few minutes and had not left the auditorium, so there's no way anybody could have got in without being seen."

Baggett showed the employee some photographs, including

one of Thornley. She was "pretty sure," but not completely certain, that Thornley was the man she saw. Library director Jack Bulow characterized the woman as very reliable, and added, "If she says she saw something, I believe her."

Another incident occurred in the same general area a few years after Whiting's sighting. An electrician who had been working in the stacks came rushing out, terrified, saying that "a man who didn't look real" had come up behind him. The electrician refused to return to work alone in the area again. When library officials showed him a group of photographs that included Thornley, he immediately pointed to Thornley's photo and said, "That's him." The unfortunate fellow was so traumatized that his company had to send someone else out to finish the job. Bulow and Baggett say they now regret that nobody thought to get the man's name so that they could learn more about his experience.

And in This Corner ...
As much time as I have spent at the Birmingham Public Library through the years, I have not had a direct encounter with Thornley's spirit. So as part of my investigation, I called on parapsychologist and professional wrestler Dr Johnny Peebles III to help make contact. Educated in California, Peebles has made a career of investigating ghosts, UFOs and other paranormal phenomena.

One stormy Tuesday evening in January, Peebles, his wrestling partner The Great Kaiser, and I met Jim Baggett to see if we could contact Thornley's spirit. As we entered the third-floor auditorium, Peebles, who had not been briefed in detail, immediately went to the location of the sighting near the kitchen. I won't reveal his methods, but we could tell that something was happening. Although we did not smell cigarette smoke, we did feel the air growing cold.

Peebles made contact with Thornley. He learned that the auditorium was where the spirit spent most of his time. Even though it was on the floor above where his office had been, he considered it his space. Thornley's spirit would return there when he needed to withdraw from patrolling the stacks or other areas of the building. Peebles sensed that Thornley was, indeed, keeping an eye on his library, and seemed to be pleased with how the it was being run.

Peebles asked Thornley if he was ready to go to the light. "He has not been summoned to the light," he reported. "He will go when he is called."

Branching Out

So far, Thornley's activity has centreed on the old library building. However, there is a small but growing body of evidence that he – or someone else, perhaps – may be watching over the newer building as well. His spirit has been spotted there by various people.

Not long ago a security guard was making his rounds before opening the main library building for the day, when he was astonished by a large, dense-looking black cloud on the third floor. The cloud did not move until the guard walked toward it for a closer look, at which time it simply evaporated. This cloud was not located near any vents or doorways.

Anne Smith, a newcomer to Birmingham, did not know about the haunting until the day she was on the escalator going down from third floor to the second. She sensed someone standing much too close to her, crowding her. Looking to her left, she observed a man's hand on the rail beside hers. When the escalator reached the bottom, she turned to give this man a piece of her mind for invading her space, only to discover she was completely alone. There is no way anyone could have run back up the escalator without being seen or heard.

Carol Hall, a local Reiki Master, reports that she smells cigarette smoke on other floors of the old library building and has now begun to sense a ghostly presence in the main building. Mrs Hall says that ghosts are attracted to people who can see them, which may explain the reason more people have not experienced Thornley's presence.

"Thornley is a benign ghost who truly does not intend to scare people," Peebles said. "He is simply trying to continue his work that was interrupted by his untimely heart attack. He feels his work is not yet completed."

The theory among the library staff is that Fant is protective of his building. Unless he sees somebody he doesn't know in an area that is not open to the public, he will leave people alone.

Jack Bulow says he sort of enjoys having the ghost around: "He brings us good luck."

THE HAUNTED CAPITOL
by Kathie Farnell

When a flock of Egyptian scarab beetles flew in from nowhere and started eating the dome of the Alabama state capitol, workers renovating the stately 150-year-old building thought they'd seen everything.

They hadn't.

Before the $33 million renovation was completed, they would be called upon to deal with a spectral woman, a haunted clock, a flock of chickens and a cat who may have been the reincarnation of a governor.

And, of course, the scarabs.

When the beetles appeared in late 1991, architect Bill Woodsmall was surprised, but not worried. He had other problems. The renovation had dragged on for six years and the cost of the project had ballooned from the original $4 million estimate. Woodsmall thought the beetles would go away. They didn't. They were eating the roof, a rubber membrane installed to help waterproof the dome.

Rubber, a natural material, sometimes attracts insects, but they usually leave when the rubber cures. This time they didn't. The scarabs, considered holy by the ancient Egyptians, kept coming back; the attacks were worst in spring but eventually the building was plagued by the scarabs every day that the temperature climbed above freezing. Woodsmall ordered an additional pesticide coating for the roof, but almost four years after the first attack, the beetles are still there. Every day a worker climbs out onto the dome, checks far scarabs and, if they're there, sprays them.

Then there was the ghost. One night in early 1992, worker James Gammage was doing decorative painting in a lift on the second floor, when he saw the figure of a woman in Victorian dress sweep dawn the hall and vanish. Gammage reported to custodian Billy Misseldine that while he was willing to work long hours on the job during daylight, he would no longer work nights in the building. Misseldine was sympathetic. He had also heard footsteps and voices.

The disturbance seemed to centre around the second floor in the area that had been the old Lieutenant Governor's office. Once,

Misseldine clearly heard voices in the office. When he looked in, it was empty, but the telephone was off the hook.

When the renovators checked back through capitol records, they found an account of a Civil War widow, a tragic lady who stalked the halls of the capitol through the 1870s and 1880s, begging officials to help her find where her husband's body had been buried.

Misseldine doesn't know whether the apparition seen by Gammage was the Victorian widow or not. Personally, he's more concerned about the clock. A clock-maker by vocation, he had taken all of the old clocks out of the building and had them repaired. The heavy marble mantel clock from the second floor governor's office was working when he replaced it on the mantel, directly under the painting of Confederate president Jefferson Davis. That night it stopped at 6.10. Misseldine examined it, wound it, and put it back on the mantel. Again, it stopped at 6.10. Since then, sometimes it works and sometimes it doesn't, but when it stops, it's always at 6:10. Once Misseldine entered the office to find the clock with its case open and the heavy glass lens cracked. He repaired it, but the clock still stops at 6:10.

A flock of chickens showed up in the building at roughly the same time the ghost was spotted. No-one knows where they came from, but a clerk who has a farm took them home. About this time, workers noticed a pregnant tortoiseshell cat who seemed at home in the building. She was a sweet-natured creature. They named her Lurleen, after the state's only woman governor, Lurleen Wallace, who died in office in 1968.

Temperamentally the opposite of her fiery politician husband, George Wallace, Governor Lurleen was a shy, conscientious woman who dreaded public appearances. Elected to serve as a figurehead for her husband, she instead took her duties seriously. Her efforts to improve conditions for the state's poor people undermined her health and probably contributed to her early death from cancer. Seeing the little tortoiseshell cat's proprietary air toward the capitol offices, some workers said this was Lurleen Wallace, come back to finish her term.

Lurleen the cat and her kittens have long since been adopted, and the capitol today is maintained as a museum. Tour guides are happy to discuss the building's history, including its ghosts.

They don't mention the beetles.

THE HAUNTED CHALET
by William Russell

In my travels I have had the opportunity to investigate several so-called haunted houses. Only one had a real ghost, although some of the other houses were haunted in a different way. But I will limit myself to the story of the real ghost.

In September 1971, my wife Helene, my children and I flew to Europe. We spent several days in London, then toured the English countryside for a few days before flying to Paris. Helene's Uncle Ben, an American expatriate, met us in Paris and drove us to his home in Larchant, 60 kilometres to the south. Ben, his French wife, Madelaine, and her niece, Charlotte, lived in a large, beautiful 15th century house.

We had expected to spend only a short time with them before touring Europe, but as October approached the weather grew colder, which made the prospect of travelling less attractive. Also, our daughter, Susy, three weeks before her seventh birthday, expressed a desire to attend the local school so she could make new friends and learn French.

Charlotte owned an enormous three-storey chalet on adjoining property. One morning Madelaine asked us if we would like to rent it for the token sum of 50 dollars a month. The 18th-century chalet, built by Napoleon III for one of his mistresses, was surrounded by a 12-foot-high stone wall that enclosed an acre of land.

We were to rent the ground floor, consisting of five large rooms and a kitchen. There was no electricity, but the kitchen had running water. There was a flush toilet in a small room that had been added to the west side of the house.

As Ben showed Helene the rooms on the first floor, I checked out the upstairs. An outside stairway led to the second floor. I entered a large chamber. It was like going back in time a hundred years. Fine linens and handmade quilts were on the beds, crystal vases and hand-blown glasses were on the tables; books, candles and various knick-knacks were on the shelves. It looked lived in. The windows were closed and no dust was visible.

In the hall I passed a library filled with books, then entered a magnificent master bedroom. In the back of a walk-in wardrobe was a large painting of a matronly woman staring boldly back at me, which made me shudder momentarily. The painting disguised a doorway. Behind it was a spiral staircase leading to the second floor, where there were two small bedrooms and a children's playroom. The playroom contained a miniature table and set of chairs, with a miniature tea set on the table. Dolls and stuffed animals were spread neatly around the room.

The temperature dropped drastically as I entered. It was 15c in the rest of the house, but this room was near freezing. I backed into the hall and it was as cold as a storage locker.

Instantly I felt desperately sad, almost suicidal. Something awful must have happened in that room, I thought.

The only prior experience that I could compare to this was when I used to visit my friend, Lee, in Los Angeles, back in the mid-'60s. Lee had an easy chair that faced a bay window with a panoramic view of the city.

The sensation of a knife

Whenever I sat in the easy chair and began to relax, I would feel the sensation of a knife slashing my throat. There was no pain, but I felt warm blood running down my neck and cool air hitting the open wound.

I nicknamed it the "uneasy chair." I was the only person who felt these weird sensations. Lee and his friends were amused by my reaction.

After repeatedly experiencing this for several months, I began insisting that Lee ask his landlord about the history of the apartment. At first he refused, saying that I was being silly, but he finally agreed to ask the next time he paid his rent.

On the first of the month Lee called me. He had asked his landlord if a violent death had ever occurred in the apartment. He intentionally did not specify the type of death. The landlord replied that three years earlier a tenant had cut his wife's throat, killing her while she was sitting in the easy chair.

Now, as I stood in the cold playroom, I wondered if the chalet, too, held the secret of a violent act that had taken place in the past. My opinion was that Lee's apartment in Los Angeles never had a ghost. I believed instead that it held a print of the murder.

Helene and I decided to live in the chalet for a while, but I chose not to say anything about the playroom.

In the following days I had times of discomfort. Sometimes when I was in my workroom making sculpted candles that I sold in Paris and Fontainebleau, I had the feeling that someone was standing behind me and watching me work, which made it difficult to concentrate.

On one occasion, when Helene and the children were out, I was sitting in our bedroom reading. Inexplicably I began to feel like committing suicide. Negative thoughts filled my brain, making me feel that life was not worth the effort. I put down the book and walked outside. It was a nice, sunny day. My depression vanished and I felt good. I walked back inside and again felt terrible. I repeated this several times, marvelling at my sudden mood changes.

Without being especially conscious of it, both Helene and I must have had misgivings about the chalet, because we spent a lot of time away. We went to Paris for one or two days at a time, cruised the local countryside or went out with Madelaine and Ben.

One day, three weeks after we had moved in, Helene said, "I suppose you know about the ghost?"

"What ghost?" I replied.

"Don't lie to me, Bill Russell. I know you better than that. You've been up in that toy room more than once."

"Oh, that ghost," I chuckled.

"Yes, that ghost." She didn't chuckle. "I've been up there once, and I'll never go up there again."

We compared notes about the coldness, sadness and whatever else we could think of. I told her I didn't exactly believe that there was a ghost. I likened the playroom to Lee's apartment in Los Angeles, but then conceded that it wasn't the same. Helene had no firm opinion, but knew that something wasn't quite right.

Several days later I was making a candle and decided to add an old, rusty railroad spike to the motif. There were some rusty spikes on the third floor, in the room past the playroom. Ben had given me permission to use them in my candles.

A wretchedly sad little girl

Ascending the spiral staircase, I played a little mind game with myself. If I sneak up to the playroom and peek in, I'll see what's in there, I thought. I quietly approached the open doorway and stood motionless for a moment, then quickly stuck my face into the entrance. At that very instant the door slammed shut, barely missing my nose. I was so shocked that it took me several seconds to regain my composure.

Suddenly my mind was filled with the vision of a wretchedly sad little girl who had slammed the door because she didn't want me to see her crying. I could see her clearly.

She was nine years old. Her soft, brown eyes contrasted with long, blonde ringlets that fell gently over her frail shoulders. She wore black, high-button shoes, a long grey dress and a brown jumper.

I opened the door slowly and entered. In one corner a small area was noticeably colder than the rest of the room. I stuck my hand, then my head, into the coldness and felt deep psychological pain, a crippling anguish.

In the following days the coldness began to frequent other parts of the house. I called it "the little girl" just to give it form. I thought that perhaps my mind had created her simply as a way of making sense of this strange phenomenon. But Helene also visualized a little girl. Her description was the same as mine, from the blonde ringlets to the high-button shoes.

One afternoon I was browsing in the first-floor library. I pushed aside some books on top of a desk, accidentally revealing a painting on the wall that had been hidden by the books. It was the portrait of a little girl. She had brown eyes, golden hair, a long grey dress; black, high-button shoes and a brown jumper. I was stunned. It was undoubtedly her.

My wife and I began comparing notes, to see if our perceptions of the entity matched. For example, one evening I had just finished tucking in the children and was lighting a fire.

"What just happened?" Helene asked.

"She just came in," I replied.

"Where is she?"

"At the foot of the bed."

"That's right," Helene said.

There was no doubt when the child was paying us a visit, or what part of the room she was in, because her presence was that strong. One would have had to be insensitive not to notice.

Her two favourite haunts were our bedroom in the evening and my workroom when I was making candles. She would stand directly behind me and look over my left shoulder. Her nearness was not especially scary to me, just bothersome. The coldness and the despair were hard to take in large doses.

Since only two bedrooms were available for our three kids, the two girls switched every so often. Peter, our three-year-old, stayed in the largest bedroom with either Susy or Julie. One night Julie was sleeping alone in the small bedroom. She woke up around 11.00 p.m.and began to panic.

"Mummy, there's somebody in here!" She said in genuine terror.

"It's okay, sweetheart. There's nobody in there," Helene lied, reassuringly.

"Damn it. She's in there with Julie," I whispered. I got out of bed to get Julie. She was so scared that the only thing to do was to bring her to bed with us.

"There, over there," she cried as I picked her up. She was pointing to a three-stair landing in the corner.

Behind the landing was a sealed-off doorway. Behind the doorway was a stairway leading up to the playroom. The entrance to the playroom was also sealed off. At that moment it dawned on me that this had been the little girl's bedroom, and that Julie was sleeping in her bed. After that night Susy slept in that bedroom, because Julie refused to sleep there again. Susy never encountered any problems there.

One day I took a load of candles to Paris and ended up spending the night there. I returned the next day to find Helene looking haggard.

"I didn't sleep a wink last night. She got into bed with me and stayed there. I finally got up and sat in a chair all night."

In mid-December the little girl and the severe winter weather took their toll. We decided to head south to Morocco. Three days before leaving, while I was watching the sunset, a full moon began to rise. I could feel its energy. It struck me that maybe I could help the little girl.

Perhaps she didn't know she was dead. After all, she sought the warmth of the evening fires and the company of a mummy and daddy. And her intense sadness seemed like the unbearable loneliness of one who had been suddenly cut out of the picture with nowhere to go and nobody to turn to.

I was unfamiliar with the concepts of house-clearing and

ghost-chasing, but I memorized a monologue in French, telling the child that she was dead, and that if she realized this, she would know what to do. I would tell her our names, our relationship to Madelaine, Charlotte and Ben, the present date, that her parents were long dead, and other things I thought might be helpful.

At 9.00 p.m.I grabbed two candles and went to the door.

"What are you doing?" Helene inquired sharply. She sensed that something was up.

"I'm going to get rid of the little girl."

"You're going to what?"

"I think I know how to do it."

I explained my feelings about the situation, and that I believed I could do something about it. Helene felt the same, but she had misgivings about my going upstairs because it was so spooky.

The hair on my neck stood up as I ascended the spiral staircase. I entered the playroom and sat on the floor. I placed one candle on my left and one on my right and waited. Within a minute she was in front of me. I could feel her.

The moon was shining through the window, giving the room an eerie atmosphere. I took a moment to collect myself, then began my monologue, repeating everything at least three times. I felt that I had the child's attention and had communicated with her.

The spirit returns

An hour later Helene and I were getting ready for bed. The children were tucked in and I made a fire.

"Damn," I sighed with resignation.

"I know. Just to the right of the fireplace."

"Oh well, I tried."

For the next three days we endured her presence.

On the morning of our departure, Ben was helping us load up the VW van that we had purchased in Nemours.

"How did you guys like living in the chalet?"

"It was nice, Ben, but it's haunted, you know." I followed up my comment with a laugh, so as to not sound too serious. I was fishing.

"Aw, everybody thinks that place is haunted." His answer was very offhand. He didn't bite.

After loading the van we walked next door to say goodbye to the ladies.

"How did they like the chalet?" Madelaine asked Ben, as they were standing off to one side.

"Bill said it's haunted."

Madelaine's response was interesting. First she glanced into the next room to see if Charlotte could overhear. She couldn't. Then she turned to me. "I'll tell you one thing; nobody has ever died in that house."

There was emphasis on the "in", as if to say that someone had died, but outside of the house. Her tone, and the way she looked at me, communicated that I had better drop the subject. I did. We said goodbye and drove off.

Dominique, Madeline's daughter from a previous marriage, lived in Cadiz. We stopped in for a quick visit before taking the ferry across to Morocco. One of the first things that Dominique asked us was how we liked living in the chalet.

"It was nice, but it's haunted, you know."

"Oh, everyone thinks that place is haunted. What kind of ghost do you think is in there? An old man, perhaps?"

"It's not an old man. It's a nine-year old-girl, with long blonde hair and big brown eyes."

Dominique's eyes widened and her mouth dropped. She backed up several paces.

"Who told you about her? Was it my mum?"

"No, your mum didn't want to talk about it. Do you want to? I would really appreciate it if you would tell me the story."

Dominique first made us promise not to tell anyone in Larchant, especially Charlotte. Then she told us her story.

"Back in the mid-'50s we went to the U.S. for a while. We stayed in Boston. I was 14. I had knew some girls who were my age. They had met a psychic who told them things about themselves; these things were true, but they were things that she could not possibly have known about. She gave the person the choice of being told about the past, present, or future. The girls always chose the past, because it's verifiable.

They thought this woman must have had some way of knowing about their private lives, but they couldn't figure out how, so they asked me to accompany them to her house, because she would have no way of knowing about me. Besides, I spoke English with an American accent, so she would probably think that I was from the States.

We went to her house one evening. The girls gave me the five-dollar fee and waited on the verandah. The lady began the session by going into trance. She visualized her mind going across the Atlantic, then described the Normandy Coast. Then she started describing the more notable landmarks of Larchant, such as the old church and some of the more dominant structures. Finally, she began to describe the house. She mentioned the old stairway railing that broke when I was ten, causing me to fall. She said that was how I got the scar on my knee, which is true.

Then she unexpectedly drifted over to the chalet. As she was describing the toy room, she suddenly screamed at the top of her lungs. I fell over backward in my chair. I quickly got up, scared to death. I grabbed her shoulders and shook her, trying to snap her out of it. She opened her eyes.

'Why did you scream?' I asked.

'Oh, that sad little girl. She's so sad, and she's still there.'

'What little girl? What are you saying?'

'She's in the yard chasing a ball, falling, can't breathe, can't breathe!'

"I stuffed the five dollars in her hand and got out of there. When I got home later, I told my mum what had happened and asked her if she knew anything about the little girl. She told me that she was the only living person that knew the story. She made me promise to keep it a secret, because it was a shameful crime of negligence that concerned our own ancestors.

A fall down a well

"The girl's name was Michelle. The date was around 1890. She was playing in the yard outside the chalet, unsupervised by an adult. The well was to be repaired and was uncovered, exposing a hole that was more than 70 metres deep. Needless to say, she fell into it and died. The body was never fished out, and the well was filled in with dirt. There never was a funeral, because the death was kept secret.

The family fabricated a story about Michelle moving to Paris to live with relatives in order to attend a private finishing school. About six months later they said that she had died from some kind of illness.

You must understand that not only would her parents have been prosecuted by the authorities, but our family would have had to live with the stigma of the tragedy even to this day, because our neighbours in Larchant are the descendants of the neighbours in Michelle's time. Not even Ben knows the story."

I was moved by Dominique's account of the little girl, Michelle, and of the overall implications of what this haunting meant. In addition to dying suddenly, Michelle had received no burial services.

Perhaps one reason we have funerals is to let the deceased know that he or she is dead. Another factor is that the unavoidable guilt that Michelle's parents must have had to deal with could have had something to do with keeping her earthbound, because they could not psychologically let her go as long as the guilt was unresolved.

It may be that a more enlightened approach to the funeral ritual would be beneficial not only to assist the disembodied soul to leave, but also to encourage the loved ones who are present to voluntarily let go, since this may have an effect on the deceased person's departure.

In May we decided that we had better go back to France and make preparations to return to the U.S., since our cash was running low.

We reasoned that since we were only going to be in Larchant for about three days, we would probably just stay with Ben and Madelaine, but as soon as we arrived, Ben ushered us over to the chalet. Relatives were visiting from Paris and they had no more room in the house.

"Looks like we'll have to endure Michelle for a few days," Helene whispered.

After unloading the van I could not resist the urge to go upstairs to the playroom. The first thing I noticed was that the room was not cold. I sat on the floor and looked out the window. Flowers were budding and birds were singing. After a few minutes I became aware that I was totally comfortable and relaxed. This was a first for me in the playroom. I wondered if Michelle was gone.

The next day Helene said that she did not feel Michelle's presence. I agreed. The atmosphere of the chalet was entirely different.

Helene had never seen Michelle's portrait, so I decided to run up to the library and bring it down so that she could see it. I went right to where the picture should have been, but nothing was on the wall except a faint dust outline of the frame.

My first thought was that Madelaine had removed it, since Dominique had undoubtedly told her that we knew the story, but that was not a possibility because Madelaine was a semi-invalid and needed assistance to ascend a stairway.

The possibility remained that she could have asked Ben to remove it. Ben did not know about Michelle, however. He was also a very guileless man who could not lie easily, so I believed that if I were to ask him about the portrait and he lied or tried to avoid the question, I would see it in his demeanour.

That afternoon Ben and I were planting some bulbs in the yard.

"Say, Ben, I wanted to show Helene a picture that was hanging in the library, but it's not there."

"Maybe you looked in the wrong place," he replied.

I had looked in the right place, though, and Ben was definitely not lying. I began to believe that Michelle had somehow managed to get rid of her portrait as a way of letting us know she was gone.

At around 9.00 p.m.Julie said to Helene, "Mummy, the monster is gone."

When I heard Julie's comment, I thought of the times from September December when the kids would play monster. One would be the monster and would chase the other two. At that moment it struck me that they had never seen a monster film.

"What monster, Julie?" I asked.

"You know, the one that lived upstairs."

"Did you ever see the monster, honey?"

"Yes, that night in the bedroom."

"What was the monster, Julie?"

"It was a woman. Not a big woman like mummy, but bigger than Susy."

"What did she look like, sweetheart?"

"She looked like Alice."

At this point Susy and Peter stuck their heads in the doorway to listen. It suddenly became clear to me that all three of the kids knew at least something about Michelle.

"Well," we laughed, "there's really no such thing as monsters. Now get ready for bed, kids."

Twelve years later, when Julie was 16, I asked her if she remembered the incident in the bedroom at the chalet.

"Of course. I was in bed, wide awake, looking toward the three-step landing. All of a sudden the blonde girl walked through the sealed-off doorway and stood there, glaring at me, as if to say, 'What are you doing in my bed?' That was when I realized that the bedroom had been hers, so I could never again sleep in that room."

HAUNTED HOLLYWOOD
by L. A. Justice

**Today's hottest stars describe their encounters with the
Other Side**

**Material Girl Madonna may be in a league of her own, but she
says she is haunted by the ghost of Evita. Talk show host Rosie
O'Donnell owns a house with a poltergeist inhabiting it. And
actor Randy Quaid watches television with his dead father.**

Hollywood is no stranger to ghosts and goblins, although celebrities
don't talk much about their mystical adventures. Perhaps they want to
avoid becoming tabloid headlines. Certainly nobody wants the flack
Shirley MacLaine endured when she went out on a cosmic limb.

Nevertheless, the paranormal stretches its long spooky arm
from New York to Los Angeles. And some of Tinseltown's finest are
dismayed to find they don't always have the starring role.

Visits from Loved Ones
Julia Roberts' dad checks up on her, even though he died from cancer
when the brown-eyed beauty was only 10.

"I talk to him every day," says the actress. "I tell him about the
good things and the bad. Sometimes he suggests things I should do."

The star of the hit *My Best Friend's Wedding* adds that she
and her dad are together all the time. "He's there whenever I want
him, day or night," she says. "It's a marvelous thing having him with
me. I know people think I'm weird, but it doesn't worry me."

Patrick Swayze, who made his *Dirty Dancing* pay off, is also
guided by his father, who died in 1982.

"We were so close that I want to cry every time I think about
him," says the star of *Ghost*. "I know he's with me. I strongly believe he
speaks to me in my dreams."

Swayze is convinced that people who are dead can come back
and visit their loved ones. "I believe death is a beginning, not an
ending," he said.

Olympic ice skater Sergei Grinkov, who died of a massive
heart attack during practice, still hovers near his wife, Ekaterina

Gordeeva. "Even though Sergei is in the cemetery in Moscow, I always feel he is here," says the Russian widow, who now lives in Connecticut. "He knows everything I am doing."

The dynamic ice skating team had been together since she was 11 and he was 15. Over the years they won four world titles and two Olympic gold medals. They married in 1991, but their fairy tale world was shattered on November 20, 1995, when the handsome, 28-year-old Sergei died suddenly.

Katya, as she is called, says the first time she returned to the ice alone she was devastated. But when the music started, she was amazed.

"I thought I wasn't going to have enough energy to skate well," says Katya. "But it was like I had double strength. I wasn't alone. I was with Sergei. That's why it was so good."

Anyone who saw her heart-wrenching performance knows that Sergei was nearby, guiding her every move, giving her the will power to go forward with the show and with her life.

Michael Landon's daughter, Cheryl, says her dad is never far away. The eldest of Landon's nine children, Cheryl developed a special bond with her dad at age 19, when he saved her life following a car crash.

When the star of *Little House on the Prairie* died of pancreatic cancer in July 1991, his daughter was devastated. Guided by her father, Cheryl wrote a biography of the beloved star. But she was too shy to promote it. Then something incredible happened.

"I was at home alone when I heard his voice clearly," says Cheryl". He promised that if I did the television show, he would show me a long-stemmed red rose."

A month later Cheryl was in New York, where she was scheduled to appear on the *Geraldo* show to discuss her book. Again she heard her father's voice, this time directing her to Central Park.

"I'd never been there before," she admits. "But I seemed to know exactly where to go. I was directed to a fountain and there was a long-stemmed red rose. Then I looked up and there was an inscription. It read, 'The Fountain of Michael the Archangel'."

A Heavenly Helping Hand

We all need a boost up the ladder now and then. Celebrities are no different. In her book *True Hauntings*, Hazel M. Denning says it's not rare for intelligent beings to communicate from the spiritual world back to the physical world.

"Their contact takes many forms, from dreams to visions," she says. "Perhaps the most common way is through intuition."

She adds that inventors, artists, writers and actors often admit they are "stuck" on a project. Then something or someone tells them what they should do in order to move forwards.

"Call it a hunch, insight, or inspiration," says Denning.

Whoopi Goldberg is one comedian who's convinced the spirits of great actors are with her to guide her career. "I'm a believer that people are still here," says the star of the Broadway play *A Funny Thing Happened on the Way to the Forum*. "A ghost to me is like perfume," she says wryly. "You get different smells at different times." Goldberg says she's had whiffs of actors like John Garfield, Bette Davis and James Cagney. "I've got a whole lot of spirits behind me."

Rosie's Search
For all her laughs and manic antics, Rosie O'Donnell is hurting inside. She was only 10 when her mum, also named Rosie, died of cancer. Now, Rosie has started attending séances at the home of a New York medium.

"Ever since I lost my mum, I've always talked to her as though she's standing right next to me," she says. "But too many things between us were left unsaid."

Friends of the funny gal say that Rosie's deep-seated insecurity is based on her mother's premature death. And although Rosie resisted turning to spiritualism at first, she has now changed her mind. Her friends add that she will never be at peace with herself until she makes contact with her mother's spirit.

While Rosie isn't blabbing about her psychic secrets, she does admit that when she makes contact she won't be able to keep it under wraps.

"I couldn't keep quiet," she says. "I'd stand on my desk and shriek, 'I just talked to my mum: What a beautiful day that would be for me.'"

Sounds of the Spirits
Musical manifestations are everywhere. Although he was shot down on a Manhattan city street some 25 years ago, Lennon's ghost is still

hanging around. Fellow bandmate Paul McCartney says Lennon has appeared several times since his death.

"The first time it happened it was scary," says the former Beatle. "I woke up at three in the morning and there was John. He just smiled and waved a bit, friendly like. I guess it's John's way of saying hello and letting me know there's life after death."

Yoko Ono says she has often seen her dead husband's ghost playing the piano in the family apartment. In fact, Lennon – a dabbler in the occult – predicted his own death after the Beatles' road manager, Brian Epstein, was killed in an accident. "I'm next," he said.

A British psychic warned Yoko before her husband's death of an impending disaster involving a man named Mark. It was Mark David Chapman who shot Lennon down.

Liberace's essence is also alive and well – at least according to Michael Jackson. The pop star says the late piano player has been visiting him for years. That could explain why Jackson's outfits seem to resemble Liberace's show-stopping costumes.

Jackson has a shrine to Liberace at his Neverland ranch. The room contains the complete collection of Liberace records, tapes of his television and movie appearances, and a huge closet filled with smoking jackets and other Liberace garb.

"He's my guardian angel," Michael once told a friend. "He's helped me get through the hard times. And when I wanted to become a dad, Liberace told me, Michael, you're a good and loving man. You should have the opportunity to be a father.'"

Down in Nashville Conway Twitty is conducting from another plane.

According to his longtime business partner and collaborator, L. E. White, Twitty sends musical memos from heaven. "He visits me from beyond the grave," says White. "I admit it sounds crazy, but Conway has come to me in my dreams more than a dozen times. We still write songs together."

After Twitty's death, White says he "couldn't write a lick". Then, in the summer of 1994 – almost exactly one year after Twitty died – the singer appeared while White was sleeping.

"He looked real," says White. "But instead of walking on the ground, he was floating on a cloud. He didn't say a word, but he gave me a big smile and began to sing. He played a beautiful little melody I'd never heard before. When I woke up I felt good for the first time."

White's been writing hits again with a little help from his ghostly pal.

Friendship Across the Divide

The late crooner Dean Martin is a busy man. Not only is he keeping an eye on his protege, Tony Danza, he's been in touch with his old pal, the cosmic redhead Shirley MacLaine.

The two were best buddies back when she was part of the Hollywood "Rat Pack", which also included Sammy Davis, Jr., and Frank Sinatra. When Dean died in December 1996, Shirley used her mystical powers to talk to him.

"He's never been happier than he is now," MacLaine told a friend. "He's been reunited with his son Dean Paul."

In MacLaine's latest book, *My Lucky Stars*, the actress admits she had a crush on the tenor. But since he was happily married, the romance never went any further than a kiss.

Shirley says that when Dean was alive, she was too shy to tell him how she felt. Now that he's in heaven, she says she can be honest.

"I can tell him he's always been the man of my dreams," she admits. "I know that some day we'll be together again – Dean, Frank, Sammy and me."

While MacLaine isn't rushing for the big reunion in the sky, she knows enough about the afterlife to realize there is nothing to fear or dread. She'll be happy with her friends for eternity.

Who Taught Tony Danza to Dance?

Tony Danza, star of *Taxi* and *Who's the Boss?*, now makes the girls scream with his Las Vegas song and dance routine. He says it's all because of his idol, velvet-voiced Dean Martin.

"I believe in angels, I believe in fate, I believe in being guided by those who have gone on," says Danza. "Now I feel Sammy and Dean working through me. When the door for them closed on Earth, I believe they deliberately opened the door for me to perform in nightclubs so I can carry on their type of act."

Danza grew up in East New York in a very unshowbiz family. His dad was a garbage man, and his mom was a homemaker. But Mrs. Danza was obsessed with Dean Martin and played his records nonstop.

"I woke up every morning to the sound of his music," says Danza.

When he made it big in Hollywood, Tony took his mother to Carmine's Restaurant, where Dean Martin was a regular customer. They got lucky one night and spotted the sexy crooner in a nearby booth. Mrs Danza went over, sat down next to him, and told him what a big fan she was. The singer was a perfect gentleman. Now Danza is convinced he has Dean's personal blessing.

"Tony spelled backward is Y NOT – that's what Dean told me," says Danza. "He says I should get on stage and just DO IT!"

Ghostly Glimpses
  • While Madonna was making the film *Evita*, she says she felt possessed by the spirit of Eva Peron, Argentina's first lady. The similarities between the two women are eerie: Both are bleached blonde Catholics who rose from humble beginnings to stardom.

"When I raised my arms to sing 'Don't Cry for Me Argentina', I felt Evita enter my body like a heat missile, starting with my feet, travelling up my spine and flying out my fingertips into the air," says the Material Girl. "Afterwards I could not speak, but I was happy."

  • Ten years after his death, handsome Cary Grant still haunts his favourite hotel. The debonair screen legend, who died in 1987 at the age of 82, is a frequent visitor – albeit an unearthly one – at the Rottingdean Club near Brighton. Even the bartender says that a good number of customers have seen the silver-haired actor in the bar and hotel – especially around room nine, where legend has it he once had a torrid affair.

  • Talk show host Rolanda Watts is guided by an angel – her late Aunt Flo, who died in 1986 at the age of 72. Rolanda says, "I feel her watching me and looking out for me. I can smell her and feel her. She even told me that I was going to show up in a TV station's board room. Now look at me."

  • Yolanda Saldivar, the woman who gunned down the 23-year-old Tejuana singer Selena, says the only thing preventing her from committing suicide while she serves her sentence in prison is the ghost of Selena.

"I dream about her every night," she says. "But for me there is no happiness."

  • Rosie O'Donnell's mansion in Nyack, New York, is haunted by the ghost of actress Helen Hayes. The 10-bedroom home was once the residence of Hayes and her husband Charles MacArthur. But their daughter Mary died of polio when she was just 19. Her presence still lingers, especially around the shrine Hayes made for her. But after plunking down a cool million, Rosie wasn't going to be intimidated by a ghost. She scoffed at the idea and called it baloney. She's not laughing anymore.

"Jeez," says the jokester after spending some time there. "I felt such a weird vibe, like someone breathing down my back." To remedy the problem, Rosie gave the house a complete makeover. But she shouldn't count on Mary vacating the premises any time in the near future.

Celebrity Hauntings

While we giggled at antics in the movie *Ghostbusters* in 1984, the unknown is no laughing matter.

"For most people, nothing is more terrifying than having an experience that flies in the face of common sense and science," says Dr Philip Stander, coauthor of *Poltergeists & the Paranormal*. He and Dr Paul Schmolling, a clinical psychologist, agree that the unfamiliar can be frightening indeed.

"When we hear disembodied footsteps or voices, or when we suddenly confront somebody who is known to be physically dead, we can be terribly unsettled and frightened," they say.

And Tinseltown is known for the restless spirits of celluloid stars who cannot let go and move on – like the one who lives with Deidre Hall.

The award-winning soap opera star says the ghost in her San Fernando Valley mansion doesn't bother her at all.

"He was a great friend of mine," says the open-minded actress. "I feel his presence in the house all the time."

Singer Englebert Humperdinck has made peace with the ghost in his three-storey Beverly Hills mansion. In fact, he and his wife Pat don't mind that the former owner, Jayne Mansfield, still visits now and then.

But actor Omar Sharif has mixed emotions about his pesky poltergeist.

"He usually comes out at night," says the star of *Dr Zhivago*. "In fact, one lady I dated for a long time refused to move in with me."

Although Sharif's penthouse suite has a magnificent view of the Eiffel Tower in Paris, the restless spirit is cramping the actor's love life.

"If I ever get married again I'll probably have to sell the apartment," he admits. "I don't think any woman wants to compete with a ghost, especially one that's moving her stuff around."

When no ladies are lurking about, Sharif is completely content to share his home with an invisible presence. And, in fact, he enjoys feeling he's not alone.

"He's certainly never hurt me in any way", says the award-winning actor. "The only time he's annoying is when I can't find my wallet or keys. But in the long run, he's easier to get along with than most roommates. There's certainly not going to be any arguments."

The X Files Ghostbuster

Gorgeous Gillian Anderson is finding that real life can imitate art. In her case, the mysterious happenings from her hit show *The X Files* are following her home.

When the actress felt a presence darting around the new home she shares with her husband and baby daughter in Vancouver, British Columbia, she was not thrilled.

"After we moved in, I felt there were spirits with us," says Anderson, who plays FBI agent Dana Scully. "It was really creepy."

Gillian was told that their home is near an old Indian burial site where many restless souls still wander.

"We had a Native American shaman come to the house and perform a ritual called smudging," she explains. "He burned herbs to purify the space. Afterward it was like the house felt lighter, as though whatever had been there was gone."

The actress, who makes a living as one who investigates UFO sightings, alien abductions, and other bizarre happenings for the television show, admits she believes in the supernatural and in the power of the mind.

"I'm not as sceptical about the paranormal as my character," admits Gillian. "It's something that I've accepted as being part of reality."

Michael Douglas is not so lucky. The actor thought a Mediterranean getaway would be the perfect place to find peace. But he was wrong. A nasty phantom haunts his $10 million mansion on the island of Mallorca.

The spectre is raising such a rumpus that a priest was called in to perform an exorcism. The ghost is rumoured to be the vengeful ex-lover of a Spanish king. According to local legend, she was killed by the king's relatives to cover up the illicit love affair. But her presence still roams the 300-acre estate, spooking Michael. "A friend of Michael's came for a visit, but she freaked out when Maria paid her a visit in the middle of the night," says one of Douglas's associates. "The ghost came into the room screaming and shouting. The frightened lady packed her bags and left, vowing never to return."

That's when Douglas consulted a priest.

"It was like a scene out of *The Exorcist*," says a friend. "The priest struggled up the hill toward the house in the dead of night. Then, while Michael waited in the living room, the priest blessed it and threw holy water in each of the rooms. Finally, they pronounced the exorcism complete and they all drank a glass of red wine."

Brooke Shields, star of the television comedy *Suddenly Susan*, thinks the set is haunted. She says that there is a "strange, ghostly presence" that she's felt on several occasions. One night when she went to the sound stage alone, she was rattled by a voice in the darkness.

"I'm an actor from another age," said the voice. "I just want to tell you there's bad luck for you here."

Shaken and petrified, Brooke approached studio executives with a request to switch sets. But they said it would be too expensive. Evidently they don't believe in ghosts.

L. A. Justice *is a Florida writer and writing coach.*

HAUNTED HOUSE IN TOKYO
By Edmond P. Gibson

Two men hanged themselves in the house. Did this explain the odd behaviour of the clocks?

THE old house stood vacant for 30 years. The landlord endeavoured to keep it in repair but 1952 found it with one upstairs shutter swinging loose, overhanging trees touching the house from both sides, the front looking forlorn with timber for needed repairs leaning against it and the garden full of weeds that encroached on the shrinking walk.

During the air attack on Tokyo even the bombers seemed to avoid the place. Fires swept around it, devastating nearby areas, but they left the house to a slower decay.

The house is of wood, built at the beginning of World War I. The builder disappeared from the job before the house was completed. For a time it stood unfinished and later the owner had another contractor finish its construction.

A German, one of the many who lived in Tokyo at the beginning of World War I, occupied the house for a time and hanged himself in it for unknown reasons.

This gave the house an unsavoury name and it stood empty for a little time. Then a Japanese rented the house. In 1922 he hanged himself in the same room where the German had died.

The Japanese are not superstitious people but two suicides in the same room in the same house did not make No. 164 Minami-Senzoku more desirable. Housing became more and more difficult to obtain in Tokyo following World War II, with much of the city bombed and burned out, but still no one seemed interested in this vacant house. According to the Tokyo *Shimbun*, it was run-down and was finally offered rent-free to anyone who would occupy it.

In August, 1952, Fujisaburo Takata, aged 32, an artist in desperate need of shelter, moved into the lonely, weather-worn house, empty since 1922. Mr Takata knew the tradition of the house but moved in anyway.

According to a story by Fred Saito of the Associated Press,

Tokyo, Takata did not find his new residence peaceful. Going to bed, he set his alarm clock for 7 a.m. but was awakened at 2:40 a.m. when it went off spontaneously at the wrong hour. He reset the clock and again it rang at the wrong hour. He took the clock to a repairman who told him there was nothing wrong with it. Mr. Takata bought himself a new alarm clock anyway but both clocks continued to go off at the wrong times in the morning. The repairman suggested that some other factor might account for their behaviour.

The books in the bookcase began to move about and books that he left closed on a table in the evening lay open the next morning. The doors of the house were flimsy and rickety. Mr Takata repaired them and fixed the locks but if he locked them at night they were open when he awoke.

The Tokyo *Shimbun*, Japan's largest evening paper, heard of Mr Takata's troubles and ran a short story about the "crazy clocks in a crazy house" in their issue of August 31, 1952. This newspaper story brought new trouble for Mr Takata.

From then on he received an average of 20 visitors a day. He had to stop his work to answer the barrage of questions from intruders who stopped at his house, day and night, to enquire about his ghost. Some of them asked to stay overnight to watch for the ghosts, while other visitors asked to share his rooms.

Fred Saito, who checked the original account which appeared in the *Shimbun*, states that Mr Takata is very shy and dislikes visitors. Mr Takata protested to him:

"I do not mind the crazy alarm clocks nor the ghosts. I do not mind the noises, the moving books and the doors that unlock themselves for no reason at all. However, I do mind these curious people. I can't get any work done with this constant interruption and if they keep on pestering me, I shall certainly have a nervous breakdown! My nerves are getting bad already!"

HAUNTED JAPAN
by Denny Sargent

Most Japanese have a healthy respect for ghosts and spirits. Even sceptics who announce that they don't believe in ghosts demur when certain spirits are mentioned. For example, the students in a class I taught became hysterical when it was jokingly suggested that we take a midnight field trip to the grave of the most famous ghost in Tokyo – Oiwasan. The most hard-headed member of the class fervently announced that it was fine to laugh about most ghosts, but not about Oiwasan.

Oiwasan was a beautiful woman who lived several hundred years ago in what is now the Yotsuya area of Tokyo, then called Edo. She resided quite happily with her handsome samurai husband. Though she was sweet and pretty, her family was not wealthy, and therefore her husband gained little financially from the marriage. Sadly, at the time, samurai received very little in the way of financial reward for their undying loyalty to their lord. It was not long, therefore, before Oiwasan's husband was attracted to the lovely daughter of a wealthy merchant family. She quickly fell under his spell and agreed to marry him. A marriage to her would be advantageous indeed, but first Oiwasan needed to be dealt with.

One night the samurai put a particularly horrible poison in Oiwasan's food. Not only did she die a painful, violent death, but the poison hideously disfigured the right side of her face. Her husband quickly disposed of the body, some say down the well, and wasted no time in marrying his new, wealthy bride. All went well for a time, until Oiwasan's vengeful spirit began to appear in the garden, crying and howling. For many nights this torment continued until, one night, the samurai could stand it no more and, grabbing his sword, rushed out of the house in anger and horror. There before him was the ghost of the wife he had murdered, her twisted face shining in the moonlight. He yelled, advanced and swiftly struck the spirit down. There a she lay, at his feet, truly dead!

He reached down, rolled the corpse over and screamed with terror. It was the dead body of his new wife who had brought him so much wealth, still dripping blood from his sword cut. Oiwasan never

299

appeared to her husband again – one assumes that she considered herself revenged. Yet the ghost of Oiwasan apparently did not find peace. Many people in Tokyo claim to have seen a beautiful woman in white wandering the streets at night, her long beautiful hair covering the right side of her face. After she approaches them, she suddenly reveals the twisted, scarred side of her face and then disappears, laughing as they run in terror.

Movie mayhem

Aside from numerous sightings of Oiwasan's ghost, tales are told about odd happenings during productions of the films made about her. Her story, of course, is perfect for a rather frightening movie, and the Japanese love ghost stories. Therefore it is not surprising that four movies have been made based on the story, each of them called *The Yotsuya Story*. The films have been made at various intervals over the last 50 years, but the most famous version was filmed in the early 1950s. Each of these productions had a number of mysterious problems on and off the set – several unexplained fires, a number of mechanical failures, film that disappeared or was oddly exposed and so on. A few people actually got hurt in weird, inexplicable accidents that scared everyone and made the news. These occurrences would stop when the cast, crew and actors (especially the actress who played Oiwasan) went to her shrine in Yotsuya and paid homage.

The last of these dramatic film hauntings took place only a few years ago. The make-up man swears that many truly odd things happened on the set, but the director refused to give in to the "hysteria and superstitions" until he mysteriously fell and broke both his legs. After that everyone went to Oiwasan's shrine to pray and the strange accidents stopped.

Devotional centres

Many swear that the spirit of Oiwasan walks the streets of Tokyo to this day and is capable of protecting women and children as well as scaring people. Her grave in Sugamo and her shrine in Yotsuya have become devotional centres filled with flowers, candles and offerings. One mysterious woman has devoted her life to taking care of the shrine. The most famous version of *The Yotsuya Story* is shown in Japan on TV at midnight every year at the height of Obon, sometime in late August. If you're visiting the country, keep an eye on the television listings.

Why do the Japanese have such a fascination with ghosts and ghouls? One reason is that there is nothing to contradict belief in these spirits in either of the country's major religions. Shinto, the animistic folk religion of the nation, and Buddhism, the national faith adopted centuries ago, have combined to create a curious and interesting mixture that accepts and propagates a belief in psychic and occult occurrences. Since there is no doctrine in Japan that magic or supernatural phenomena are manifestations of evil, Japanese society has generally been tolerant of these ideas.

The native and adopted beliefs that are the root of Japanese culture stress that there are a number of spirits (*boddhisattvas* or *kami*) inhabiting our world. They exist in many places and forms, and they can hurt or help you. Powerful people who die can become kami that can help (or hurt) the living.

Ancestor worship was an important part of ancient Japanese thought, and it is still a common belief that one's ancestors (called *shugorei*) constantly watch and guard the living. Many people also believe that if a person dies violently, his or her kami might come back and terrorize the living, so a shrine, or *jizo*, is built to offer repose to the spirit.

During the Edo period (1600–1868), especially, legends and ghost stories were spread, codified, and passed down from generation to generation. Stories of ghosts and *obake* (monsters) are now used to frighten or entertain children, but they were once widely held, serious beliefs. To this day many Japanese people won't swim in lakes, though they've forgotten that this avoidance originated from stories of malicious little water monsters called *kappa*. Traditions like this are strong and have made lasting impressions upon the Japanese, even those who profess disbelief. Because children are raised to believe in a universe swarming with kami, it is not unusual to encounter many intelligent, inquisitive people who deeply believe in spirits and ghosts.

Curse of the kami

One of the most famous ghosts in Tokyo is considered a kami. He is Taira no Masakado, the powerful warlord who was the leader of the unsuccessful Tengyo Rebellion. In A.D. 940 Masakado tried to make himself emperor of eastern Japan, but he was defeated and beheaded in what is now northern Tokyo by another famous lord, Fujiwara no Hidesato. Taira's body was buried in what is now Marunochi and his head was taken to Kyoto to be displayed. His head was later stolen by sympathizers and buried somewhere near Kanda Myojin shrine. Because of the nature of his death, his spirit was unleashed.

Masakado's often-seen ghost was said to be responsible for a number of miracles in Tokyo, but his curse was definitely on the house of Hidesato, especially the Sano family. Masakado's kami was eventually enshrined at Kanda Myojin shrine in central Tokyo. This caused a political rumpus, and at one point the Emperor Meiji even declared Masakado's kami evicted from the shrine. In any event, members of the Sano family were forbidden to walk in front of the shrine, and when the shrine had a festival, all the doors of the Sano house (in nearby Yushima) were closed up tight.

Many peculiar things happened to members of the Sano family because of this curse, but the most interesting came about because of a friendship. In the late 1700s, a man named Kanda Oribe lived near the shrine. He was a descendent of Masakado and wore his crest. He was friends with Sano Goemon, a member of the Sano family, and frequently went out with him. One day, they went drinking, but Sano felt that his formal kimono was inappropriate so Kanda lent him one of his. Suddenly Sano collapsed and went into fits. He became so ill that onlookers feared for his life and immediately called for doctors.

Kanda hurried after his friend, who was rushed back home. When he arrived, Kanda was shocked to find his friend completely recovered. Sano related that as soon as the borrowed robe (and the Masakado crest) was taken off him, the pain stopped. Both men were convinced of the continuing power of the curse of Masakado, just as most people in Tokyo still believe in the power of Masakado, for good or for ill. It is said that even today the descendants of Sano won't go near Kanda Myojin shrine.

Masakado has also caused havoc in the Marunochi section of Tokyo, where his ghost is held responsible for a number of deaths and disasters. Over the last 100 years, his grave, situated as it is in the middle of a quickly growing urban area, has been slated for relocation on several occasions. Yet every time a move has been attempted, accidents have occurred and people have died of mysterious diseases. This has happened at least four times, and almost everyone involved swears that Masakado's ghost possesses workers and either shocks or kills them. Cranes have fallen over, stones have shifted, cables have snapped and phantoms have been seen. The grave is still in its original location and there are no current plans to move it.

Obon: festival for the dead

Some of the dramatic events that you will see every August in front of Kanda Myojin, as well as in thousands of other places across Japan, are the dances, parades and bonfires that mark *Obon*, the time when the shades of the dead return to Earth.

Obon is a commonly accepted twilight time in Japan. The festival, which is older than anyone can date, commemorates the time when the veil between the worlds of the living and the dead is parted and one's ancestors return to Earth and commune with their living relatives. They are welcomed with strange dances and rites from August 13 until around the end of the month. The most famous of the dances, the circular dance called *Bon Odori*, is a lively entertainment that conceals an ancient, spooky ritual. The original object of Bon Odori was to call forth the shades of departed relatives so participants could dance with them, which is why everyone dances alone. If you carefully watch the more dedicated dancers, you might see an otherworldly gleam in their eyes. Many a strange ghost picture and odd phenomenon has been recorded around Bon Odori circles.

During Obon it is also traditional for the family to visit the ancestral *haka* or grave. Usually a large number of relatives are buried in the haka. The grave is cleaned and the departed's favourite sake, cigarettes or food offered, along with the more common flowers, incense, mekans and mochi sweets. The families that remember the older traditions also make a small horse doll out of aubergines and place this on the grave. This is so the spirits of the dead may use it to ride back to the material world and visit.

Though it is nice to visit those long gone, keep them up to date on the family and ask for some help, it is also a good thing that they don't hang around too long. Japanese legends abound with horror stories about ghosts that decided it was better to stay than to return to the realm of the dead. So, at the end of Obon season, great bonfires are built to help send the ghostly visitors back to the beyond. The most famous example of this fiery goodbye is the Daimonji festival in Kyoto, where the bonfires take the form of huge characters on seven hills surrounding the city. After this send-off, Obon is over and the world returns to normal.

One of the less serious Obon pastimes is telling ghost stories around a bonfire or in a dark room. It is traditional for all the participants to huddle together in a dark and desolate place surrounded by 100 lit candles. After each ghost story is told, one candle is blown out. This continues until the last candle is extinguished.

"One plate, two plates..."

One of the popular stories is that of the plate-counting ghost. The story of Okiku, the "well ghost", is a tragic tale that is known by almost everyone in Tokyo. Though she seems to have found rest, unlike Oiwasan, one can still terrify Japanese kids by sneaking up behind them and saying "one plate, two plates, *three plates...*"

During the Shoho era (1644–48) a certain samurai who served a local lord had a set of 10 dishes that he valued above all things. The man was married to a nasty, vindictive woman and, as was usual, they had a maidservant who took care of the house. This shy young woman was treated horribly by the wife, who was jealous of her youth and beauty. One day, the wife broke one of the plates by mistake and, fearing the wrath of her husband, threw the pieces into the well. She then accused the maid of stealing it. The samurai was furious and in the heat of anger beat the maid and cast her out. The innocent maid, in despair, supposedly either hung herself by the well or leaped into the well and drowned herself.

Soon after, her ghost began to appear near the well, and every night the samurai and his guilty wife awoke to a voice saying, "One plate, two plates, three plates, four plates..." and so on. After the ninth plate was counted, there was only hysterical sobbing. This would die down and then the ghostly plate counting would be repeated again and again until daybreak. This strange occurrence became known to all the other samurai.

One, a friend of the now deeply disturbed master of the house, agreed to see what he could do. He hid by the well, and when the ghost of Okiku appeared, he was ready. When she started counting, he crept closer, and when she got to "nine plates" and was about to cry, he yelled "ten plates!" and she disappeared, never to be seen again. It would be easy to discount this story except that there are detailed records of it, and the maid's grave is clearly marked in a graveyard in Kichijoji, one of the larger Buddhist temples in Tokyo.

Protection from spirits

It was in a Buddhist temple like this that a friend's encounter with a ghost recently occurred. She was attending the funeral of her grandmother with her family when, as they were leaving, her younger sister turned to them with an odd expression and began talking in her grandmother's voice. She told them that all was fine and that the service had been wonderful. Such hauntings and possessions are not uncommon, according to Japanese legends.

It is also from Buddhist temples (or nearby shrines) that one can obtain spiritual defences against ghosts if a not so familiar one takes a particular liking to you. You can, as most Japanese do, obtain and carry an *omamori*, a magical charm. These come in assorted styles and vary in function from protecting against traffic accidents to facilitating pregnancy. You can get a *mayoke omamori* that wards off general bad fortune, and this should ward off ghosts. An *ofuda* can also be purchased at a temple or shrine. This is a rectangular paper amulet that contains the name (and thus the power) of a Buddhist or Shinto deity. It should be placed near one's doorway where it will repel all ghostly visitors or, if imminent attack is foreseen, it can be placed on the forehead as one faces the nasty spirit and recites prayers.

For a devout Buddhist, there is another way to blast ghosts back to the netherworld: by chanting mantras (*okyo*) and brandishing *juzu*, or prayer beads, at the ghost. In popular films and folklore this is a sure bet, but one has to have at least some spiritual clout for this method to work. Most people simply experience the presence of a ghost with a mixture of resignation, fear and excitement.

An amazing number of Japanese people claim to have seen ghosts. The stories are often surprisingly similar and can be typified with two contemporary examples. If you ask around, you will hear hundreds of stories similar to these:

Keiko M. suddenly awoke in her bed covered with the sweat of fear. She was paralysed and couldn't move a muscle or make a sound. Suddenly, at the foot of her bed, she noticed the figure of an old man. He floated there and gestured at her. Then she passed out. She has no idea who he was, but this experience has happened several times.

Yasuyuki O. was riding home on his bicycle late at night. He came to a hill and began to coast down it. He felt something cold at his back and turned around. He saw a beautiful, white woman clinging to his back and laughing. He screamed and crashed his bike. When he regained his senses, the apparition was gone.

Traditional Japanese ghosts are easy to differentiate from Western ghosts. The Edo-period image of a ghost, still quite popular in tales, is of a transparent being wearing a white kimono and a white triangular headdress. Its arms are extended and bend down at the wrists. Japanese ghosts never have legs and always float above the ground. Ghosts seen in Tokyo nowadays usually are legless and white, but otherwise they seem to have evolved more contemporary appearances.

One thing that hasn't changed is the widespread fascination with ghosts. TV shows, magazines and even cartoons constantly reinforce an idea that has been held by the Japanese for centuries – that the living are merely links to long chains of ancestors that stretch off into another world, a world they too will someday inhabit. To most people in Tokyo, the mundane and spiritual lie side by side, and there are moments where the two meet and mingle. The *torii* or gate of every shrine sitting amidst the gleaming modern skyscrapers of the city announces the entrance to another world, the realm of the spirits.

So if you are wandering past a graveyard late at night in a shitamachi area of Tokyo during Obon and you hear "Huuuuuuuuuuuuuu dorodorodoro... urameshiya!!!!" it would be best if you held your omamori tightly in your hands and quickly walked away toward a more modern area of the city.

Denny Sargent is the author of Global Ritualism *(Llewellyn Worldwide, 1994) and an ecological textbook. He has also taught English as a second language and has worked as a journalist.*

⚲ THE HAUNTED TRAIN AT EASTER TIME ⚲

Some 40 years ago, at Easter, I was returning home from Plumas, Manitoba, where I had been teaching. I had an experience that, viewed in retrospect, is most peculiar. I thought nothing about it at the time, though.

I got on the train at suppertime. The short days, though getting longer at this time of the year, still made for a long night.

Sometime during the night, all the passengers going north – my way – got off the train at their various destinations. I slept through it all.

I awoke during the night to find an exceedingly old couple, man and woman, on the train in my coach. They sat across the aisle and two seats behind me. I saw them at first peripherally. On turning, I found them with happy expressions on their faces. They had the appearance of being from the past. Their luggage was in hand-woven baskets. They didn't speak to one another or to me. I don't remember speaking to them.

The woman's hair was at one time blonde but was now greying. It was voluminous. It was braided in a style I had not seen before. The two braids were brought down behind the ears and pinned on top of her head.

I remember with strange vividness their gnarled hands which each held in their laps, motionless.

Their baskets were of a type I had never seen before. Was she wearing a sweater, but not buttoned up? She had a tight, ruffled collar. I was sensibly struck by the joy in their oval faces – but more in hers than his. Did the man have a grey windbreaker? They looked like a very long-married couple – perhaps each a hundred years old or more. A great, palpable love seemed to radiate from them. I am astonished at how clearly I can see them now, across the span of 40 years!

I must have dozed after the train passed Dauphine, and awoke at Ethelbert, up the line, to find the old couple gone, baskets and all. When getting off the train at The Pas, I asked the conductor where the old couple had gotten off. He said I was the only passenger on the car all night!

I have often wondered over the years about the event, and have no explanation for it, or indeed its significance. It was as if the train had moved back 100 years in time. At the time I thought nothing of the event – it all looked so normal! The womans braids were tight, as if freshly braided for her trip.

    – Walter Krivda, The Pas, Manitoba

THE HAUNTING ON
SOUTH SHORE DRIVE
by J. Anthony

**"Look at what I've done," the spectre said, extending the
bloody stump of his arm.**

In the crisp Minnesota autumn of 1979, Dave M. and his family moved
into an empty house, nestled along a windy stretch of road just outside
Albert Lea. The blue two-storey house blended in naturally with its
rural setting. A large maple tree stood in the front garden, and a lake
wasn't far away.

Dave felt uneasy about the move. He believed that something
was terribly wrong with the house. Even so, his wife Selina loved the
house for its roominess and design, and she convinced Dave to give it
a try.

As they moved in, their landlord mentioned that the previous
tenants had left abruptly, abandoning many of their possessions. They
even left some of their things strewn across the driveway, indicating
that they had departed in a hurry. The landlord had received no prior
notice of their departure.

From the beginning, Dave felt he was always being watched.
The sensation was strongest in the attic. Selina's sister Tina also felt
odd in the house. She visited the family often and frequently babysat
for the couple's two sons, Nathan, age two, and Nick, nearly one. Like
Dave, she sensed that someone was watching her. She saw
unaccountable shadows glide past the living room window. Many times
she felt compelled to check on the safety of the young boys, who
shared an upstairs bedroom.

One evening, Selina looked in on her sons, believing that they
had been asleep for hours. She opened their door to discover Nathan
standing up in his crib with his eyes wide open, searching the room
aimlessly.

"Honey, why aren't you sleeping?" she asked.

"I can't, Mummy," he replied. "I don't want the hand to get
Nick."

He spoke with such conviction that Selina looked around the
room.

"What hand, Nathan?"

"The hand. The hand that came out of the floor," he answered.

She smiled and assured him that he had been dreaming. He denied it. But as she left the room Selina couldn't help feeling a hint of alarm at what Nathan had said. After all, he didn't appear to have been sleeping at all.

Nothing more was mentioned until two weeks later, when Nathan asked, "Mum, when is the hand coming back?" Dave and Selina thought his question was a bit odd. Why would a two-year-old still be thinking of a long-ago dream? The event prompted Dave to find a new home for the family.

Years later, in June of 1987, they had moved into a new home not far from the old place. Nathan was in the year four at a nearby school. His baby brother, Kris, the newest member of the family, had been playing at a park close by, when suddenly he burst into the house crying for his mum. A lady at the park had spanked him. Selina needed to know why, and she headed for the park with Kris.

They had a few words, and the lady apologized, blaming her mood on her pregnancy. Selina and the woman, who introduced herself as Janet, found themselves deep in discussion as they watched their children play. Both women were young and married, both had sons named Nathan, and both had recently moved into new houses. In fact, the Reed family had just moved into the house on South Shore Drive.

When she learned that Selina had lived there, Janet asked if she had experienced anything odd in the house. Selina was a bit shocked by the question and told her only that they had sometimes felt uneasy about the place.

"Did you ever experience anything dealing with a hand?" Janet asked. Selina told her of the dream Nathan had had of a bloody hand appearing out of the floor, floating around the room and then moving in Nick's direction. Now she wasn't so sure it was a dream.

Janet nodded. She told Selina that her daughter was using the upstairs bedroom.

One night, while her daughter fought a fever, Janet felt compelled to stay in the room with her and watch over her.

Late that night she began dozing off. Suddenly she opened her eyes. A man's dark silhouette was standing before her. His murky features were vague, yet it was clear to her that it was an outline of a man's figure. He looked distorted, like exhaust fumes from a car. Janet swallowed hard and tried to get a grip on herself, but nothing could prepare her for what was about to happen.

She saw the man's arm stretch toward her. Unlike his body, the man's arm seemed solid. It was as if he were trying to show her something. His arm was clad in dark clothing, but he seemed to have a bloody wrist with no hand.

Suddenly the spectre spoke. With a deep, shaky voice he said, "Look at what I've done. See what I have done." And then he was quiet. She lay there motionless, staring up at him. Then she ran to the door to get her husband. She hesitated before leaving the room, realizing her daughter was still sleeping there, and turned back for a second glance. But the spectre was gone. Janet said she and her husband searched the house most of the night, but found nothing unusual.

Selina couldn't wait to tell Dave. Dave asked friends in the county records office to search the files for the history of the house. All the paperwork seemed routine.

The Reeds eventually divorced and both moved away from the community. As far as Dave and Selina know, however, the house is now vacant.

Or is it?

J. Anthony was born and raised in Albert Lea, Minnesota. He now lives in Glenville, Minnesota.

THE HAUNTED HONKY-TONK
by *Patricia Bowskill*

**Bobby Randall Mackey never dreamed of owning a bar –
especially not a haunted one.**

In the 1970s he had built a successful career playing in nightclubs in
nearby Cincinnati and was building a nest egg for his big move to
Nashville. He had always dreamed of becoming a country star. Yet one
day he felt compelled to take a look at a vacant nightclub on the banks
of the Licking River in the small town of Wilder, Kentucky.

To this day, he can't say what made him look at the antiquated
structure. He only knows that when he first entered it, a strange sense
of déjà vu came over him.

Bobby says that he knew every nook and cranny as if he had
been there before. He knew what the stage, the bar and even the
storage areas would look like. Buying a bar, especially this particular
bar, went against all logic. It was bigger than Bobby needed for a
country music bar and in desperate need of repair. With one small
child at home and one on the way, Bobby's wife, Janet, thought it was
the wrong time to begin a risky business venture.

But Bobby put in a bid on the property, and it was quickly
accepted. Janet decided that it was easier to be a part of her husband's
dream than to fight it. Little did she imagine the fights she would soon
face.

In the spring of 1978 Janet prepared for the bar's grand
opening. While she cleaned, a ladder began swaying for no apparent
reason. According to Janet, it seemed to walk toward her. Frozen with
fright, Janet watched as it fell. A maintenance man intervened and
saved Janet from harm.

Bobby didn't believe that this was a "ghost attack". He simply
asked Janet to get more rest. He worried that something was wrong
with his wife and her pregnancy, but he refused to believe that there
was anything wrong with the bar.

But the incidents didn't stop. One day as Janet filled a bucket
at the bar's sink to do some scrubbing, an invisible force pushed her
head under the faucet. The water turned blood red as Janet fought to
keep from drowning. Luckily, the maintenance man was there once

again to rescue her and was able to pull her away from the mysterious violent force.

The most damaging attack occurred when Janet was nearly six months pregnant. She says she was flung down a flight of steps after hearing a raspy voice say "get out." The attack led to the premature birth of their second child.

The bar has a long, violent history. In 1802, 11 people were arrested for worshipping Satan in the building that is now Bobby Mackey's. At the time, the building was a slaughterhouse. A well was dug under the property so that animal blood could drain directly into the Licking River.

In 1896, a pregnant woman named Pearl Bryan was beheaded less than two miles from where the bar now stands. Alonzo Walling and Scott Jackson were hanged for the crime on March 21, 1897. Walling swore from the gallows that he would curse the area and the people who lived there for all eternity.

Pearl Bryan's head was never found. Some say it was dumped in the bar's well.

In the 1930s, the bar was a mob-connected establishment called "The Latin Quarter". Johanna, the daughter of a Cleveland mobster, became pregnant by a club singer named Robert Randall. Johanna's father had Randall killed. In revenge, she poisoned her father and killed herself.

Could Robert Randall Mackey be the reincarnation of '30s crooner Robert Randall? Mackey doesn't believe in reincarnation or ghosts, and doesn't know how to explain all the eerie coincidences surrounding his bar, but it's not a subject that he likes to talk about. Until recently, he also forbade his staff to talk about ghosts sharing the building.

Mackey said he doesn't try to understand why his career goals changed mid-stream or why he remained on the banks of the Licking River. He simply lives for the weekends when he can play for the crowds, even if the crowds may include a few unseen patrons.

HORATIO AT THE BRIDGE
by James L. Choron

A phantom tank from World War II holds the bridge in the 1991 Russian upheaval.

It was August 1991, and the Soviet Union was in the grip of yet another revolution, the fourth major revolt in the space of 175 years.

For the third time in a century, barricades spanned the streets of Moscow, and a partisan army – old men and women, students and a handful of professional soldiers – stood on makeshift walls of cast-aside rubble and faced the tanks of the finest mechanized army on the European continent. They were armed with Molotov cocktails, knives, pitchforks and a few guns that they had taken from the Museum of the Soviet Army and, ironically enough, the Museum of the Revolution.

Ten kilometres outside Moscow's outermost ring road, a barricade spanned the Tula Highway, just south of the bridge over the Moscow River. The redoubt was held by fewer than 100 volunteers determined to hold the bridge and not allow reinforcements to bolster the Moscow garrison, which, under the control of the Kremlin Old Guard, was attempting to overthrow the reformist government of Mikhail Gorbachev and reinstate hard-line Communism in the country. The battle lines swung back and forth, but, even with the weight of world opinion on the side of the reformers, it was only even odds that they could win through if the Moscow garrison was not reinforced from outside.

The defenders of the Tula Highway barricade were spread thin. In order to obstruct the approach to Moscow completely, it was necessary to block not only the bridge, but also the shallow, natural fords on either side of it. For three days, they had been lucky. No reinforcing column had yet appeared from the direction of the massive state arsenal and military complex in Tula.

Just before dawn, a motorbike with a single rider dashed toward the barricade at breakneck speed. The motorcyclist was a courier from an advance post some 20 kilometres farther down the highway. The defenders, of course, did not have anything so sophisticated as a radio.

The Armour Arrives

The news was grim. Tanks. About 60 of them, followed by infantry in armored carriers. It was an airborne armoured brigade, and it would be at the barricade well before midday. The time to stand had come.

The rag-tag little army began to prepare. Some made their peace with God as they filled bottles with petrol. Others cleaned and loaded the antique Nagant rifles and PpSh submachine guns that they had liberated from the museums. Only about half of them had a gun of any kind. Their leader, Viktor Ivanov, a grizzled old veteran of World War II and a former infantry sergeant, cleaned his pistol and whistled a tune. It was, he thought, as good a day to die as any. What he wouldn't give for a single tank, he told his second in command, an Afghan veteran named Pavel Ordinov. At least they could block the bridge and buy some time. It had worked back in '42 at this very place. The two men lounged in the shadow of the bridge abutment on the Moscow side of the river.

Many of the defenders took catnaps. Soon enough, they would need all the strength they could muster. As the sun rose higher in the sky, heralding the new day, the growling roar of a heavy motor rumbled up the highway from the direction of Moscow.

"We're finished!" Ivanov told his younger colleague. "They've broken the barricade at the ring, and they're coming to finish us off. We're in a vice."

Ordinov grimaced and got to his feet. Hastily he started barking commands and mustering half of the defenders to face the new threat from the north. Things were looking pretty bleak.

A Tank to the Rescue

Shortly, the outline of a tank became visible, plodding up the highway from Moscow. It was a single tank, and not one that Ordinov recognized. As it drew closer, he could make out what it was. Crawling up the road toward them, exactly in the middle of the four-lane asphalt ribbon, was a T-34, an aging veteran of World War II. Undoubtedly, it had not fired a shot in anger in more than 40 years. Clinging to the hull was a squad of infantry. Flying from the radio antenna was a large red banner. *Unbelievable*, Ordinov thought. *They got one of the museum exhibits running* – not that it would be much help against modern armour. Well, at least, they could block the bridge. The thing was heavy; it would take time to push its gutted, burned-out hulk off the road.

Closer and closer the ancient behemoth crept. The soldiers were armed with the same kind of antiques that Ordinov's troops carried. They were dressed in uniforms, but what uniforms! *They must have raided the museum right and proper*, he thought to himself.

In five more minutes, the old tank was close enough to read the banner that it flew: a standard Soviet flag, across which, in bright yellow paint, were written the words *Za Rodina* ("For the Motherland"), a common enough sight in the Great Patriotic War, as World War II is called in Russia.

"The Fascists Will Not Pass"

Growling past the startled defenders, the tank's commander, a pale-looking man in his mid-30s, leaned over the rim of his cupola hatch and shouted, "Clear a path. We will block the bridge. The Fascists will not pass us easily – or cheaply."

Ordinov complied, and the venerable old veteran parked itself sideways across the bridge, with its diminutive 76mm gun pointing down the roadway. Silently the ten soldiers who had been clinging to the hull jumped down and began to dig in around the bridge. They spoke not a word to anyone around them and would not answer questions.

The sun rose in the splendour of summer's last dying fling, and the heat of the morning set in. The old tank, completely buttoned up, must have been like an oven. Not once was a single hatch opened for air.

About midday, the dreaded, anticipated threat from the south materialized. The sound of 60 T-80 main battle tanks and the same number of BMP II armoured personnel carriers rent the air as the force of their engines shook the ground like an earthquake. The ancient T-34 came to life as the column came into view from below a low hill. Slowly the turret began to move and the gun elevated.

Then a miracle happened. The advancing column stopped some two kilometres from the barricade, and a lone WuZ Jeep raced toward the bridge, stopping in a cloud of dust only 50 metres from the T34 and the entrenched soldiers. It contained a driver and a single officer, dressed in camouflage and the distinctive blue beret of a paratrooper.

The short, stocky officer stood and shouted toward Ivanov, Ordinov, and their troops. He didn't appear to notice the turret of the old T-34 as it rolled toward his Jeep.

"I am Colonel General Alexander Lebed. This is my command, the 26th Airborne Armoured Brigade. Join us, comrades, in breaking the siege. We stand for God and freedom – and the rightfully elected government of this country."

The rest, as they say, is history. Lebed's column, joined by the defenders of the Tula Highway barricade, rolled into Moscow an hour and a half later, and the "August Coup" was all but over. Within the space of a few days, Gorbachev was released from his *dacha*, where he was being held prisoner, and the rightful government once again took control. As the armoured column passed the bridge, the old T-34 began to move slowly. No one paid much attention to it after that. They just assumed that it would join the end of the column and come into Moscow at its best speed. It certainly wasn't as fast as the modern equipment of the 26th Airborne Armoured Brigade.

It was never seen again...

Mystery Tank Recovered
This tale circulated around Moscow for years. Everyone wondered as to the identity of the mystery tank. In May 1998, the puzzle was solved, at least for many. It was at that time that construction crews began to widen the Tula Highway and replace the old, two-lane bridge that bottlenecked traffic on the four-lane expressway as it crossed the Moscow River. As they demolished the old bridge, they made an astounding find.

As they began to excavate the bridge abutments on the Moscow side of the river, they found the hull of a T-34 tank and the remains of the crew. As they continued to dig, they found the remains of ten infantrymen who had apparently been deployed, along with the tank, in the summer of 1942 in an attempt to hold the bridge against the advancing Germans until reinforcements could arrive. Of course, they never did. The Germans were stopped, but much closer to Moscow.

THE HOTEL COLORADO
by Jared Hargrave

The historic Hotel Colorado is located in Glenwood Springs, Colorado, at the intersection of the Colorado and Roaring Fork rivers. The Ute Indians believed that the spring water possessed healing powers. Attracted by the legends, a rich engineer named Walter Devereux bought Glenwood Springs and the surrounding ten acres. There he built the hotel in 1893.

Over more than 100 years, the Hotel Colorado has housed thousands of guests, some of whom died during their stay. The hotel's staff sometimes wonder if the deceased ever left.

Jolyn Nauman worked at the Hotel Colorado during the summer of 1995. "Late one afternoon," she said, "I was cleaning a room on the third floor. I had just made the bed and was ready to wash the bathroom. I searched through my cleaning cart to get my bathroom disinfectant and found that I had run out. I knew that one of the other housekeepers was cleaning a room down the hall. So I left the room, locking the door behind me. I got some disinfectant from my co-worker and came back to the room, but the door would not unlock. I kept trying. The lock would not budge. None of my other keys would work either.

"So I called to my co-worker and she tried her key. Her key wouldn't work either. I tried my key one last time before going to the manager, and this time the door unlocked as if there had never been a problem. When I looked in the room, the bed I had just made was completely mussed. And the bed sheets and covers had been thrown off the bed and onto the floor."

According to Nauman, there was nobody in the room. She also noticed that the room was very cold, as if the window had been left open on a winter day. But it was late July and the window was closed.

She reported other unusual phenomena, such as the cigar smoke aroma that would occasionally drift through the lobby when nobody nearby was smoking. According to a night auditor, strange events often occurred between 2.00 and 4.00 a.m. The lift has moved between floors with nobody on it. Doors have opened and closed for no reason. And in the rooms in the bell towers, a mysterious woman has awakened several male guests, standing over their beds.

One guest awoke in the middle of the night and notified the staff that doors and drawers in his room were opening and closing by themselves. When he got back home after his holiday, the activity continued in his own bedroom. He concluded that he had brought the phenomenon with him. He packed his bags and spoke aloud to the gremlin-like force, saying that he was returning to the hotel. After this second trip, he never was bothered by the entity again.

One of the hotel's more tragic events happened in the 1890s. A little girl fell from one of the balconies while chasing a ball. Since then, some guests have reported seeing their children in the corridor playing ball with a girl dressed in Victorian clothing.

One night in 1987, a woman said that she had been awakened by a little girl standing by the foot of her bed. Positive that she had locked her door, the woman called the front desk and asked the night clerk if he had given a key to a little girl. The clerk said he had not. The woman returned to the hotel several more times, always checking into the same room to visit the ghostly girl.

Another supernatural disturbance occurred after extensive remodelling of the hotel's forth floor. Workmen hung wallpaper in a room and left for the night. When they returned in the morning, the wallpaper was rolled up on the floor. They reapplied the wallpaper twice with the same results. Finally they decided to try an experiment. They left three different rolls of wallpaper on the bed and left for the night. When they returned the next day, two of the rolls were on the floor and one was still on the bed. They glued the paper that was left on the bed to the walls, where it still remains.

Is the Hotel Colorado haunted? Nauman said that she frequently felt inexplicable chills as she walked the hotel's corridors. For its guests and employees, the history of the Hotel Colorado is more than entries in a dusty ledger.

Jared Hargrave *is a freelance writer and college student who grew up near Glenwood Springs.*

SLEEPING IN A HOUSE OF HORRORS
by Janet Brennan

Overnight in the Lizzie Borden house.

Nothing says "holiday" like a gory double murder.

At least, that seems to be the feeling among the thousands of overnight guests and day visitors who have flocked to the Lizzie Borden Bed & Breakfast Museum since it opened for business on August 4, 1996, the 104th anniversary of the day the famous axe murders were committed.

The 1892 crime caused a sensation, and Lizzie Borden's trial in 1893 was the O. J. Simpson event of its century. The brutal murders shocked the community: Wealthy businessman Andrew Borden, 70, and his wife Abby, 64, were hacked to death with multiple blows in their own home. Their 32-year-old spinster daughter Lizzie and 26-year-old Irish maid Bridget Sullivan were on the premises, yet both claimed not to have heard or seen anything.

The crime was immortalized in the children's jump-rope song: "Lizzie Borden took an axe, gave her mother 40 whacks, when she saw what she had done, gave her father 41."

Now, 111 years after the crime, interest in the unsolved mystery remains as high as ever. Countless books, documentaries, websites, college classes and even an opera and a television movie starring Elizabeth Montgomery rehash the events of that terrible August morning in Victorian New England. There's even a *Lizzie Borden Quarterly* published every three months that announces new theories and research findings on the century-old crimes. But nowhere is this macabre fascination more prevalent, and more irresistible, than in Fall River, Massachusetts, Lizzie Borden's hometown and the scene of the crimes.

The Mecca for murder fans is the Borden house at 92 Second St in Fall River. People come from all over the world to immerse themselves in the crime scene, even – for those who dare – sleeping in the bedroom where Lizzie's stepmother Abby Borden was killed, the bed just inches from the spot where her hacked body lay undiscovered for over two hours in a pool of blood and brains.

I had heard of this unusual B&B and the hordes of people

who are Lizzie Borden "groupies". I decided to spend a weekend at the inn, to see for myself what motivates these people in their creepy obsession. What I discovered was that the inn's guests are about evenly divided among true-crime aficionados who have a scholarly interest in either the criminal, legal or sociological aspects of the case; the ghost-hunter types who have less interest in the facts of the case but plenty of interest in the rare chance to stay overnight in a house that, I found, is most definitely haunted; and the merely curious who are on a weekend away at what is surely the country's most unusual B&B.

I had thought I'd write this story from a cynical, "people are weird" perspective. But almost immediately upon arriving I found myself falling under the Lizzie spell. The beauty and comfort of the house, so meticulously restored, and the knowledge and graciousness of the staff – from our hostess right down to the cook and cleaning lady – got me completely caught up in the mystery. Even my husband, Michael, a reluctant companion on this eerie outing, got into the spirit (excuse the pun). Proclaiming "I'm just the chauffeur," he planned to skip the three-hour tour offered to overnight guests. Instead, he ended up happily playing the part of Lizzie's father in our hostess's re-enactment, lying on the couch while a heavy hatchet matching the suspected weapon stopped just inches from his head.

I would encourage anyone with an interest in old mysteries or spirit activity to spend a night at the inn. If that is impossible for you, then come along with me now as I share with you my spooky experiences at Lizzie's house.

Alone in Lizzie's Room
We arrived in Fall River on a Friday afternoon last July and found the Bordens' 1845 Greek Revival home looking as it did the day of the crime, though the neighbourhood around it has changed from residential to business. There is a bus station across the street and an old printing shop next door, which now serves as the gift shop for the Borden house and museum.

We were let into the house by Michael, the caretaker. He informed us that we were to be the only guests that night. He also was the first to inform us that the house was haunted. He said many visitors have photographed glowing orbs of light in the kitchen and basement, and a researcher for Dean Koontz, the horror writer, picked up a male voice on her tape recorder in the basement.

Michael showed us to our rooms – we were staying that night in the "Lizzie and Emma Suite." As he entered the tiny bedroom that had been Lizzie's, he said, "Oh yes, I can feel the energy here."

On that ominous note, he left us to explore on our own. My first impression was that the house looked exactly as I remembered it looking in the Elizabeth Montgomery movie. The only difference is that some of the Bordens' closets have been changed into guest bathrooms. (There were no bathrooms in Lizzie's day, just one toilet in the basement.) And air conditioning and electricity have been added – in Lizzie's day paraffin lamps and candles lit the house, as the miserly Mr. Borden refused to install electricity.

We went from room to room, taking pictures. The house has little of the Bordens' original furniture, but thanks to extensive police photos after the crime, the inn's owners have been able to recreate the rooms with exact replicas of the Bordens' furniture and decorations. Though we were alone in the silent house, we did not find the atmosphere of the place spooky, thanks to the summer sun streaming in through the many lace-curtained windows, and the colourful floral rugs and wallpaper. Even the front guest bedroom where Abby's body was found did not spook me, as the decor reminded me so much of my grandmother's bedroom that I felt perfectly at home. The only macabre note was the gruesome crime-scene photos in the bedroom where Mrs Borden was killed as she was making the bed and in the sitting room where Mr Borden met his fate some 90 minutes later as he took a pre-lunch nap on a sofa.

I took many photos of the murder spots, hoping that when they were developed I would see a ghostly outline. That did not happen, though I did get an orb of light in the kitchen, like those Michael had described. Though I saw nothing when I took the photo, the print shows a small, golden globe hovering in the corner above the wood-burning stove where Lizzie burned a dress three days after the murders – a dress she claimed had been paint-stained for months. The police had not found any bloody clothes in their search of Lizzie's belongings (nor any paint-stained ones, either), and the destruction of the dress certainly seemed suspicious. Luckily for Lizzie, a judge would rule that eyewitness testimony about the dress-burning could not be used at trial, and it was this and similar rulings in her favour that would get her acquitted.

Another odd effect appeared in the photo of the bedroom

murder scene that I took from the front stairs. The family's maid, Bridget Sullivan, testified that on the day of the murders, she heard Lizzie laughing from the top of the stairs. In the Elizabeth Montgomery movie, Lizzie is laughing delightedly because, as she stands on the stairs, she can look under the bed and see the dead body of her hated stepmother lying on the floor of the guest bedroom. For my photo, I stood on the stairs and shot into the bedroom to recreate Lizzie's vantage point. An orange shadow appears in front of the left doorjamb, though at the time the area was bright with afternoon sunshine.

It was a treat to have the house to ourselves, but we had to leave for the evening, as we had plans to meet friends for dinner and attend a play in nearby Rhode Island. The play we saw at Theater by the Sea, "The Secret Garden", was excellent, but in our circumstances a poor choice. It was about death, and the majority of the cast played ghosts.

We returned after midnight and let ourselves in. Michael was asleep in the attic, and all was quiet. We prepared for bed; I would sleep alone in Lizzie's little room, and my husband would stay in the adjoining large bedroom that belonged to Lizzie's sister, Emma.

One of Lizzie's dresses is on a dressmaker's dummy next to her bed. I wondered if I would wake up in the night and be frightened by that dress glowing white just inches from my face. I decided to sleep with the covers over my head.

The house that seemed so cheery in the daylight was not so nice at night. Though the cosy bed felt welcoming, I avoided going to the bathroom because it would have meant passing the open door of the death bedroom. I got very little sleep, as every time my husband moved in his bed my heart would skip as I thought, *Is that a ghost?* When I finally did doze off, my dreams were peopled with "Secret Garden" ghosts haunting the rooms of the Lizzie Borden house.

Ghosts Galore

The next morning, I found some guest books inside a writing table in Emma's bedroom. Many of the entries give tantalizing hints at other guests' experiences, like this one written April 18, 2003: "Dear Lizzie, Thank you for the visit last night. It was a good thing that the window did not break. I hope to see you next year. – Jo-Jo."

I was glad I had not read that before sleeping in Lizzie's room!

Or this one: "Lizzie, I don't know if you were speaking to me last night, but thanks to whomever for the appearance on tape and video. – K. Rowland."

On October 15, 2002, Mary Sooy wrote: "When we first arrived here a picture fell in Emma's room and shattered. Then later that night we heard a cat meow even thoughren't any living cats here."

Another entry mentioning cats was written by Stephanie Soares and Judy Bullock on August 5, 2002: "We heard some cats cry when we were in the driveway and we heard footsteps on the third floor."

Several other entries also dealt with goings-on in the third-floor attic: "July 13, 2002, 12 a.m. Third-floor bathroom lights go out, find our way to the door, light switch was DOWN. – Shelly Collins."

And this anonymous one written August 3, 2002: "At about 11.30 p.m., while in the Andrew Jennings room [an attic bedroom], we were speaking about whether Lizzie was guilty, and the bedside lamp turned itself on!"

After reading those notes and others in a similar vein, it was with some trepidation that we went down to breakfast for a recreation of the final meal eaten by the murder victims. At 8 a.m. on August 4, 1892, Mr. and Mrs. Borden and their overnight guest, John Morse, breakfasted on coffee, cookies, bananas, three-day-old mutton broth, and "johnny cakes," a traditional New England pancake made from white cornmeal. The B&B serves the same meal at 8.00 a.m. every day, though thankfully leaving out the spoiled mutton broth and adding eggs, ham, home fries and banana bread. For a whimsical touch, the inn substitutes the Bordens' molasses cookies with sugar cookies in the shape of a hatchet. Guests may lose their appetite for the yummy breakfast when they learn that the bodies of the Bordens were laid out in the dining room, and Mrs B's autopsy was conducted right on the dining-room table!

Dave, an affable retiree, cooked the breakfast for Michael and me. Dave doesn't believe in ghosts, dismissing all the strange experiences in the house as the result of guests and staff "seeing what they want to see". His no-nonsense attitude was reassuring after my nearly sleepless night. He did allow, though, that when serving breakfast he often overhears guests talking about their dreams, and very often it will happen that everyone in the house has had the same dream.

Shortly after the pragmatic Dave left the house, Jean, the

housekeeper, arrived. She quickly brought us back to the twilight zone. She told us that once when she was alone in the house, she heard footsteps going up to the third floor, and that she felt the invisible cat rubbing against her legs in the kitchen.

When I told her about the "cat meowing" entries I had read in the guest book, she explained that Lizzie was said to have decapitated her stepmother's kitten after it bothered some guests Lizzie had over to tea. Later that night, Shelly, our hostess, told us that many people have heard the meowing. Shelly said she felt the cat jump on the bed when she was spending a night in Mrs Borden's bedroom, and many other guests have felt the same thing, on that bed only.

Jean also told us the story of the chambermaid who was cleaning the John Morse bedroom, where Abby Borden was killed. The worker had just finished making the bed and had turned to put some towels on the dresser. When she turned back to the bed, she saw the clear impression of a body lying there. She ran out of the house and never returned, refusing to enter even to pick up her check.

The Lizzie Tour

The only bad thing about staying at the Borden B&B is the fact that guests are kicked out between the hours of 10.00 a.m. and 3.00 p.m. to accommodate the public tours that are given between 11.00 and 2.30 daily during July and August and on weekends in May, June, September and October. But for the murder-obsessed, there are plenty of other "Lizzie sights" to see in Fall River, and the inn provides a map to them.

We made the pilgrimage to Oak Grove Cemetery, where arrows painted on the road lead visitors to the Borden family plot. Lizzie and Emma are buried right behind their father, mother, stepmother and a sibling who died in infancy. I was surprised to see many pennies and other coins placed on Lizzie's individual headstone as well as the large family monument. Her headstone is inscribed simply "Lizbeth," the name she chose for herself after the murders (she had been christened "Lizzie") in a useless attempt to change her identity. That did not prevent the city from ostracizing her for the rest of her life.

A few blocks from the cemetery is Maplecroft, the 13-room mansion Lizzie and Emma moved into just five weeks after Lizzie's trial ended. Lizzie lived at Maplecroft for the rest of her life – she died in 1927, at age 67, of complications from gallbladder surgery. Emma, the older sister who had been like a mother to Lizzie after their own mother died, lived with Lizzie at Maplecroft for 11 years. She moved out in 1904 when Lizzie took up with an actress. Emma told a friend she could "no longer tolerate what was going on" – scandalized perhaps by Lizzie's parties or, it is hypothesized, her lesbian relationship with the actress. Emma moved to New Hampshire and died in a fall down some stairs just nine days after the death of her infamous sister.

Neither sister ever married. Emma left her half of their father's half-million-dollar fortune (a sum worth many millions today) to various church groups and charities. Lizzie left all her money to an animal shelter – perhaps to make amends for killing her stepmother's cat?

We dined that evening at Lizzie's church. The former Central Congregational Church now houses a restaurant, the Abbey, run by a culinary institute.

We returned to the inn just in time for our private tour. The inn had ten guests booked for that night, but the couple who were to have stayed in the bedroom where Abby died checked out shortly after their arrival, claiming sudden illness. So the remaining eight of us gathered in the parlour with Shelly, our hostess for the evening.

Shelly displayed a comprehensive knowledge of the crime, and the evening passed quickly as she took us from room to room, discussing the events that happened in each location. In a bedroom, she picked up a hymnal and sang the song Lizzie paid a professional singer to perform at her own funeral – a funeral that took place in Maplecroft. According to Lizzie's wishes, it was attended by only one person – her maid – and the singer. Shelly re-enacted both murders using her own real hatchet, with my husband and a teenage guest playing the victims. To actually see that hatchet being swung repeatedly – Abby received 18 blows and Andrew 11 – really brings home the terrible brutality of the crimes. It's no wonder the jury could not believe that Lizzie, a prim, slight, oh-so-proper Victorian lady – a member of the Temperance Union who taught Sunday School to the children of Chinese immigrants – could commit such a violent, heinous act. Twice.

Shelly showed us a dress Elizabeth Montgomery wore in the movie and a movie prop: a bottle of prussic acid, a poison Lizzie attempted to buy the day before the hatchet murders. Lizzie told the druggist she needed it to kill moths, but the suspicious man refused to sell it to her. That juicy tidbit of information was never told to the jury. The judge ruled that, since the murders were done with a hatchet, the attempted purchase of poison had no relevance.

It is not surprising that Lizzie got off scot-free, yet she is convicted night after night in her own home as the inn's guests vote on who they think did the crime. Among our group, the jury was not unanimous. Most thought Lizzie did it, but a few holdouts thought it could have been the maid or a stranger some neighbours had seen in the garden.

We were so focused on the fascinating minutiae of the crime that we forgot about the paranormal aspects – until we got to the basement. It is here that most believe Lizzie cleaned up and disposed of the murder weapon, here that the victims' blood-and brain-spattered clothing was dumped after the autopsy and here that much of the paranormal activity takes place. Globes of light have been photographed, voices have manifested on tape recorders and one of the inn's owners, when she was living in the house as a teenager, saw a female ghost in Victorian clothing glide across the floor.

Our group was standing around a coffin that held a headless mannequin – a prop for the inn's Halloween haunted house – when the heavy, wooden coffin suddenly crashed to the floor with a loud bang. It seems that two of the three saw-horses on which it lay inexplicably collapsed at the same time. The whole group was badly shaken, some to the point of weeping. I was just grateful to have ten unbroken toes inside my sandals.

After our tour, Shelly brought out some snacks as we continued to discuss the case and watched some of the inn's extensive video collection of documentaries done on the crime. Finally, past midnight, it was off to bed. This time we slept in the Irish maid's attic bedroom, as the other suites had already been booked.

We passed an uneventful night in the quiet house, and the next morning at breakfast found out the other guests had also rested in peace – except for the meowing of that cat.

Janet Brennan, a newspaper editor, believes Lizzie did it with the help of Bridget the maid. Emma, who left town shortly before the murders for a rare holiday, might have known of their plans.

HOUSE WITH THE EARTHBOUND SPIRITS

By Lady M. S. Lawford

It was a large and beautiful house – but strangely lacking in privacy. Guests were spied on nightly through fanlights by unseen presences.

My son, Peter, was about eight years old when our little family returned from a voyage to Tahiti, Australia and the Hawaiian Islands.

Arriving in London, we were met by the usual downpour and leaden skies; it was anything but warm, although it was August.

Among my post I received a letter from a friend who wished to rent us his house on the island of Madeira for the coming winter. Even though we were half unpacked we all decided to take the house. My husband, Gen. Sir Sidney Lawford, booked our passages on the next outgoing steamer.

We were enchanted with the house. The garden and grounds were full of Lilies-of-the-Nile, plus Bougainvillaea in all shades of glorious colour. In addition, the butler, cook and two upstairs maids went with the house.

We settled happily into our new environment, prepared to enjoy tennis, drives, bathing and other recreation available on the delightful island. The house was too large for us – four or five bedrooms and bathrooms, a drawing room, dining room, and one huge room which the servants called The Ballroom. My husband and I slept in a large room with three windows overlooking the sea; it also had three doors with glass fanlights opening onto the corridor. Peter slept in a smaller room just off ours, with no door and separated only by an archway with curtains.

After we had lived here two or three months we were invited to a big Portuguese wedding and did not return to the house until about 1.00 a.m. As our son was already asleep, we went quietly to bed.

At 4.00 a.m. I awoke with a start. Peter stood by the side of my bed and his white, China-silk pyjamas were sticking to his body as if he had gone swimming in them.

"What on earth?" I gasped.

"I can't sleep in my room. Someone keeps looking at me. Let

me stay here – please!" Peter pleaded.

After rubbing him dry and changing his pyjamas I put him to sleep on one of the couches in our bedroom. When General Lawford woke in the morning and saw him there, he said, "A fine way to spoil the child!" and indicated he did not believe Peter's story.

Every night our son went to bed in his room, and every morning we found him covered by one of his blankets on the couch in our room. After a week or 10 days of this I, too, began to wake up with the feeling that someone was watching me. My chiffon nightgown would be clinging to my body and my pillow wet with perspiration.

I awakened my husband who murmured, "Mass hysteria" and went back to sleep.

However, about a week later, around midnight, *he* woke *me* and said someone or something was looking at him from the fanlights.

Next day my husband told the butler to glue some brown paper on the inside of the threefanlights and that night he removed the keys after locking the bedroom doors.

The following morning I awoke, grateful for an undisturbed night, only to look at the floor and find it covered with pieces of brown paper – paper torn from the inside of the fanlights by unseen hands.

After some discussion my husband and I decided to take the next ship to Lisbon. The friends we had made on the island then gave us a nice farewell party.

At the party an elderly gentleman said to me, "I wondered how long you would stay there. Six months is about the limit!"

When I asked him why, he promptly answered, "That house is full of earthbound spirits – two murders and a suicide in the big bedroom!!"

HOYNE AVENUE GHOST
by Cathleen Lapkoff

I first met Greg Lapkoff, my husband, in the spring of 1976. At that time his family was experiencing an ongoing series of poltergeist phenomena. The haunting would continue for nearly ten years and go from harmless antics to eerily threatening activity. The events would finally culminate in a family moving from their home; it would also provide some evidence of life after death. This is my husband's true story, in his own words.

The beginning

I was the first one to notice it. No-one else in the family believed me. Through the years, however, each member of my family would encounter the presence that haunted our sprawling apartment on the near northwest side of Chicago.

The house was built approximately 90 years ago. It is a well-kept brick flat with a beautiful greystone facade. Standing in the middle of a shady, tree-lined, working-class neighbourhood, it couldn't have looked more sedate or normal. It was anything but normal.

We moved in halfway through the warm autumn of 1965. My family consisted of myself (then a 16-year-old high school student), my 14-year-old sister Lynn and my two brothers, Jeff and Butch, aged six and 23.

Mom and Dad rounded out the group. My father was a no-nonsense truck driver, and my mother was a nurse who had absolutely no belief in anything paranormal.

Our apartment was mostly bright and cheery. It was on the third floor and had seven rooms. A long hall connected the dining room to a den that we used as a TV room. Two bedrooms also opened off this hall. A third bedroom lay directly off the living room, which was the easternmost room in the house.

Later, manifestations and incidents would occur in every single room of this house, including the back verandah, and were experienced by everyone, including our dog, Rex.

My older brother and I shared one of the bedrooms that opened to the long, interior hall. Our room was dark and gloomy and filled with an eerie "dead calm". A thunderstorm raging in the night could barely be heard inside my bedroom. Other noises, though, could be heard quite clearly.

Several weeks after moving in, on a humid autumn evening, I was awakened in the middle of the night by heavy laboured breathing coming from my brother's bed, directly across the room from me. My brother, being in his 20s, kept significantly different hours from me. Sometimes he would arrive home late and get to bed without my ever hearing him.

On this night I assumed that he had come home late and that the strange breathing was coming from him. "Butch, Butch," I whispered. There was no answer.

The breathing, long and drawn out, continued. I stared into the impenetrable darkness toward his bed. Then I got out of bed and walked over to his. He wasn't there.

I went back to my bed totally perplexed, trying to think of a reassuring reason to explain the sounds I had heard. Finally, I concocted the complicated scenario of my father breathing heavily in the next room down the hall, and the sound waves bouncing off my partially open door and angling over to my brother's bed, then back to me.

Still, I lay awake, and the breathing continued. I was beginning to lose confidence in my theory, for I could now hear my father's snoring and the breathing at the same time. I was about to bolt from my room, when I heard my brother's footsteps coming up the front hallway stairs. His key turned the front door lock and I clearly heard the door open and shut.

I heard Butch walk past my bedroom, down the long hall, and into the kitchen. I happily got up, excited to tell him of the strange, gasping sounds in our bedroom. I ran into the kitchen – but Butch wasn't there. No one was there!

I switched on the lights in the dark kitchen and retreated to my bedroom, where I also turned on the lights. I kept them that way until my brother really came home.

The eerie breathing sounds tormented me for the next several weeks. They seemed to happen only on the weekends when I was alone in my room. I developed a way to escape the sound. It was quite simple.

I began a mental countdown to liftoff: "10, 9, 8, 7, 6, 5, 4, 3, 2, 1, liftoff!" At lift-off, I would dash madly out of the room.

No-one believed my story, and after a time things quieted down. This was to become a pattern during our time living in the apartment.

There would be a series of incidents, followed by a period of quiet. As the years progressed, the incidents gained in power.

The middle years

My older brother got married. He moved to an apartment just down the block from us and started what was to be a very successful general contracting business.

I was now left to deal with my private haunting alone. It seemed that as soon as Butch left, back came my noisy companion. I knew the sound was real, and that it wasn't the radiators or my father's long-range breathing. I also knew that sooner or later someone else in the family would be affected. It happened that summer.

Butch's self-employed status, and his close proximity to us afforded him the luxury of often stopping over in the afternoon. One particular time he stopped by when no one was home. He was about to leave when he heard heavy, laboured breathing coming from my sister's room.

He started to walk toward the room, then decided that it must be my mother sleeping, and that she must really be tired. It would be best not to disturb her. So he left without checking the room.

He called later and told her jokingly. "Boy you must have really been tired this afternoon. I heard you snoring all the way by the dining room."

She told him she hadn't been home at all, that she had switched her off days that week. In fact, no one had been home when he heard the sound.

It appeared that the presence had now moved to my sister's room. Lynn began to complain of breathing noises coming from her bedroom cupboard. Ordinarily, this would have been laughed off as the old cupboard monster. We didn't laugh it off, though.

A certain uneasiness began to grip the family. My experiences were no longer isolated. I felt both vindicated and more fearful as I realized that what was happening could be real. My father began to call the unseen guest "Charlie". It was his way of reducing the fear factor.

Once again, the noises stopped for a while. A new family member was happily received in May of 1968. His name was Rex, our family dog. Rex would later have several significant encounters with Charlie.

The summer of 1968 was the "summer of love". Acid rock was king and the tumultuous national Democratic convention would bring worldwide attention to Chicago.

Perhaps the unseen presence in our house drew energy from these turbulent times, for during this period the ghost would be visible for the first time.

I was 19 years old then, working part time and enjoying the interval between high school and college. I spent many late nights out with my friends and sometimes would not come home until the next morning.

One night my father was kept awake all night. He was very concerned by what was happening in the hall outside his bedroom. He assumed he was seeing me pace up and down the hall all night long, wearing what he called "crazy white pyjamas."

The next morning he approached me about what was troubling me. Much to his chagrin, he found out that I had not even been home. My friends and I had taken a spur of the moment trip to Wisconsin the night before.

So now my older brother, my sister, my father and myself had all had direct contact with the spirit. The next two contactees would be my youngest brother Jeff, who was now nine years old, and our intrepid mutt, Rex.

I guess Rex knew that there was something unseen in the house. He was always hesitant about entering the hallway area after dark. But, luckily for Jeff, on his first encounter with Charlie, he was accompanied by Rex.

It was Jeff's duty to take Rex out in the evening. Rex always loved this outing. He would race down the stairs in anticipation of his evening jaunt. One particular night Rex began his usual run down the stairs with Jeff following close behind.

Suddenly about halfway down, he stopped cold and froze in position, growling ominously. Jeff was scared, but he could not see or hear anything in the stairwell. Suddenly Rex did something strange. He began to back up the stairs, one step at a time, growling with every step. Every so often he would viciously snap at something in front of him.

Deciding that discretion was the better part of valor, Jeff beat a hasty retreat all the way back up to the house. Rex arrived a few minutes later, none the worse for wear.

To this day, Jeff wonders what would have happened had he walked down those steps alone.

And so it went. The pattern was now evident. Each cycle seemed to produce more powerful manifestations. We hadn't yet considered moving. I do recall, however, once debating whether or not to contact Hans Holzer after he made an appearance on a local talk show. I still wish we had.

So far, there didn't seem to be any real threat in the manifestations, but as time wore on, my mother began to be drawn into the circle. Once she was involved, the presence became aggressive and began to show a true physical side.

I got married in 1971, and my direct participation in the happenings on Hoyne Avenue came to a close. The incidents, however, now seemed to accelerate. My sister, Lynn, was already married.

This left Jeff as the only remaining child in the house. He was entering those awkward teenage years, the years most associated with poltergeist activity.

Jeff and Mum now became the centre of several dramatic encounters. During this period my mother worked the afternoon shift at the hospital. She normally arrived home at 3.30 p.m. My father was working nights. Jeff got home from school at about 2.30.

He had an hour to kill before Mom arrived. He would normally have a friend come over to keep him company. They would play guitar, sometimes too loudly, in my infamous bedroom off the hall.

One particular afternoon Jeff and his friend Al were playing guitar. Jeff was facing the wall and Al was facing the open bedroom door. In the middle of a particularly loud riff, Al abruptly stopped. "We're in trouble," he said.

"Your mother just came home."

"Way too early," Jeff responded.

"No, she's here all right. I just saw her walk by in that white uniform."

The old fear began to rise in Jeff. He put down his guitar. It was a half hour too early for Mum to be home. He didn't want to, but he forced himself to walk through the house.

No-one was there except him and Al. When this information registered, Al left. He never again accepted invitations to play guitar with my brother.

Now Charlie's interest turned to my mother. The time was opportune, with father working nights, and Mum and Jeff were in the house alone. The breathing started again, this time in my mother's bedroom. With her first direct experience came belief, and her belief seemed to give Charlie power.

A not so subtle change in the timbre of the events began. They were more physical, and consequently more threatening. The cyclical nature of the phenomenon stayed the same, but the comings and goings now centred around my mother.

The lights in my mother's room began to come on in the middle of the night. She would get up and turn them off only to have them come on again. Just when she began to feel overwhelmed, the events would stop for months at a time. Then it would start again, stronger than before.

The final cycles

After a period of respite, the light problem began in my mother's room again. I know she was frightened, but she wouldn't admit it. She is a very stubborn woman. Events on one humid night in the autumn of 1974, however, would forever banish my mother from the room she shared with my dad.

Mum went to bed at about 10.00 p.m. Dad was still working nights, and she was working the morning shift at the hospital. Jeff retired to his room (my old room), which had been oddly free of any phenomena for over a year.

After my mother had been sleeping for several hours, her bedroom light suddenly came on. She awoke with that old stab of fear in her stomach and got up to turn the light off. Then she lay in her bed, wide awake, fully expecting additional harassment. She was not disappointed.

The light came back on. She switched the light off and struggled to hold on to her wits. She still professed some doubts as to the reality of the whole affair. This night, however, would end her doubts forever.

The light was off for over ten minutes. Mum settled back down to sleep, when someone suddenly got into bed next to her. She felt the bed jostle and the mattress depress as it absorbed the weight of another person.

Her mind raced. Her husband was working and her son was sound asleep in the next room. She thought of the possibility that the house had been invaded by a burglar.

Then her opportunity for thinking was over. A hand softly gripped her by the shoulder and attempted to gently pull her toward whatever lay in bed with her. Mom violently tossed the covers aside and ran through the hallway.

"Get the hell away from me!" she screamed.

Jeff came bursting out of his room "What's wrong!" he shouted. He sprinted into her now deserted room. Nothing was there.

Jeff's encounter

Jeff was now 15. As with many teenagers, he began to experiment with smoking. This did not sit well with our visitor.

One night Jeff was home alone watching television. Mum and Dad did not like his smoking. He normally kept a pack of cigarettes hidden in the dining room cabinet.

This was a large piece of furniture built directly into the wall, and it dominated one whole side of the TV room. It had heavy oak and glass doors and exhibited that Old World craftsmanship that is seldom seen today.

Jeff opened one of the cabinet doors and discovered that the cigarettes were gone. Dismayed, he left the door open and began to rummage through a nearby desk.

As he straightened up ready to abandon the search, the heavy glass door of the cabinet slammed shut, the sound reverberating throughout the room. Startled and scared, Jeff decided to leave the house for a while and go out to buy more cigarettes.

When he returned, things seemed normal enough. He didn't go back to the TV room, though. He sat down in the dining room.

Reaching for a cut-glass ashtray, he lit one of the new cigarettes and took a long drag. As he was about to flick the ashes into the ashtray, it exploded into fragments before his startled eyes.

That was it for Jeff. He left the house, returning only after he was certain that someone alive was home.

The ghost's identity is revealed

These events involving my mother and Jeff finally led my family to move. Before the move was to take place, however, a tragedy provided a partial answer to the haunting.

The building was owned by a kindly Polish couple, Arthur and Jennifer. One early spring day, while driving home from work, Arthur suffered a massive heart attack and died instantly. We had lost a dear friend and mourned him like a family member.

We attended the wake and met the people who had lived in our apartment many years before us. We learned that their mother had died of lung cancer.

Suffering horribly, she expired in the room that later became my bedroom. She had extreme difficulty breathing near the end. Cigarette smoke would have been very aggravating to her.

It wasn't long after that that my parents finally moved from the Hoyne Avenue building. Charlie, or the suffering spirit of a dying old lady, still walks through those halls, alternately thrilling and terrifying those who live there.

I can honestly say that I am thankful for having undergone this experience. It has taught me and everyone else who lived through it that there is much more to this world than what we can reach out and touch. Sometimes that something more reaches out and touches us.

ICELAND'S FARM POLTERGEIST
by The Rev. Sveinn Vikingur

An on-the-spot report of an unusual case from the chief executive of the Icelandic Society for Psychic Research.

In the north of Iceland there is a small farm called Saurar where Gudmundur Einarsson, a 72-year-old farmer, lives together with his wife, Margret Benediktsdorrir, and their two grown children, a daughter called Sigurborg and a son called Benedikt.

On Wednesday, March 18, 1964, at 1.40 a.m. Einarsson and his wife were woken by a sudden noise. They occupied separate beds and between their beds, under the window, stood an oval table a little more than a yard in length and weighing about 44 pounds. They noticed that this table had been moved away from the window and now was standing well out into the room. At first they supposed this had been caused by an earthquake although, strangely enough, no other objects in the room had changed position.

In the afternoon of the next day Mrs Margret Benediktsdottir and her daughter, Sigurborg, were working out of doors when they heard a big crash from inside the house. No-one was inside when they hurried in. There they saw that the kitchen table had been moved to the centre of the floor and a pile of crockery which had been placed on top of it now lay broken on the floor. Every now and then throughout the rest of that day they noticed things being moved to and fro.

The night after, Mr Einarsson and his wife were awakened once more at 4.20 a.m. by the dining room table being moved.

Next day, March 19, a reporter from the newspaper *Morgunblaoio*, MrThordur Jonsson, came for a visit, together with his chauffeur. He has said that, after having sat for sometime in the lounge conversing with the farmer and his wife, they were invited into the kitchen for some coffee. The two old people went in first, the reporter followed and last came the chauffeur. No one remained behind in the lounge. As the chauffeur entered the kitchen a noise was heard from the lounge. He immediately returned to the lounge, the others following him. There the table had been pushed a couple of yards across the floor.

The same day another son of the elderly couple, Bjorgvin,

turned up at Saurar for a few weeks stay.

On Friday, March 20, at 2.30 p.m. the daughter was in the kitchen, her mother was speaking on the telephone in the lounge, and the father was out of doors with his two sons, when suddenly Sigurborg noticed that a big cupboard standing against the wall was beginning to move. She hastily caught a small wireless set which had been placed on top of the cupboard and, no sooner had she done so, than the cupboard crashed to the floor.

The next morning, March 21, at 9:30 a.m. the cupboard again fell flat on the floor. No-one was in the kitchen at that time. The old woman was in the adjoining room with her son, Bjorgvin, when they heard the noise. The daughter had left home about an hour before this. She was going to stay with her sister at Rekjavik for a few weeks as she was beginning to suffer from nerves.

The news of this phenomenon had by now reached the capital and the place was invaded by hordes of reporters and curious persons.

On Saturday I travelled to Saurar on behalf of the Society for Psychical Research, together with some other members of the board. We stayed at the farm for three hours. The medium, Hafsteinn Bjornsson, accompanied us. We did not witness any telekinetic phenomena but we were shown the broken crockery and the cupboard in the kitchen which had now been fastened to the wall. The farmer's wife told us that while the family was having lunch in the kitchen that day the table at which they were seated suddenly began to move and they hurriedly put their hands on the crockery so that it would not fall on the floor.

We organized a séance with the medium but it did not result in our discovering the causes of the mysterious phenomena.

After discussing the matter with the residents I am convinced that none of them has deliberately caused the phenomena to occur.

One of the most eminent geologists of Iceland came to the farm and concluded after his research that the theory of an earthquake was out of the question. Later, another specialist turned up, bringing with him a seismograph, but he found no traces of an earthquake either.

The phenomena continued almost every day until April 3, the last week being the most eventful. The big table in the lounge was moved many times a day, even tipped over, and in the end it had to be tied to the wall. Then the top was broken off. Framed photographs fell down from the walls of the lounge, together with other small objects, several of which were smashed.

Between the lounge and the kitchen there is a small room in which the daughter slept before leaving for Rekjavik. In there some objects began to move also. A small tray hanging on the wall was thrown across the room several times onto the bed where the girl had slept.

In the kitchen, objects were seen to move and in the pantry, which is fitted with shelves full of various things, plates from one of the shelves repeatedly were thrown to the floor where they broke into small pieces, while objects standing on the other shelves did not move at all.

On April 3 Mrs Margret Benediktsdottir was taken to the hospital, about 30 miles away from the farm, on account of some illness. She remained there for eight days. In the meantime the phenomena ceased completely. But two days after her return they began once more, although with much less frequency and vigour than before. A little later they totally ceased, and since then there has been no recurrence.

At the end of May the American parapsychologist, Mr W.G. Roll, Project Director of the Psychical Research Foundation in North Carolina, came to Iceland. I accompanied him on two trips to Saurar for a further examination of the phenomena which by then, unfortunately, had ceased to occur. We both concluded they must have belonged to the so-called "poltergeist" type of phenomena. We questioned the residents very thoroughly regarding the nature of the phenomena and were shown which objects had been moved and in what way. The main points we discovered were these:

1. Apparently the objects were moved chiefly from west to east, although some moved in other directions. It should be noted that the lines of direction crossed each other at a certain point on the kitchen floor.

2. The objects were moved, sometimes damaged or ruined, totally without regard to their ownership in each case.

3. The forces behind the phenomena did not seem to be endowed with intelligence. The moving objects did not appear to respond to anyone's

thoughts or wishes, nor was there any kind of teasing connected with any particular person living at the farm.

On the other hand there are several indications that the phenomena may have been connected in some way with the old woman. The direction of movement of most of the objects pointed to the kitchen where she worked every day. She was the only person always present when the phenomena occurred. They ceased as soon as she left for the hospital and started again shortly after her return to the farm. They continued after the daughter left for Reykjavik and while the farmer and his son, Bjorgvin, were out fishing. They also occurred while the younger son, Benedikt, was not at home but up in the mountains tending the sheep.

IN SEARCH OF THE PINK LADY
by Joshua P. Warren

A ghostbuster hunts for the mysterious spirit who haunts a posh southern resort.

"Excuse me."

I snapped out of my little world of scientific readings and raised my gaze to the puzzled woman before me. She stared down with a wrinkled brow as I stooped beside an antique chair. "Yes?" I said.

"I don't mean to be nosy," she said, her head cocked to the side, "but I was wondering what sort of gadget that is."

I looked down at the electromagnetic field meter in my hand. To end her questions, I gave her the first conventional answer that came to mind. "It's a light meter," I said. I continued to take readings from the chair.

She was quiet for a few moments more before saying, "It doesn't look like a light meter to me."

I realized this woman wouldn't just go away. She was curious. There she was in the Grove Park Inn, the finest resort hotel in the Blue Ridge Mountains of North Carolina. and she had found a man taking readings from a chair. You don't run across that sort of thing every day.

Remembering that the hotel wanted my work done as confidentially as possible, I was slow to tell her the truth. "Well, there have been some – how should I put it – strange goings-on in the Grove Park Inn."

Her eyes brightened and she beamed. "You're looking for ghosts, aren't you?" she asked.

"You might say that."

She grew even more excited. "Tell me all about it!" she exclaimed.

I sat down beside her, and, after making it very clear that there was much I could not discuss, I told the story of the Pink Lady. It is, without a doubt, the most famous legend concerning the classic hotel. Built in Asheville by E. W. Grove in 1913, the Grove Park Inn has seen more famous faces than one can easily list from memory. From Thomas Edison, Henry Ford and Franklin D. Roosevelt, to Richard Nixon, Dan Aykroyd and a host of other celebrities, scholars and politicians, the Grove Park Inn is not impressed by big names. There are lots of stories of guests here, but none of them are as popular as the one about the lady in pink.

On a chilly November night sometime in the late 1910s or early 1920s, a young woman wearing a long, pink gown was staying in the hotel. Her room was in the Palm Court, the core of the Main Inn, where six levels of rooms encircle a spacious drop to the lounge below. It is said that the young lady somehow fell to her death there. No-one knows whether her fall was accident, murder or suicide. Ever since the event supposedly occurred, however, employees and guests have been reporting unexplainable phenomena throughout the historic building.

Since the first documented occurrences in around 1940, people have encountered everything from a pink phantom gliding through the hotel to a rash of mischievous and unexplainable events. Occurrences range from small events such as objects moving around, doors of vacant rooms being locked from the inside, lifts being called to empty floors and typewriters typing by themselves, to large events like bellmen being physically pushed by invisible forces and every guest room light in the empty hotel turning on at once.

The witness list includes people from all walks of life, from bellmen and maids, to doctors and chiefs of police. Although in the most extreme encounters, employees have left their jobs and guests have been moved to different rooms, the occurrences are always benevolent. There has never been a malicious story attached to the elusive, and somewhat forlorn, phantom.

For years, hotel administration forbade its employees to gossip about the ghostly encounters, unsure of how the public would react. In November 1995, however, the Grove Park Inn hired me to research the phenomena for the first time in history. My results were to appear in a media release about the Pink Lady. Rather than allowing the rumours to continue, the hotel decided to officially recognize the phenomena and make sure that they were accurately portrayed to the public.

This was as far as I got with the woman in the hotel lobby. The investigation was still pretty much under wraps at that point. She begged me for more details, as well as my results, but I held true to my pledge of secrecy. I was about to continue my work, when she said, "At least tell me this. Have you gotten any positive results yet?"

I looked back at her and replied, "Oh yes ... ooooh yes." With that, I disappeared into a crowd moving toward a wing of the hotel. I didn't look back, but I knew that I had driven her crazy.

I had been studying that chair in the lobby for a reason. At approximately 5.30 a.m., on December 30, 1995, I had captured a strange image in a photograph of the chair. Using Kodak 1000 speed film and a 35mm camera, I had inadvertently snapped a photo of a grey mist hovering over the chair. At the time the photograph was taken, there was no visible indication of an apparition, and no instrumentation was in use. After the photo was developed, it was examined by four photographic experts. None of them could give me a conventional explanation for the image.

In addition to our 35mm cameras (some of them able to photograph in the infrared and ultraviolet range), I and my colleagues Mark-Ellis Bennett, Tim Vandenberghe and Tim Pedersen used devices such as ultra- and subsonic audio recording equipment, a night vision scope, electromagnetic field detectors, a video camera, a Wimshurst generator, a Van de Graff generator, and a Tesla coil. It is my belief that spectral materialization is achieved by a high concentration of electrical ions (accompanied by fluctuating electromagnetic fields). Devices such as the Wimshurst and Van de Graff generators produce a great number of ions and were sometimes employed with the hope of enhancing ghostly activity. Of course, the Tesla coil can be used to manipulate the electrical environment in a number of ways.

Though my colleagues worked with me at irregular intervals, I ultimately stayed in a total of 20 rooms at the Grove Park Inn over a period of ten nights between December 29, 1995, and May 27, 1996. During this time, we took five photographs (four with 35mm 1000 speed film and one ultraviolet photograph) that contained some sort of inexplicable image. When we took the photographs, we often detected a strong, fluctuating electromagnetic field.

From the start it was apparent that the Grove Park Inn vas highly conducive to supernatural activity. Strong, fluctuating electromagnetic energy fields (sometimes up to 8 milligauss, the amount found one inch from a television screen) randomly passed through secluded areas of the massive granite structure and then mysteriously disappeared. Although we tried to find conventional sources for the energy, in most cases we were unsuccessful.

Over the course of the investigation, two events significantly affected our research. The first one began on the afternoon of January 4, 1996. Mark-Ellis Bennett (a specialist in infrared and ultraviolet photography, as well as audio recording) noticed something odd about a photograph made the night of December 29, 1995. It was a photograph of Tim Pedersen and me standing on the fifth floor of the Palm Court. We posed for the photo (taken by an lift operator) simply to commemorate our first night of research. In the background of the photograph, however, an unusual orange glow appeared outside room 545. Bennett felt the room should be investigated, and I wholeheartedly agreed.

We tried to enter room 545 with the maid's key – a credit card type key passed through an electronic slot – but the door would not open. After several more tries, the door still would not unlock. Next, we obtained the guest key. Once again the door wouldn't open after several tries.

We eventually had to have security personnel open the door. Once inside, we detected massive fluctuating energy fields throughout the room. Bennett and I decided to come back that night with the equipment necessary to conduct formal research. However, upon our return, the activity had died down.

The next night, after midnight, I returned to room 545 with Mark-Ellis Bennett and Tim Vandenberghe. We set up the electromagnetic field meter on the arm of a chair and observed it from a distance. We patiently watched it for quite a while, but the meter read little or no energy. Suddenly, the meter detected a small energy gain, which grew and began to fluctuate. We fired away with our cameras and after a few moments, Bennett rushed to the site and held his hand over the meter. He exclaimed that he felt a strange sensation on the surface of his skin. Vandenberghe and I raced over and held out our hands as well. At first I felt nothing. Then I suddenly experienced one of the strangest sensations of my life.

An unexplainable feeling of weight pressed down on my hand and the hair on my knuckles stood up. The force felt full of static but neutral in temperature. After a few seconds it was gone, and Vandenberghe exclaimed, "I feel it!" Then it left his hand as well. We all described experiencing the same sensations. After that, the energy in the room seemed to die down.

By the end of our investigation, I concluded that room 545 was the most supernaturally active room in the hotel.

The night of January 20, 1996, marked another major event in the investigation. Tim Vandenberghe and I had set up a Van de Graff generator in Elaine's, the hotel's nightclub. There had been countless sightings in the club, and we regularly picked up strong readings there. After the generator ran a few moments, it began dispersing electrical discharges of approximately four inches. Vandenberghe viewed the scene through an infrared night-vision scope.

After approximately thirty minutes, the electrical discharges from the generator began to grow in size. They reached a peak of a little over a foot long and then branched out in midair, as though they were drawn to some invisible conductor. I took many photographs and Vandenberghe continued to use his scope while lying on his back and looking upward. This continued for a while, and then the activity seemed to lessen in intensity.

When I returned to the scene later, Vandenberghe, his face pale and his eyes large, said, "I saw something!" He claimed that while lying on his back, he had seen a white streak of illumination. Eager to rule out a conventional cause, we reproduced the circumstances, watching for reflections and light sources. After two attempts, we could not recreate the effect. We found no natural explanation for what he claimed to have seen.

I was amazed when I later developed the photographs from that night. A photo of the generator, made only ten minutes before the sighting, showed a white streak of illumination in the upper right-hand corner. Vandenberghe claims to have seen something very similar.

Although paranormal activities can and do take place all over the hotel, by the end of the field research, I had pinpointed the two most active sites in the hotel. By *active* I mean sites having the highest potential to host a paranormal experience. These two sites are the fifth floor of the hotel (particularly room 545) and Elaine's nightclub. If the legendary Pink Lady died from a fall, it's likely she stayed in room 545 and fell from the fifth-floor balcony outside her room.

Though I interviewed a number of people and searched through many records, I was not able to uncover the identity of the Pink Lady. The Grove Park has virtually no guest records until recent times.

If the Pink Lady died in a fall, the tragedy may have been kept secret. When I asked a previous hotel employee if anyone had died in the hotel, she replied, "I imagine if anyone did die, they slipped them out of there without letting the employees know. It's not one of those things that they would advertise."

During our investigation, we did confirm that strange things are happening at the Grove Park Inn. The identity of the Pink Lady, however, remains an enigma.

Joshua P. Warren *is the author of* Haunted Asheville *(Shadowbox Publications, Asheville, North Carolina).*

❦ LOST SOULS OF THE ISLES OF SHOALS ❦
by Janet Brennan

*A beautiful lover abandoned to guard pirate treasure, a
ghastly butcher wielding a knife and a petty thief running
amok on a deadly killing spree – these spirits are among the
Lost Souls of the Isles of Shoals*

Captain John Quelch began his career on the right side of the law. As
a young man, he was commissioned to sail from Boston in pursuit of
the pirates who were devastating the Atlantic shipping business. But
Quelch soon discovered that piracy was more profitable, and the
pursuer became the pursued.

Historical records show that in 1702 he buried $100,000 in
several places on White Island – half of which has yet to be found – and
$275,000 on Star Island. Unfortunately for Quelch, he never had a
chance to spend his plunder. He was caught and hanged in Boston in
1704 along with five of his crew.

Quelch was one of the first pirates who left treasure on the
islands known as the Isles of Shoals. The nine small, treeless islands are
situated nine miles off the southern coast of Maine. Five of them –
Appledore, Smuttynose, Cedar, Duck and Malaga – belong to Maine.
The other four – Star, White, Lunging and Seavey – are New
Hampshire's.

Altogether the nine islands total barely 206 acres. Any passing
sailor looking at these flat little bits of rock poking out of the Atlantic
Ocean would never guess that such a barren, uninteresting-looking
place claims a history of still-buried pirate treasure, grisly murders,
tragic accidents and a contingent of resident ghosts.

For at least the last 400 years the islands have attracted a
rather rough-and-tumble population. A stone cairn of unknown origin
on Smuttynose may have been erected by Vikings or even earlier Celtic
explorers. In the early 1700s the Isles became a favorite stopover for
pirates, and it is from this point that the strangeness began.

Pirate Treasures and Tragedies
After Quelch, a more infamous pirate arrived to hide his treasure on
the islands. Edward Teach, better known as Blackbeard, terrorized the

Virginia and Carolina coasts from 1717 to 1718. Despite Blackbeard's penchant for piracy and abducting civilians to hold for ransom, the colourful sea captain somehow managed to find the time to marry more than a dozen women. He took his final bride – number 15 by most accounts – to the Isles of Shoals for their honeymoon. Their holiday was cut short when Blackbeard spotted a British fleet on the horizon. He beat a hasty escape, leaving his new bride to guard the treasure he hid on Smuttynose Island.

Blackbeard never returned for his wife or his riches. He was killed in a battle with a Virginia government ship off the coast of North Carolina in November 1718. His widow faithfully remained, awaiting his return to Smuttynose. She died there in 1735.

Some 45 years after her death, a resident named Samuel Haley found four bars of solid silver hidden under a large rock on Smuttynose. The silver was worth about $4,000 – a fortune in the 1780s. He used the money to build a seawall connecting Smuttynose to Malaga Island, creating a small, safe harbour that still exists.

Another pirate who left both his treasure and his woman to guard it on the Isles was one Captain Scott. Scott had been a comrade of Blackbeard, sailing and stealing with him until Scott acquired a ship of his own. He first came to the Isles of Shoals in 1714, bringing with him his beautiful teenaged lover. Before leaving on a pirating excursion, he carried the girl to the site of his buried treasure and made her swear to guard it until he returned, even if she had to wait until Judgement Day. Unfortunately for the girl, Scott never did return. It's believed he went down with his ship when it sank during a battle with a British warship. But Scott's lady, due either to great love or great fear, fulfilled her vow to wait for him forever.

During the ensuing two centuries her spirit was seen on several of the islands. The first published account of the apparition was a newspaper article in 1826, written by a man who was holidaying on Star Island. One morning, he wrote, he rowed over to explore Appledore Island where he found a young woman standing on the shore, her gaze fixed on the eastern horizon. When he spoke to her, she turned to him, stared with "the most melancholy blue eyes I ever beheld," and said quietly, "He *will* come again." She then disappeared.

When the visitor returned to Star Island, he asked a local fisherman about the ghost. The resident told him she was Captain Scott's woman and was often seen on the islands; the fisherman himself had seen her.

Fascinated, the man returned to Appledore almost every day of his stay and saw her many more times. The sad woman never spoke except to say, "He *will* come again." He described her as wearing a dark cloak and as having golden hair that flowed loosely over her shoulders. When the wind blew, her hair did not move, and when she walked no sound of rustling gown or crunching shingle could be heard.

Many decades later her appearance was documented on uninhabited Duck Island. Celia Thaxter, a famous Victorian-era poet who lived on Appledore, boated over to Duck Island with a party of friends for a picnic. A gentleman in her group was walking around by himself when he saw someone staring at him through the window of a deserted shack. Thaxter wrote that he described the face as that of a "woman, wan as death; a face young, yet with a look in it of infinite age .... It looked as if it had been watching and waiting for me since the beginning of time." Keeping his eyes locked on the mournful visage, he approached the hut and entered it, but found it chillingly empty.

Ghosts of Appledore

While Captain Scott's faithful lady has been seen on several islands, another apparition that is linked to pirate treasure haunts Appledore Island exclusively. This ghost doesn't guard pirate gold, but seeks it. The ghost is known on the Isles as "Old Babb". Nathaniel Hawthorne, while holidaying at a hotel on Appledore in 1852, interviewed people who had seen Babb's ghost. Hawthorne later wrote about the haunting, but erroneously described Babb as being a member of Captain Kidd's pirate crew.

In truth Philip Babb was never a pirate – he earned plenty of money legally and on land. Yet apparently the riches he earned in life didn't satisfy him enough to keep him from seeking more after his death.

Babb was a prosperous tavernkeeper, butcher, and constable on Appledore Island. He rendered his hogs at a small cove on Appledore, and for some reason he became convinced that pirate treasure had been buried there. Babb dug a deep pit in the cove in an unsuccessful attempt to find it. Babb died in 1671, never having found any treasure. But his spirit stayed at the site and was seen over the next two centuries.

Celia Thaxter, the poet, never saw Old Babb herself, but she talked to plenty of other Appledore residents who had. She wrote that they described him as wearing "a coarse, striped butcher's frock, with a leather belt to which is attached a sheath containing a ghostly knife, sharp and glittering, which it is his delight to brandish in the face of terrified humanity".

Those people unlucky enough to see Babb close-up said he had hollow eyes in "a ghastly face", which bore a "devilish expression of malice".

Celia's brother Oscar Laighton lived his whole life on the Isles of Shoals. Nine years before his death at the age of 99, he wrote a history of the islands. Laighton saw Old Babb plenty of times. "At dusk on pleasant evenings we would see Babb's ghost standing at the head of his cove near the pit he dug," Laighton wrote. The ghost "was very real and no Islander would venture near after nightfall."

Ten Miles Out, a guidebook to the Shoals first published in 1949 and revised in 1972, contains this pithy comment on Philip Babb: "Dug for hidden treasure. Died in 1671. His ghost still walks."

Babb's pit remained on the island some 200 years after he dug it. Laighton said a storm in 1851 finally filled the pit in. Later in the nineteenth century the Coast Guard built a boathouse over the site. After that, Laighton wrote, Babb's ghost was not seen again.

Captain Scott's woman and Old Babb are not the only ones who haunt Appledore. Hawthorne, always fascinated by the supernatural, wrote about a spirit that made a brief appearance in his friend Celia's home. One day, the Thaxter family's nurse walked into their parlour and encountered "a little old woman in a striped gown" who ignored the nurse when she spoke to her. The old woman drew a chair up to the fireplace, sat down, and stretched her legs out to warm her feet near the fire. The nurse left the room for a moment, and when she returned the woman was gone.

The Thaxters never figured out who their uninvited guest could have been. In later years, though, Celia Thaxter invited other ghosts into her home, and welcomed their friendly visits.

Celia Thaxter died peacefully in her Appledore home in 1894. In 1914, her family's popular hotel on the island burned down, and Appledore ended its era as a busy summer resort. Celia and most of her immediate family lie buried in a tiny cemetery there, silent guardians of the ghost town Appledore has become.

Watery Deaths

Shipwrecks have been a common occurrence at the Isles since the 1600s. Samuel Haley, the man who found pirate silver on Smuttynose and used it to build a safe harbour, saw so many ships wrecked during the 1700s that he kept a fire on his hearth and a light burning in his window 24 hours a day as a beacon to any shipwrecked person in need of shelter.

Being a practical Yankee, Haley often salvaged what he could from the wrecks for his own use. A Spanish ship was wrecked near Smuttynose in 1813. Haley used the timbers that washed ashore to build a house, which he called The Mid-Ocean House of Entertainment. How fitting that later shipwreck victims found shelter in the house built from the wrecked ship's remains.

Of course, ships' timbers were not the only things to wash up on the islands after a wreck. Fourteen sailors' bodies were also recovered from the Spanish shipwreck and buried by the island inhabitants. The cemetery on Smuttynose where the Spanish sailors are buried can still be seen today.

Many people have been caught in the bloodthirsty clutches of the Isles' surrounding waters. A freak event on dry land in September 1848, involving Nancy Underhill, the beloved schoolteacher of Star Island, devastated the residents. Underhill had a favourite spot that she would escape to for a few moments of solitude – an oceanside cliff with a large rock at the top in the shape of a chair. One day Underhill was sitting in the rocky perch high over the ocean, gazing at the view, when a huge wave suddenly came from nowhere and dragged her out to sea. Her body washed up on York Beach in Maine, some 12 miles away, a week later. "Miss Underhill's Chair" remains a Star Island landmark visible to passing sailors, an eerie sight for those who know its tragic history.

Almost 54 years later another tragedy saddened a new generation of islanders. In 1902, a group of young people was spending the summer working at the Oceanic Hotel on Star Island. On July 17, they decided to enjoy their day off by sailing around the islands. A party of 14 waitresses and two waiters hired a local fisherman, Captain Frederick Miles, to take them on an afternoon jaunt. Five other girls also had planned to go, but when the time came to board they inexplicably refused – perhaps saved by their angels or their own intuition. Instead they remained on the pier, watching their friends happily sail away.

Because the wind was picking up the sailors stayed close to the islands. At times they were so close to shore they could call out to other friends on land. Guests relaxing outside the Oceanic Hotel on Star Island and the Appledore Hotel watched the antics of the merry party and became inadvertent witnesses to instant horror. The boat suddenly capsized 200 feet off Appledore, near Babb's Cove, and sank like a rock, sucking all 17 boaters under.

A minute after the boat hit the ocean floor, bodies began bobbing to the surface. Island onlookers dashed to their boats to attempt a rescue. The first man to arrive grabbed two girls, but the strong waves knocked him out of his boat. He managed to keep a hold on both girls, however, and dragged them to shore. It was only when he began resuscitation that he saw to his horror that one of them was his own sister. She was already dead. The other waitress was brought back from the brink of death after 30 minutes of resuscitation efforts. Only one other waitress and Captain Miles survived the ordeal. Twelve waitresses, the headwaiter, and his assistant drowned.

A Night of Terror

Over the centuries the ocean has killed scores of people at the Shoals, but the single most horrific event in the islands' history was caused not by heartless nature but by a most heartless man. A double murder committed during a robbery gone awry on Smuttynose Island in 1873 stands out as the Shoals' most terrible tragedy.

In March of 1873, there were only six people on Smuttynose, all related and living in one house: John and Maren Hontvet; Maren's sister Karen Christensen; Maren and Karen's brother Ivan Christensen with his bride, Anethe; and John's brother Matthew Hontvet. All were recent immigrants from Norway, and the men were self-employed fishermen.

Karen Christensnen had worked as a companion to Celia Thaxter's invalid mother on Appledore for two years. Two weeks before the murders, Celia arrived from her winter home in Massachusetts to take care of her mother, so Karen went to stay with her sister and brother on Smuttynose. Karen was 39 and, Celia wrote, rather melancholy over a lost love back in Norway.

The men went to Portsmouth, New Hampshire, on March 5 to sell their catch and buy supplies. There they happened upon another fisherman, Louis Wagner. Wagner knew the family well, as he had lived in an apartment in their house on Smuttynose the years before. The island men told Wagner they would be spending the night in Portsmouth. Wagner saw an opportunity for what he thought would be the perfect crime. With the women home alone on the otherwise deserted island, he could easily steal the several hundred dollars he knew John was saving to buy a new boat.

Wagner waited till dark, and then rowed the 12 miles to Smuttynose. Apparently he wasn't planning any violence. He brought no weapon with him, carrying only a stick of wood that he planned to insert in the latch of Maren and Anethe's bedroom as they slept, safely locking them in while he searched the house for the money. He didn't know Karen was also in the house.

Wagner arrived at the island around 11.00 p.m. and waited until the house windows went dark. At 1.00 a.m. he peeked through the bedroom window and saw Maren and Anethe asleep. He entered the house, slipped the wood into the bedroom latch, and quietly began searching for the money.

Suddenly, pandemonium broke out. In the bedroom, Maren's little dog began to bark frantically. The noise woke Karen, who had been sleeping in the kitchen. The women started to scream. Startled by Karen, Wagner grabbed a kitchen chair and began beating her with it. She fell against the bedroom door and dislodged the stick he'd placed through the latch. As Anethe crawled out the bedroom window, Maren opened the bedroom door, grabbed the nearly unconscious Karen, and dragged her into the bedroom. Then she pushed a bed against the door as a barricade. Wagner ran out of the house and saw Anethe standing in the snow, paralysed with fear. He grabbed an axe that was leaning against the house, and chopped at the helpless Anethe until she died.

Wagner re-entered the house and pushed his way into the bedroom. Seeing Maren attempt to escape out the window with her dog, he swung the axe in her direction. The axe handle hit the windowsill and broke and the blade flew out of the window. Wagner went outside to retrieve it and Maren fled into the darkness.

While Wagner was outside, Karen crawled to the door of Wagner's old apartment. Wagner found her there, chopped at her viciously with the broken axe, strangled her with a scarf and finally kicked her body under his own bed.

By this point, totally demented, Wagner brought Anethe's body in from the garden and dumped it on the kitchen floor. Then, covered in blood, he brewed a pot of tea, gathered food from the pantry, sat down at the kitchen table and calmly ate with Anethe's mangled body at his feet. Having eaten, he searched the house for John's money, leaving bloodstains on everything he touched. He came within inches of the $200 hidden among linen folded in a bureau, but missed it. He found about $17 in change.

Wagner then began looking outside for Maren, but he was unsuccessful. She had run, barefoot and in her nightgown, over the icy rocks to a cave at the far end of the island. As dawn approached, Wagner gave up his search and rowed back to the mainland. Maren shivered through six hours of that frigid, terrible night, with only the dog in her arms to keep her warm.

Crazed with fear and frostbite, she shouted to another Norwegian family on neighboring Appledore and was rescued. Celia Thaxter was attending to Maren's frozen feet as the Smuttynose men returned home and discovered the bodies of their loved ones. Their horror was outweighed only by their heartbreak. Wagner was arrested that day in Boston, and executed at Thomaston, Maine, in 1875, in a hanging so botched and gruesome that it prompted the state to temporarily abolish the death penalty.

In 1875 Celia wrote a lengthy account of the event that was published in the *Atlantic* magazine. The Hontvet Christensen house burned down in 1885. Smuttynose Island, haunted or not, is now almost deserted.

A Supernatural Theory
What caused Louis Wagner, who left the mainland as an unarmed petty thief, to turn into a maniacal murderer once he was on the island? Why did ruthless pirates feel at home on the isles, using them as their honeymoon haven? And what keeps ghosts tied to the place hundreds of years after their deaths? Perhaps an answer lies in the shoals geology.

People had long assumed that the islands were the summit of a submerged mountain. But geological studies begun by Dr Katharine Fowler-Billings in 1959 prove that the isles are in fact the base, not the peak, of a mountain. Geologists believe the mountain was formed by volcanic action 400 million years ago. Its top was then sheared off by the last glacial ice flow 10,000 years ago, and carried far out into the Atlantic. What remains for us to walk on is a horizontal cross-section of the mountain's core. The rocky ground, sparsely covered with vegetation, is mostly granite. Geologists have found, lying on the surface, quartz crystals as large as footballs and smaller crystals of black tourmaline and red garnet glinting in the sun.

Could the quartz crystals attract paranormal activity? Quartz crystals are used in radios, radar, and television sets to amplify electric signals. Might the Isles act as a giant crystal radio set, pulling in electromagnetic waves from the atmosphere and amplifying them? Could some people who are "tuned in" to the islands' frequency feel good there, while other people go crazy?

Whether the Isles of Shoal's violent and macabre history is the result of quartz crystals or bad luck remains an open question. As for the bleak islands themselves, they continue their legacy as homes better suited to spirits than the living.

Janet Brennan *is a newspaper editor in Portland, Maine, and a* FATE *stringer.*

JAPANESE SPIRITS
by Matthew Braaten

Not long ago, I returned home to Minnesota after working as a teacher in Japan for two years. I lived in a city surrounded by mountains located about three hours north of Tokyo, on the main island. Before going to Japan I had done a considerable amount of reading and research about the history, culture and various other aspects of Japanese society in order to acquaint myself with some of what I thought I might experience. However, you cannot prepare for the unexpected.

My combination of patience, persistence and luck put me in several strange situations; it also uncovered some amazing true-life paranormal accounts.

A Ceremony

As a secondary school English teacher, I had four schools in the city under my jurisdiction. In Japan, a teacher's duties far exceed the boundaries of the classroom as I often accompanied classes on field trips and other school excursions as part of my job. One field trip in particular stands out for not only being a lovely weekend spent camping in the mountains, but also because something bizarre occurred.

After the students and teachers had cooked the evening meal, eaten and cleaned up, some of the teachers began piling wood to make a large fire. The notion of a campfire seemed familiar from my experience of camping in the wilderness back at home. I asked if I should bring my guitar, but the assistant principal (*kyoto sensei*) said it would not be needed.

As darkness fell, the students, all in ordered groups, began gathering around the fire. They seemed as jovia as usual. However, after a few minutes of waiting around the huge bonfire, everyone suddenly grew silent. The other teachers organized the students into a tight circle and I was among them. Some of the students were handed torches which they lit from the fire. Everyone stood in silence until a small drum was struck several times by two students who stood out of the circle.

Three figures gradually emerged from the shadows. They walked in a triangle, approaching slowly, and wearing dark-coloured hoods that hid their faces. They were led by one person in the centre, who, as it turned out, was the *kyoto sensei*. The other two were students, one male and one female. Everyone was very serious; nobody even cracked a smile. The *kyoto sensei*, with his hood still covering his face, began chanting to the fire. After a while, he asked everyone to repeat several of the phrases. Although at the time I understood very little of the Japanese being spoken, I had one of the teachers translate it for me.

The chanting, as it was explained to me, was a call to keep evil spirits and bad luck away, and for good fortune to follow the students throughout the year. The students on the trip were just beginning their third (and final) year of middle school. The transition year between middle school and senior school is probably the most significant year in a Japanese student's life – the results they receive on their final middle school exams will determine which senior school they attend, which in turn determines which college they will go to. Hence, there is an immense amount of pressure put on third-year middle school students in Japan.

The bonfire ceremony was very pagan in appearance, but this should not have come as a total surprise. Japan's national religion is Shinto, which was developed over thousands of years. Before Shinto, the Japanese followed numerous polytheistic pagan religions. There are still aspects of these in the Shinto religion today. Most notably, gods in nature are still recognized as part of Shinto. In fact, one of the four Shinto affirmations is the fervent "Love of Nature". Shinto is a vague, hard to define religion – just like all others, I suppose.

That night, when the ceremony was finished, everything returned to "normal". The kids went back to their cabins to sleep and the teachers and I had several good luck drinks together.

Visiting the Dead

It's not easy to get Japanese people to discuss their views on spirituality, let alone the paranormal. It usually takes a good deal of trust, determination and alcohol to coerce them into opening up, but when they do it can be fascinating. One night during my second year in Japan I realized perhaps the most important element in the search for paranormal events – luck.

I was attending a party given by a friend who lived in a small village outside of the city. Around midnight, I stepped outside for some fresh air and observed a small group of people walking past the house. They appeared to be heading towards the Shinto cemetery (*bochi*) which sat on a nearby hillside. I recognized one of the group as an acquaintance of mine. After a brief conversation, he asked if I wanted to join them.

Being the adventurer I am, I consented. Before I knew it I was walking up the narrow hillside path trailing behind my friend and his family. Although the purpose was still unclear to me, I jumped at the chance to experience something new. We walked silently up the path passing under several traditional Shinto archways (*torii*), which often line sacred or spiritual paths in Japan.

The group consisted of my friend's wife, his teenage daughter, his younger brother and their mother. We passed a small temple (*tera*) and proceeded into the heart of the well-kept graveyard aided only by the light of the moon.

When we reached the stone they were looking for, the family formed a half-circle around it. I stepped back. My friend's mother lit an incense stick and placed it in a dish of sand on the stone. They took each other's hands after a cue from the mother. She began to speak in a dialect which was unfamiliar to me.

Finally, she repeated the word "*Otousan*" (which means father; husbands and wives in Japan often refer to each other as "father" and "mother"), calling it out several times. After a long silence, I felt a sudden chill come over my body. There was something there. I could sense activity all around us, but I couldn't see or hear anything distinct.

The old woman asked, from what I understood, why "he" (the father, her deceased husband) had been appearing to her sister lately. At this, I began to feel dizzy and nauseous. Trying desperately not to draw attention to myself, I stepped away from the group until I felt I had to sit down. I recall them all staring at me at one point, at which time I saw my friend on his hands and knees bowing in front of the grave.

The next thing I remember is being led back down the path by my friend and his family. I reached the party again safely, but there was something different among the family. The mother, in particular, seemed to stare at me suspiciously. Then they left.

Although I saw my friend again several times over the next year or so, we never again spoke of the incident except for one time, when he told me: "You should not have come with us that night, but that was my fault."

"Why?" I asked.

"Because father said he could not speak in the presence of a stranger," he replied.

The Honeymoon Picture

An American friend and I often gave parties in our apartments which were attended by other foreign teachers from the area (three Americans, a Scot, an Aussie and a Brazilian) and about half a dozen Japanese friends of ours. Late in the evening during our first annual Halloween party, the foreigners began relating ghost stories. We all took turns sharing our tales, translating them for the non-English speakers. Our Japanese friends grew more intrigued by these stories as the night progressed. The telling of "ghost stories" was a totally foreign notion to our Japanese guests. This is probably because speaking of the deceased is somewhat taboo in Japan and the witnessing of an apparition is taken very seriously.

And so, when one of our Japanese guests, Masumi, suddenly said she had a story, it came as a big surprise. Her story remains as one of the strangest and most intriguing reports I have ever heard. She made me swear that I would never mention her full name in conjunction with the story. (The Japanese are also a modest, private people.) After another drink, she worked up the nerve to tell us. What's interesting to point out is that while we foreigners were just telling stories, she felt that in order to share, she had to tell a dark family truth.

The story pertained to something that happened to her aunt Keiko a few years earlier. Keiko was with her husband on their honeymoon in Miyagi Prefecture. They had spent the day at the beach enjoying the summer weather. Later that afternoon, they climbed up to a scenic viewpoint. After enjoying the view for a while, they asked someone to take a photo of the two of them standing on the steep cliff with the ocean in the background. Then Keiko wanted to take a photo of her husband alone.

He backed up near the edge of the cliff while Keiko was focusing the camera. Just as she snapped the picture, her husband screamed and fell off the edge to the rocks below. He did not survive the fall.

Keiko was utterly grief-stricken for the next several months, but gradually her state improved. At long last she took the film from the honeymoon in to get developed. She dropped the film off at her neighbourhood photo shop, just as she'd always done in the past. After a few days she returned to pick up the photos. The moment she came in the door, the two young female employees began acting very strangely. When Keiko asked for her pictures, both employees went in the back to get the manager. He returned alone with an extremely disturbed expression on his face. Keiko greeted him, nonetheless, for they had known each other for years.

He made small chit-chat with her, but something seemed wrong. When at last she asked for her photos the man's face grew even more serious. He said he could not hand over her photos. This incensed Keiko and she asked again more sternly. To this he replied that there had been a problem and he tried to dissuade her from seeing the photos. Finally, she demanded the photos as they were the last ones of her husband alive. The man burst into tears and yelled for one of the workers in back to bring the photos. As he handed Keiko the photos he said: "Please forgive me, I tried to warn you." A chill came over her.

She waited until she got home to open the envelope. Keiko described the strange reception she received from the shopkeeper to her mother, who sat down beside her. Together they began going through the pictures, her mother looking first. There were pictures of the couple on their first day of the honeymoon, and others of them at different places they'd gone together on their trip. Then they came to the pictures taken that day at the beach. Keiko and her husband looked so happy.

Finally, they came to the picture of the two of them together on the cliff. Keiko's mother studied the next picture, while Keiko stared longingly at the photo of her and her husband together. Suddenly, her mother gasped and dropped the picture. She said nothing, but only shook. At this, Keiko picked up the photo she had taken of her husband. She saw the horrified look on her husband's face as dozens of hands and arms pulled him over the cliff.

Masumi later learned that the cliff has a history. It was on that spot hundreds of years before that the local Shogun falsely accused a group of young men from a nearby village of treason and forced them off the cliff to their death. I asked if it would be possible to see the photo, but Masumi said she was told that the photo was "missing", and that her aunt remains in a state of deep depression.

Mr Mogi's Passenger

During another of our cross-cultural theme parties, a friend of mine named Mogi-san sat me down alone and said he had heard about my interest in true stories about apparitions (*yuureh*). He said that his father had had something very strange happen to him a few years before, and Mogi-san felt compelled to tell me the story.

Mogi's father worked in the downtown area of the city. On his way to work, he drove what came to be known to me as the river road. (Although it has an official name, we just called it the river road because it runs alongside the river.) People take it in order to avoid the traffic on the main road. I often used the river road for the same reason; in fact, I used to wonder why more people didn't use it until I drove it myself the first time. It's very narrow, and at most points there are no guard rails between the road and the river below.

Mr Mogi had been driving the river road for years without a problem until one morning, as he was driving along, he suddenly realized that a man was sitting in his passenger seat. Mr Mogi asked, obviously shocked, "Who are you?" The man introduced himself as Mr Takahashii.

Mr Mogi asked, "What do you want?"

The man replied, "Do you mind if I just ride along?" Mr Mogi didn't know what to say; he wasn't sure if he was hallucinating or what.

His passenger, Mr Takahashii, continued to appear for the next several days on the morning drive. Mr Mogi grew so distressed over the matter that he took a week of sick leave from work, and sought professional help. After seeing doctors and having multiple exams, they could not find anything physically wrong with him. So he went to see a psychiatrist. After Mr Mogi reluctantly told his story, the doctor gave him some very good advice.

"If the man appears again," she said, "ask him why he is there, and then ask him if there is anything you can do to help him."

The following Monday morning, Mr Mogi resumed his drive to work along the river road. Once again the man appeared in the passenger seat. Recalling the advice of the doctor, Mr Mogi asked the man why he was appearing along this stretch of road. The man replied, "I used to drive this road every day, too, and one winter day I met a car that was going too fast. I swerved to miss it and crashed into the river. I died."

Mr Mogi pondered this for a moment, then asked, "What do you want from me? Can I do something to help you?"

The man replied, "Yes. Please go to my wife and give her this message…"

The man gave Mr Mogi specific instructions along with his full name and address. Mr Mogi felt he had no choice but to do as the dead man had asked.

That night after work, Mr Mogi found the house of the dead man's widow. He knocked on the door and when a woman came, he introduced himself. It was extremely difficult for him to do, but he briefly explained the situation. Mrs Takahashii at first thought he was crazy and tried to close the door, but Mr Mogi begged her to listen and told her he had instructions from her deceased husband. About this time the woman's sons arrived.

Mr Mogi asked, "Are you having any financial problems, or problems proving that the house is yours?"

The woman and her sons studied him suspiciously. "Perhaps. Why?" she asked.

"Your husband has told me how to help you, if you let me in," replied Mr Mogi.

He then stepped into the house and went directly to the kitchen. He immediately got down on his hands and knees and started feeling the floor along the base of the wall. Mrs Takahashii and her teenage sons stared curiously at him.

After a few minutes of searching, Mr Mogi found a loose floor panel. He strained and yanked until he pulled it off. Then he reached into the space, feeling around, until he found a large manila envelope covered in dust. He gave it to the woman who carefully, still very wary of Mr Mogi, opened the envelope. Inside were the apparently "missing" deeds to the house and some other land owned by Mr Takahashii, a will, and other legal documents. The woman thanked Mr Mogi repeatedly.

Mr Mogi continued driving the river road to work in the mornings and evenings, but he never saw the mysterious passenger again.

LA LLORONA,
THE WEEPING WOMAN
by Steven Narbonne

She is called La Llorona, pronounced *Lah Yo-row-naw*, which means "the Weeping Woman". Her origins have been lost, and her name, the place where she was born, and even the name of her people have long been forgotten. Though there is more than one tale of La Llorona, certain aspects remain remarkably consistent, no matter who tells the story.

She lived, according to legend, shortly after the Conquistadors, the Spanish conquerors, had arrived in MesoAmerica. It is said that she was very beautiful, with the high cheekbones of her people, and flashing brown eyes. She had the long black hair of her tribe as well, and its highlights gleamed in the sun. Her figure was full in a way that drew the eyes of men, and she moved with the fluid grace all women strive for but few attain.

She was ready with a laugh at most times, but also quick to anger. Too quick, if later events are any indication.

In a way, all her attributes were a pity. Possibly if she had been less pretty her laughter less happy, she would not have attracted the attention of a young Spanish noble. He looked upon her and found her desirable. She looked at him and found him pleasing, too, as well she might have.

The young noble was rich and powerful. He sat on his charger proudly, with his back stiff and straight as his sword. He, too, had a ready laugh. He, too, was quick to anger.

The two began to meet, and soon they became lovers. No-one dared say anything to her for fear of the noble's wrath. No-one would have dreamed of reproaching him. Was it not his right to take what he wanted? Do not all men sow their wild oats? It was just a fling. It would pass. For him, it did.

It was not just a passing diversion for the young Indian woman, however. She loved him with all the fire of her youth and culture. She gave her all to him, and after she had borne him two sons, she was sure that he would soon give his world to her.

Eventually, however, she heard rumours that disturbed her. Those gossip mongers, common to all ages and eager to spread hurt, spoke of the forthcoming marriage of the young man to a Spanish lady of his own station. The Indian woman refused to believe at first, but the uncertainty was too much to bear and she went to speak to her lover.

It happened that she chose the day of his wedding to confront him. She dashed past the guards at the young man's hacienda and ran to face him. She demanded her rights as the mother of his two sons. Then the youth did a cruel thing: He laughed in her face.

Marry her? He, a nobleman of Spain, should lower himself by marrying a common Indian? She should be glad he had deigned to even notice her, much less honour her with his attentions. He had his guards drive her from his house.

The young woman was mad with rage and humiliation. She raced to her hut, head lowered to avoid the mocking looks of those who despised her for consorting with the Spanish. Inside were her two young sons, eyes wide with fright at seeing on their mother's face a fury such as they had never seen before. "Her sons?" her unleashed emotions asked. No. His sons.

In her madness she advanced on the boys. She took hold of them and dragged them whimpering to a distant spot on the bank of the river, far from the village. There she pushed the helpless boys' heads under water and held them until their struggling stopped. There, it was done. Now her lover would share her pain.

Maybe he did. Then again, maybe not. The young noble faded into richly deserved obscurity after marriage. He would have been on his honeymoon when the bodies were found.

When the boys' corpses were discovered, the authorities were notified. The young woman had made no effort to leave her community, and she was taken into custody. Everyone knew what had happened, and Spanish justice was swift. A trial was held. The woman was convicted. Three days after her sons' deaths, she was executed. A tragedy, but not the stuff of legend – except for the events that followed.

Returned to Earth

According to legend, the woman's spirit was brought before God for judgment. God asked where her children were. Of course, she had no answer. God was wrathful and sent her back to Earth to find her children. She would not be allowed peace until she did. She began the search where she had murdered them by the river, and she continues to search for them to this day, always by bodies of water.

It was not long before she was observed in her sad task. Reports came from various sources about the apparition that appeared by the river and keened for the lost children. For some, the weeping ghost seemed a good lesson of divine justice. Others found her an object of pity. There was fear, too.

As in all areas where there are bodies of water, there is a price to be paid for the advantages of living there. One price is that people will drown, especially children. In places where La Llorona was seen, the inevitable drownings were blamed on the spirit. It is only to be expected. If a child drowns, the natural reaction of a parent, besides grief, is guilt. The "if only's" start. If only they had watched the child more closely. If only the warnings about the river had been more stern. Blaming the drowning on supernatural malevolence absolves the parent of that guilt. My research, however, has failed to uncover a single documented case of La Llorona having harmed a person. Even the fright she inspires in witnesses seems accidental rather than by design.

The following story, obtained through a translator during conversations with Mrs Librada Lopez of Coachella, California, provides a typical example of an encounter with La Llorona. This incident took place near Lopez's village, Michoacan, Mexico, in 1940. The fisherman's name has been forgotten after more than 50 years.

The fisherman worked quickly at setting his fishing lines. It was Lent and only fish were to be eaten, no meat, and this gave urgency to his task. It was evening and dark, but he had walked the path beside the creek often before and the moonlight helped. At last he came to the end of his line, but, as he cast the last hook in, he spotted someone sitting on the opposite side of the creek. It was a woman, head bowed demurely, hands in her lap. A washerwoman, he wondered? She was close to the water and roughly where the village women did their laundry. No, it was too late in the day. A prostitute? He dismissed the thought almost as soon as he had it. The village was too small and poor to support such a dubious luxury, and the women too vigilant.

He suddenly smiled in realization. Of course. She was here for a rendezvous. No doubt she had sneaked out unnoticed or she had made some excuse to her parents.

The young fisherman glanced at the moon. It was still early. He would have some fun with this mysterious woman, then return to the village.

Agilely, he jumped the little creek. "Ay, chiquita, como esta?" he said. The woman continued staring at her hands, not responding to his polite "How are you?"

He walked several steps toward her. He could see her more clearly now. She was attractive, with straight, black hair shining in the moonlight, and a shapely figure that her long garments could not hide. Her clothing was strange though. All white. So white it seemed to be softly glowing. He could not see her face, but she was obviously beautiful.

He walked closer still, slowly, so as not to frighten her. At first the young man confined himself to forward but polite comments on her looks, but her continued silence emboldened him. He began to make pointed remarks on those areas of her figure that interested him most. He started to whistle and make wolf calls at the woman.

At length she rose gracefully and began to walk away. The man decided to pursue her a short distance, then be on his way. He was enjoying himself.

He strolled behind the woman, offering witty observations on late boyfriends, and his lip noises were reaching their artistic peak when they reached a widening of the creek. The woman crossed it.

She appeared to glide over the water. She showed no effort, made no leap. There was just a smooth transition from one side of the creek to the other.

The fisherman hurried over to the spot the woman had just left and judged the distance. He decided that he could have crossed it, but only with a running start. There was no way he could have just stepped across as she had. There was no way she could have done it the way she did, either.

Coldness came over him as he watched her retreating form. Something was wrong, terribly wrong. He began to shout after her, "Who are you? How did you do that? Answer me, *bruja*." The woman he had called bruja, which means "witch", stopped. She slowly turned and then showed him her face. He gasped in horror, for her face was not that of a desirable young woman, but that of a desiccated corpse.

Parchment-thin skin tightly covered a skull face, and her eyes were so sunken in their sockets that he only saw black holes. She began to grin. Her cracked lips strained upward in a hellish parody of a young woman's smile of invitation. The macabre sight snapped him out of his trance. He turned and ran blindly away from the scene. As he ran, he heard the specter crying "Ay, mi hijos, mi hijos [my children, my children]." At that moment, he knew he had seen La Llorona.

From this example, one can see that this spectre, unlike many, not only does not try to inflict herself on others, but appears to actively avoid doing so. I suspect that the solitary search through her personal purgatory has effectively erased any desire to further harm others. Left alone, she will probably continue to search in her inoffensive though sometimes frightening manner.

Like most phenomena of this kind, a multitude of sightings are dubious at best, mistakes or outright frauds. People have reported La Llorona miles from any water, in the rearview mirror of their cars, for example.

Another Sighting

While there still remains a good deal of solid anecdotal evidence supporting the crying woman's existence, it is always wise not to be too credulous. Maria Valdez of Palm Desert, California, offers the following example of too-quick belief.

In 1947, Maria and her husband bought a small house in Harlingen, Texas. Soon they and their three young children were moved in and happy with the house, except that, like many in those days, they had no toilet. People dug outhouses or paid a small fee to empty their chamber pots into neighbour's toilets. The Valdez family arranged to use their neighbour's toilet, as had the family before them.

Harlingen is in southeast Texas, a land of agriculture amid scrub brush. It is also hot and humid in the summer months.

It was Maria's duty to empty the chamber pot. She performed this task in the late hours of the evening, around 11.00 p.m. At that hour, she avoided the sun's heat and the embarrassment of being seen by the neighbours.

Despite her caution, however, insomniacs and night owls did see her. Rumours began to spread about a beautiful but mysterious woman, dressed in a long, white gown, roaming through the scrub-land late at night. It did not take very long before the watchers were sure they knew who the woman was. Who else would be prowling about the sage and tumbleweeds so late? Who else would be beautiful, dressed in a long, white gown and sporting flowing, black hair? It was La Llorona. Any fool could see that.

Maria Valdez has long since moved from Harlingen, but when she last heard, the local legend was still going strong. She has often been tempted to set the record straight but never had the opportunity to do so. She does so now.

Curiously, I have not found reports from anyone except Mexicans or Hispanics concerning La Llorona. No Anglo has ever reported seeing her. Possibly this is because an Anglo seeing her would not know her identity, and, unable to understand her cry, would simply believe he or she had seen a ghost.

Poetic Justice

Perhaps La Llorona is getting only what she deserves for her crimes. Wandering forever, in search of that which cannot be found, to pay for a crime that cannot be righted, has a certain poetic justice. After so many years, however, is justice still a legitimate concern? Will mercy never enter the equation? Possibly those of you who read these words and believe, as I do, that it has been long enough, can intercede for La Llorona with your guides and saints, or direct your prayers to the Creator. It is time for her sorrowful journey to end.

Steven Narbonne *became interested in the paranormal after having a near death experience as the result of an accident. He currently lives and works in California.*

THE LAMBERT HOUSE
by Randall Heddon

A father's spirit still haunts his family's home.

I always considered myself spiritually agnostic. While accepting that there are many things in this life I will never know, I believed only in what I could see and touch. This changed forever on a dark night in April 1993.

I grew up in a large isolated house on Lambert Street in Portland, Oregon. After my father's death at the age of 77, my family reluctantly decided to move my mother, who had been diagnosed with Alzheimer's disease, to a smaller residence. We sold the house in 1989, and my mother went to live in a nursing home.

Three years later, however, the person we had sold the house tostopped sending his monthly payments, and we were forced to repossess it. We reclaimed the house in April 1993 to find it neglected, badly in need of paint and repairs. We were divided about whether to move my mother back to the house or leave her where she was.

I spent the day we reclaimed the house with my friend Don Basem, who helped me move some boxes and furniture we needed to store there. It took three trips in Don's van, and it was about 9.00 in the evening when we arrived with the final load.

Friendly and inviting during the day, the house took on a foreboding appearance after dark. Don and I began unloading boxes and carrying them upstairs. As we finished lowering a particularly heavy box to the floor, Don stopped and looked around. He said that he felt strange. I laughed, but I had been aware of a cold area in the main upstairs hall and an uncomfortable feeling of being watched. I agreed with Don that it did feel odd, but we still had a lot to do, and I was certain the weird feelings were the result of being alone in a cold, empty house.

We went back outside and brought up another box to put into the small bedroom at the top of the stairs. I walked into the room and immediately knew that something was there with me. Goosepimples covered my body as I felt whatever it was walk directly into me.

Don felt it too; he wouldn't even enter the room. I turned

around to see him staring into the room, attempting to see something that wasn't visible. He grabbed me, and in a daze we ran downstairs and away from the presence. My eyes had started to water when I entered the room, and by the time we made it downstairs, tears were running uncontrollably down my face.

"I'll tell you one thing," Don said, leaning on the wall for support. "Whatever's going on, the thing in this house is hurting."

I, too, was aware of a sadness that permeated the house. I had to get out of there. We drove into town and got a pitcher of beer at a local bar. Tears were still streaming down my face; my body had not yet recovered from the shock.

Don said that he had lived in an apartment years ago where he had felt something similar. He asked if anyone had ever died in the house. I told him my father had died in one of the downstairs bedrooms five years earlier. "That's it," he said. "It's your father. That's why he walked into you, and why you keep crying. You have to tell him to go to the light."

I disagreed. First, I wasn't crying; I just couldn't stop my eyes from watering. Second, why should I send my father back to the light if he had gone to this much trouble to make his presence known? I didn't even know for sure we were dealing with my father.

It was late when we returned to the house, but we had to finish unloading the van. I also knew that for my peace of mind I had to go back and confront the presence. Several glasses of beer helped my resolve.

Neither of us wanted to go inside, but we steadied ourselves, unlocked the door, and went in. The main floor was dark and cold, but uninhabited. We slowly walked to the stairwell, then up to the small bedroom where we had felt the presence. The entity was not there, but it had left a peculiar cold feeling behind. We went to another bedroom and again felt the unnatural cold, but nothing else.

We walked into the third bedroom and stopped. Both Don and I felt the presence in front of us. Don said, "Go to the light. You have to go to the light."

"What do you want?" I yelled. Tears rolled from my eyes.

We stood staring at the space the entity occupied in the dark, and at the same moment, we sensed it begin to move, walking by us and out of the room. As soon as it left the room the temperature seemed to change and we could breathe normally.

We chased the entity through the house, finding it first in the rooms upstairs, then in a small kitchen alcove, and finally in the room where my father had died. Every time we tried to talk, it would leave the room.

At 1.30 in the morning I decided it was time to go. I pitied the entity. I felt as though we were forcing it to run from us. The sadness still hung over the entire house. I agreed with Don – whatever it was, it was most certainly in pain.

Another Witness

The week after my encounter my brother Brad hired a salesman named Dave from San Francisco. Brad told him that we were fixing up the family house and if needed he could use it until he got an apartment in Portland.

The following Sunday I returned to the house and went back to work, cleaning the outside, clearing brush and organizing the garage. I didn't go upstairs, and I intended to leave before the sun went down. I was in no mood to confront the situation that day.

Dave drove up as I was finishing. We talked for a while. As I was getting ready to go, he said, "You know, the house is haunted."

It came out of the blue. I'm sure the surprise showed on my face. He looked somewhat sheepish and said, "Well, I'm sure it's probably just my imagination. Don't tell Brad I said anything – I don't want him to think I'm flaky."

Dave said that when he had first arrived it was late at night. He went inside and immediately felt he wasn't alone. He went to his car and got a pistol he had brought with him from California. He walked through the entire house until he was satisfied that no-one else was there. Only then did he unpack his clothes and bring his cat in from the car.

The first two nights in the house passed without incident, though he did notice that lights that he left on upstairs at night would be turned off the following morning, and that windows left open would be closed.

On the third night Dave awoke feeling uncomfortable, and from his bed could see the hallway light become dim and then bright again. He looked to the window where the light reflected and realized he was seeing what resembled a figure walking back and forth in front of the light.

The next day he left on a two-day sales trip. When he returned, his cat, which had been left inside, came bounding out the door looking wild, never to be seen again.

I told Dave what had happened to me, and I promised I wouldn't tell my brother what he had said. I still hadn't figured how to tell Brad about my own experience. I knew that he and my sister Barbara would think I was demented.

The Family Investigates

With much trepidation I called Brad. I bluntly told him the family house was haunted and prepared myself for his scepticism. A somewhat conservative businessman, he didn't take much stock in haunted houses, but he went to the house that afternoon.

I was out of town, so he called me that evening. "It feels warm and nice, and I don't get any hint of ghosts walking around," he said. Try it at midnight, I thought. I didn't mention Dave's experiences, but I said, "It's time to get someone professional in."

When my niece, Tina Zander, heard that I thought the house was haunted, she walked through it herself. She said she felt a presence, and she called a friend of hers. Mrs Stone (not her real name), a woman in her 70s, offered to "read" the house at no charge.

Mrs Stone, Tina, and Brad met outside the house. Mrs Stone told Brad to change the colour of his aura before he walked in. He pictured the colour red. She said, "No, not red, another colour." Brad was surprised that Mrs Stone knew what he had thought of. He decided on yellow. "Yellow's fine," she said, and they walked in, my brother amazed.

They walked through the house for about an hour. Nothing out of the ordinary happened. As they were preparing to leave, Mrs Stone said, "He's here."

"Who's here?" asked Brad and Tina.

"Your father," Mrs Stone said, "and there's someone with him. They're holding hands. I think it's a small girl." She talked to herself for a minute and then turned to my brother.

"He wants you to be a man," Mrs Stone said. "You have to do the right thing!" She said my father was angry that my mother was in a nursing home, and he wanted her brought back to the house immediately, with care-givers to watch over her.

Brad thought this information was all interesting, but he

dismissed what he was hearing. The three of them began walking outside when suddenly he fell to his knees and began crying.

"I felt something walk up behind me," he said. "I knew I could walk away from it, or just sink into it. The next thing I knew I was on the ground with this huge wave of emotion."

Mrs Stone described the scene for me later. "Your father walked around behind your brother and put his arms around him," she said. "When he did that your brother collapsed."

Brad went back inside alone, sat on the upstairs landing, and talked to the house, promising to move my mother back in as soon as possible.

A Second Opinion

Our intention was to move my mother back in the house when it was ready, but I was nervous. Barbara had heard about my brother's experience, but she would not believe the house was possessed. We agreed to get a second reading on the house from an impartial source.

This was the first and only time I have ever tried to find a legitimate psychic. I didn't want to call a 900 number, so I called Portland's newspaper, the *Oregonian*, and asked if they could help me contact any psychics used either by them or by the police. From the five names I was given, I finally decided on Alice, a young woman who seemed to be the most level-headed and intuitive. I told her nothing except that I felt the house might be occupied.

Two days later, at 7.30 in the evening, Alice met us at the house. Barbara, her son Hans, and Tina's family all came to hear what Alice had to say.

As soon as we walked into the house Alice looked at me and said, "First of all, you're not crazy. There are two entities in here." She walked to the kitchen alcove where Dave and I had both experienced the presence, and stood for a long time. She turned to me and said, "Your father's dead, isn't he? On the phone I had a feeling it was your mother, but your father is here."

Alice turned back to the alcove. "There is a woman here, too," she said. "She doesn't like me at all. She's very small. It could be a child, but the energy is that of a very dominant woman."

She walked through the house, followed by the entourage. We eventually went upstairs and sat in one of the rooms where I had first encountered the presence. As we gathered around Alice on the floor, she said that my father was very upset.

"He didn't mean for this to happen," she said. "He's glad to see everyone, but he didn't want this to become a circus."

I suddenly felt guilty. Most of us there were sceptical and had come to debunk the haunting. I believed my father had made his presence known to me for a reason, and I was turning it into a sideshow. I decided never to do it to him again.

It became obvious that Alice's attempts at communication were taxing her. She repeated that it was difficult because my father was so upset. I again felt the heavy sadness fall over the room like a weight. Alice said my father wanted "Weezie" (his nickname for my mother) to come home. It was the same basic message as before. He thought my mother was unsafe where she was living, and he wanted her back in the house.

We were in the room for about two hours. My hair stood on end and my eyes watered the entire time. Alice was shaken by the experience. I tried to find evidence of fraud, but she was much too accurate on too many points to be dismissed.

Alice was exhausted, so we called it a night, locked up the house, and said goodbye. Alice started to leave, then suddenly turned back, took my hand, and said, "Bring your mother back."

Three weeks later we moved my mother into the house. For the first few weeks I stayed on the main floor as my mother got settled. Family members would exchange glances when my mother would ask, "Where's your father? I just saw him." Occasionally at night I felt the presence nearby, though the fear I had initially experienced was gone.

My mother has been back in the house more than three years, and we have been lucky to find two people who have taken wonderful care of her. We decided not to tell them anything. Lately, however, they do mention that when they go upstairs, the windows are open if they had been closed, and the lights are turned off if they had been left on. They say things like, "I think your father got warm during the night," or "Your father hates to waste electricity." They seem to know he is still there, watching out for my mother.

Randall Heddon *is a musician who has worked in television and in the movies. He currently produces commercial music in Portland, Oregon.*

THE HAUNTED LEMP HOUSE
by D. Douglas Graham

Tragedy stalked a famous St. Louis family

For decades, fame and tragedy haunted the Lemps, one of Missouri's most famous families. In fact, Edgar Allan Poe's story, "The Fall of the House of Usher" could have been modelled on the lives of the Lemp beer-brewing dynasty. All the elements of the fictional account can be found in the Lemp family history: obsession, decadence, dark secrets and self-destruction. Today some consider their fading, white-washed mansion one of the most haunted homes in North America.

The Lemp family rose to prominence quickly after John Adam Lemp arrived in St Louis in 1838. John had been a brewer in his native Germany, and when he landed in the American city he found it full of German-speaking expatriots. The new Americans had been weaned on full-bodied German beer. American brew, however, was based on old British recipes – which simply didn't satisfy them. The entrepreneurial John Adam Lemp introduced a new lager beer to a thirsty city and became an overnight success.

In less than two decades, John Adam's brewery swelled to the size of several city blocks. At the time of his death, Lemp Beer was becoming a national institution.

Early Success and Sudden Death
The history of conspicuously wealthy families seems to follow a classic pattern. The founder creates the fortune, his offspring embellish it through hard work, and the last of the line squander it away. The Lemps fit that mould.

John Adam's fledgeling enterprise went international under the stewardship of his son, William. William lived for Lemp Beer, and by the 1880s the brand was as recognizable as Budweiser is today.

William groomed his first-born son, Frederick, to take over the family business. Frederick took to the task with gusto, burning up his youth promoting Lemp Beer. Unfortunately, Frederick worked too hard and died of exhaustion at the age of 28.

William was shattered. Three years later he shot himself, hoping perhaps, to join his favourite son in the next world.

Will and Lil Take Over

All the Lemps were peculiar, but Will, Jr., the next Lemp to head the family business, pushed his eccentricities beyond acceptable limits. When his reign began, Will, Jr., immediately set out to plunder the family fortune. He bought houses, horses, property and art – much of it imported from Europe and Asia. In 1899, he acquired another pretty ornament: a young wife named Lillian Handlan.

Lillian soon became a willing accomplice in Will, Jr.'s, spending spree. Every morning Lillian was given a $1,000 bill and instructed to spend it before sunset. By all accounts Lillian never failed to meet her husband's demands.

Will, Jr.'s, behaviour grew increasingly bizarre with time. By middle age, he had become a curmudgeon, and he was well on the way to becoming a full-fledged misanthrope.

John Adam Lemp had built his brewery over a network of caverns known as the Cherokee Caves. It was located just a few blocks from the family mansion on De Menil Street.

Will, Jr., used the caves to travel to and from his office, in order to avoid the sycophants and riff-raff he was certain were shadowing him. Over the years he also built a ballroom, a vaudeville stage and a swimming pool in the caves – and they remain intact to this day.

Will, Jr., ruthlessly persecuted his enemies, both real and imaginary. Eventually Lillian also fell into this category, and shortly after the turn of the century Will, Jr., asked her for a divorce.

By this time the Lemps' crazy ways had infected Lillian's behaviour as well. She customarily appeared around town clad from head to foot in lavender. She also outfitted her horse and carriage in lavender, a habit which earned her the nickname "Lavender Lil".

The Lemp divorce was the biggest thing to hit St Louis since the Civil War. The courtroom was mobbed with reporters, gossip mongers, and the riffraff that Will, Jr., had always feared.

Everyone had a field day when Lillian laid her husband's oddities on the table for all to see. Will, Jr., would sometimes try to run over people he didn't approve of with his carriage, she said, and when his wild behaviour fell short of making its point, he followed up with a pistol shot. Will, Jr., steadfastly denied all charges, counter-charging that Lillian sometimes smoked in the house.

The latter shocking disclosure was all that was needed to make him a free man. Lillian survived the separation – and her ex-husband – by many years.

By 1922, John Adam's brewing empire was practically bankrupt. When the brewery was sold that year, it brought slightly more than half a million dollars. Just a couple of years earlier the plant had been valued at seven million dollars.

Heartbroken, angry and stupefied by his long run of bad luck, Will, Jr., shot himself on December 29.

The Mystery of the Monkey-Faced Boy

Will, Jr., had a roving eye, and his frequent affairs may have been the primary motive behind his divorce. It is possible that at least one child, a boy, was brought into the world as a result of these extramarital dalliances. The boy was reportedly deformed and retarded, and like a tragic character in a gothic novel, he spent much of his life locked away in one of the attics of the family manor.

Rumours about the monkey-faced boy persist to this day, and while it would be easy to dismiss the stories as romantic fluff, certain eerie phenomena seem to support them. Some people remember passing the Lemp house as children while a deformed boy gazed down at them from a dusty attic window.

Even today, strange sounds sometimes come from inside the attic: a child's pathetic whimpering and a soft, disembodied voice calling for "mama." Some people report hearing a child yell, "Hi Mum, Hi Mum," when they enter an empty room. Tables shake and levitate, cups and plates move about – all of it allegedly the work of the mysterious monkey-faced boy. The ghost seems anxious to take credit for these shenanigans: His face often appears on photographs taken in the basement, bar and dining rooms.

Elsa Lemp: The Curse Follows Her

One of John Adam's daughters, Elsa, was unhappily married. She did not live at the infamous Lemp Mansion, but she carried all of its misery with her to her new residence in the city's Central West End. Elsa killed herself there, and today the house at 13 Hortense Place is said to be haunted, yet another casualty of the Lemp family curse.

When Paul Pointer worked as a radio host, he interviewed a man who lived at 13 Hortense Place. The guest unhesitatingly confirmed that the house was haunted and that the haunting seemed to follow a classic pattern. A ghost would appear at the top of the staircase, travel slowly down, and finally disappear into a wall. When the paper was torn from the wall, a secret doorway was revealed. Only later did the guest realize that he was living in the same house that Elsa Lemp had also lived and died in.

Charles Lemp: An Oddball Among Oddballs

After Will, Jr.s, death, Charles Lemp presided over the dynasty. Though he had the means to live elsewhere, Charles was attached to the house on De Menil Street, and he insisted on staying there despite its dismal history. The grim ambiance of the house gradually worked its black magic on Charles. He became an oddball even by the standards of his odd family. Like the late Howard Hughes, he lived in terror of microbes. He even wore a pair of white gloves to protect himself from contamination.

He lived to a ripe old age, but ultimately could not deny the siren call of suicide. In 1949, he shot himself, shortly after his seventy-seventh birthday.

Edward, the Party Animal

Charles' successor, his brother Edward, was apparently the smartest of the Lemp line. Unlike his unfortunate siblings, he did not live in the family home. Instead he bought a huge property in the neighbouring city of Kirkwood and devoted the rest of his life to spending the family fortune.

Eddie's estate was a popular spot for the socialites of the time. Wild animals freely roamed the grounds, and Eddie threw frequent and extravagant parties.

Eddie could not bear the thought of being alone. His parties continued all day and night, and when there were no parties, the servants remained in the house to keep the old man company. He lived well into his nineties, but died alone and childless.

When Eddie died there were no Lemps left in the world – no living Lemps, at least. Like the family that built it, the Lemp mansion went into a long, downward spiral. In the 1950s and 1960s it was converted into low-rent housing. It was around this time that the well-dressed shade of Charles Lemp began to materialize at various points on the estate.

But these random appearances were only the tip of the psychic iceberg. By the 1970s the Lemp mansion erupted with paranormal events, even attracting the attention of national media and paranormal investigators. When *Life* magazine published an article on prominent haunted houses in 1982, the Lemp mansion was listed among the most ghost-infested real estate in the country.

A former resident came across the piece and wrote a letter to the current owners, the Pointer family. At that time the Pointers were trying to turn the place into a restaurant, and a few of the workers were reporting unusual incidents.

The writer indicated that he had lived in a basement apartment in the mansion during the early 1950s. One night he was travelling the murky labyrinth of the basement on the way to the restroom. Passing a large reception room, he looked up suddenly and saw a well-dressed man appear from nowhere.

"He looked steadily right at me, smiling," the letter read. "He wore a neat, expensive, dark suit. His shoes were especially clean and new-looking. I have never seen any pictures of a Lemp family member, but I know this was the ghost of Charles Lemp who died in that basement place. He was not large, just about 5' 7". His hair was dark and combed straight back. All this took only a second to see.

"I panicked and took one step to run, but then I stopped. I wanted to appear unafraid. As I stopped, I turned to look at him again. He was not there. He simply vanished."

Ghost Carriages

During renovations orchestrated by the Pointers, a painter and his wife lived in a second-floor bedroom of the mansion. Each morning the wife complained that ghostly horses had kept her up all night. The sound of hoof-beats on cobblestone was driving her nuts, she said.

As summer dragged on, the grass began to recede into little squares. When landscapers dug up the yard, they found a tiled courtyard just inches below the topsoil. (The landscapers used the tiles, some of which were inscribed with dates as old as 1878, to spruce up the basement floor.)

As work on the house progressed, the new owner's son was hired as night watchman. He had a Doberman pinscher who followed him everywhere – everywhere, that is, but inside the Lemp mansion. One night the dog would not enter the house. She growled, whined and even nipped at her beloved master. Since she wouldn't cooperate, he tied the dog to the back porch. Thirty minutes later, she disappeared.

Three years after the house was restored, a little old lady dropped in for lunch. The woman had been a Lemp employee in her younger days, and she had known the Lemps personally.

She said that after Charles committed suicide, his body was found in an upstairs bedroom. She had seen the body – and that of the companion Charles had taken with him to the hereafter, his devoted Doberman pinscher.

Not the Last of Lavender Lil

The spirit of Lavender Lil is also thought to haunt places she inhabited in life. Lillian died in the 1960s, and since that time, the unidentified ghost of a woman has been repeatedly observed hovering near the top of the third floor stairwell and in virtually all the bedrooms and hallways of the Lemp Mansion. She is particularly fond of the first floor bathroom, which Will, Jr., outfitted with all the latest innovations available at the time, including a standing shower imported from Italy. The bathroom (currently the ladies room) is essentially the same today as it was in Will, Jr.'s, time. The original fixtures remain, and the toilet is enclosed behind a stall of oak and frosted glass.

Many patrons have claimed that they heard disembodied voices as they were using the facilities. One elderly customer heard someone milling around the sink. The customer announced with some irritation that she would be done in a moment. The person outside the stall responded by moving closer to the stall, her small figure clearly visible behind the frosted glass door. Then, suddenly, the figure simply evaporated.

As the shaken woman washed her hands she saw that there was only one way to enter or leave the bathroom, and she confirmed that she had heard no-one come in after her.

As Paul Pointer was relating the woman's strange encounter to one of his employees, a waiter stood by listening intently. The waiter later revealed that his girlfriend had gone through exactly the same thing. So similar were the two stories that the waiter assumed Paul was describing his girlfriend's experience.

At the beginning of the twenty-first century, the Lemp house shows no sign of giving up its ghosts.

"We sometimes have a tremendously difficult time keeping car alarms from going off in the parking lot," Pointer admitted. "It can really get bad when the alarms are connected to the horn – then you get both going off at the same time.

"People come here expecting to experience weird things," Pointer said. "Fortunately for us, they are rarely disappointed."

D. Douglas Graham *is a writer and investigator of paranormal phenonmena whose interest in these topics began at the age of 12. He has contributed articles to* UFO Universe, UFO Magazine *and various books about haunted houses.*

THE BERNARDSVILLE LIBRARY GHOST
By Randolph W. Liebeck

The public library on Morristown Road in Bernardsville is located in a beautiful eighteenth-century building in rural Somerset County, New Jersey. Built in 1710 and listed in the National Register of Historic Places, the building served as a tavern and farmhouse before its current incarnation as a library.

Like countless other libraries throughout the U.S., the Bernardsville library serves as a meeting place, resource centre, and quiet sanctuary for local citizens. Helpful and knowledgeable librarians answer questions and guide intrepid readers through book racks. Unlike most other libraries, however, Bernardsville is cheerfully inclined to point out that one of its card holders has never checked out a book. The holder of that library card is Miss Phyllis Parker. She is a ghost.

Since the late nineteenth century there have been documented reports of paranormal phenomena in connection with the building, but it is popularly believed that the origins of the haunting can be traced to early 1777, when the building was the Vealtown Tavern. (Vealtown was Bernardsville's original name.) Troops from General Washington's Continental Army frequented the tavern on the campaign from Princeton to Morristown. The innkeeper, Captain Parker, ran the tavern with the help of his daughter Phyllis, who was reportedly in love with the local physician, Dr. Byram.

In January 1777, General Anthony Wayne and his staff stopped at the inn for a night of relaxation. While there, the General's courier pouch containing vital secret documents was stolen. Everyone in the tavern at the time of the theft was accounted for with the exception of Dr Byram. When Captain Parker described the doctor to Wayne, the general immediately recognized him as the notorious Tory spy Aaron Wilde. Byram/Wilde was kept under surveillance and soon arrested by Continental forces with the stolen documents on his person. He was tried, convicted and hanged on the spot. Captain Parker retrieved Byram's body and, determined to provide a proper burial for the man his daughter loved, secured the body in a wooden crate and returned it to the inn to await burial the next day. Parker told his daughter the crate contained the body of an executed spy, but he could not bring himself to tell her it was her beloved Dr Byram.

Late that night, soldiers heard the sounds of chopping and tearing wood. It is not known why Phyllis frantically tore open the crate with a hatchet, or why she may have suspected Byram was inside. Perhaps she overheard Wayne's troops talking about it earlier that evening. The next sound heard was the horrendous, night-shattering scream of a young woman whose mind snapped upon the sight of her lover's dead body. Local history maintains that the event left Phyllis hopelessly insane. There is no record of her life after this point, or of her death, but it is believed that the ghost of Phyllis Parker returns to the site of this tragic occurrence on cold winter nights to replay the drama for new and unsuspecting audiences.

The Hauntings Begin
While there were earlier local rumours about the house being haunted, the first solid reports of haunting activity began in about 1875 when the property was being used as a private residence. The occupants reported various auditory phenomena such as footsteps, the sounds of rustling clothing and windows opening and slamming shut.

On a cold January night in 1877, the lady of the house was home alone with her child. While sewing, she was startled by the sounds of slow, heavy footsteps on the kitchen verandah and what sounded like several men carrying a heavy object. Frightened, the woman listened to the sound of the kitchen door opening, footsteps crossing the wooden floor and a heavy crate or box hitting the floor. The footsteps then travelled out of the back door. Silence followed and the woman sat in her room, afraid to look in the kitchen.

Soon the noises started again with the sounds of wooden panels being ripped, pounded and torn apart. The baby, in an upstairs bedroom, screamed in fright. The mother bolted from the sewing room and ran upstairs. She grabbed her child and latched the bedroom door as the terrible cry of a woman's incomprehensible grief erupted from the kitchen, echoing into the night. The scream gave way to a series of mournful sobs that slowly faded away into silence. A later search revealed that the house was locked, empty, and undisturbed.

The kitchen referred to in this account was formerly the dining room where Byram's casket was set in front of the fireplace. At the time of this incident the story of Dr Byram and Phyllis Parker was not publicly known, only later uncovered by historians.

Various stories circulated about the house over the next few decades, but the next documented case was nearly a century later, one January evening in 1974. By this time the public library was in operation at the site. A staff volunteer walking from her car to the library saw through the front window an apparition of a man dressed in eighteenth-century clothing. A search revealed that the building was empty. Haunting phenomena have continued sporadically since then.

Former library employees Martha Hamill and Maria Mandala individually reported unnerving encounters in the early 1980s. One winter evening, Hamill was working alone after hours preparing an annual report when she heard murmuring voices coming from somewhere in the building. Thinking someone may have entered the library, she searched the building, but found it empty, with all doors and windows secured. Returning to her report, she heard the mumbling voices again, which she compared to "children talking, sharing secrets". The only place she had not checked was the basement, which she remembers as being too frightening to enter. Feeling very apprehensive, Hamill put her work away and left the building.

Staff-member Maria Mandala also regularly worked alone after the library had closed. On several occasions she reported hearing what sounded like a woman softly humming or singing, but when she searched in and around the building there was never anyone there. Mandala claimed she was not upset by the ethereal music, but one incident did frighten her. She was alone in the building one night having coffee when she noticed all the extension indicator lights on the library's several telephones were lit, implying the lines were in use. The phones had not rung and no one else was in the library. Mandala picked up one of the phones to listen, but no one was on the line.

Former library director Geraldine Burden told FATE that while strange sounds and events continue to this day, the last report of an apparition was in late November 1989. A three-year-old boy was attending the library's story hour with his mother and older brother. While his mother was checking books out at the circulation desk, the child wandered to the doorway of the reading room (the aforementioned dining room of earlier days). Yelling for his mother's attention, the boy stood staring into the room. The mother walked over to the tot and they entered the reading room. The boy pointed toward the fireplace saying, "There it is. There!"

According to the mother and the children's librarian, no one else was in the room. The child was insistent and kept pointing. When his mother asked him what he saw, he pointed again and said, "The lady."

The mother reported feeling very disturbed, with "chills running up and down her spine," and wanted to get out of the reading room immediately. The apparition, visible only to the youngster, was of a dark-haired lady with a long dress that reached the floor. The boy told his mother that he said hello to the lady but got no response.

The library ghost is also well known to the Bernardsville Police Department. Former Police Chief John Maddaluna revealed that in 1950, when he was a new recruit in the department, he was walking the midnight beat with his training sergeant. While checking doorknobs and shining his torch into shop-front windows, he noticed movement inside the library. Aiming his flashlight through the window he saw a female figure wearing a long white dress that trailed on the floor. Then he lost sight of her. Thinking there was an intruder inside, Maddaluna ducked down and sneaked around to a couple of other windows. Once again he saw the figure, only to lose it again. Alerting his sergeant, he was told not to worry. It was "just the ghost", which the sergeant himself had seen several times.

Police Officer Nicholas Valente told FATE that a regular routine for officers on the night shift is to park across from the library, hoping to catch a glimpse of Phyllis while having their sandwiches and coffee.

Library Ghost Hunting

The library has attracted the attention of a few noted ghost hunters. In 1976 the prolific and controversial psychic investigative team of Ed and Lorraine Warren visited the library. Lorraine, who claims to be clairvoyant, reported sensing strong haunting activity immediately upon entering the building. She identified a couple of highly active areas marked by pockets of "psychic cold", and she described the spirit of Phyllis Parker quite specifically.

In 1987, psychical researcher Norm Gauthier attempted to record evidence of electronic voice phenomena (EVP) at the library. Sophisticated recording equipment using sealed tapes provided by local news reporters was set up on January 29, the day believed to be the anniversary of Phyllis' traumatic discovery. (Notably, most of the phenomena have occurred in the winter.)

The all-night session by Gauthier and several reporters resulted in the recording of possible EVP, including the sounds of furniture moving, dishes and glasses banging (tavern sounds?), and a fleeting male voice, unintelligible except for the word "please." The reporters all agreed that they heard none of these sounds during the taping session; they were audible only during later playback.

With the cooperation of the library staff, I organized a full field investigation at the library on the night of April 7, 1995. I arrived with fellow police officers and paranormal investigators Peter Villani, Art Vernon and Gerry Wyhopen. Anne Jones, a civilian psychic who has worked with New Jersey law enforcement, also joined our team. Library staffers Pam Clancey and Brooks Mullen were on hand to assist us. The library was closed and locked for the night and the investigation was under way at 8.35 p.m.

Anne pulled me aside – out of earshot of the others – and told me she had walked through the building and had experienced extremely strong feelings of negative energy or pressure as she went down the steps to the basement.

Meanwhile, Peter was touring the building and recording the layout with a camcorder. When he returned he pulled me aside and said he felt very strange when he walked through two locations – the bottom of the stairs leading to the basement and a dark aisle of bookshelves in the far right corner of the first floor balcony. He described the sensation as one of "atmospheric pressure or compression", He had not spoken with Anne yet and had no knowledge of what she had sensed in the basement. I scanned these areas for unusual electromagnetic fields with a Tri-Field Meter but with negative results. Peter felt the strangeness had left the areas. I didn't tell anyone about Peter's sensations because I wanted to see if they would pick up independently on anything in the upper balcony area.

We did background scans of all rooms to record ambient electromagnetic (EMF), electrical, and radiation levels. Everything was within normal parameters. I accompanied Anne on another in-depth tour, instructing her to note any locations where she felt a presence so I could re-scan the area for spikes or anomalous readings. Unfortunately, Anne reported she felt the presence had left the building or become dormant. I repeated these controlled excursions with the other team members, but everyone felt the earlier negative atmosphere had lifted. Further EMF and radiation scans throughout the night were negative.

At about 12.30 a.m. Anne and Gerry did another tour of the facility. Gerry has demonstrated strong psychic sensitivity in the past and has been working with Anne to develop this gift. Peter and Art videotaped the premises. Art was also using extremely sensitive audio surveillance equipment, typically used by law enforcement, in an attempt to pick up any anomalous sounds that might be beyond the sensitivity range of the human ear and the videocameras.

Anne and Gerry called to me from the upper balcony, wanting me to run an energy scan in the far right aisle. Anne said she again felt the negative energy she had experienced in the basement. Gerry reported that he felt a cold, tingling sensation in his arm and a feeling of "pressure, an oppressive atmosphere", Neither of them knew of Peter's encounter in the exact same location.

When I reached the aisle, I couldn't sense anything unusual. Anne said she could feel the presence leaving. She said she had also felt the presence in the ground floor aisle below this one. Scans at both levels revealed normal background EMF levels. I set up infrared-thermal surveillance units covering the two active aisles, as well as one in a quiet aisle to be used as a control.

At about 2 a.m. I was standing outside the staff kitchen with library assistants Pam and Brooks. Art was in the reading room running electronic surveillance. Pam and Brooks had been telling me how the ghost often plays havoc with the library's computer system, leading employees to suspect that Phyllis does not like the intrusion of modern technology into her house. They pointed out that Phyllis might be put off by the equipment our ghost-hunting team had brought in.

As I stood in the hall with my camera in my right hand, we were startled by a loud electrical pop. The camera's motor drive and handle-mount strobe began firing on continuous, rapid fire mode on its own initiative. I sat the camera on the kitchen table, and it continued advancing and flashing wildly until the roll of film was used up.

An inspection revealed that the batteries in the strobe's power pack had exploded. These were newly bought and installed brand-name alkaline C-cells. In 13 years of advanced photography experience, I had never experienced anything like this before. Everyone was a little spooked by the incident, but we logged it as an untimely coincidence.

In earlier investigations I had been at another reputedly haunted house with a television news crew whose fully charged camcorder power packs mysteriously went dead when they entered the house and at another site where my camera gear suffered complete electronic failure, only to start working again when I left the haunted area. I had brought backup cameras and flashes to Bernardsville, just in case. There were no problems with the backup gear.

At about 3.15 a.m., the computer-controlled infrared detectors picked up moving heat sources on both the upper and lower aisles where our investigators had felt subjective sensations earlier. No one was near the aisles when the units were triggered. The control aisle did not trigger any response.

No further events occurred, and our investigative team packed up and left at about 5.00 a.m.

It is interesting to note that the area with past activity, the reading room, did not trigger either subjective or objective response during our investigation. The two shelving aisles that elicited subjective human and technical (infrared) responses had no prior haunting history. The basement landing, however, does have a history of activity according to library staff.

The monitoring of EMF levels, which has brought intriguing results in other ghost investigations, yielded nothing in this case. Careful review of over eight hours of video surveillance footage revealed no visual, magnetic or energy anomalies. Continuous audio surveillance revealed no unusual sounds or EVP. The overloading of my camera equipment is as yet unexplained.

While we had hoped for a more direct and dramatic appearance by the ghost of Phyllis Parker, we agree that the cumulative effect of the series of small incidents, subjective and objective, is highly intriguing and perhaps more than we were actually expecting. The library deserves further study.

THE POSSESSION OF MAGDALENE GROMBACH
By John P. Bessor

They destroyed her house as the white spirit had ordered.
And in the dry well they found out why.

FOR the best evidence of conscious, personal survival after death we must bypass the séance room (which all too often is the scene of conscious or subconscious impersonation) and study the accounts of spontaneous phenomena manifesting in the form of haunted houses and haunted people.

One such account concerns Magdalene Grombach, a young peasant girl who lived in the little village of Orlach, in Wurtemburg, Germany. Magdalene was one of four children. Her father, industrious and honest, was a devout Lutheran and reared his family in his faith.

One morning in February, 1831, Magdalene went out to perform her daily chore of milking the cows in the cowshed. She was amazed to find that the cows' tails were plaited together "as if the finest lace weaver had been at work." Thinking it some trick played by one of her schoolfellows, she disregarded it. But when the cows' tails were plaited in the same way on subsequent mornings, she and her family became perplexed and concerned and finally determined to keep a nightly vigil on the cowshed. For several weeks they watched and for several weeks the cows' tails were plaited by an invisible agency.

One day when Magdalene and her father were in the shed and she was sitting on the milking stool, she suddenly was dealt a severe blow on her ear by an unseen hand. Her cap was thrown against her father some distance away.

The Grombach family became convinced that some supernatural agency was at work. Often they saw strange birds and cats going in and out of the cow-shed. Trifling, yet puzzling, things such as these occurred during an entire year and then were followed by manifestations of a more serious nature.

On February 8, 1832, when Magdalene and her brother were busily engaged in cleaning out the cowshed, they were amazed to see a bright flame burst up from the floor. With the help of neighbours the flame finally was beaten out but no-one knew how it had started. On the next day strange fires of an identical nature broke out in their house. It was necessary to take all their furniture out into the garden. Subsequently for several days mysterious fires ignited in various parts of the cottage, even though friends and neighbours kept constant watch inside and out.

During this period Magdalene first saw, while out in the cowshed with her father and brother one evening about eight o'clock, a "closely swathed", grey, shadowy woman who spoke to her in a far away voice, "Remove the house; remove the house. If it be not removed before the fifth of March next year, great misfortune will befall you. The house has been set on fire by an evil spirit; but unless it be pulled down before the fifth of March next year, I cannot protect you from great misfortune. Promise that the house shall be destroyed."

Magdalene promised.

Her father and brother heard the voice but could not distinguish what was said. Neither did they see the apparition. Magdalene saw and conversed with the spirit frequently after that and apparently grew very fond of it. The apparition gave no reason for tearing down the house but simply said that it was necessary.

Further conversations revealed that this spirit belonged to a woman born in Orlach in 1412. She said that she had been forced to become a nun, much against her will, that she was bound, in a way she could not tell, to a "black spirit" who now was intent on effecting harm on the family, and that it was her purpose to ward off this evil. She admitted that during her earth life she had been guilty of many crimes (which she refused to name) and expressed regret that she had committed them. Magdalene always referred to her as the "white spirit".

On St John's Day, 1832, all save Magdalene attended church. She remained home to prepare the dinner. As she was thus engaged she heard a loud explosion in the cowshed. She was about to investigate this noise when her glance fell on a heap of strange, yellow frogs on the hearth. Wishing to show the frogs to her parents on their return from church, she was about to pick them up and place them in her apron when she heard a voice call to her, seemingly from the ground beneath, "Magdalene, let the frogs go." At once the frogs all vanished.

This event seemed to herald more awful phenomena. The

poor girl was pursued by apparitions of frightful animals, by derisive voices and scornful laughter. One midday, when she was in the meadow making hay, the apparition of a "black man" approached her and demanded, "What does she want who comes to thee? Do not thou speak to her; but speak to me and I will give thee the key to the cellar beneath thy house. There are eight firkins of wine there and many rich things." Saying this he gave a contemptuous laugh and vanished.

For several days thereafter, when she was in the hay field, the "black spirit" appeared to her. She steadfastly refused to converse with him. He derided her father for carrying a Bible about him and told her that the Mass was "much finer and grander". He tried to induce his unwilling listener to have Mass said "to keep the weather fine" and threatened her with all manner of evil should she not cease conversing with the female spirit whom he called that "bag of bones". He said that he was a monk and Magdalene always saw him dressed as such. Sometimes he mimicked the voices of her friends, seeking to have her answer, but she seemed to know his imitations and would not reply.

Very often he foretold the future with accuracy and one day he promised to give her, as proof of his friendship, a bag full of money. The very next evening, when Magdalene and her sister were at work in the cowshed, they saw a small bag fall near their feet. Upon opening it they found it contained 11 gulden and several thalers. The next evening Magdalene encountered the "white spirit" who told her not to keep the money, that it was from the "black spirit" in fulfilment of one of his promises. The "white spirit" told her that for her obedience she would have other money given her and she requested Magdalene to buy a hymn book with it.

The next day Magdalene and her father drove to Hall and presented the bag of money to the orphanage there. On their way home a shopkeeper hailed them and asked Magdalene if she were not the girl of whom he had heard so much. She modestly replied that she was and he gave her a gulden "to buy a new hymn book with".

The apparitions created by the "black spirit" were now so frightening that Magdalene often swooned or fell into a cataleptic state. Frequently she lay rigid for hours. Sometimes, during these seizures, she would strike out violently at anyone who approached her – always with her *left* arm and leg which were icy cold, while her right side was warm and quiescent. These attacks increased in frequency and her frantic parents sought the aid of both doctors and clergymen but they could not help her. Magdalene stated that, just prior to lapsing into these states, a black and frightful monster would appear and lay an icy hand upon the back of her neck. During an attack she would cry, "The black spirit – it is he that plagues me."

The doctors bled her with leeches, as was the custom at that time, but she would cry, "This will do no good. I am not ill. No physician can help me." Asked who could help her she would emerge suddenly from her trance and exclaim joyfully, "I am helped; the white lady has helped me."

At this time the "white spirit" told Magdalene that the "black spirit" must, for a while, completely possess her physical body but that she would lead Magdalene's soul to a place of safety during these intervals when the "black spirit" was in control.

The attacks became more frequent and more violent. Magdalene said that even when she was doing housework she could discern the outline of a monk's form, all in black. She never clearly saw his face. He would say, "Wilt thou still give me no answer? Take care, I shall plague thee." Then she would feel his icy fingers grasp the back of her neck and his body press against her left side. Always this was her last conscious sensation. Then she would lie as in death. The pupils of her eyes turned inwards and her left arm and leg either moved up and down or extended ready to strike. Her left side was always cold while her right side was quiet and warm.

These attacks would last four or five hours. During them Magdalene's voice was hoarse and masculine – in every way similar to that of her tormentor. They always terminated in an "extraordinary" struggle between her right and left sides. When she had recovered she said that she was not aware of having spoken in a man's voice, but that she thought she was, during these intervals, attending church, singing and praying with a congregation. These attacks occurred over a period of five months.

On March 4, 1833, when workmen were tearing down the Grombach cottage, the "white spirit" appeared to Magdalene in dazzling white robes. She entranced Magdalene and spoke through her lips, saying that she had been seduced by the monk who now tormented Magdalene and had aided him in his crimes. She told of centuries of anguish and penitence and of her faith in an eventual release through the grace of Christ. With a wonderful and thankful prayer the "white spirit" left the body of Magdalene.

The spirit of the monk then took possession and from Sunday night until Tuesday noon Magdalene remained possessed. She ate nothing. On Tuesday a large crowd gathered to witness the final demolition of the house and to question the monk's spirit. Through Magdalene he answered questions in a deep, masculine voice and he also expressed great joy that he would soon be delivered from his earthly penitence. He described the countryside and it looked in the 15th century and said that the ancient monastery of Krailsheim once stood on the site where the Grombach house and farm were now. An antiquarian present stated that the descriptions given fitted the known history of the district and represented knowledge which Magdalene could not possess.

Magdalene was taken to a neighbour's house some distance from her home. Still entranced and with her face livid, she spoke excitedly as the demolition of the Grombach cottage progressed. Her voice was deep and masculine. The workmen had torn down the walls and were digging in the cellar when they came upon an ancient piece of masonry under which they discovered a large, dry well filled with rubbish and human bones. Among these were the skeletons of several infants.

Immediately upon discovery of this ancient well Magdalene, though some distance away in the neighbour's home, awoke from her trance. Her skin resumed its normal colour and she, confused on seeing so many strangers around her, hid her face and wept.

Finally she regained her composure and gradually became, once again, the normal, healthy girl she had been nearly 18 months before.

From that day on Magdalene never heard, saw, or experienced any further phenomena.

Had it all been in her mind or were the spirits of a penitent nun and monk, which had roamed the earth for four centuries in despair, finally released from the scenes of their infamy? In this girl, had they found a medium through whom they could tell their story?

I MARCHED WITH GERMAN SOLDIERS
By Ernest Heckler

IN 1911 I HUNTED for a vacant room in one of the villas on the out-skirts of the southern German city of Heilbronn-am-Neckar, state of Württemberg (Schwabia), famed for its Infantry Regiment No. 122, named in honour of Kaiser Franz Joseph of Austria.

In pre-war Württemberg a high school graduate had the prerogative of taking a one-year military training, instead of two or three years required for the common soldier, depending on the branch of service, and of being trained as a future reserve officer. A one-year trainee could choose his branch of service, but had to pay for his own food and living quarters, pay a soldier to keep his field-uniform clean and if he turned out to be a poor sharp-shooter on the field-range, bribe his superiors for extra ammunition.

I tried not to rent an officer's house, but unsuccessfully. A very courteous, charming lady showed me the vacant room in her house. I agreed to take it, paying her a month's rent in advance. Then when I entered the house that night in the semi-dark I saw an officer's cap hanging on the rack in the entrance hall. The landlady had not told me an army officer was staying in the house.

I was to report for duty at 8.00 o'clock the next morning, but I did not get up in time. At about 10.00 o'clock the landlady and her officer-husband entered my room to enquire about me.

The officer spoke rebukingly to his wife, "But I told you, my dear, not to rent this room again." I explained to them that I had a terrible nightmare in which I fought, for what seemed hours, with forces of super-human strength bent upon my destruction. The dream terminated when someone went up and down my spine with a chisel, beating upon my helpless body, as I was unable to move or cry aloud.

"You see! You see!" nodded the officer to his wife.

I finally managed to get up and noticed in the mirror my drawn face, sunken eyes and sallow complexion, quite foreign to me then. I was exhausted and sick. No, it wasn't a hangover, as I had not been drinking the night before.

The officer volunteered to take me to the camp where I would have to give an explanation for my failure to report in time. When we entered the office he offered me a chair facing two other officers, one of whom gave me a quick, stern look, while the other one turned to my landlord with the question "What! Again!?"

Oddly enough, they seemed to understand what had occurred to me. One of the officers made a reservation for me at a nearby hotel, told me to move there temporarily, go to bed again and report for duty the next morning. This I did.

I was in the camp for several days before I finally understood the mystery of all this. I learned that the officer in whose house I had the frightening experience, was for some time on sick-leave. He had been gradually loosing weight and strength, complaining of repeated and terrifying nightmares. He was a puzzle to his doctors. He had been a superior to two corporals, who had incurred his continual displeasure. They had complained of maltreatment and had asked for transfer which was denied them. In desperation they had killed each other in a suicide pact, shooting each other in the mouth with army rifles. Their brains had been spattered all over the walls. To make matters worse, it was thought that their spirits were haunting the house of the officer, where I slept that one night.

I had no opinion or occult knowledge about haunted houses but I soon became aware that there was much maltreatment in the German army. A major not getting along with his chief, the chief not liking his lieutenant, the lieutenant despising a corporal and the corporal physically abusing the newly recruited boys was not at all uncommon.

Württemberg people were mostly peasants (Bauern) and shepherds, known for their amiable dispositions (Gemütlichkeit). Some of their youngsters were markedly awkward and slow to learn and for that reason had a rough time in the army under the German military discipline then existing, although the majority of the boys quickly learned goose-stepping and saluting, and mastered jumping over every increasing barriers on the obstacle course.

Ordinarily, when the young soldiers marched through the city singing, the teenage girls would open their windows and throw flowers and kisses at them. But one day one officer worked my company so hard that the older men passed the word "No singing!" When the order came to sing, a few voices began feebly . . . "O Deutschland hoch . . ." and the effort died out. On a repeated command by the now enraged officer, no-one tried to sing. In a frenzy he marched us back to the field, where he made us practise *creeping* in a freshly cow-manured pasture. After an hour or so the chief deserted his company, turning us over to the sergeant. When we marched through the city this time, the windows were hurriedly closed.

    – *La Mesa, Calif.*

MISCHIEVOUS SKELETON
By Pauline Saltzman

Strange things happened when the bones of an ancient Roman were put on display in the museum.

RIVA is a small village on the shore of Lago di Garda in Italy. In the days of ancient Rome this lake was known as Benacus Lacus. Lake Garda has been a showplace for thousands of years. Its climate is ideal and in the surrounding country are medieval castles and some of the finest Roman ruins in existence. At the present time, Riva is also the scene of what may become a classic haunting.

In the summer of 1954, a group of workmen who were digging a ditch suddenly struck a hard substance with their shovels. As there have been previous discoveries of old Roman relics and ruins, the labourers dug with extreme care and caution.

They finally unearthed an ancient Roman sarcophagus which contained some human bones. The local archaeologists examined the findings and judged that they were approximately 2,000 years old. They also concluded that the skeleton, whose head was missing, was that of an old Roman who had been beheaded for some crime.

The bones of this decapitated skeleton were strung into place with bits of wire, and the Rivan authorities then replaced the assembled skeleton in its coffin.

The famous municipal museum of Riva prominently displayed the coffin and skeleton in its main hall.

One morning the curator arrived at his post, to find that the sarcophagus had been removed. Various objects were scattered about the room. The authorities made a careful investigation but found that all doors and windows had remained securely locked for the night as usual. Furthermore, a museum guard, on duty all night, had heard nothing.

The curator and his aides were mystified. They shrugged their shoulders and closed the stone coffin. As an extra precaution all the museum's locks were changed.

Nothing untoward occurred during the next two weeks. However, at the beginning of the third week when the director of the museum arrived at his spot as usual he found that the sarcophagus had again been opened during the night! This time an antique Roman lamp, the kind once used by burglars, lay at the feet of the assembled skeleton. The mystery was further intensified when the authorities discovered ashes sprinkled before an exhibited altar. It was as if someone had been worshipping Jupiter!

Once more the museum guard was questioned. He had heard no-one! The new locks apparently were untouched and had remained locked. Not a shred of evidence existed to suggest that someone had stolen into the museum!

A few days later, still another mysterious disorder was disclosed by museum authorities. This time there was evidence of a severe struggle. Some modern weapons, which had been on exhibition nearby, were scattered about the main hall and an ancient Roman dagger, was embedded in the museum floor, as if it had ben driven brutally into it.

In 1050, a young girl named Juliet Tewsley, who lived in the village of Holywell, fell deeply in love with a handsome reed cutter named Tom Zouls. He was a rough fellow, and preferred the company in low-down taverns in the area. Tired of Juliet's charms, he spurned her for another.

On one of those brooding, melancholy days of low-lying mists peculiar to the fen country, heartbroken Juliet hanged herself from a willow tree on the riverbank. Because she was a suicide, it was forbidden to bury her in the sanctified ground of the parish churchyard.

Instead, according to custom, the villagers buried her, still clothed in her pink gown, at a crossroads – in this case, close to where she hanged herself. The site was also where the ferry made its daily crossings over the river, linking road to road. People crossed themselves when they passed by the grave and avoided it altogether after dusk.

Sometime later, probably in early medieval times, the Ferry Bloat Inn was built close to the ferry crossing at Holywell. The building foundation surrounded Juliet's tombstone, which was incorporated into the bar of the inn. Just when whispers arose that Juliet's ghost had taken to haunting the inn cannot be ascertained, but according to legend, her restless spirit has returned to it again and again over the centuries. The stone slab remains a part of the flooring to this day, and it has been trodden on by countless generations of customers.

From all accounts, the pink-clad wraith of a young girl is seen to materialize above the stone slab and then drift away in the direction of the river running by outside. The most significant day for this spectral materialization is March 17 each year, the date Juliet is believed to have committed suicide.

Old oral tradition is a strong factor in the community life of East Anglia and the fen country of England. So, despite a lack of proof for the story of Juliet's life, the presence of the gravestone in the floor of the heavily beamed bar of the Ferry Boat Inn has long aroused interest among people far and wide. For many years now people have gathered at the inn – especially on "Juliet's Night", as March 17 is called locally – to watch for the wraith's appearance at midnight.

In 1952 the landlord went so far as to obtain a late extension.

Two years later, in 1954, hundreds of curious people invaded Holywell on Juliet's Night. So great was the crowd that police from the nearby town of St Ives had to be drafted to cope with it. People jostled for space in the packed inn as the tension increased by the hour.

Sometime later, intrigued by the sensation caused by the haunting, the Cambridge Psychical Research Society sent a team of investigators to the inn, but no ghostly figure materialized. Clairvoyants have also visited the inn and have tried to contact Juliet.

All manner of odd happenings have taken place at the inn. Strange sounds have been heard, and patrons have claimed that doors left shut have opened in mysterious fashion. Old-fashioned music, rather like a dirge, is occasionally heard, seemingly coming from nowhere. Described as haunting and strangely beautiful, the music can only be heard by women in the bar area. Dogs do not like being in this room. Some will growl and bristle with fear if guided too close to the gravestone slab.

There would most certainly seem to be something supernatural centred around this room in the inn. It is not a place to be in alone after dark. Local women are reluctant to go near the inn on the night Juliet is said to rise up from the floor and head for the river. They are fearful lest they encounter the unknown. The ghost of a lovelorn girl who cannot rest has become part of the history and the haunting of the Ferry Boat Inn at Holywell, beside the River Ouse in Cambridgeshire.

Joyce Rushen *is a writer currently living in Norwich.*

More Haunted Inns
England's Ferry Boat Inn is not the only such establishment of haunted repute. There are many other inns throughout the country and the world that claim to have ghostly inhabitants.

The Stagecoach Inn, located in Ventura County, California, was supposedly haunted for 85 years. The ghost there was believed to be that of Pierre Duvon, a mountain man who was murdered while sleeping in the inn during a stay in 1885. The inn was destroyed by fire in 1970, and a replica of the building replaced it. Some of the photos taken during the blaze showed the mysterious face of a whiskered spectre. Perhaps it was the face of Pierre Duvon.

The East Wind Inn, in Tenants Harbor, Maine, plays host to a number of apparitions. Psychic Annika Hurwitt believes the chief ghost is that of a woman killed in the inn by her husband in the late 1800s. The ghost creates all kinds of havoc on the top floor of the three-story inn, which was built around 1860. Other ghostly residents include what Hurwitt believes is an old sea captain who sits in a chair looking at the water and smoking a pipe. The ghostly captain is aware of the phantom "crazy lady" on the top floor.

From London to San Diego and various points between and beyond, haunted inns dot the countryside. What draws and keeps the spirits to these places remain a mystery. Perhaps the spirits feel these places are perfect for an eternal stay.

– *Frank Spaeth*

A NIGHT IN LOUISIANA'S MOST HAUNTED HOUSE

by Marjorie A.E. Cook

The *Wall Street Journal*, the *CBS Morning News*, and the Smithsonian Institution have all called the Myrtles Plantation in St Francisville, Louisiana, "The Most Haunted House in America." Many visitors and staff agree that the 200-year-old structure, built upon a desecrated Indian burial ground and the site of at least 10 murders, has earned this distinction. Especially in agreement are those who have glimpsed one of the dozen or more ghosts reputed to roam its expansive grounds and elegant rooms.

When I first toured the so-called "Dark Lady" in 1994, I viewed a Gothic mansion resplendent in stained glass, gold leaf, and Italian marble. Amid the tour guide's tales of wealth and grandeur, the plantation's murderous legacy was revealed. Its ghostly aftermath was not. Several months later, I learned of the home's haunted history while watching a Halloween edition of *National Geographic Explorer*. It was these "ghosts on the Bayou" that drew me back to the estate on Halloween weekend 1996.

After spending the holiday in our favourite New Orleans haunts, my husband Thomas and I traveled the Great River Road to one of the South's most legendary homes. As we neared our destination, the traffic along Highway 61 slowed to a halt. Police officers posted at the Myrtles' gated entrance directed visitors to enter the estate on foot. Ours was the only one in a long line of cars allowed to turn into the plantation's winding, tree-lined drive. Because of the popularity of the home's ghost tours, parking on the grounds is prohibited – unless you spend the night in the house.

A melee of expectant sightseers mingled with tour groups and lawn statuary in front of the house. As a light rain began to fall, people crowded onto the impressively ornamented, 120-foot-wide gallery. Others took refuge beneath some of the 150 moss-draped oak trees that stand sentinel over the mansion. The nearby restaurant, formerly the plantation kitchen, bustled with preparation for a costumed dinner to be held that night.

Thomas and I checked in at the reservation desk and followed a narrow path to a broad patio at the back of the estate. In contrast to the rest of the plantation, the patio was as still as a sealed crypt. In the centre of the semi-enclosed brick courtyard, a triple-tiered fountain offered a watery accompaniment to the rain. A scattering of tables and cast-iron chairs enticed guests, perhaps both Earthly and ethereal, to enjoy the serene surroundings.

As we approached the back of the house, we discovered four couples – the other guests of the bed and breakfast – who ushered us to the second-floor bedrooms. Our room was one of six available to guests. It was beautifully outfitted in furnishings dating from about 1834, its walls of a colour reminiscent of the glow of a sunset seen through lace curtains. A white satin canopy hovered like a pale spectreabove the massive four-poster bed. The bed, wardrobe, and high chest of drawers were carved of mahogany and were of the grand proportion befitting the plantation lifestyle.

Downstairs, the other overnight guests exchanged introductions. We were graciously welcomed into the discussion by Laura Eagle and James Skinner, a couple from New Orleans. Laura had brought James, her fiancé, to the Myrtles as a surprise birthday getaway. She thought the eerie locale would appeal to a man born on Halloween. James, a digital imaging professional, had developed an affinity for spook-inspired birthday celebrations, but he wondered if a night in a haunted house wasn't a bit much. He confessed that he didn't believe in ghosts, but he didn't disbelieve either. As a 20-year student of the paranormal, I confidently told him that the chance of encountering anything otherworldly was remote at best.

Of course, I'd never spent the night in "America's most haunted house."

Murderous Legacy

By 11.00 p.m., the crowd of several hundred tourists dwindled to about two dozen. When the final tour was about to commence, Thomas, James, Laura and I strolled to the front gallery to wait beneath the arches of filigree, grape clusters and vines. When the front door opened, it felt like a portal to the past.

We were greeted by a woman attired in evening dress. At her invitation, we stepped across the threshold and into an ancient, elegant foyer. Standing on the main staircase, she introduced herself as our tour guide. But unlike most tours of historic homes, this was not going to be merely a textbook history of names and dates.

Instead, we would hear the true stories of ill-fated lives, murderous encounters, and ghostly manifestations.

The staircase on which the guide stood played a part in her first tale. This is where one former owner died after opening the front door to a murderer. Prominent lawyer William Winters had owned the Myrtles for a decade prior to that evening in 1871. He felt no cause for concern when he responded to a voice beckoning from beyond the main entrance. Opening the door to investigate, the unarmed attorney was fired at. From the second floor, his wife, Sarah Mathilda, heard the gunshots resonate. She reached the landing in time to witness her husband staggering upstairs, clutching his bloodied chest. On the seventeenth step, almost within reach of Sarah's comforting arms, William collapsed and died. The drama has played out time and again to startled visitors and staff. A woman's desperate cry for "William" is heard, followed by the appearance of a frock-coated spectre struggling up the staircase. We're told Mr Winters' demise was even captured on camera 125 years later.

While Mr Winters seems bound by his moment of death, another former resident carries on as if she's still among the living. She is Chloe, a house slave prone to nocturnal wanderings.

Chloe was the mistress of another ill-fated owner, Judge Clarke Woodruffe. The judge was so taken with Chloe that he installed her in the main house to care for his children. Eventually the judge's interest in Chloe waned, and he reassigned her to the plantation's kitchen.

Whether this was before or after he cut off her ear is unclear.

Chloe had always had an annoying habit of eavesdropping on the family's conversations. This became an intolerable offense when Judge Woodruffe caught her listening in on a shady business deal. As punishment, he sliced off her left ear. Chloe's response to this brutal attack was even more horrifying.

Feigning an attempt to make up with the judge, she offered to bake a special cake for a family birthday celebration. Judge Woodruffe accepted, unaware that what made the cake special was the lethal addition of oleander leaves to the recipe. During the celebration, Judge Woodruffe was called away on business. His family indulged in the birthday confection without him.

We're told that Judge Woodruffe's wife and two little girls died uncomfortable deaths.

For her deed, the judge's former mistress was hanged from one of the towering oaks that loom over the grounds. Her body was cast into the river.

Still, Chloe finds her way back to her old home. Hers is the apparition most often encountered. Sometimes she is glimpsed floating from bedroom to bedroom as if checking on the sleeping inhabitants. Several unfortunate souls, including a couple on their honeymoon, have awakened to find the green-turbanned spectre tucking them in. Those who have witnessed Chloe's roamings often say she appears to be looking for someone.

Perhaps she is searching for the Judge's daughters. The flaxen-haired sisters, perpetually dressed in long, white gowns, are said to still reside in the house. More than one person has had the unnerving experience of being peered at by the ghostly pair – through the second-storey windows.

Ghosts in the Photos

My attention was diverted by a sharp jab to my right hip. I turned, expecting to find a prankster taking advantage of the eerie atmosphere, but no-one was standing behind me. No-one was within five feet of me, for that matter. I was sure I hadn't bumped into anything; the closest piece of furniture was several feet to my left, and behind me was a wall. I was perplexed, but decided to forget about it and keep listening to the story. I might not have given the incident another thought had it not been for what happened next.

A surge, like static electricity, suddenly traversed the lower two-thirds of my body. Unlike a shock to the skin, this energy seemed to permeate my skin, bones and organs. When I tried to describe the sensation to Thomas, I had difficulty finding the words. I've read hundreds of descriptions of tactile sensations, like cold spots, encountered in haunted places, but nothing like this.

For the rest of the tour, my thoughts wandered to that strange episode in the foyer. But the tour won my full attention with its dramatic, startling conclusion.

Beneath the languid glow of the dining room's Baccarat crystal chandelier, we were offered a tangible argument for the existence of ghosts – a photo taken by Teeta Moss shortly after she purchased the estate. I, too, have a snapshot from the same vantage point. Both photos show the rear of the house, the line of rocking chairs tucked into the cool shade of the white pillared verandah and the simply constructed slave quarters built adjacent to the main structure.

But Teeta Moss's photo shows something mine does not.

Standing in the breezeway between the main house and the slave quarters is a woman of African ancestry dressed in a simple gown. The details of her countenance and attire can be clearly discerned against the background of white clapboard siding.

Her head is covered with a swath of fabric tied into a turban. Her headwear sits askew, pulled low on one side to conceal the top of her left ear. I had seen her image before, on the *National Geographic* special.

It is Chloe, the Woodruffes' vengeful, eavesdropping slave.

An expert at a Houston crime lab determined the photo to be unaltered and not the result of double exposure. An enlargement made during analysis also shows Chloe to be "a shadow of her former self". What appeared to be a solid human form in the original is actually translucent. You can see through her to the clapboard siding on the house.

In the same photo are two less noticeable images. On the gently sloping roof, crouched among the dormer windows, are the forms of two little girls. Are these the daughters of Judge Woodruffe, hiding from their murderer?

The photo incited a flurry of questions from the audience. Our guide patiently answered each query. Satisfied that they had, in fact, seen a photo of a ghost, the tourists wandered back to their cars. After all the questions had been answered, the only people left were the tour guides, the overnight guests and two local women who thought it best to wait until the very end to make their unusual request.

The women asked to see "the photos kept in the office".

A friend and former employee of the Myrtles had told them of a little-known collection of photographs kept in an envelope in the business office. It seems that some former guests have captured more than fond memories in their vacation photos.

Teeta Moss has received numerous letters from people who believe they've photographed a ghost. Many of the "anomalies" are simply reflections or camera straps that have strayed in front of the lens.

There are others, though, like the photo taken by Moss, that are nothing short of astounding.

Our tour guide obliged us first with a photo of the home's facade, taken in the light of midday. The details of the house and grounds – the wrought iron ornamentation, the lush plantings – can be clearly seen in the photo. Also visible is the statue of a woman near the front entrance, apparently floating in mid-air.

Next was the photo referred to during the tour. It shows the staircase, and on it a man dressed in the style of William Winters' day.

Another, taken near the small pond on the grounds, shows a band of battle-weary soldiers engaged in an eternal march.

The final photo was most affecting of all. Also taken near the pond, the colour print reveals a ghastly scene from the Myrtles' tragic past. Through it we witnessed a phantom funeral. A man dressed as a priest holds a small book in his folded hands. Four others hunch forward with the weight of the coffin they carry. The most disturbing image is of a fifth man, hanging by his neck. His body is ramrod-straight, his chest and shoulders collapsed inward.

A Night in the Voodoo Room

Our tour guide then asked if we'd like to hear the ghost stories attributed to each of our rooms. Most of us were already anxious with the prospect of spending the night in the house. We knew we'd seen and heard too much, but like witnesses who've stumbled upon some gruesome scene, we were unable to turn away. Hesitantly we agreed to listen.

We learned of a phantom child who frequents the first-floor suite. She's fond of jumping on the bed, whether it's occupied or not.

The guest room with two beds was once shared by the daughters of Judge Woodruffe. This is the room where they slept, played and died.

Ours was once the bedroom of one of two Sarahs who had lived at the Myrtles. One of them was still a child when she contracted yellow fever, a disease that ravaged the South. Her parents enlisted the finest doctors, but despite their best efforts, the girl's health deteriorated. Sarah's father vowed to try anything to save her. He put his last hope in the magic of Voodoo. Arrangements were made to bring a slave named Clio, reputedly a powerful Voodoo priestess, from a nearby plantation. Upon her arrival, instead of gratitude she received a desperate decree: She must save Sarah's life or lose her own.

In the bed where we would sleep that night, Sarah succumbed to the fever. Her grief-stricken father hanged the priestess from the chandelier in that same room.

Some nights, Clio comes back to perform her healing rituals. She is sometimes seen standing over the prone form of Sarah, shaking her magic gris-gris bag. Less frequently, an incantation, intoned in a mysterious and foreign tongue, can be heard reverberating through the sunset-coloured room.

The stories ended with a "Goodnight and good luck," and we were left alone and outnumbered – ten overnight guests versus 14 ghosts. For a long time, we stood on the darkened verandah, talking in whispers like mourners at a funeral. Travel-weary Thomas was the first to go upstairs. I was the last. Long after midnight, I finally slipped into the still house and beneath the covers.

I didn't know how late it was when the creaking of wooden floorboards coaxed me from my sleep. I recognized it as the sound of a rocking chair. This was strange enough considering that the only other person in the room was lying beside me. Even stranger was the fact that there was no rocking chair in the room.

Thomas stirred beside me. I asked in a whisper if he, too, heard the sound.

"The rocking chair?" he asked.

He had heard it earlier. Soon after he crawled under the lace-trimmed coverlet, the floorboards beside the bed had begun to creak. The rhythmic sound actually helped lull him to sleep.

When the rocking stopped, I spent an hour waiting for the quiet to be interrupted again. Satisfied that our phantom rocker wouldn't return, I fell asleep.

Around 3.00 a.m., we were awakened with a jolt, as a thunderous bang resonated from the home's rear entrance. It was the sound of the back door slamming heavily, as if someone had left in a hurry. It didn't make sense that someone was coming in at this hour. The door was locked and the house staff wasn't due for hours.

Slow, weighty footsteps ascending the narrow stairwell told us that someone was indeed coming. At the top of the stairs, the footsteps ceased.

More curious than scared, I climbed out of bed. Bracing myself against the wall, I opened our bedroom door. Our nighttime visitor had vanished.

Gone with the Wind

The rest of the night passed without incident. We didn't see or hear another soul, living or dead, until we met the other guests at breakfast. Over steaming plates of eggs, bacon and grits, we told James and Laura about our phantom rocking chair. James appeared tired, but claimed that the night had passed quietly. Not even our nocturnal visitor on the stairwell, who had awakened everyone else on the second floor, had roused our dining companions.

But after we finished our meal and left the restaurant, James confessed. The evening hadn't been nearly as peaceful as he'd claimed, not by a long shot. Something happened around 3.00 a.m., the haunting hour at the Myrtles, that James would never forget.

He had been awakened by a sense that someone was in the room besides him and Laura. James assured me that he had been fully awake for what happened next. He felt a gentle pressure on the edge of the bed, as if someone were sitting down next to him.

"Then," he said, "whatever it was went through me. My body shuddered with the force of it."

As he searched for a logical explanation, it happened again. He then heard the sounds of children, he thought, running in the attic.

I understood immediately what James was describing. I suspected that we'd had physical contact with a particularly "spirited" little pair of ghosts: the daughters of Judge Woodruffe. Several facts supported my assumption: the sound of children running, James's two bedside visitors, and the jab to my hip during the story about the murdered sisters, as well as my sensation of being walked through, which I experienced in the lower two-thirds of my body. It would be reasonable to guess that the older daughter might have stood about four feet tall.

All the speculation led me to question the owner. Finding Teeta Moss, I asked if another lesser-known spirit, other than Sarah or Clio, had ever been encountered in our guest room.

Teeta told me one had: the ghost of Sarah's mother. It's believed her name was Kate, and we know she kept watch at Sarah's bedside from the day the little girl fell ill until she died. Kate rarely left her daughter's side during her two-week illness, and some say she's still there. Her presence is evident by the sound of the rocking chair, long since gone from the room where she held her vigil.

Marjorie A. E. Cook *is a Wisconsin writer and teacher and the founder of the Society for Hauntings Investigation & Research.*

HELLO MR ALLISON
by Genevieve Nichols

Before my husband and I sailed for England in 1949, I purchased a used Hartmann wardrobe trunk. It was a beautiful piece of luggage and looked brand new. I was especially impressed with the lock, which guaranteed that the trunk wouldn't fly open.

After our arrival in London, we found a flat in a 300-year-old house. The walls were about a foot thick and made entirely of brick. Our flat was on the upper floor.

Between us we had three trunks and, after they were emptied, we decided to lay them on their sides and throw a large velour cloth over them. With a few pillows they made a wonderful window seat.

We had barely turned out the light and got into bed that first night when we heard a knocking coming from inside my wardrobe trunk. We got up, turned on the light, and opened the trunk, but we found nothing. We relocked the trunk with care, making sure the lock was secure and could not cause a noise.

The knocking stopped that night, but the next night the same thing happened.

Scotty, my husband, said, "All right, Mr Allison, that's enough!"

I asked who Mr Allison was and he said that when he was about eight years old, his mother and stepfather had purchased a farm in Michigan for a very reasonable price because it was said to be haunted.

Mr Allison, the former owner, had built the house himself. It was a two-storey affair and part of the second floor had not been finished.

Mr Allison had slipped and fallen backwards onto a nail that had not been hammered down, and it went through his back into his heart. He was found several days later hanging on the nail. The farmhouse had remained vacant for years until my husband's mother and stepfather bought the place.

The children weren't told about the former occupant, but

upon starting school they soon heard the rumours. Scotty said his mother treated the matter in a most unusual and wise way.

She said, "Poor Mr Allison. He must be very lonely. Let's set a place for him at our table."

The children thought it was a great game and would share their food by putting bites on Mr Allison's plate. Mr Allison became an accepted member of the household.

The children were no longer afraid of unexplainable events, such as entering a room and finding the rocker rocking. They would just say, "Hello, Mr Allison!"

When the family left the farm, Scotty said it was too bad they couldn't take poor Mr Allison. He would be all alone again.

Now, all these years later, it seemed that Mr Allison had returned. Once Scotty said, "Hello, M. Allison," the knocking stopped and was not heard again for a year, until it was time for us to return to the U.S.

The day before we started packing, we had just turned out the light when Scotty said, "O.K. Mr Allison, it's time to come out!" We started to laugh, and with that there was a loud click and the trunk's lock flew open.

Scotty got up, opened the trunk, and left it open. There was no more knocking that night.

As soon as we returned to Hollywood, Scotty entered the Veterans Hospital and I advertised the trunk for sale.

I had kept it way back in the closet, with the door closed. I had heard a muffled knocking only one time.

The first person who called to see the trunk purchased it. She said she was taking it to her little granddaughter on a trip to the Hawaiian Islands.

This same little granddaughter later became a famous actress, whose name I'll not reveal – but if she reads this and has a knocking trunk – she'll know it must have been poor Mr Allison.

THE ELLUSIVE MR EDISON
by Linda Lauren

The rumpled figure with the shock of white hair could only have been Thomas Edison's spirit.

As a writer of historical paranormal romance, I often find myself, in the course of my research, in the homes of some very memorable people. Most recently I visited Glenmont, once the home of Thomas Alva Edison. Built in 1880 by architect Henry Hudson Holly, the lovely pink Queen Anne style house in Llewellyn Park in West Orange, NJ, is situated on 15 acres of luscious green pasture and is an awesome sight to behold.

Stepping onto the side veradah, I was transported to another, simpler time. On this particular day I was the sole visitor to the estate and therefore fortunate to have the guide's undivided attention. Walking across the same polished hardwood floors that Thomas Edison once walked, I revelled in what I learned of the lives of the large Edison family, their servants and their friends. As I followed the guide through each room, I drifted about in history, in a time before electric light – and at its advent.

The kitchen was the next-to-last room I was allowed explore and the most recent opened to the public. Standing by the large butcher's block table, my eyes travelled to a cupboard, where I spied several drawers once filled with various herbs and spices.

I took a deep breath and turned questioningly to my guide. "I smell coffee," I said.

My guide shook her head. "That's impossible. Food and drink are not allowed in the house. Not even for the guides."

Her denial did not remove the aroma that wafted through the kitchen, assaulting my senses. I definitely smelled coffee.

The tour was over too soon. But as I said good-bye to my guide, she told me that if I would like to pay my respects to Thomas and Mina Edison, I should go around the back of the house because both are buried on the grounds. I thanked her and headed in what I assumed was the right direction.

It was hot that day. The temperature reached 100 degrees. I

walked the 15 acres in the intense heat at least three times, covering more ground than I had intended. My search was futile and I still did not come across the resting place of the inventor and his wife. Tired of going in circles, I sought rest on a wrought iron bench under a shady tree. There I took out my personal quartz crystal and meditated awhile, contemplating where the small cemetery might be.

I got up and looked around the neatly cropped expanse of lawn. In the distance I saw a man. He had shocking white hair with a side parting, and his dark brown suit with thin lapels seemed to drape around him as if he'd been sleeping in it for days. To say this man looked like Mr Edison would be a gross understatement.

Dismissing the very idea and hoping he was perhaps a caretaker, I waved to him and started across the lawn. He silently turned and pointed to my right. I looked to where he pointed, and when I returned my gaze to him, within a mere blink of an eye, he had disappeared. Near where he had stood, there were no trees for him to slip behind, yet he had vanished.

Puzzled but dismissing the incident as merely odd, I walked to the area he had pointed to, where I came upon a horseshoe hedge. There within the hedge was Thomas Edison's final resting place beside his beloved Mina. Two marble stones marked the graves. The stones could easily go undetected if one were looking for the traditional headstones of our day. Tears sprang to my eyes and I began to tremble. I said a prayer and made my way back to my car.

Did Thomas Edison show me the way? I believe so, for there is no rational explanation for the man's disappearance or his resemblance to the inventor. I know what I saw and who I saw, and I believe that I am one visitor who was afforded the rare experience of two guides.

MURDER BY A GHOST
By James Crenshaw

*The colonel emptied his gun at the cowled shape. Then he was
bent backwards by strangling hands.*

I HAVE talked with a man who was an eye-witness to a murder by a
ghost!

Gerardo Murillo, or Dr Atl – the name by which he is
popularly known – has long been prominent in the social, political and
artistic life of Mexico, where he was born more than 70 years ago. Dr
Atl first mentioned the strange murder in his book of reminiscences,
Gentes Profanas en el Convento (Profane Persons in the Monastery).
Then in conversations growing out of his interest in my own book,
Telephone Between Worlds, he described with greater detail certain
remarkable features of this very weird crime.

During the confusion that followed the assassination of
President Caranza and the accession of General Obregon in 1920, Dr
Atl became a resident of *El Convento de la Merced* (Monastery of
Mercy) in Mexico City. The ancient *convento*, which had been taken
over by the government, was occupied only by a porter-caretaker,
Angel Gutérrez and his family, an army colonel, presently out of favour
with the new regime, and his *asistente* (orderly).

Dr Atl, who was politically involved with both factions of the
1920 revolution, was given refuge by Angel, a former soldier. Angel
apologized for the presence of the colonel, describing him as *"muy mal
encarado"* (very evil-faced) and as having a reputation for having killed
many people.

The porter lived with his wife and two young sons in a room
near the entrance to the large patio. This patio was enclosed by two
tiers of arches, so that the arcades formed a quadrangle with rooms
opening into it on the ground and first floors. Dr. Atl moved into one
of the cells on the first floor, where the colonel and his orderly also
stayed.

The first hint that there might be other occupants of the
monastery came when Angel confessed he feared the ghost of a *fraile*
(friar or monk) that he claimed walked about the corridors at night. He
admitted he had not seen the ghost but had felt the cold air when the

phantom passed him.

The colonel, on the other hand, frequently saw the ghost of the friar so plainly, according to Angel, that he stalked it through the shadowy arcades, now and then firing his pistol at it. The officer swore to send it back to the cemetery whence it came.

Angel maintained that there were other unnatural manifestations in the ancient cloister; that there were long processions of ghosts who could not be seen but whose murmured prayers were sometimes plainly audible. His children were often disturbed at night by a suffocating pressure and had to be held by their parents so they could sleep.

The colonel, too, sometimes complained of a heavy weight on his chest at night and he described the misty figure of a brown-cowled monk gliding among the pillars and archways. His *asistente* declared that he likewise had seen the monk, though not so clearly as the colonel. He saw only the outlines, the hood and a white ribbon running down the front of the monk's habit. He never saw a face, only a huge hand grasping the folds of the garment. The orderly confessed it made him very nervous and he would not have stayed except that he feared reprisals from the colonel more than he feared the ghost.

Since one of the religious holidays on which Angel contended the most pronounced manifestations occurred was now at hand the caretaker invited his guest to sit up with him during the night and watch for the ghost. Dr Atl said he was not much interested, having little belief in spirits but, out of courtesy, accepted Angel's invitation.

On the appointed night the children, being extremely nervous, were taken to a neighbour's home. Dr Atl and Angel sat in the middle of the courtyard and waited. Dr Atl dozed but was awakened around midnight by the porter, who said the voices had begun. Dr Atl heard nothing. He splashed water on his face from the fountain in the patio to be sure he was fully awake. Then, following Angel into one of the corridors, he distinctly felt a wave of ice-cold air.

First he put his hand out to feel the current and then stepped into it, following as it moved up the wide stairway to the second level of arcades. Now he could hear the eerie murmuring of many subdued voices, as though in prayer.

Halfway up the stairs; the experiment was interrupted by a blood-chilling scream from Angel's room, The two men ran down to find Señora Gutiérrez in hysterics. She sobbed that a terrific force had pushed her against the wall and had held her there until the moment of her scream. On the wall she indicated they found two enormous hand prints in the hard surface.

"The impressions were like those left by pressure on wet cement except that these were made on a wall that had been standing for many years," said Dr Atl.

The prints had not been there before. Angel swore he recently had whitewashed the wall and knew they were not there then. But they remained, says Dr Atl, until the wall was torn down during demolition of that part of the building many years later.

Following this terrifying experience nothing further occurred that night.

One Sunday shortly afterwards at about twilight, when everyone had left the monastery except Dr Atl, he went out onto about twilight to the balcony and stood looking down into the patio. He heard the main door open and close with a bang. He supposed it was Angel returning but instead saw the colonel and his *asistente* go to their rooms. A few minutes later they reappeared and crossed the patio toward the large entrance in one of the interior walls.

This is Dr Atl's statement of what he thereafter witnessed:
"Part way along they paused. The orderly stopped exactly in the middle of the courtyard. The colonel advanced until he was under one of the arches. His attention seemed riveted on something inside the large entrance.

From the spot where I was, some 20 metres from the scene, I could observe with exactness the movements of each man. I saw the colonel advance again slowly and pause. With a slow movement he took his revolver out of its holster and extended his arm toward the opening in the wall. He aimed his gun at something I could not see.

He fired again and again, five times in all. Then he managed to reload his gun but something knocked it to the ground and he abruptly put his hands up to his neck as if trying to free himself from some strangling force.

He moved his head from side to side in desperation and then I saw what was indeed most strange; his body fell slowly backwards, being held in mid-air by an invisible something or someone. His body continued to lean slowly backwards in this impossible manner until he lay on the floor.

There he fought violently for a little while. A groan or a growl, like that of a wounded beast, ended the fight. Meanwhile the orderly fainted, completely overcome by fear.

The death occurred so suddenly I did not even think of moving from the spot where I was until I heard the colonel's stifled groan. I then threw myself down the stairs and ran to the body.

It was limp and motionless. The face was purple. The tongue hung out. I stooped down to observe the neck. It was badly scratched and showed the traces of three enormous fingers."

Moments later Angel and his wife entered the monastery, followed by a group of neighbours who had heard the shooting. Police from a nearby headquarters also heard the shots and came to investigate. Dr Atl and Angel told them all they knew and they were ordered detained. The body of the colonel and the unconscious orderly were transferred to the police station.

The police *comisario* (inspector) asked whether there could have been anyone else in the monastery at the time of the murder. Despite the incriminating implication, Dr Atl insisted there was only the colonel, the orderly and himself.

"I am sure," he added without qualifying the sentence, "that whoever strangled the colonel was not visible to me."

The *comisario* said that "justice cannot admit the participation of a phantom in a crime," but Dr Atl promptly retorted that he had not spoken of phantoms, only of what he had seen and not seen.

It appeared that Dr Atl was going to be charged with the murder until he suggested a closer examination of the fingerprints on the body. A physician already had verified that death was by strangulation. He was asked to compare the marks on the throat with the fingers of the suspect. As a morgue attendant uncovered the face and neck of the body, revealing the traces of three large fingers, Dr. Atl extended his hand. The physician reported it was quite apparent that Dr Atl's fingers – the small, delicate fingers of an artist – in no way corresponded to the marks on the corpse. Nevertheless, Dr Atl was ordered held until the *asistente* could be revived.

The following day, having regained his senses sufficiently to talk coherently, the orderly went with Dr Atl and the police to the monastery for a re-enactment of the death. The trembling soldier in a state of near-hysteria, was firm in his insistence that the colonel had fired at the shadowy outline of a cowled monk.

"My chief fired one shot and then four more," he told the police. "The phantom kept coming forward and I had a dreadful fear. I was aware that my chief reloaded but when he raised his arm to fire again, a great hand came out from the shadow and took him by the neck."

His story dovetailed perfectly with that of Dr Atl from this point. The orderly described how the monstrous hand choked the colonel and slowly forced his body backward until it was prone on the patio floor.

The inspector was forced to concede that, thoughalthough he could not in his official report attribute the crime to an apparition, he also could not accuse either of the two witnesses or Angel. The murder, it was clear, was by "a person or persons unknown".

Dr Atl states that various psychic manifestations continued in the monastery for approximately a year and a half. Then he and Angel discovered a secret burial place within the abbey; government officials were informed and some 120 skeletons were removed, whereupon the supernatural phenomena ceased.

As a rational thinker Dr Atl is still reluctant to believe that he is one of the few men in modern times – possibly the only one – to witness a murder by a ghost.

MY DEAD AUNT IS ALIVE!
by Martins Agbonlahor

As a young man travelled through a foreign country, he faced the shock of his life.

I was sitting on my balcony one Friday afternoon, when a middle-aged man in a long white robe walked past me. He rang a bell with his right hand and bellowed in a guttural voice, "Turn from your evil ways, for there is life after death."

His pronouncement gave me food for thought. Is there really survival after death? I wondered. But all my pondering didn't prepare me for the event that answered my question: I ran into my aunt at a fair in Turin, Italy – and she had died and been buried three months earlier.

Winifred Osinfade was my mother's younger sister. I was as close to her as I was to my own mother. In fact, I even called her Mummy. She had given birth to a baby boy in the mid-1950s, but he died in his infancy. When I was born in 1964, my aunt took me to a fortune teller, as is the tradition in my African hometown. The *Baba lawo* peered deep into my infant eyes and concluded that I was the reincarnation of my dead cousin. He offered several proofs, including a big round mole I have on my right knee – just like the one her son had on his knee. Auntie swept me off my feet and happily carried me home, announcing to everyone that her child had come again, this time to stay.

Aunt Winnie was also my godmother. I remember how she used to shower me with gifts, and she always treated me kindly. When I grew up and decided to move to Italy, she wept profusely at her "lovely son's" departure. Crying, she stroked my head and said, "Honey, go in peace and don't you worry, as I shall see you again."

On January 27, 1995, I went to bed early, because I planned to rise early the following day for the 1,300-kilometre journey to Turin. I slept soundly, with no inkling of who I would meet there.

Turin hosts a weekly fair in Porta Palazzo, a large marketplace. Shoppers choose from a wide array of imports, antiques and jewellery at bargain prices. When I was there, I was lost among a teeming crowd. Suddenly someone slapped my back. At first, I didn't really notice, but then I was pulled by the collar. I turned and there was Aunt Winnie, laughing, with her arms held out to me. I was delighted to see her and we embraced.

I asked her why she hadn't replied to the series of letters I had written during the last several months. She told me she just hadn't had the chance. I pulled out my camera for a snapshot, but she angrily turned me down with a wave of her hand, saying there wasn't time for that.

For the first time in my life, I wondered what was wrong with Mummy. She had never raised her voice to me like that before. I wanted to follow her home, but she ruled it out and instead gave me her address and asked me to come see her the next day.

I woke up the following morning and headed straight for 43 Saluzzo Street. I had to take a cab, as I didn't know my way around Turin. The drive took about 35 minutes. The house was dilapidated and looked abandoned.

As luck would have it, an old woman strolled out. I asked her if she knew my Aunt Winnie. To my surprise, she said my aunt had moved out just a few days before. Dumfounded, I decided to phone my parents and ask them for my aunt's new address – and complain about her shabby behaviour.

My mother answered the phone. When I told her that I had run into Aunt Winnie and that she had invited me to her home, my mother shrieked, "God forbid!" and dropped the phone. I later learned that she had fainted when I mentioned her sister's name. After waiting for about five minutes, I redialled the number. This time my Uncle Dickson answered. He told me in a voice touched with emotion that Aunt Winnie had died three months earlier. They hadn't told me because they knew I would be upset, and because I would be unable to go home for the funeral.

HAUNTED NEW ORLEANS
by Charles Coulombe

*Cultures mix in a town where the ghosts outnumber
the living.*

**One night, you may find yourself sitting at Antoine's, a fine New
Orleans restaurant. Your waiter brings you a sazerac cocktail,
oysters Foch, a bottle of Mouton-Cadet, alligator soup,
pompano en papillot, puffed potatoes and, to finish, *café brulot
diabolique*. But while you bask in such elegance and savour the
delicious tastes, remember: You may well be dining at the gates
of the unearthly.**

Louisiana is a world apart from the rest of the United States. Its law is
based on the French Napoleanic Code and its counties are called
parishes. While the northern half of the state has much in common
with neighbouring Mississippi and Arkansas, the south is Catholic, and
as late as World War II, was almost wholly French speaking west of
New Orleans. That southern half is an amazing kaleidoscope of
cultures.

    The Creoles, now almost completely assimilated into English-
speaking culture, are the descendants of the original French and
Spanish settlers. Their ancestors brought in African slaves, taught them
French, converted them to Catholicism and sometimes had children
with them; the offspring of these unions were the Creoles of Colour,
who dominate New Orleans politically today.

    After the American purchase in 1803, Anglo-Saxons arrived
from the southeastern U.S., followed by Irish, German and Italian
immigrants. As early as 1765, Acadians, driven from their Nova Scotia
homes by the British, sought refuge in the prairies and bayous west of
the city, where their Cajun descendants live today. South of New
Orleans, in St Bernard Parish, Spanish settlers, called Islenos after the
Canary Islands where they originated, arrived about the same time.
The so-called Florida parishes across the Mississippi River provided
refuge to Loyalists fleeing the American Revolution. To complicate the
mix further, Dalmatians from what is now Croatia came as oyster and
fishermen, settling the lower reaches of the Mississippi.

    Such an ethnic and cultural stew produced the landscape we

have now. Each group arrived with their own customs. Some they kept, some they discarded, others they traded with other folk also settled there, adapting things to their liking. So it is that gumbo, a stew indigenous to the South, made with or without chicken, sausage, shrimp, seafood, tomatoes, okra and peppers, is found in a hundred different styles.

Everyone celebrates Mardi Gras, but each does it in their own way. Many people set up a St Joseph's Table on that saint's day. And of course, on the Feast of All Saints, a state holiday, everyone goes to visit their family tombs.

In New Orleans, in the South Louisiana countryside, and even in non-Louisiana, culturally connected Gulf towns like Biloxi, Mobile and Pensacola, candles light up the cemeteries on that night, the eve of All Souls, when the dead in Purgatory come back to visit the living. On such a night, in such a place, the traveller thinks himself in Haiti, the French West Indies, Mauritius, Brittany or anywhere other than everyday America.

Antoine's Ghosts

As might be expected, such an open acceptance of death and the unseen, fed by the folklore of a hundred different peoples, permeates the area. Citizens in New Orleans take such things for granted, and there is not a house in the old French Quarter, the *Vieux Carre*, that does not have its own ghost. Even at Antoine's, the elegant atmosphere, impeccable service, waiters and classic Creole cuisine cannot alter the fact that something else lingers there besides waiters and diners.

Located at 713 St Louis Street, Antoine's has been in the hands of four generations of the same family since it opened in 1840. One night last year, M. Henri Alciatore, head waiter and a descendant of Antoine himself, saw what he took to be a busboy dressed in white enter the Japanese Room. He attempted to follow, only to find the room locked – from the outside! He entered the room to find it empty. On another occasion, while transporting records upstairs, Alciatore looked up the staircase and saw an indeterminate, slightly glowing figure, which quickly disappeared.

One waiter thought he saw Alciatore entering the Mystery Room. Finding it empty, he went into the front, only to find the head waiter there. Since then, he will not go into the room. Even the main dining room (featured in the Oliver Stone film *JFK*) is not secure from the supernatural. One night, a cashier glanced into the dining room, and noticed a man in tuxedo standing by the first table. The cashier blinked, and the man was gone.

Ghostly Bookstore
The quarter boasts many fine second-hand bookshops. Crescent City Bookstore, at 204 Chartres Street, is renowned for its selection. But some visitors have encountered a child ghost on the ground floor, and four more on the second. The third floor is used as storage and is off limits to customers. This is probably just as well, since the appearance of the black man in 1930s clothing who bled to death from a stab wound or the hippie girl who overdosed there, might disturb them.

Stories of this kind are common in New Orleans, but several houses stand out even there. Across the quarter from the bookshop, at 1113 Chartres Street, is the Beauregard-Keyes House. A national historic place, it was home at different times to General Pierre Beauregard and author Frances Parkinson Keyes, whose most famous book is Dinner at Antoines. Although many have seen and felt strange things there, it is apparently neither the gallant Confederate officer, nor the vivacious and pious writer who has returned. It is said that after dark a group of four figures emerges from the upper side and rear galleries. They creep along, until suddenly other phantoms open ghostly fire on them. The bullets enter their bodies, they bleed, three die and one jumps from the gallery. As he hits the ground, bodies and blood disappear, as does the scene, apparently a recreation of a nineteenth-century mafia gunfight.

Turkish Delight
Stranger still is the story of the Sultan's House at 1240–42 Burgundy Street. After the Civil War, the house was rented by its impoverished Creole owner to a wealthy Turk, who had arrived in New Orleans with a fortune in gold and jewels and a retinue of eunuchs, harem girls and young lads – the first for security, the latter two for pleasure.

Ensconced in the Burgundy Street house, the Turk and his entourage gave themselves up to private amusements. It was said that he belonged to the Ottoman royal family; indeed, he was rumoured to be no less than a younger brother of the sultan himself. If so, this would explain what happened, for in those days it was the custom of the House of Osman that each new sultan had all of his brothers (potential rivals for the throne) killed.

One morning, neighbours saw blood streaming through the garden gates and into the street. Summoned, the police broke in on a scene of horror. The inhabitants of the house had been raped and sliced to pieces with swords. The Turk himself had been buried alive in the front yard, presumably spared the other indignities because of his exalted status. The neighbours had heard nothing. Not surprisingly, subsequent tenants have heard piercing shrieks and seen strange figures.

Horror at LaLaurie House

More scandalous still to New Orleans society were the happenings at the LaLaurie home at 1140 Royal Street. In the 1820s and '30s, Mme Delphine Macarty LaLaurie, daughter of an aristocratic Irish officer in the French service, was a well-known socialite among the elegant and exclusive Creoles. Invitations to her home were much sought after. But on the night of April 10, 1834, a fire broke out in the kitchen and the house slaves were unable to put it out.

Fire fighters arrived and spread through the house. In the attic they found slaves chained to the wall and in cages. Some had had organs removed. One woman had had all of her bones broken and reset in strange ways. Another was missing all her limbs. The abominations went on. Most of the slaves were dead, but some still lived.

News of the atrocities spread through the city, and soon a mob assembled outside the house, eager for the blood of the sadist they had so long respected. Suddenly, LaLaurie and her doctor husband appeared in a carriage drawn by four horses. Galloping through the crowd, they rode down to the dock and onto a waiting ship for France.

Although she died in exile, Mme LaLaurie was eventually secretly buried in local cemetery. The house stood empty for years. But six decades later, some of the Italian immigrants who were then crowding the quarter settled in it, ignorant of its history. Residents saw visions of chained and tortured slaves, pets died horrible deaths, children were menaced by the apparition of a white woman with a bloody whip and blood-curdling screams were heard.

Tenant turnover was rapid. Eventually, the building became a bar which did quite well. After it closed, another business attempted to take its place. But after two successive mornings of finding his shop interior covered with disgusting filth, the owner gave up. Today, with the building divided into luxury apartments, all seems well – but for how long?

Voodoo Queen

Not all the peculiarities to be found in the city are ghostly. In New Orleans, as throughout the southern half of the state, Voodoo is practised. In the old days, of course, it was closer to the Caribbean prototype. It was whispered that zombies were made, and the Voodoo deities rode their human horses at dances on Congo Square and at the Bayou St John. Most frightful of all were the orgies held on that night of magic, the eve of midsummer – St John's Eve. This was as strange a time as ever it was in Old Europe.

For many a year, the dancers on the Bayou St John were led by a woman who to this day is revered in the city: Marie Laveau. Born in 1794, Marie Laveau married in 1819 and was widowed in 1826. From that time on, she became known as a powerful Voodoo practitioner. Her *gris-gris*, little collections of such things as feathers, stones, and animal parts (the exact makeup of each differing according to the desired result), were much sought.

A well-known hairdresser, the mulatto Voodoo Queen had access to all the best houses in the city and built up a regiment of spies among the servants of the wealthy. There was, however, another side to Marie Laveau. She was a faithful communicant at St Louis Cathedral, assisted the priests during the various yellow fever epidemics and helped to organize covert resistance to the Yankee occupation during the war between the states. Her death in 1881 was accompanied by the Last Rites of the Catholic Church, and it is said that by that time she had already retired from the practice of Voodoo. In any case, her daughter, also named Marie Laveau, took over where her mother left off. Marie Laveau II's death in 1897, however, left a vacancy which has not been filled.

Congo Square is now the relatively sedate Beauregard Square, and the Bayou St John is today enclosed within City Park. But the tomb of Marie Laveau in St Louis Cemetery # 1 is still much visited, and several tons of "goofer dust" (as graveyard dirt is called in Voodoo) have been extracted from around it for magical uses and dutifully replaced by cemetery workers. All sorts of strange gifts are left there and those wishing certain items enchanted leave them overnight on June 23, St John's Eve.

To be sure, Voodoo is still very much alive in New Orleans, particularly as far as the making of *gris-gris* and other such things are concerned. The F & F Botanica at 801 North Broad Street is typical of the many stores that supply the faithful in the city. The Historic New

Orleans Voodoo Museum, at 724 Dumaine Street, offers exhibits on New Orleans Voodoo as it is practised today, Voodoo tours of the Quarter, and a working Voodoo altar.

Los Angeles-based **Charles Coulombe** *writes extensively on folkloric, religious, and historical topics. He is a frequent contributor to FATE.*

Supernatural Cajun Country

Leaving the city behind does not mean escaping the supernatural – far from it! Cajuns have their own tales of witchcraft and ghosts, and are often happy to share them. But there is more than this in Cajun country. While seeming mysterious to outsiders, the bayous were both refuges and larders to the early Cajuns. Where the early Puritans saw in the trackless forests of New England a wilderness under the devil's dominion, Cajuns viewed the bayous as a source of wonder. What darkness there might be, humans brought with them. Even the devil might easily be banished with the Sign of the Cross or holy water.

But what strange beings the men brought! The *letiche* is a spirit of a dead unbaptized child who wanders about the beds of living children, hoping vainly to somehow share the graces enjoyed by the christened. Deep in the bayous, you may see the glowing torch of a *feux-follet*, a will o' the wisp, who will lead you astray, and then laughing, leave you to find your own way out. Most fearful of these denizens, however, is the *loup-garou*, the werewolf.

Wherever the French settled, in France itself, in Quebec, the West Indies, Mauritius and Reunion, and most especially Louisiana, the loup-garou followed them. In Cajun country, it is believed by many that while some loups-garous are cursed to their fate (and thus fairly docile), others acquire their shape-shifting abilities through magic, rubbing themselves with a special grease to achieve the transformation. Vicious and bloodthirsty, they fear only two things: frogs and salt. The evil loups-garous hold balls at Bayou Goula, particularly on St John's Eve.

While these beliefs enthrall the humble among the Cajuns, their social superiors in the plantation houses that dot the state are not immune. Destrehan Plantation, on the River Road west of New Orleans, is renowned for its ghosts, and some of them have been captured on film. Kenilworth Plantation below the city has a pair of loving apparitions who mount the stairs hand in hand – and headless. In brief, the state is a haven for those interested in such things.
– *Charles Coulombe*

NORTH RIDGE
by Richard Sellers

Ghostly guardians appear in the Oklahoma morning mist.

On November 22, 1970, at 5.30 a.m. on a cold, crisp Oklahoma morning, the sun in the distant east was spreading a fine dusting of light over last night's stars. The crunch of the icy ground under my feet was the only sound I could hear as I made my way along the well-worn trail manufactured by men and cattle. The air was still and the mist was thick. From a distance behind me I heard my uncle call out a warning to "stay on the main trail and stay away from the North Ridge."

For several days I had heard my relatives talking about the North Ridge as though it were a place of instant doom. Without turning I waved in acknowledgment and continued into the silence of the misty gloom ahead.

This was the third morning of my hunting trip at my relatives' home in northeastern Oklahoma. My uncle's neighbour and close friend invited us (my uncle, cousins and me) to hunt on his land. Their spread consisted of several thousand acres of hilly grazing land for a variety of horses and cattle, including a small herd of Brahma bulls that had taken up residence near the North Ridge.

It seemed to grow darker the further I walked along the westbound trail. The air was extremely still and silent. I had been on the same trail the day before at high sun, but now it looked like another world. I knew the trail twisted for miles and eventually made its way west and north around the hills to my right. After a short forever (or maybe an hour), the mist had grown incredibly thick. I knew the sun had risen much higher behind me, but the visibility had not changed.

I stopped in the middle of the trail and was instantly bathed in the silence of the cold, dark, never-ending mist. The silence was broken only by the sound of my heartbeat. Only then did I realize that I was not breathing. I looked at the trail ahead and could only see a few feet. I looked to my right and said aloud, "Just how bad could this North Ridge be?" Then I turned right and headed for the higher ground.

I followed what appeared to be a small animal trail up to the edge of a steep, rocky, heavily forested hillside. The trail ended at the base of the hill. I stopped for a moment to look up the hillside ahead and then took a quick look behind. The lower trail meant miles of boring mist. I turned toward the hill, shouldered my rifle, and said, "How dangerous could a bunch of lazy cows be?"

The trek up the hill's southern side was steep and rough. The trees, brush and branches were thick, and most of the rocks were covered with slippery, moist moss. If there was anything dangerous at the top, it had plenty of warning of my impending arrival. After almost crawling the last 100 yards, I was relieved when the ground suddenly levelled and the forest broke into a grassy clearing. I stood at the edge of the clearing to survey the next leg of my journey and to ponder the warnings I had been given about my chosen path.

The clearing was covered with a low mist a little more than ankle deep. There was a small pond ahead and slightly to my right. The additional elevation provided a bit more light than below. This allowed me to make out the boundaries of the clearing. It was almost a perfect circle, as though by design rather than by nature. Since my intended destination was straight north, I chose an exit about 400 yards across the clearing.

I slowly began to cross the centre of the clearing and instantly became aware of the sound of moist leaves rustling behind me. I stopped and the sound stopped. I started and the sound began again. I stopped again and slowly turned to investigate. As I finished my about-face, I saw 20 to 30 ominous-looking Brahma cattle that seemed to grow out of the fog.

After forcing myself not to react too quickly, I could see that they seemed to be both watching me and grazing at the same time. They were enormous and obviously capable of doing great harm to unwelcome intruders. They did not seem to be immediately menacing, so I turned back to the task of traversing the clearing.

When I turned around, I found that I was completely surrounded by several hundred Brahma. The warnings, the cold mist, and the cattle stirred a moment of panic within me, and I quickly readied my already unslung rifle.

They all seemed to stop grazing at once. Then they raised their heads and appeared to focus on me and my rifle. From somewhere in the herd I heard a few snorts like those one might hear at a bullfight. There was also some mild stirring and some stomping of hooves. I calmed down enough to realize that I was facing several hundred Brahma with a rifle containing only five rounds.

Once I realized the futility of fighting, I lowered my rifle in a gesture of truce. Suddenly the Brahma directly in front of me stepped aside a few feet. The group behind them followed the lead and slowly opened a gauntlet in the direction of my goal. I stepped forward unhindered into the tunnel provided for me. Although they were barely more than an arm's length away, they made no aggressive moves toward me as I walked. Their heads and eyes followed me as I made my way toward my exit from the clearing. The heat from their bodies and breath cause the low lying fog to swirl in a slow, ghostly way. I could smell the musty dew on their greyish-white skin.

Vanishing cattle

With much relief I finally arrived at the northern edge of the clearing, and without hesitation I stepped into the forest. I walked about ten paces and turned for a last look at my escorts. They were gone!

I stepped back to the edge of the clearing, but there was no sign that they had ever been there. The air was still, the mist was unmoved, and not a single Brahma was in sight. I stood there for a few minutes watching to see if they would reappear. I quickly turned and headed down the north face of the North Ridge.

I arrived at the meeting place designated for the hunters to compare kill or sighting stories. I told my uncle, cousins and the land owner what had happened.

They all responded with laughter and disbelieving looks. The land owner told me that he only has about 20 Brahma on his entire property and they rarely gather in one place.

I left Oklahoma two days later to return to California. I never had the opportunity or received an invitation to return to the North Ridge. After all these years my uncle insists that I saw nothing but fog that morning. I am convinced that what I saw was real and unimagined.

THAT'S NOT MY DAUGHTER!
by J. P. Delaney

The frightened ghost of a young accident victim almost ruined the life of an 11-year-old girl.

I first met Missy and her mother, Pam, in my office on May 5, 1994. Missy was a beautiful 11-year-old with a friendly smile – despite the chronic pain her mother had described on the phone. In the previous six months, Missy had been plagued by headaches, jaw and neck soreness, fatigue, mood swings and depression. The young student was even losing her short-term memory and the ability to concentrate. Meanwhile, Pam had been helplessly watching her child waste away. "That's not my daughter," she told me.

Pam had taken Missy to an astounding 36 physicians, including pediatricians, ear, nose and throat doctors, optometrists, dentists, orthodontists, neurologists, chiropractors, physiotherapists, and rheumatologists.

Nothing helped. In fact, Missy's health was continuing to deteriorate. Finally, the last doctor had recommended a child psychiatrist. "As I looked through the yellow pages to find one," Pam told me, "I stopped and said, 'No, I refuse to do this.' Something made me turn to hypnotherapists, and I found your name."

In our initial phone conversation, Pam made an appointment for Missy. I asked her to call me if she thought of anything else I should know. Within an hour, she called back. "I don't know if this has anything to do with Missy's problems," she said, "but I'll tell you anyway."

A Ghostly Encounter

"Beginning in June 1992, Missy had her first encounter with a spirit," Pam said. "She described it as a little girl. Missy was sleeping and it shook her bed. Missy then reached out to touch her and realized that her hand passed totally through her."

Pam herself had seen an almost clear substance dripping down her bedroom mirror. At times, the family would come home to find all the lights on, inexplicably. Money was frequently missing.

Missy had first experienced pain on November 6, 1993. As she walked through the kitchen, she screamed, "Somebody pulled my hair!"

As the weeks went on, her knuckles, wrists, and hands unexplainably became brown and discoloured.

One other puzzling event had marked the past few months: For no apparent reason, Missy was suddenly terrified of crossing railroad tracks.

I thought I knew the answer: Missy seemed to have been attacked by a confused, earthbound spirit. It wasn't the first time I had encountered such a situation.

Any number of things – such as fear, ignorance and guilt – can keep a spirit earthbound. Dr Edith Fiore's book *The Unquiet Dead* is an excellent work on the subject. I use it frequently in my work as a hypnotherapist.

During my first session with Missy, I explained what hypnosis is, what it is not, and how we were going to use it to help her. That day, I did a basic relaxation session, combined with an emphasis on increased self-confidence. I surmised that her health problems had taken a toll on her self-esteem.

I tape-recorded the session and asked Missy to listen to it at night as she fell asleep. This would help her relax, get a good night's sleep, and prepare her mind to follow my voice. She agreed. Missy was ready to get well.

A week later, I saw her again. Missy said she had been listening to her tape every night. She seemed a little more "up".

During our second session, I asked Missy if she had ever had any strange experiences. She exploded into conversation, telling me stories she hadn't even told her mother. Here was my opening.

I asked Missy if she had seen the movie *Ghost*. She had. Then I called her attention to the scene where Patrick Swayze is killed in the alley, but at first does not realize he is dead. Then I reminded her of the very last scene where Swayze's character goes into the light. Missy immediately saw the connection between the movie and her own experiences.

"Fortunately, this situation is an easy one to fix," I said. "That is, if you are willing. I will not do anything without your permission."

She was willing.

Spiritual Healing

Missy jumped into a comfortable armchair. I put on some soft music and dimmed the lights. I said, "You know, Missy, this session is as much for the earthbound spirit as it is for you." She nodded in agreement.

I gave Missy a few minutes of general relaxation suggestions. Then, using a script from Dr Flore's book, I continued:

"Imagine you have a miniature sun, just like the sun in our solar system, deep within your solar plexus. This sun is radiating through every atom and cell of your being. It fills you with light to the tips of your fingers, the top of your head and the soles of your feet. It shines through you and beyond you an arm's length in every direction…above your head…below your feet…out to the sides…creating an aura, a brilliant, dazzling, radiant white light that completely surrounds and protects you from any negativity or harm."

I paused for a moment.

Then I spoke directly to the spirit that was with Missy.

I told the spirit that it was not Missy. I said that it had once had a body, personality, ideas and attitudes – and that something had happened to its body and it died. In my practice, I have found that many spirits remain earthbound because they simply do not realize they are dead.

I continued speaking to the spirit.

"Then, at one point, you joined Missy. That's where you made an even worse mistake. Up until that point, you had just been hurting yourself, keeping yourself from the wonderful life you could have been having in the spirit world with your loved ones. When you joined Missy you started hurting her. The very least you've done is to use her energy, causing her to be tired. And you may confuse her because she can't tell your thoughts, wishes and needs from her own."

I spoke slowly, giving the earthbound spirit time to understand what was being said.

Then I directed the attention of the earthbound spirit to its loved ones, also in spirit form. "They're so happy to see you because they have really been worried about you. They've been looking for you, searching for you and longing for you … and now they've found you … and they're overjoyed to see you. Look at them … they're reaching out their arms for you … now they're embracing you, giving you warm, wonderful hugs."

I always pause for a few minutes here. I've found that spirits frequently remain earthbound because they feel guilty and fear retribution. I want them to know that they are loved, appreciated and welcomed into the spirit world.

"In a few minutes, you're going to leave Missy," I said. "When you do, you're going to find yourself in your very own spirit body. Your rightful body. To use as long as you need to. It's a perfect body in every sense of the word. It's a youthful and attractive body. A body that will never age, never get wrinkled or be sick, never have anything wrong with it. If you're male, you'll find yourself in a male body, strong and healthy. If you're female, you'll be in a lovely, healthy, youthful female body."

I paused again. Then I pulled out the clincher. "Now, just in case you're afraid of going to hell, I want you to know that there's somebody here from the spirit world, a teacher of religious education, who is going to explain to you that there is nothing to fear, because there's no such thing as hell. If you were brought up as a Catholic, this teacher is a nun or priest. If you're a Protestant, it's a minister of your own denomination. If you're a Jew, this being is a rabbi. Whoever you need is here to explain to you that you have absolutely nothing to fear."

Go to the Light
Next, I directed the spirit's attention to the Light as it moved closer to them. "You have a beautiful new life waiting for you. You'll be with lots of loved ones, family and friends. The worst is over…and the best is yet to come.

"Go with our blessings and our love," I said. "Go in the name of the Father, the Son, and the Holy Spirit, in peace, and light, and love."

Then I slowly counted Missy back to a wide-awake state, back to her body, back to the present moment. The entire process took just 15 minutes. Missy's eyes were huge. She was crying.

"How do you feel?" her mother asked.

"Almost all of my pain is gone," Missy replied. "I only have a very mild headache." Pam wanted to ask more questions, but I stopped her. "Let her relax and we'll schedule our next session," I said.

We made an appointment for the following week. My intuition told me that Missy's problems were over, but I wanted one more session with her. I wanted to teach her how to protect herself in the future.

Pam called me that night to tell me about their 45-minute trip back home. "When we left, Missy wanted to talk about what she had experienced. By this time, she was in no pain. We were both crying happy tears."

Missy had told her about the spirit that occupied her body. "The spirit was a child who had been killed in an accident between a car and a train," Pam said. "Missy said, 'Mum, there were three people in the car. The two people in the front seat were arguing and the little girl was asleep with her hand under her face. The accident happened right as they crossed the railway tracks. A train hit them. Mum, that's why I was so afraid of crossing railway tracks.'

"Missy had even felt the impact," Pam said. Perhaps that accounted for her headaches and forehead, jaw, and neck pain.

The next week, at our third and final visit, a bouncing, dancing, bright-eyed Missy entered my office. She practically jumped into my arms. She bubbled with conversation, telling me how good she felt.

"There's one more thing we have to do," I said. "I'll show you how to protect yourself in the future."

I told Missy how to picture herself surrounded by protective white light. I also advised her to avoid hospitals, nursing homes, cemeteries and ouija boards. And I gave her a copy of Dr Fiore's book so she could learn more about earthbound spirits.

Two and a half years later, Missy is still healthy and happy. She is once again a student – who just happens to have learned a life lesson most of us will never have to face.

J. P. Delaney *is a certified clinical hypnotherapist in New Orleans, Louisiana.*

THE HAUNTING ON OCEAN AVENUE
by Audenreed Meehan

Our family has been a magnet of sorts. We have had a variety of unwanted guests wherever we have lived. Ghosts, poltergeists or spirits have taken up residence with us many times. Since I can remember, there have been problems with hauntings. I did some research and learned that certain things will invite spirits. Sometimes you can invite them without knowing it. Other times, they are just there. And still other times, they're there and you never know it. We always knew of their presence.

Documentation

Subsequently, I decided to document these hauntings. The following is one of the first hauntings I can remember.

I was 12 years old in the spring of 1972. My family, (Mum, Dad, my two sisters and I) had just moved into a five-room apartment on Ocean Avenue in Brooklyn. It was an old building, the kind only found in the familiar New York skyline. The building's exterior had seen better days, but the inside was well kept, with hardwood floors, plaster walls with framed borders and tall ceilings – very art deco. There was a large, rounded bay window in the dining room with a window seat, an outside courtyard with a garden and a fenced-in front garden where children could play safely.

The former tenant, a man in his 80s, had just moved to Florida to live with his children. His wife had recently passed away. I met this man only once, when we originally viewed the apartment. Even as a young child, I could tell his heart was broken at the loss of his wife. He was teary eyed and was drinking a can of beer as the movers took his things to the truck. We moved in a few days later.

Our new dwelling was a corner unit that provided a lot of sunlight no matter what time of day it was. It was apartment number 14 on the third floor. It was great to be moving from our confining four rooms to a much more spacious five-room place. Last to be brought into our new home weres Tim-Tam and Ping-Pong, our Siamese cats.

While we unpacked, Tim-Tam and PingPong darted through the house, not playfully bouncing about, but tearing through each

437

room. At first we laughed at their energy and thought they were having fun exploring. But it didn't stop; they wouldn't quit. After a few hours, they had knocked over glasses and knick-knacks, slid off of furniture and scratched the wood. It was as if someone were chasing them around. They were in fear, ears back, tails puffed out and the hair on their backs standing up. Finally, we had to catch them and put them in a box.

After three days of this behaviour, and being afraid they would have a heart attack, we gave the cats away. They hadn't eaten nor had they used the cat box. We knew it was for the best. It was obvious that there was something in the apartment that caused their behavior. The minute they were taken out, they settled down.

My mother let us pick out the décor for our bedroom. It was a 10-by-12 one-window room with a door leading right into the bathroom. *The Brady Bunch* was my favourite show. I wanted a room just like Marsha, Jan and Cindy's. My sister and I picked pink as our colour scheme: pink and white bedspreads with white daisies, pink curtains, big fuzzy pillows and a new light fixture: a pink, tulip-shaped chandelier (with white and yellow daisies). The superintendent installed the light that afternoon. It hung from the ceiling on a long, white chain. The light was considered very "mod"; we thought were so cool. That night, however, we wished the light fixture had never been installed. Something or someone didn't like it and didn't hesitate to let us know.

The Whizzing Chandelier

My younger sister Ruth and I were in bed early. We had school the next morning. I faintly heard my older sister, Catherine, calling out, "Mum! Come here!" She was shouting from the landing right outside of our bedroom. I was still half-asleep, but I heard my mother say, "Oh, my God!" At that point I was wide awake. Both Ruth and I sat up in a fright. The room was dark. I nervously asked, "What's wrong"? Catherine and my mother were looking up at the ceiling. My mother turned the light on. I looked up and saw the chandelier whizzing around on its chain as if someone were using it as a lasso. It was spinning so fast that it literally made a whizzing sound. I screamed and ran out of the room.

We tried to come up with an explanation, but nothing made sense. My mother stayed quiet. We slept on the sofabed that night. I remember sleeping in fear each night after that. I had to be totally exhausted in order to fall asleep. But even then, I had dreadful dreams.

My father worked on night shifts as a bartender at a restaurant bar we owned. We greeted him early that morning when he came home and told him the strange story. He didn't say much; he just listened and dismissed it as four females being hysterical.

A few days later, my father arrived home from work at his usual time, 5.00 a.m. It was just getting light. His normal routine was to eat breakfast, watch the news and wake my mother up at 6.00 a.m.; then he would go to bed. She would open the restaurant bar at 8.00 a.m. and work until 6.00 p.m., when he relieved her.

This particular morning, my father sat at the dining-room table having breakfast and watching the news. Without warning, he was rocked from his chair by an explosion that came from the kitchen. He got up, a little disoriented. The dining room window had been blown out into the street. Only blowing curtains remained. He went to the kitchen but couldn't get through: the stove was knocked over and the washing machine was in the middle of the floor. The window in the kitchen was also gone.

We heard the sound and went running into the dining room. The whole building heard the blast. The fire engine was there within minutes; then came Brooklyn Union Gas. There was a lot of confusion, with neighbours in the hall, people going through our house, and so on.

They began their search but could find no reason for the explosion. My mother asked if it was a gas leak. The gas man said "absolutely not." There was no leak, all the pipes were fine, there was no fire and there was no sewer-gas buildup. The men checked the other apartments in the building, but nothing unusual was found. Needless to say, the landlord was not a happy man, having to replace two large windows. My mother and father spoke about the possibilities, but they too came up with no real reason. We never did find out what happened.

The Strange Air Conditioner

It was mid-July and the days were getting very hot. Everyone was running air conditioners, especially at night. At 3.03 a.m., my mother woke up because the air had gone off. Immediately, she thought the fuse had blown. The house used the old screw-in fuses, and you had to go to the basement in order to change them. She decided to wait for my father to get home.

Finally, the room became too hot, so she got up to take a look. She turned the knob; the air came on immediately. It made no sense to her, but she went back to bed.

The next night at 3.03 a.m. and every night after for three weeks, the same scenario played itself out: air turned off, Mother turned it back on. It was never a blown fuse.

Other events such as exploding tomatoes on the kitchen window ledge, items constantly disappearing, and puddles of water on the floor in the cupboard every morning were daily happenings. Sounds of footsteps, faint cries of a woman, hot and cold areas in the house, exploding sounds in the kitchen and an unseen door slamming all became commonplace. My father, sound asleep and alone in the house, would be awakened by a woman calling out his name. Someone was angry and they didn't mind letting us know.

My only sleepover was enough for friends to never come back. Four girl friends arrived at 6.00 p.m. We sat in the living room and played games, talked about boys, watched TV and told ghost stories. Our goal was to stay up all night and watch the late-late show on CBS. We were perched on the sofabed with our potato chips and Cokes. The lights were off. *My Friend Irma* was the first late movie.

It was about 1.30 a.m. when the noise started. First, there was a banging sound, as though someone were slamming a door shut. I thought it was the next-door neighbours. The noise grew louder, then stopped all at once. A grey/white "blob" shape moved from the hall closet through a door that was slightly ajar. It hovered there for a moment, then moved toward the sofabed. We didn't make a sound; no one moved. We stared in amazement at this smoky, floating blob thing. I could hear the scuffing sound of slippers on the floor as it moved past the bed and into the dining room and turned into the kitchen. Once out of sight, there was a second of silence; then everyone screamed in unison. We were terrified and turned on the lights immediately. The slumber party was over. Three of the four girls called their parents to come pick them up. The bravest one, Theresa, stayed. We left the lights on all night and didn't sleep until daylight.

One of the last events: Mother's two brothers, Bobby and Jim, came to our house for a visit. Bobby had just arrived from England. It was the first time he had been in this apartment.

Self-Closing Curtains

Jim, Bobby and my mother sat at the dining-room table having some tea. My mother told them about the happenings in the house. Uncle Jim laughed and made little jokes. Bobby told her, "That's rubbish." As soon as he spoke, as if on cue, the curtains in the dining-room window (which were held back by ties) closed on their own. Both uncles looked at the window, then to my mother, then to each other. Without a word, they got up and ran out of the house, leaving my mother sitting at the table. Bobby called up to the window to have my mother throw his coat down to him. He never set foot in that apartment again. They both advised that we move right away.

The year was nearly over, and without anyone saying it out loud, we knew we'd be moving again soon.

Early one evening, my mother, an avid reader, sat in the dining room reading a book. Out of the corner of her eye, she saw a transparent, whitish figure come from the closet and move toward her. She heard the familiar sound of scuffing slippers as this shape came closer. Paralysed with fear, she sat staring at the book but no longer reading. The sensation of hot air, like someone breathing on her neck, made her hair stand up. Finally, she had enough. This had to stop. She slammed both hands down on the table. All her fears, anger, and concerns rolled into one gave her the strength to shout into the air, "Your husband went to Florida to live with your kids! He's not here any more! Go to Florida and see him! Now get the hell out of here!" Instantaneously, the heat and the sound were all gone. For the first time in almost a year, there was nothing. No unfriendly presence in the air. This spirit must have been the wife of the former tenant looking for her husband. To her, we were intruders and didn't belong there.

This torment took a toll on everyone. Because of the constant fear, nerves were running high at all times. There were arguments and squabbles. No one wanted to be in the house. Sit-down dinner was a thing of the past. My older sister's personality changed. She became withdrawn and aggressive. She got into fights at school, which was unlike her. Mother was taking tranquillizers. I was slightly more accepting of what was happening but nervous and confused by it all. Ruth, the baby, was simply scared to death. She wouldn't go anywhere alone, not even to the bathroom.

Even though this was clearly over, we were left with unseen scars. I never was able to sleep in total darkness again. I prayed a lot and found strength there. But a full year of trepidation was a huge emotional and physically draining encounter.

We moved a few months later.

Audenreed Meehan *now lives in Pennsylvania, but is a former resident of New York, Scotland and Ireland.*

HAUNTING ON THE HUDSON
by Jo-Ann and Cecil Corsiatto

Bodies of water have a special appeal, but to us, rivers have a fascination of their own. Unlike lakes and oceans, rivers have a destination. Recently, we have come to know the beauty of the Hudson River. From its source in the Adirondack Mountains to its jaw at the battery on the south side of Manhattan, the Hudson River runs for 315 miles. Once, as we watched a piece of wood floating with the current, we sensed a power about the flow of the river, a dependability, as the wood travelled on its way with obvious ease.

Nyack, N.Y., is a sleepy little community of some 6,400 people, located on the west side of the Hudson River, about 45 minutes north of New York City. It's an area steeped in American heritage and Revolutionary War history. Less than 100 feet from the river, located in one of the oldest sections of town, is a splendid 18-room, three-storey Victorian mansion built in 1900.

Residing in this mansion for more than 24 years were three loving, giving ghosts who made their presence known to the fourth owners of the house, Helen and George Ackley and their family. The Ackleys purchased the dwelling after it had been vacant for seven years. An article published in *Readers Digest* gave this house and these ghosts national acclaim in 1977.

We drove up to see the house in February, 1994. We were unable to go inside, but we wandered around the area, looking at the newly painted exterior as long as the penetrating rain and wind would allow.

The house of the spirits
As I looked at the stately old mansion, I thought, "If a ghost alone in such a house became aware that it was suddenly sharing its quarters with strangers, would it not endeavour to make its presence known?" The ghosts on the Hudson did exactly this by creating a variety of rappings, tappings, thumps and unusual odours.

These phantom inhabitants, contrary to most ghosts, are said to have given gifts on special occasions. The story is like a love story between a warm and caring family and their three loyal, unseen friends.

Teenagers used to call the house haunted long before the Ackleys ever arrived. Just before they moved in, some of the neighbourhood children ran over to ask the Ackleys, "Did you know you bought a haunted house?" Two of the children reported seeing a ghost when peeking through a window while the house was vacant.

One of the first indications that the house may indeed have been haunted happened during some early renovations. The local plumber was recreating the water system when he heard footsteps overhead. He looked around upstairs several times, but he could not find anybody.

George and Helen Ackley were not in the slightest way perturbed by the ghostly intruders. In fact, they welcomed their presence. As time went on, the Ackley family became used to the unexplained happenings in the house – things like lights going out a few minutes after they were turned on, and ghostly rappings on the doors and walls. There were also the footsteps.

Every morning, between 8.30 and 9.15 a.m., the unseen visitors were heard walking from the third to the second level. And then, every evening around 9.00 p.m., footsteps could be heard going back up to the third level. Were these ghosts arising in the morning and retiring at night as they did during their earthly existence.

Every morning at exactly the same time, Cynthia, one of the children, was awakened by someone shaking her bed. If Cynthia didn't get up right away, the bed would shake harder. When Cynthia, before going to bed at night, explained to her invisible roommate her desire to sleep a little late in the morning, the shaking stopped.

Cynthia, who was in her teens at the time, was in bed one warm summer night when an apparition entered her room. The air suddenly chilled. There, in a glimmer of light, was a young woman in front of the bedroom mirror, brushing her long hair. The misty figure was wearing a long, white, lace gown with a high neckline. Her sweet, gentle face was smiling at Cindy in a friendly way.

At first Cindy was frightened. Her heart was thumping so loudly that she was sure it could be heard. She lay perfectly still, hoping the image would disappear, but it came nearer.

It came so near she could almost touch it. When Cindy called out to her family, the young woman vanished. The young woman appeared in Cindy's room a number of times after that, often wearing a long, dark cloak. Like the rest of the family, Cindy eventually became used to the appearance and disappearance of the young woman.

Over the years, as the Ackleys restored the old mansion with much love, and I am sure, much expense, odd things continued to happen. While painting her living room, Helen, perched at the top of an eight-foot ladder, felt someone watching her.

Since George was at work and the children were at school, Helen felt a bit anxious. As she continued to paint, she felt the presence of someone come even closer. As she looked over her shoulder, there he was, a cheerful little man with a ruddy, round face, white hair and piercing blue eyes.

Helen spoke to him. "I hope you like the colour," she said. He nodded and smiled. "I hope you're pleased with what we are doing in the house." Again he smiled and then slowly faded out of sight. Helen was certain he approved of the renovations. She told me, "He seemed happy, and I was proud to have met him."

When I asked Helen how he was dressed, she described him in an immaculate light blue suit with a short, unbuttoned jacket turned back over white shirt ruffles at his wrists. Below his knee-length breeches were white hose and black, shiny pumps with buckles. Helen didn't know why she saw him then, and she never saw him again.

Unafraid, believing that good outweighs the forces of evil, the Ackleys filled their home with peace, contentment, love and happiness. Many curious incidents convinced them that their ghosts were just like family. Through the years a bond between the family and the ghosts continued to grow.

When Cynthia was to be married, she cut short a college term and came home to Nyack. Just before her wedding day, she awoke to find a dainty pair of silver sugar tongs on her dressing table.

Since no-one in the house knew how the sugar tongs found their way to an empty dressing table, the family assumed that it was left as a wedding gift for Cindy by the family ghosts. It has been 20 years now, and, amazingly, Cindy's tiny silver tongs have never tarnished.

Two years after her marriage, Cindy again came home to Nyack, to have her baby. After the birth of the baby, the family tried to purchase a baby's ring small enough to fit the infant. No ring seemed to fit. On the morning Cindy was leaving Nyack to join her husband, who was serving in the military, she awoke to find a tiny baby's ring on her bed side table, a ring that fit the baby's finger perfectly. A ring was also left in the hall for the Ackley's younger daughter, Cara Lee.

When Helen and George arrived home from being out of town, Helen noticed the small ring on Cara Lee's finger. "Who gave you the ring?" Helen asked.

Cara Lee answered, "It was left for me." When asked how she knew it was for her, she answered, "Because it fits me."

There were many observations of the ghosts in Cindy's room and on the second floor. Once, when a relative was an overnight guest, she was astounded to see a young man, wearing a white wig and early American clothing, enter her room. The entity walked toward the bed, sat down and opened a book in mid-air; he slowly turned the pages, as if he were looking for something. He then closed the book, stood up and vanished from sight.

It was assumed that this was the same young military man seen previously by the Ackley's oldest son. Later the family identified the uniform as that of a lieutenant in the U.S. Navy.

Unlike the disturbances of poltergeists, little is known about apparitions, phantoms and spirits that can be seen. They are far less common than poltergeist cases. When seen by observers, apparitions are usually wispy and witnessed only briefly, with little observation of detail. Furthermore, it is quite unusual for observers to feel the emotions of an entity.

Throughout the years, the three spirit beings who were very much a part of this Hudson River mansion continued to convey emotion and companionship to the family. One winter evening, as Helen stood at the dining room window, she could see the view of the Hudson clearly. The trees were bare, and the shore lights were visible across the water.

As she stood there, basking in the magnificent view of the Tappan Zee Bridge in the distance, feeling perhaps a little lonely, wondering when her husband would return from his trip, a chill engulfed her left side. Every hair on her neck stood up. As she slowly turned her head she saw nothing, but felt a presence right next to her, making her aware she was not alone. "It's beautiful on the river, isn't it?" Helen asked aloud. As she spoke, a sense of calm came over her. She stood for a few more minutes, and then turned to leave.

She felt the presence of the entity walk right beside her. Helen hesitated at the door, and so did the spirit. "Thank you for sharing the view with me. I'm going to bed now," Helen said, as she walked down the hall to her bedroom. Her invisible companion remained behind.

How three separate entities arrived at this house on the Hudson can only be speculated. In our research of the house we learned that the first owners were a family named Perry. Prior to the construction of the house around 1900, the property was an apple and possibly a cherry orchid.

A psychic was invited to view the exterior of the house. She sensed that the spirits there had perished in a boat fire.

Fatal steamboat fire

Through extensive research, we learned that steamboat racing on the river was common in the mid-1800s. Two of these boats lost over 100 passengers, who perished in their fires. Could the Ackley ghosts have been passengers on either of those boats? Did they make their way to the orchard, which later became the site of this grand home? Only the spirits know the answers to these questions.

After George's death, Helen decided to sell the house and move. In 1989 a young bond trader and his wife made an offer to buy the mansion. When they heard about the hauntings they changed their minds. The case went to court and, after a spirited debate, an appeals court in New York ruled this Nyack house "legally haunted".

When another buyer surfaced, Helen knew she would be leaving behind some memories and some dear friends. When her daughter was moving a major portion of the family furnishings out, a large, three-section living room mirror came crashing off the wall. Everyone ran from all directions to see what had happened. Not only was the entire mirror shattered, but the durable wires that had supported it were broken into many pieces.

The Ackleys felt that the spirits were expressing their sadness and anger because the family was moving. When moving day arrived, just before Helen closed the front door for the final time, she looked back at the empty rooms and whispered with tearful eyes, "Goodbye, I wish you could come with us."

One might think that this story ended in 1989 when the Ackleys moved out of the house. But a bond of feeling and fond memories remains alive to this day in Helen Ackley's heart.

THE GHOST ORBS OF ANCIENT JAPAN
by Frank Joseph

The human soul has long been envisioned in numerous cultures around the world as a sphere. In the Western Hermetic tradition, the very soul of God was defined as an intelligible sphere whose centre is everywhere and circumference is nowhere. Edgar Cayce, America's "Sleeping Prophet" of the early 20th century, claimed his "spirit body" assumed the shape of an orb whenever, during a trance state, he projected his consciousness into another dimension.

The ancient Egyptians believed the soul was like a bubble formed of two main parts – the *ba* and *ka*. The *ba* represented human striving toward spirituality, the ideal, beauty, self-sacrifice – all those loftier qualities which separate us from mere beasts. This striving of the *ba* made it rise to the top of the bubble, drawing it toward higher, more refined levels of being. Its counterweight was the *ka*, which embodies our basic needs to survive, experience pleasure, and exercise control over our surroundings. If we were comprised only of the *ba*, existence in this material world would not be possible, because we would fly uncontrollably into the heavenly regions. If we were only made of *ka*, we would sink into the Earth as mere materialists, no better than any other animal interested in subsistence, self-indulgence and dominance. Together, these twin aspects of the soul enable it to float, as it were, through eternity, the *ka* serving as ballast for the *ba*. At death, the *ba* is freed to soar into the spiritual regions that are its natural home, while the *ka* sinks back into the Earth for material recycling.

The Tamayura of Japan
The concept of the human soul as a differentiated sphere did not vanish with ancient Egypt but is still familiar to modern Japanese. They refer to it as the *tamayura*, a kind of luminous "ghost orb" occasionally inhabiting cemeteries or haunted locations. In the British Isles, such orbs are known as fairy lights often, although not exclusively, associated with prehistoric standing stones such as Stonehenge, Avebury and other megalithic sites. The *tamayura* were

first mentioned in the *Kokin-syu* (Book of spirit power), among Japan's oldest written documents, which describes folk beliefs long antedating its first publication in the 11th century. It was followed by the *Sin Kokin-syu* (New edition of the book of spirit power) and tells how "ghost bubbles" carry the souls of the dead from this world to the next. The *tamayura* were said to have used Japan's oldest stone monuments as gateways for passing back and forth between the material and spiritual realms.

Most outsiders are unaware of the numerous although remotely secluded megalithic sites found, with difficulty, across the main island of Honsu, where *tamayura* are commonly reported. Many of these standing stones are virtually indistinguishable from the far better known Neolithic structures in Western Europe, with which they share more than a passing physical resemblance. Remarkably, many of Japan's standing stones are contemporary with their megalithic counterparts in Ireland, southern England, Brittany, Portugal, Spain and Majorca. At least a few of the Japanese Neolithic sites even demonstrate the same astronomical orientations featured in Stone Age Western European sites.

All this leads some unconventional scholars to speculate that seafarers travelled back and forth between Japan and Western Europe, 5,000 and more years ago. Be that as it may, the same phenomenon – fairy lights in the West, *tamayura* in the East – supposedly occurs around megalithic centres in both lands.

A collection of Japanese standing stones where spirit bubbles are said to appear is located in Tokushima prefecture. Its very name, Iwagami, or "Place of the Stone God", suggests the paranormal phenomenon observed at this site. But the location with reportedly the greatest number of orb encounters is found in Ohita prefecture, in the southeastern part of Honsu. Recorded sightings among the 13-foot-tall monoliths of Kyoseki go back more than 800 years, to the *Kokin-syu*, or "Book of Spirits" cited above, and continue today. According to most observers, bubbles of blue light are seen to sometimes float among the stones, moving with deliberate, conscious action, before vanishing into thin air. The *tamayura* do not appear like clockwork, however, nor are they invariably seen by every visitor at all times. When I first visited the Kyoseki site four years ago, I saw nothing out of the ordinary. Nor did any of the five other persons with me. But we most definitely sensed a distinct presence. The Greeks referred to such feelings as instinctual human reaction to the *genius loci*, the spirit of place, associated with sacred sites of real spiritual power. The sensation is much the same as the awe visitors experience when they enter Saint Paul's Cathedral or Carlsbad Caverns.

But Kyoseki is not easy to find. There are no roadside signs providing directions. To reach the site, the services of a local guide are required for anyone outside the nearby town of Ajimu. The megalithic site itself is not overgrown, however, but open to the sky. Its quartet of massive stones evokes a mystical atmosphere area that residents identify with by draping a knotted hawser or rope over one of them. Known as a *gohei*, it is traditionally used by Japanese throughout their islands to define and set it apart from the mundane world as a holy object.

A year before to my earliest encounter with the Kyoseki stones, a visitor from far away Yokahama documented the existence of the *tamayura*, or ghost orbs, for the first time. On May 7, 1999, Mrs Chieko Kohama was walking among the monoliths with some friends when she noticed more than half a dozen light-blue bubbles unaccountably drifting among the huge stones. The noiseless objects seemed to phase in and out of reality, and everyone belonging to her party of 20 men and women saw them. In an attempt to prove they were not optical illusions of some kind, she raised her 35mm Minolta camera and photographed the site.

Orbs on Film

To her amazement some days later, after returning to Yokahama, the developed print not only captured the blue orbs, but showed some of them in far greater detail and higher definition than her own rather nebulous sighting. Photographic experts closely scrutinized the apparent bubbles in her print and concurred that they were real objects, not the result of distortions brought about by intrusive lighting conditions or any imperfections in the film. They were just as much a part of the environment as the trees and megaliths around which they danced.

Mrs Kohama gave her photo to Prof. Nobuhiro Yoshida, a multilingual expert in Asian archaeology and the best-known scientist in Japan. He was gracious enough to share it with me after we visited the Kyoseki site together. I asked him why the *tamayura* are better photographed by cameras than seen by human vision.

"This phenomenon is largely and most often invisible to the naked eye due to the sensing capacity of its wavelength," he explained. "The superior sensitivity of film enables a camera to photograph this ultrahigh wavelength radiating from its point of energy. The human retina and film have their own specific receptive frequencies for sensing these various ranges of light."

Piezoelectric Effect

There may be another explanation for the ghost orb phenomenon, if not its preference to be photographed, than perhaps its more earthbound origins. *Tamayura* may be variations on the well-known geologic visual marvel referred to as the "Andes glow". This is a luminous cloud or aura sometimes seen flitting above a mountaintop like incandescent gas or even lightning streaks. When subjected to the tectonic stress of seismicity, mountains containing large amounts of quartz react in a manner similar to old crystal radio receivers, which "jumped a spark" under pressure from a tightening screw.

Known as the piezoelectric effect, it is produced by certain crystals which generate voltage when subjected to pressure, and, conversely, undergo mechanical stress if subjected to an electric field, alternately expanding and contracting in response to an alternating electrical field. The principle is still found at work in modern microphones. The so-called "corona discharge" produced by the piezoelectric effect is a mysterious-looking light appearing in a variety of shapes – including, on occasion, blue orbs.

The same electrical process is at work among mountains of high crystalline content situated in seismically active areas. Before or during an earthquake, tectonic stress squeezes the quartz to produce the bluish Andes glow. Although the phenomenon derives its name from the famous South American mountain range, it has been observed and photographed around the world wherever crystal-rich mountains are found in seismically sensitive regions, including Japan. True, the Kyoseki stones are positioned over an active fault zone, but then the entire country is earthquake-prone.

Orb Websites

Contradicting geological explanations of the enigmatic orbs are their common sightings around the world, most commonly at graveyards, churches and in private homes during family gatherings. American photographer Alan Meyer has posted some remarkable images on his website (*www.alanmeyer.com/custom4.html*) of ghost bubbles congregating above a collection of antique fire engines. Could these orbs be the lingering spirits of long-dead firefighters?

Another website (*http://members.lycos.co.uk/sldocs/orbs.html*) features the phenomenon hovering over the bloodstained battleground of Gettysburg, scene of the American Civil War's crucial encounter between Union and Confederate armies in 1863. The images featured by these websites are remarkable, because the orbs they show are identical to their *tamayura* counterparts captured in Mrs Kohama's photograph at the Kyoseki standing stones in Japan. Their shared resemblance argues persuasively on behalf of an actual phenomenon.

Moreover, the ghost bubbles are likewise reported by survivors of NDEs (near-death experiences) and observers during a death watch at the time of passing. Outside corroborating evidence is cited in the Hawaiian Islands, where the same ghost bubbles have often been reported and photographed floating above ancient temple platforms. Known as *heiau*, these prehistoric structures were never used for burials, although the native Hawaiians practised their most sacred and profane ceremonies within the stone enclosures. The very walls of Hawaii's *heiau* must still resonate with powerful energies running the gamut from community prayer to cannibal feasts. Perhaps the luminous ghost bubbles often observed at the old ruins are the souls of petitioners and victims alike, come back to haunt the site of their former lives on Earth.

Whether the result of natural forces in our planet or human souls drifting from one plane of existence to another, the blue orbs are real and unquestionably merit further study by scientists and psychics alike.

Frank Joseph *is a regular FATE contributor and editor of* Ancient American.

OUT OF AFRICA
by Cynthia Hind

A Zimbabwean parapsychologist shares ghostly tales from her homeland.

Most of Africa's traditional religions are based on ancestral spirits. Some are welcome, some are to be carefully monitored, and others are truly malevolent and are to be avoided at all costs. There are also certain rituals that have to be performed at the time of death of an immediate family member. To ignore these is tantamount to inviting disaster.

Among the Mashona of Zimbabwe (other tribal beliefs are not dissimilar) the spirit that passes from a person at death is called the *mudzimu*. When called by its children, the spirit returns home and looks after its dependants. It is important that the mudzimu comes gently and not in anger. The people are not afraid of these spirits.

The wandering spirit is another matter. It has no purpose for remaining on the earthly plane, so it seeks to express its identity through another person or medium (*avikiro*). The *chitokwane* is the unfortunate spirit of one resurrected immediately after death by a scheming medium who can control it to do damage to his enemies.

These different kinds of spirits come in various guises and paranormal roles. Very often they are not seen as the Western ghost is seen, but they are just as effective. The head messenger of the Native Affairs Department reported in the NADA magazine that when he was a young fighting man in the days of King Lobengula of the Matabele tribe in Rhodesia (now Zimbabwe), his regiment was stationed in the Gweru District.

One day Nkabi, son of a local leader, Chief Gambo, was herding cattle with another man near the Vungu River. Here they met up with two men from the Balozwi tribe who had been conquered by the Matabele, but on the king's instructions, they were to be left in peace in their own haunts.

One of the Balozwi men mentioned that he had a pair of brass tongs. These tongs were used by the people to pick up red hot embers from open fires for lighting their pipes. They were made by old artisans and were often very beautiful and greatly prized by the owners.

The tongs took Nkabi's fancy but the owner refused to part with them. After some argument, Nkabi forcibly took them. The owner pointed out that Nkabi was disobeying the king's instructions and would only bring misfortune and evil to himself, but Nkabi ignored the man and left with his companion, their cattle and the tongs.

A while later, they stopped for a drink. Nkabi had put the tongs in leather hoops at the back of his shield. After he had his fill of water he picked up the shield, but the tongs were gone. He knew his companion had not touched them, so he was deeply disturbed by their disappearance.

His demeanour became strange and he began singing and talking rubbish. Before long it was obvious that he was out of his mind. When the men arrived at their *kraal* (village), Nkabi was so disturbed that he had to be tied up.

The matter was reported to the king, who felt Nkabi had had his just desserts for disobedience. The king asked some of his soldiers to help find the tongs and their rightful owner. This did not take long; the owner lived on the southern edge of the Somabula Forest. But when the owner was interviewed, he laughed and produced the tongs, saying his ancestral guardian spirit had returned them to him. He asked them to bring Nkabi to him so that he could change his condition.

The soldiers collected Nkabi and waited until dark. A big fire had been made and they produced a piece of cloth. A bowl of hot water was brought and some herbs were placed in the water. The piece of cloth was placed over the bowl and three *assegais*, long-bladed spears, were driven into the ground to form a triangle around the fire. Three dogs were brought to stand guard at each assegai. They were not tied up.

Nkabi, still bound tightly, was brought into the triangle while the observers watched. The owner of the tongs and the medium through whom the ancestral spirit had passed to Nkabi began to chant and appeal to the spirits. They rubbed some substance on Nkabi's lips. After a while they said the ceremony was over and that Nkabi was cured.

They gave the men a pot of beer of which Nkabi also partook, although he had refused food and beer for many days. They removed Nkabi's bonds and he joined in the drinking and eating quite normally.

Nkabi lived a long life and produced a large family before he died.

What had actually happened to the tongs? They were a sacred heirloom and, according to Matabele custom, could be held only by the person to whom the spirit had passed them. In other words, the tongs could belong only to their rightful owner and Nkabi was stricken with insanity for removing them. But how the tongs disappeared in the middle of the bush and finished up with the owner is something not even the district commissioner could explain.

Grandma's Ghost

For some time now, a young Zimbabwean, Gunter Hofer, has been helping me obtain ghost accounts from the people of this country. Recently he brought his grandmother, Cleo Rossin, to have tea with me, and she told me several stories that many of the people believe. She said that a long time ago she met a man named Timot and he told her of an incident that had occurred in his village.

One day a strange old man came and picked out a young woman and took her with him to some caves nearby (she had been hypnotized by the man to follow him, Cleo said). Later, her family and other villagers went to the caves to look for her, but they could not find her. They believed that a large round stone nearby gave access to grounds underneath the cave, and when they moved the stone they could see a cave beneath it. But no one wanted to go down there; they were too afraid.

The family of the woman who had disappeared started to cry. They thought they would never see her again. But the other villagers told them, "No, don't cry. If you cry she will never come back."

This was in August of that year, and after a week or two, the woman unexpectedly returned. She brought with her a lot of fresh fruit, although it was not the season for that type of fruit.

"Where did you go?" the villagers asked her.

She replied, "I am not supposed to tell you where I have been."

But they asked, "Where did you get all this fresh fruit?" and they pressured her to tell them. Eventually she said she had gone beneath the caves. She said there were gardens there with fresh vegetables and fruit. She said it was a very big place, but if she showed them where it was, she would die. All this took place on the other side of the Kafue River, not far from where Cleo's father had his farm.

Cleo also recalled that when she was about 15 years old and living on the family farm at Chirundu, one of the fields was planted with peanuts and the children were sent to pick them. The nuts had all been taken up and heaped in a pile, and it was just beginning to grow dark. There is very little twilight in this part of Africa, as it is close to the equator and night falls rapidly.

It was then that Cleo saw a woman coming out of the surrounding bush. She called to everyone: "Come and see, come and see. This woman is carrying her baby upside down on her back. How can she put a child on her back upside down?" The legs of the baby stuck out on top of the mother's back and the head of the child was covered at the bottom of her back with the traditional wrap-around back cloth.

The woman was dressed all in black. She was walking fast, not very far away from Cleo but on the edge of the field, toward the place where her father had planted some lemon trees. Suddenly, it looked as though the lemon trees were on fire. Cleo called to her mother (who is now an old lady of 100), and she saw it too, but she said very quickly, "Don't go there. Come here. It's a ghost."

When the woman walked past the lemon trees, she was also glowing, and then suddenly, she disappeared.

The Spirits Speak

Apparently this type of apparition is not uncommon. My grandfather, Marcus Grill, came to what was then Rhodesia (now Zimbabwe) in 1896. He had taken the train from Johannesburg, South Africa, where he had been temporarily employed, to try to find the "streets paved with gold" that were promised to new immigrants to Rhodesia. He had ridden the train as far as it went in those days – to Mafeking – and from there he had walked, with two friends of his, to Bulawayo, a journey of some two months.

Things were no better in Rhodesia than in South Africa, and the only way he could make a living was to set up a small store selling cheap food to the local people and catering to the small tourist trade that began when the railway was extended to Bulawayo.

After a while, he had enough money to send for his wife and five children and he struggled to make a living for his family. When he was offered a stuffed crocodile by a passing hunter, he quickly agreed to purchase it, as he was sure it would prove an added attraction for the tourist trade. Very soon, he managed to fix the crocodile over the doorway to the shop and indeed, the tourist trade did increase. However, he soon noticed that his African customers began deserting him. They were the mainstay of his living and he became quite worried.

It was a particularly dry season and the evidence of drought could be seen everywhere. The crops were dying and the land was sere and lemon-yellow in the tremendous heat. Cattle and goats were rib-thin all around him.

One day the district commissioner called on him. "Mr Grill," he said, "you'll have to remove that stuffed crocodile over your doorway. The local witch doctor said the spirits told him that it brings bad luck and stops the rain."

My grandfather was bemused and refused to take the crocodile away. After all, the crocodile was a big attraction with the tourists and they admired it each time they passed. But after a few weeks he realized that he was losing too many customers and would have to pander to the witch doctor if business was to revive.

He called in one of my uncles and told him to take the crocodile down and hide it somewhere in the loft. This my uncle did. Within 24 hours, there was a most terrific rainstorm which not only broke the drought, but almost flooded the shop. They had to pack sandbags at the door to stop the water coming in. My grandfather's shop prospered, too, for now all his old customers returned and business was better than it had been.

Many years later, when the shop was rebuilt and improved, my uncles discovered the old stuffed crocodile and quickly buried it sometime during the night a good way from where they could be seen.

Cynthia Hind *lives in Zimbabwe and is MUFON's Coordinator for the African Continent. Her most recent book is* UFOs Over Africa *(Horus House Press). Cynthia shared her thoughts on the most important UFO events of the past half century in "Fifty Years of UFOs" (FATE, June 1997).*

PABLO AND THE PUGOT
By Ruth Ellen Smith

They call it a "Pugot" in the Philippines, but except for name, it seems to be the same thing as our own "Poltergeist."

Supersticious beliefs in the Philippines vary with the localities. Unknown entities are given names. The goblin called Kibaan is general throughout all provinces. In the province of Batangas there is in addition to the Kibaan the Aswang, the Tiyanak, the Nuno, a dwarf called the Dwende and the Capre. Some are good and some are bad. Then there is the Pugot, who is noted for his mischievousness and disconcerting ways. In the Ilocos region in northern Luzon, many people have seen or come in contact with this variable sprite, the Pugot.

Recently a friend of mine, Miss Gerarda Florendo, wrote me of a *Pugot* in their cousin's home when she was a young girl. Her family had brought an orphan boy from the mountains to work as their house-boy. The lad, Pablo, was about 10 years of age at the time. He had not been in the house a week before strange things began to happen there.

First came the throwing of pebbles. When Pablo was in one room alone somebody unseen would throw pebbles into the room. At first his mistress thought that some boys in the neighbourhood might be using sling-shots or flip-jacks to heave the stones in.

But as time passed the rain of pebbles came even if the whole family was present with the boy. Whenever the barrage began the members of the family would rush to the windows and shout for whoever it was to stop at once. The bombardment would continue until the mistress of the house would run angrily around the house to try to catch whoever was playing tricks on them. But nobody was ever found. At times the pebbles fell on the floor as fast as little Pablo could sweep them out.

This kept up for several weeks, much to the irritation of the entire family. But then they noticed that the shower of pebbles occurred only when Pablo was present. One day the boy ran into the house greatly excited and said that someone had thrown a big rock at him and it had struck him on the shoulder.

The rock proved to be as big as a large orange yet Pablo insisted he was not hurt by it. While he was telling his story, still another rock fell near him. Rushing inside the family closed all the windows and doors and made the sign of the Cross. After that the stones ceased to fall for a week or more.

Many of the neighbours had now heard of the strange happenings at the cousin's house and wanted to see the phenomenon for themselves. The authorities took a hand and guarded the place night and day. With the house full of government officials and the grounds surrounded by police, the stoning began once more. Dozens of persons beheld the thing and stood helplessly by, not knowing what to do.

They closed all the windows and doors but the rocks kept on falling! They apparently came through the closed windows without damaging the panes and after they had fallen they arose and flew about the rooms without volition.

Terrified, the police, the neighbours and family climbed onto chairs and furniture, thinking the ceiling the safest place, but the shower of stones continued undiminished for several hours. The strangest part was the fact that even if the rocks struck someone, as they often did, they did not inflict injury. They felt like sponges and did no more harm than rubber balls. Yet once they had fallen the stones were heavy and injured toes and fingers when dropped by the people on themselves. They tried all sorts of experiments to find out all that they could of the strange matter.

They marked the stones and placed them in a chest and closed the lid. Those same marked stones came out of the box and fell in the room over and over again. After a while the stones lay quiet and the mischief was ended for that day.

Shortly after this demonstration the *Pugot* changed tactics and turned his attention to uprooting plants in the garden and to digging out and destroying potted plants kept on the back verandah. Every day while nobody was near, one plant was uprooted.

About this time the *Pugot* became visible to Pablo. One morning while the family was at breakfast, Pablo gave a big yell and rushed to the back verandah, shouting that there was a man there who was uprooting a potted plant. Everyone rushed out to see but nobody but the boy could see anyone at all. Pablo insisted there was a man dressed all in white and that he was at that very moment slowly walking away from them. There was the usual plant lying broken by its pot without visible reason but there was nothing else. They decided that Pablo was letting his imagination run away with him and decided to forget the matter.

After that morning Pablo saw the *Pugot* quite often. Sometimes the figure in white would be roosting in a treetop, sometimes it would appear walking about the garden, breaking the branches off the shrubbery or picking and throwing aside the flowers growing there.

At last a friendly priest advised the boy to talk with the *Pugot* on his next visit and find out from him what he wanted. Timidly, Pablo followed this advice and spoke to the *Pugot*.

To his surprise the *Pugot* responded and asked the boy to set a table laden with rice cakes, cigars, buyo and betel leaves in the garden for him. Then he was to await the *Pugot's* coming. Pablo rushed to the house and told his employers about the conversation and they allowed him to grant the *Pugot's* wishes.

After the feast, the *Pugot* told Pablo to return at once to his home in the mountains. When he reached his majority he would become a great healer of the sick, the *Pugot* said. Pablo promised to do as he was told and went at once to bid goodbye to the family for whom he worked.

His employers, though sorry to lose such a good house-boy, were greatly relieved to see him go if it meant that the *Pugot* would also stay away. Sure enough, the *Pugot* ceased at once to annoy them and all the mischief about the place ended.